AT THE FOREFRONT OF A NEW CENTURY
Montgomery

Montgomery

At the Forefront of a New Century

By WENDI LEWIS

Corporate Profiles by MARTY ELLIS

Featuring the Photography of ROBERT FOUTS

Produced in cooperation with the
Montgomery Area Chamber of Commerce

Montgomery
AT THE FOREFRONT OF A NEW CENTURY

Produced in cooperation with the
Montgomery Area Chamber of Commerce

41 Commerce Street, P.O. Box 79
Montgomery, Alabama 36101
(334) 834-5200

By Wendi Lewis
Corporate Profiles by Marty Ellis
Featuring the photography of Robert Fouts

Community Communications, Inc.
Publishers: Ronald P. Beers and James E. Turner

Staff for *Montgomery: At the Forefront of a New Century*
Publisher's Sales Associates: Dahlia Smith Davis and Paula Haider
Executive Editor: James E. Turner
Managing Editor: Lenita L. Gilreath
Design Director: Camille Leonard
Designer: Camille Leonard
Photo Editors: Lenita L. Gilreath and Camille Leonard
Production Manager: Corinne Cau
Editorial Assistants: Linda Pegram and Katrina Williams
Sales Assistant: Annette Lozier
Proofreader: Wynona B. Hall
Accounting Services: Sara Ann Turner
Printing Production: Frank Rosenberg/GSAmerica

Community Communications, Inc.
Montgomery, Alabama

James E. Turner, *Chairman of the Board*
Ronald P. Beers, *President*
Daniel S. Chambliss, *Vice President*

Table of Contents

Prologue
AT THE FOREFRONT OF A NEW CENTURY

Montgomery is poised for growth at the dawn of a new era. Although life in contemporary Montgomery is shaped by the city's rich historical legacy, the city's best days lie ahead.

Chapter 1
A STRONG FOUNDATION

Montgomery has been dubbed "Center Stage in the South," partly because of its central location in the state and the region, but also because of the role it has long played as a turning point for events in the Heart of Dixie. Through events both fabulous and phenomenal, Montgomery has been a pivot point.

Chapter 2
TAKING CARE OF BUSINESS

The lifeblood of any city is its business community. A healthy, thriving business and industry base ensures jobs for citizens, tax revenues necessary for maintaining public property and roads, and a healthy overall economy—which is, in turn, good for business.

Chapter 3
A MILITARY SALUTE

Maxwell Air Force Base, home of Air University, is responsible for the education of the best and brightest high-ranking Air Force officers. Maxwell's Gunter Annex and the Standard Systems Group are key components in information technology as they develop software for the Air Force and Department of Defense. As a result, Montgomery is recognized as a center of excellence in this area.

Chapter 4
GOVERNMENT IN PROGRESS

State and federal government plays a large role in the life of Montgomery because of its pervasive presence in the downtown area and its position as an economic mainstay of the city and a stable employer for thousands. Local government provides clean streets and safe neighborhoods for the people of Montgomery. A synergism between the government and the public continues to explore new avenues of growth and progress.

Chapter 5
PORTRAIT OF OUR PEOPLE

More than bricks and mortar, a city is built by the people that make up her community. From world-class achievers in business, politics, and the arts to the neighbors who care—in Montgomery you can find the best in people.

C h a p t e r   6

CORNERSTONES OF THE COMMUNITY

Montgomery is a big city wrapped in small-town charm. From its educational institutions to its inspirational places of worship to its charming neighborhoods, families are considered the cornerstone of the community.

Page **102**

C h a p t e r   8

DOWNTOWN RENAISSANCE

Montgomery's skyline seems to change almost daily, as a wealth of new construction is springing to life downtown. At the heart of the downtown renaissance is the Retirement Systems of Alabama.

Page **160**

C h a p t e r   1 0

LET US ENTERTAIN YOU

Put down that luggage! You don't have to travel to New York to experience the wonder of the arts. It's all right here in Montgomery. World-class theater, symphony, ballet, art—all find a home in Montgomery.

Page **204**

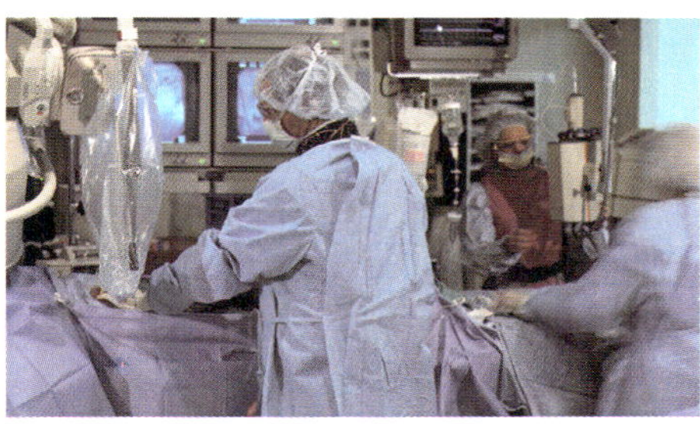

C h a p t e r   7

A HEALTHY ATTITUDE

Montgomery offers an extensive health care system, with four full-service hospitals and numerous specialized care facilities located in the Capital City.

Page **142**

C h a p t e r   9

TIME OUT

We've got sporting events to thrill the serious athlete, the weekend enthusiast, and the armchair quarterback; our area parks and attractions provide countless hours of fun for the whole family; and Montgomery is host to some of the best special events in our region.

Page **178**

Chapter 11

NETWORKS

The area's transportation, communications, and energy firms keep people, information, and power circulating inside and outside the Montgomery area.

Chapter 12

MANUFACTURING, DISTRIBUTION & TECHNOLOGY

Producing and moving goods for individuals and industry, manufacturing, distribution, and technology firms provide employment for many Montgomery area residents.

Chapter 13

BUSINESS AND FINANCE

Montgomery's business, insurance, and financial community offers a strong base for the area's growing economy.

Chapter 14

PROFESSIONS

From law to accounting, architecture to public relations, Montgomery's professional firms are recognized as leaders in their fields.

Foreword

The Montgomery Area Chamber of Commerce is pleased to present *Montgomery: At the Forefront of a New Century.* We believe this beautiful book brings to life all the warmth, inherent charm, and subtle sophistication of Montgomery's people. In vivid photographs and eloquent words, the local authors and photographer touch each of Montgomery's fascinating and considerable assets in a sweeping brush stroke of Montgomery's social, economic, and cultural life.

The Montgomery area is steeped in tradition dating back to the days of Indian settlements and frontier battles between the English and French. From the tumultuous times when Montgomery sprang forth as the Cradle of the Confederacy and gave rise to the Civil War, to the turbulent times of the 1950s and 1960s, when Montgomery sowed the seeds of the movement for Civil Rights, Montgomery has been the birthplace of the two most cataclysmic events in American history.

It is the journey from those troubled and historic times to the economic prosperity and diversity of Montgomery today which this book so richly portrays. Perhaps that is why we felt the title, *At the Forefront of a New Century*, so appropriate. Not only are we celebrating the past, but we are also looking to the future. There is a momentum in Montgomery right now, an excitement and vitality evidenced by the renaissance of downtown and the changing skyline along the hills and bluffs of the Alabama River.

It is also appropriate that Montgomerians are turning their vision for the future to the banks of the riverfront. This gentle, rolling stream which twists and turns through Montgomery on the way south to the Gulf of Mexico has been the lifeblood of Alabama's Capital City throughout much of its history. How fitting that the river is now emerging as a centerpiece in the Chamber's economic development efforts.

So, it is with a great deal of pride that I, on behalf of the board of directors of the Montgomery Area Chamber of Commerce, present *Montgomery: At the Forefront of a New Century.* From the historic landmarks of Civil War and Civil Rights, to the modern-day hallmarks of a successful metropolitan area, Montgomery shines throughout these pages as a city poised center stage to meet the challenges of a new day.

Randall L. George
President
Montgomery Area Chamber of Commerce

Preface

There's a saying in the South—a Yankee is a person from the North who comes to visit and then goes home. A Damn Yankee is one who stays.

By that definition, I have to admit I'm a Damn Yankee. Sure, I've made Montgomery my home since the age of four (with the exception of a year spent in Colorado), but I wasn't born here. Therefore, I'm not a native.

Worse, my parents and lineage are from the heart of Ohio, and I never really even got much of a Southern accent, so those born and bred in the Heart of Dixie can pick me out as a "Northerner" right off.

Despite this character flaw, I have embraced the South, and Montgomery in particular. And the South, and Montgomery in particular, have embraced me right back.

This is my home, but it's also more than that. Montgomery is more to me than a return address or a street or house. It's more than a place to work and pass the days.

In part, Montgomery is tree-lined streets dotted with shade and the warm breeze of a hot summer day. It's history alive in every day, as busy commuters pass over brick streets worn by the wheels of buggies and the tracks of electric streetcars.

Sitting in the Court Square noontime sun, listening to the soft rippling and splashing of the historic fountain, you can look straight up Dexter Avenue to the Capitol Building and, depending on your viewpoint, see Jefferson Davis standing on its steps taking the oath of office as the President of the Confederate States of America; Dr. Martin Luther King Jr. leading crowds in swelling protest songs; or busy heads of state government bustling about the business of policy and protocol.

In part, Montgomery is the churning waters of the Alabama River under the wheel of a riverboat; fireworks exploding in the summer air; the smell of grilled onions and polish sausages hovering against the backdrop of the pulsing lights and throbbing music of Jubilee CityFest or the South Alabama State Fair.

In part, Montgomery is crowds of school children piling eagerly out of bright yellow school buses, mouths agape and eyes wide in wonder as they take in the sights and sounds of downtown Montgomery, from the glimpse into the past that is Old Alabama Town, to the sparkling, bright-white glare of marble columns housing history and government.

In part, Montgomery is the golden glow of light pouring into an evening sky over the banners of the Alabama Shakespeare Festival; the faint strains of music emanating from the stage door of the Davis Theatre, as inside the magic of the Montgomery Symphony Orchestra, the Montgomery Ballet, or the Alabama Dance Theatre holds an audience enthralled; and the hushed echoes of admiration for art and artists of the Montgomery Museum of Fine Arts.

From the quiet calm of cool grass and warm sunshine to the crisp excitement of a roaring crowd packed into Cramton Bowl— this is Montgomery.

Montgomery is so many different things, and she changes and grows every day. Each time I stop to take a look around, there is something new to see, something else to discover. And I think again how blessed I am to call Montgomery home.

I'd like to dedicate this book first and foremost to Dr. Robert Evans at Auburn University at Montgomery, without whose enthusiastic encouragement I would not be a writer today. Dr. Evans, "Time!"

Also, I want to dedicate this book to my husband, Eric, for his support and encouragement; to my mother, for giving me a love of language through her endless gifts of books; and my dad, for believing in whatever I do.

Wendi Lewis
Author

Part One
MONTGOMERY

Prologue

AT THE FOREFRONT OF A NEW CENTURY

Montgomery. She's a Southern belle. She's a city slicker. Somehow, she manages to take the big city and wrap it up in small-town charm.

Throughout her life, she has provided fertile ground for growth and change that has affected the city, state, nation, and even the world. She was the capital of the Confederacy and the birthplace of civil rights.

The accomplishments of the past can still be found in the people, places, and culture of Montgomery. The city seems to have saved what was best of days gone by and mixed it with a vision for the future. Photo by Robert Fouts.

Her people have stared in wide-eyed wonderment at steamboats chugging into port on the Alabama River, the first electric streetcars whizzing down Dexter Avenue, and the mysteries of flight as the Wright brothers worked their magic over Maxwell Field.

Today, the accomplishments of the past can still be found in the people, places, and culture of Montgomery. The city seems to have saved what was best of days gone by and mixed it with a vision for the future, piecing together a colorful quilt with patches made of memories, dreams, and plans.

An Old-South charm infuses the architecture of the city, with stately white-columned mansions harkening back to antebellum days. The people, too, greet newcomers to the Capital City with an openness born of good old-fashioned Southern hospitality.

Amid the bustle of the busy city, there's still time to take things slow, to stop and say, "Hello."

But don't mistake our Southern drawl for standing still. Montgomery is constantly growing and changing, anxiously moving to the forefront of a new century. "It's a very traditional town, but with a strong desire to go places," said Randy George, president of the Montgomery Area Chamber of Commerce. "Montgomery is a long way from satisfied with the status quo, but also cherishes its history and traditions, and the finer aspects of Southern life."

Of course, change does not come without a price. But through the payments our history required has come a solid sense of the value of what we've bought.

But built upon the turbulent history of the fight for civil rights is a foundation of cultural diversity. The idea of tolerance and understanding that must exist between people of different races, the same message preached by Dr. King, can still be found today as people of all races, not just black and white, work and live side by side to make up the community that is Montgomery.

As a reminder of the sacrifices made during the fight for civil rights, and as an admonition for racial harmony in the future, stands the Civil Rights Memorial, located in downtown Montgomery at the Southern Poverty Law Center. Constructed in 1989, the monument was designed by Maya Lin, who also designed the Vietnam Memorial.

Inscribed on the monument are the names of 40 people who lost their lives during the fight for civil rights, either through peaceful protest, as innocent targets of racial hate groups, or as victims of violent retribution against events or sites of civil rights protest.

The theme of the monument is water, with a waterfall cascading down a black granite wall on which are inscribed the words, ". . . until justice rolls down like waters and righteousness like a mighty stream—Martin Luther King Jr." The words, taken from the Biblical book of Amos, were used by Dr. King not only in his "I Have a Dream" speech, but also at a rally for the boycotting of the Montgomery public bus system.

Water also runs over a circular black granite pedestal, which is inscribed with the 40 names, and also with significant dates in the struggle for civil rights.

In an article written by William Zinsser in *Smithsonian Magazine,* dated September 1991, artist Maya Lin states that the quote by Dr. King inspired the idea of using water as her theme. She hoped to show how the people and events of the movement worked together to shape history, Zinsser reported. She began the quote at ". . . until," omitting its actual beginning of "We will not be satisfied" in order to emphasize that the fight for equality—among races, sexes, or in any fashion—is one that is ongoing, Zinsser says.

Adding to the cultural diversity of Montgomery is Maxwell Air Force Base and Gunter Annex, which brings in top military leaders from throughout the world. When members of the military leave Montgomery, they take a bit of the city with

them in their hearts. And we, their hosts, are left with a broader picture of the world.

Within Montgomery itself, horizons are expanding—both literally and figuratively.

On the literal side, the skyline of Montgomery is rapidly changing, as the downtown area now enjoys a booming revitalization. The Retirement Systems of Alabama (RSA) has created a showplace for doing business, and other agencies have followed suit, filling the sky with modern towers of glass and granite.

Those who haven't traveled Dexter Avenue in a while are greeted with a pleasant surprise of bubbling new fountains and expanses of green, grassy parks.

Near the historic train shed, the Embassy Suites Hotel and scenic Overlook Park keep watch over the Alabama River. Surrounding the new hotel are quaint sandwich shoppes, coffee houses, and even a brew pub, a unique fixture in Montgomery.

It's an interesting mix, this town. The quaint, old-fashioned side by side with modern technology. From history-rich Old Alabama Town to the cutting-edge Alabama TechnaCenter, this old girl is young again. **M**

The people of Montgomery greet newcomers with an openess born of good, old-fashioned Southern hospitality. Photo by Robert Fouts.

CHAPTER ONE

A STRONG FOUNDATION

A popular slogan used to describe Montgomery is "Center Stage in the South."

It has been thus dubbed partly because of its central location in the state and the region, but also because of the role it has long played as a turning point for events in the Heart of Dixie. Through events both fabulous and phenomenal, Montgomery has been a pivot point.

Visitors to Old Alabama Town are treated to reenactments of daily life in Alabama's early years, enjoy old-fashioned musical "jam sessions," and can even eat lunch in a restored home dating to the 1800s. Photo by Robert Fouts.

In its earliest days, Alabama was occupied by the Alabamu Indians, who were the ancestors of the tribe later called Creek. They made their home on the rich lands by the Alabama River, which today curves around the modern structures of downtown Montgomery.

Although a few early pioneers made the trek into the territory, including famous explorer Hernando de Soto in his quest for gold in 1540 (unsuccessful in Alabama), the land was not open for settlement to any but the most hardy and brave until 1814, after the Battle of Horseshoe Bend.

But the land around Montgomery, particularly in the area north of Montgomery, in what is now Wetumpka's historic Fort Toulouse/Jackson Park, was continually occupied for about 2,000 years, and intermittently occupied for about 5,000 years prior to its widespread settlement in the early 1800s, according to Ned Jenkins, archaeologist and manager of Fort Toulouse/Jackson Park.

Archaeologists are able to determine the different dates of land occupation by the "point styles," or different styles of what most people commonly call arrowheads, Jenkins said.

According to most recent history, he reports, it is known the English inhabited the land where the park is now located around 1680. In 1717 the French were invited to inhabit the land by the Alabamu Indians, who were part of the Creek Confederacy. The Indians wanted the French to occupy the area to prevent the English, who treated the Indians badly, from holding a monopoly on trade, Jenkins explained. The French built Fort Toulouse. They held the land until 1763, when the treaty ending the French and Indian War gave all French holdings east of the Mississippi to the English.

In 1814 Andrew Jackson built Fort Jackson on the site. The Treaty of Fort Jackson, signed at the site, ceded more than 20 million acres of Indian land, including that now occupied by the city of Montgomery, to the United States government.

Early settlers farmed the land, fished the river, and hunted game.

In 1816 the Mississippi Territorial Legislature (which included Alabama) decided to call the new area Montgomery County, in memory of Major Lemuel Purnell Montgomery, a hero killed at Horseshoe Bend.

In 1817 Alabama became a territory distinct from the Mississippi Territory, of which it had formerly been a part, and the area now occupied by Fort Toulouse/Jackson Park became the first county seat for Montgomery County, and Fort Jackson served as the first brig for the county jail, Jenkins said.

In 1819 the county seat was moved to Montgomery, and later that year the fort was decommissioned.

But people can still visit Fort Toulouse/Jackson Park and enjoy the sights and sounds of the eighteenth century as costumed volunteers create a Living History Book presentation several times each year. These special events bring to life such periods and events of history as the French period (eighteenth century), The War of 1812, and an eighteenth-century Indian village.

During the reenactment events, visitors to Fort Toulouse/Jackson Park enjoy demonstrations of everyday life on the new frontier, including cooking, tanning hides, craftsmanship, and blacksmithing. Also, visitors can purchase authentic replicas of eighteenth-century items including clothing, axes, knives, glassware, pipes, tomahawks, toys, and more.

The French built Fort Toulouse and held the land until 1763, when the treaty ending the French and Indian War gave all French holdings east of the Mississippi to the English. Today, visitors can enjoy the history of Fort Toulouse/Jackson Park. Photo by Robert Fouts.

Chief of the Lower Creek Indians, William McIntosh agreed to the removal of his people to the west in the 1820s and was subsequently assassinated by distraught members of his tribe. Photo courtesy of Fouts Commercial Photography.

Montgomery County was named in honor of Major Lemuel Purnell Montgomery, a hero killed at Horseshoe Bend. Photo courtesy of Fouts Commercial Photography.

Attorney Andrew Dexter purchased land on the Alabama River from the United States Land Office in 1817. He decided to call his settlement "New Philadelphia." Photo courtesy of Fouts Commercial Photography.

General John Scott bought land west of Andrew Dexter's property and decided to call his town "Alabama Town." Photo courtesy of Fouts Commercial Photography.

The pace of the settlement of Montgomery was slow until 1817, when the United States Land Office announced land on the Alabama River for sale. Andrew Dexter, an attorney, purchased the land and was determined to see a city grow from it.

Dexter decided to call his settlement "New Philadelphia." One of the first streets laid out in the town was called Market Street, and it ran east to a hill on which Dexter raised goats, and west to a natural artesian well. Today, that street is called Dexter Avenue, and on "Goat Hill" stands the State Capitol building, while keeping guard over the site of the artesian well is the famous Court Square Fountain.

Another man determined to see a city established on the wild land along the Alabama River was General John Scott. He bought the land west of Dexter's land and decided to call the town "Alabama Town." Scott Street in downtown Montgomery was named in memory of this founder.

Relations between the two cities did not go well in the beginning, as Scott and Dexter argued over boundaries and attempted to block each other's plans for expansion. Finally, in 1818, the two decided to meet and merge.

In 1819 Alabama was made a state. Representatives from the brand new state approached the brand new legislature and proposed to create the City of Montgomery. The bill passed and the new governor, William Wyatt Bibb, signed it into law.

As the city grew, commerce expanded as well. More and bigger boats came to the wharf on the banks of the Alabama River. In 1821 the first steamboat, the *Harriet,* docked at the city wharf. From steamboats and paddle wheelers to modern-day industrial barges, the Alabama River has provided the channel of commerce that has helped the city grow.

As trade increased on the river in its earliest days, stores grew up along the waterfront, and business boomed in the city. Today, the river helps corporations move their goods in a cost-efficient manner to railway yards and seaports.

Beyond the industrial pluses, the Alabama River serves as a great natural source of beauty. Riverfront and Overlook Parks lie above the winding expanse of water, and the *Betsy Ann* riverboat docked at its shore hearkens back to days gone by. Visitors to the Capital City can travel back in time on the authentic stern-wheel riverboat. Day cruises, parties, dinner cruises—all will transport passengers to a quieter place in time in Montgomery history. City and Chamber leaders are working to make riverfront development the centerpiece of the area's economic development strategy in the coming century.

As the port at the Alabama River brought in more people and news from beyond the borders of the young city and state, the town truly began to turn from frontier to civilized.

Acting on the increased information available from both the river travelers and the new "Pony Express" mail service, several newspapers began operations.

Because of a growing population, it was decided an organized place of worship was necessary, and the city's first church was built on the corner of Court and Church Streets in 1827. It was shared by Methodists, Presbyterians, and Baptists.

"Culture" came to call in 1830, when the first theater was constructed and named the Montgomery Theatre.

Finally, in 1846 the city was established enough to be considered a home for the state capital. The legislature approved the motion to move the state capital to Montgomery, and the building was located on "Goat Hill," where it stands today. Visitors to the Capitol building can view its original section, restored to its former beauty, down to the authentic carpeting and trompe l'oeil painting. In later years, the two "wings" of the Capitol were added at each side of the original structure.

But as the city flourished, there was an undercurrent of unrest flowing throughout the South. The nation was talking of abolishing slavery.

In those days in the South, including Montgomery, there was a feeling that the slave owner was good to his slaves, providing them security and looking to their needs. Slaves were viewed as valuable property, and plantation owners had long relied on the use of slave labor to assure the operation of their businesses. The owners feared change and resisted the idea that slavery was cruel.

The intersection of Dexter Avenue and Court Street in downtown Montgomery marks the merging of the two earliest settlements in this area. Andrew Dexter developed "New Philadelphia," which included the land where the Court Square Fountain and the State Capitol building are now located. General John Scott purchased land along the riverfront, which he called "Alabama Town." In 1818 these two parcels were merged to form the City of Montgomery. Photo courtesy of Fouts Commercial Photography.

As the city grew, commerce expanded and more and bigger boats came to the wharf on the banks of the Alabama River. Photo courtesy of Fouts Commercial Photography.

1885 CONSECRATED TO T
FAME'S TEMPLE BOASTS NO HIGHER NAME;
NO KING IS GRANDER ON HIS THRONE;
NO GLORY SHINES WITH BRIGHTER GLEAM,
THE NAME OF PATRIOT STANDS ALONE.

Antislavery supporters, including those from the South, argued that it was morally wrong to consider another human being as property. Slave owners and merchants who dealt in cotton feared the industry would collapse if slavery were abolished, because the business depended so much on the slave labor. They feared financial ruin and the disappearance of their way of life.

Because the issue of slavery so greatly affected their daily way of life, leaders of Southern states argued the question should be left to each state to decide, not dictated from a Union government that they felt did not fully understand their plight.

Anxiety grew when Abraham Lincoln was elected president in 1860, and the talk of secession increased. In January of 1861, Alabama representatives called strongly for secession. By the beginning of February, Alabama had joined six other states in seceding from the Union.

A week later, they selected Jefferson Davis to be president of the Confederate States of America, and he was sworn in at the State Capitol building. Today, a bronze star on the front steps of the building marks the spot where Davis was sworn in, and just across the street still stands the First White House of the Confederacy, preserved as a historical landmark and open for tours.

After the establishment of the Confederate government, talk of war was incessant as the Union government strove to bring the Southern states back into line. The breaking point came when President Lincoln sent troops to occupy Fort Sumter, located on the coast of Charleston, South Carolina. Confederate President Davis issued an ultimatum, ordering that Union troops evacuate the Southern fort. When this did not occur, Davis issued the order for Confederate troops to fire on Fort Sumter, beginning the War Between the States. This historic telegram was sent from Montgomery, where today a historic marker stands on Dexter Avenue, next to Court Square, in front of the law offices of Balch and Bingham, the former site of the telegraph office.

Although the South lost the War Between the States, the men who fought and died in its battles are remembered today. Groups made up of descendants of Confederate soldiers meet to keep the memories alive.

On important days of the Civil War, these groups often hold special memorial services, many including full authentic Confederate costume. Many of these ceremonies are held at historic Oakwood Cemetery.

Oakwood Cemetery, established by donations of land from city founders Andrew Dexter in

The Confederate Monument, erected in 1868, pays tribute to those men who died for the Southern cause, but whose names were not discovered upon their death. Photo by Robert Fouts.

In early 1861 representatives selected Jefferson Davis to be president of the Confederate States of America, and he was sworn in at the Alabama State Capitol. Today, a bronze star on the front steps of the building marks the spot where Davis was sworn in. Photo by Robert Fouts.

1817 and General John Scott in 1818, is the oldest cemetery in Montgomery and, therefore, rich in history. According to historic records, the early part of the graveyard was known as Scott's Free Burying Ground, and was open to all of Montgomery's people, from soldiers to statesmen, prominent or poor.

The cemetery covers approximately 154 acres of land, according to caretaker Gary Legere, and there are more than 200,000 people buried on its grounds. Of that number, there are more than 4,000 Confederate soldiers buried at Oakwood. In addition to soldiers killed in action during the War Between the States, Oakwood is the final resting place of those who served in the Confederacy and lived, and were later buried at the end of their natural lives among their fallen compatriots. Markers provided by the Sophie Bibb Chapter of the United Daughters of the Confederacy mark each grave occupied by a man who served as a soldier of the Confederacy.

Two prominent monuments stand in tribute to the soldiers who fought on the Confederate side in the Civil War. The first, the Confederate Monument over the Unknown Confederate Soldiers, was erected by the Ladies Memorial Association in 1868 and pays tribute to those men who died for the Southern cause, but whose names were not discovered upon their death. An inscription on this monument reads, "They do not die who in their deeds survive, Enshrined forever in the hearts of men."

The second Confederate tribute is the "Camp Lomax 1861-1865" monument. Three square columns are inscribed on all four sides with the names of the soldiers who served in this local Confederate veterans' organization.

Additional Confederate memorial ceremonies are held throughout the city during the year. A monument erected at one side of the Capitol building recalls the contributions of the Confederate soldiers to the history of the city and state. This is a popular site for ceremonies and events remembering the contributions of Montgomerians who served the Confederacy in the Civil War.

Oakwood is also the final resting place of at least 25 Union soldiers. The Civil War Federal Soldiers' Memorial, decorated with an American flag, marks the site where 25 Union soldiers are buried together. The monument was erected May 30, 1908, by the Federal Memorial Association of Montgomery. Seven of the soldiers buried at the site are named, and the other 18 are unknown. The monument also lists the names of 10 other Federal soldiers buried in other locations throughout Oakwood Cemetery.

Oakwood Cemetery is the oldest cemetery in Montgomery and is rich in history. More than 4,000 Confederate soldiers are buried at Oakwood. Photo by Robert Fouts.

In 1893 the body of former Confederate President Jefferson Davis lay in state in the Alabama Capitol on the way to Richmond, Virginia, for final interment. Photo courtesy of Fouts Commercial Photography.

UNKNOWN
SOLDIER
CSA

F M HURST
CO I
54 ALA INF
CSA
JUN 22 1864

UNKNOWN
SOLDIER
CSA
MAR 22 1862

I PORTER
CO A
22 ALA INF
CSA
JUN 14 1864

eople of all nationalities come to Montgomery each year to visit the sites of the historic battles for civil rights, including the pulpit of the Dexter Avenue King Memorial Baptist Church, from which Dr. Martin Luther King Jr. presented many messages urging a course of nonviolent action to bring about change.

In 1954 Martin Luther King accepted his first pastorate at the Dexter Avenue Baptist Church in Montgomery. He devoted his life to the fight for full citizenship rights for the racially oppressed. Photo by Robert Fouts. Archival photo courtesy of **The Montgomery Advertiser.**

Rosa Parks became a central figure in the Civil Rights Movement when she sparked the Montgomery bus boycott by refusing to give up her seat on a city bus to a white passenger. Photo courtesy of Alabama State University.

In addition to Civil War history, Oakwood Cemetery is rich in Montgomery history as the final resting place of prominent citizens, political leaders, and founding fathers. Among those buried at Oakwood are Governor Benjamin J. Fitzpatrick, General John Scott, Governor Thomas Hill Watts, William Burr Howell (the father of Mrs. Jefferson Davis), Colonel Tennant Lomax (Montgomery's War Between the States hero), Justice Anthony D. Sayre (father of Zelda Sayre, who married F. Scott Fitzgerald), Jack Thorington (mayor of Montgomery 1839-1840), and many more.

In addition to Scott's Free Burying Ground, much of the cemetery was purchased by the City of Montgomery and sold as plots. There is also a Catholic cemetery and a Jewish cemetery included on the grounds.

Oakwood Annex is adjacent to Oakwood Cemetery and is under private ownership. It also contains many graves of historical importance, the most noteworthy probably that of Hank Williams, which is visited by hundreds of tourists each year.

An interesting feature of Montgomery is that the landmarks of the Civil War stand so close to the landmarks and memorials of the second great battle to be fought in this Capital City, the battle for Civil Rights, fought almost a century later.

Although the Union victory in the Civil War brought blacks their freedom, it was many years before they won their right to equality. It is significant that the fight began in earnest in the same city that cheered the election of the Confederate president.

In the years before Civil Rights, conflicts and turmoil had been building between blacks and whites throughout the country because of the issue of segregation. Supposedly "free," blacks were barred from "white-only" restaurants, clubs, parks, and schools. Both literally and figuratively, they were made to sit at the back of the bus— which is where the war began.

In December of 1955, Rosa Parks, a black woman who lived and worked in Montgomery, was taking the bus home after a long day on her job as a seamstress. As white people began to fill the bus, the driver told her and some other blacks to give up their seats and move to the back of the bus. Parks sat quietly still in her seat.

She was exhausted. Her feet hurt, and her eyes were blurry from staring at the needle all day. But more than that, she was tired of being made to give up what was hers, simply because her skin was black and not white. So when the bus driver asked her again if she were going to move from her seat, she quietly, calmly told him no.

"It was time for someone to stand up—or, in my case, sit down. I refused to move," Parks recalls in her book about her role in the events of the Civil Rights Movement, *Quiet Strength: The Faith, the Hope, and the Heart of a Woman Who Changed a Nation.*

Because she would not yield her seat, Parks was arrested, sparking a boycott of the city bus system by blacks. Black leaders in the community, including a young preacher by the name of Reverend Martin Luther King Jr., banded together to support the boycott. Beginning the next Monday, and for the next 381 days, not one black person rode the city buses.

The focus of the nation was now on the issue of Civil Rights, and Montgomery was the battleground where the issue would ultimately be fought. It was not only a contest for the courts, but also a literal battle that brought destruction and bloodshed. It was a see-saw of victories and violence.

The Reverend Dr. King traveled the country bringing a message of nonviolent protest, encouraging such demonstrations as sit-ins by blacks at all-white lunch counters.

A peaceful march through Selma and west Alabama was planned to show the unity of commitment of the black community. As the approximately 600 marchers left Selma, led by Dr. King, they were stopped on the Edmund Pettus Bridge by armed state troopers. When they did not follow the troopers' orders to turn back, they were beaten and doused with tear gas.

In a separate incident, "Freedom Riders" coming through the city to show support for Civil Rights were beaten severely when their buses stopped in Montgomery.

Hank Williams made Montgomery his home in the early 1940s. His grave site is located in Montgomery's Oakwood Cemetery Annex. Photo by Robert Fouts.

In the late 1800s Montgomery laid trolley tracks from Commerce Street all the way up to the Capitol on Dexter Avenue. The first trolley ever to run on electricity ran that route, dubbed "The Lightning Route." Photo courtesy of Fouts Commercial Photography.

Ultimately, the courts were in agreement with the calls of the blacks for equality. In the summer of 1965, the Voting Rights Act was passed by congress, and signed into law by President Lyndon Johnson.

It has been a long, hard road from civil rights on paper to civil rights in practice, but with each new generation the ideas of equality and justice are strengthened through education and cooperation.

Thousands of people of all nationalities come to Montgomery each year to visit the sites of the historic battles for civil rights, from the pulpit of the Dexter Avenue King Memorial Baptist Church, from which Dr. Martin Luther King Jr. presented many messages urging a course of non-violent action to bring about change; to the Civil Rights Memorial, located appropriately in front of the Southern Poverty Law Center, which strives today to champion the civil rights of those who cannot defend themselves, and to educate people through a program of teaching tolerance.

Today, people of all ages are able to learn about the important contributions of black people to Alabama history, visit the sites of landmark civil rights events, and are taught the importance of race relations.

From a turbulent and sometimes violent era has grown a strong understanding of the cost of racial division, and the value of racial harmony.

New battles in the defense of the civil rights not only of people of color, but also of women, children, and citizens from myriad different beliefs and walks of life are fought every day in the United States. Today, people can stand unafraid and speak out for what they know is right, and equal.

Because Rosa Parks had the courage many years ago to keep her seat, knowing in her heart she deserved as much as any other human being to sit in the front of the bus, thousands of American citizens can today claim the benefits and birthright of the Civil Rights Amendment to the Constitution.

Because the events of the Civil War and the Civil Rights Movement had such a significant impact on the nation and, in some cases, even the world, it is easy to lose some of Montgomery's other accomplishments in the shuffle.

The city was home to many fascinating people and was the setting for a number of "firsts."

In the 1880s, Montgomery laid trolley tracks from Commerce Street all the way up to the Capitol on Dexter Avenue. The first trolley ever

to run on electricity ran that route, dubbed "The Lightning Route."

While advances were being made in ground travel, Montgomerians also began watching the skies. In the early years of the 1900s, Wilbur Wright came to Montgomery in search of a place to locate a pilot training school. He and his brother, Orville, had made the first airplane flight in 1903 and were working on a business of manufacturing airplanes, or "flying machines," as they were called at the time.

They settled on a large piece of farmland, where they constructed Montgomery's first airfield. Maxwell Air Force Base, home of Air University, which trains the best pilots from all over the world, now stands on the same ground where that first airfield, called Maxwell Field, was built. The grand jet runways and fine buildings that house the Air University are a far cry from the converted hay barn that served as the Wright brothers' first hangar.

The Wright brothers' school began in 1910, dazzling farmers and townspeople with the sight of a flying machine soaring overhead. Later, the first ever night flight was made by the Wright brothers at Maxwell Field.

Several famous artists have also called Montgomery home. Scott Fitzgerald was stationed at Camp Sheridan, located just outside Montgomery, in 1917, where he attended officers' training camp as a member of the 17th Infantry Brigade. The camp worked to prepare soldiers who were scheduled to be sent overseas to fight in World War I. However, the war ended before Fitzgerald was sent, which is reported to have been a sharp disappointment for him. While stationed at Camp Sheridan, Fitzgerald worked on a revision of his novel *The Romantic Egoist,* which had been turned down for publication by Charles Scribner's Sons publishers in New York. After rewriting the work in each moment he could spare from the duties of his military training, he

Camp Sheridan, located just outside of Montgomery, prepared soldiers to be sent overseas to fight in World War I. Red Cross volunteers delivered roses to the soldiers. Photo courtesy of Fouts Commercial Photography.

Firefighters stand ready for action at the Scott Street Fire Station in 1910. Photo courtesy of Fouts Commercial Photography.

As the main street leading from Montgomery's first center of trade and industry, the riverfront, Commerce Street naturally developed as the city's center of business. As pictured here in the mid-1930s, the area was a bustling hub for shopping. Photo courtesy of Fouts Commercial Photography. (top right)

Saturday afternoons spent at the movies were a popular pastime for Montgomery youth in the 1950s. Photo by John E. Scott Jr. (bottom right)

resubmitted it to Scribner's, but it was again turned down.

It was also during this period that Fitzgerald attended a dance at the Montgomery Country Club, in July of 1918, and there he became enchanted by Montgomery's leading belle— Zelda Sayre. After a tumultuous courtship, during which the pair became engaged in February of 1919, and "dis-engaged" (by Zelda) in June of that same year, they were "re-engaged" in November of 1919 after Fitzgerald sold his novel *This Side of Paradise,* and the couple finally wed April 3, 1920.

Zelda, too, was an artist in her own right, painting and writing much of a novel called *Save Me the Waltz,* before suffering a nervous breakdown.

Nat King Cole also was a native of Montgomery. The famous musician is known throughout the world as the singer of such popular hits as "Unforgettable" and "Mona Lisa."

Perhaps the most famous Montgomery singer was Hank Williams. Although he grew up in Georgiana, Alabama, Williams made Montgomery his home in the early 1940s, when he moved here with his mother. As a young teenager, Williams began singing in talent shows and before long was appearing all over Alabama

as news of his talent spread. In 1946 he cut his first record.

Williams is a solid part of country music history, with hits like "Your Cheatin' Heart," "I'm So Lonesome I Could Cry," and "Jambalaya" still popular today. His grave site is located in Montgomery's Oakwood Cemetery Annex, and local legend has it that if you visit his grave at midnight, you can faintly hear Old Hank singing "Your Cheatin' Heart."

The influences of the many types of art and music that are a part of Montgomery's history make it possible to find a variety in the arts today. Folk artists such as Mose T. are respected for their primitivism. The Montgomery chapter of the Alabama Jazz Federation keeps the beat alive in the city by hosting guest artists and supporting local jazz musicians. Country, rock, classical— there's something for everyone.

Montgomerians are treated to a smorgasbord of musical entertainment each year during Jubilee CityFest, held each Memorial Day weekend. The event brings entertainers ranging in style from zydeco to classic rock to country, and draws thousands of fun-seekers from throughout the Southeast.

Montgomery is a patchwork quilt, past and present blending in harmony to create something beautiful.

Montgomery is proud of its past. The Landmarks Foundation works to preserve bits of living history. Historic markers can be found scattered throughout the city, from Scott and Zelda's home in the charming Old Cloverdale neighborhood, to the elaborate gingerbread trim and breathtaking river views of the Cottage Hill district. Even in the bustling downtown business district, it isn't unusual to be stopped short by the sight of a preserved antebellum mansion resting in splendid grace between busy modern towers.

Just across the street from a sparkling new highrise office complex you will find Old Alabama Town. Authentic stores, a church, a schoolhouse, homes, and even a doctor's office line the streets of this trip back through time. Visitors to Old Alabama Town are treated to reenactments of daily life in Alabama's early years, enjoy old-fashioned musical "jam sessions," and can even eat lunch in a restored home dating to the 1800s.

Montgomery is looking forward to its future. Yet we remain ever conscious of the importance of the past. The past is our foundation, it is our teacher, and it reminds us of who we are. And from that groundwork, we build a strong tomorrow. *m*

SHERWIN-WILLIAMS
PAINTS
JOHNNY WEISSMULLER
"JUNGLE MOON MEN"
ALSO TWO GUNS AND A BADGE

TAKING CARE OF BUSINESS

The lifeblood of any city is its business community. A healthy, thriving business and industry base ensures jobs for citizens, tax revenue necessary for maintaining public property and roads, and a healthy economy overall—which is, in turn, good for businesses.

Whether moving people or goods is the objective, Montgomery's transportation system gets the job done. Photo by Robert Fouts.

Creating a good business climate is not a job any one business can do by itself. It takes work. Montgomery's citizens, members of the business community, government officials, and the Chamber work together to make it happen in the Montgomery area.

In 1992 the Montgomery Area Chamber of Commerce developed a community plan designed to move Montgomery boldly into the forefront of economic development. Called, appropriately enough, *Forefront Montgomery*, the plan had an ambitious goal—to create 10,000 jobs in the Montgomery area within a five-year time frame.

In May of 1995, the Chamber of Commerce announced "the five-year vision of 10,000 jobs has been surpassed—13,400 jobs [were] created for the Montgomery area in only three years." The plan had achieved 134 percent of its original goal. But rather than being satisfied with success, the Chamber set a challenge goal for itself and the tri-county area in which it plans to create a total of 20,000 new jobs by 1997, the end of the original five-year plan.

What is the secret of Montgomery's success in business? "If business is going to come to Montgomery and be successful, or expand in Montgomery, it needs to find a climate conducive to business," said Randall George, president of the Montgomery Area Chamber of Commerce. "We work to ensure that a positive environment for business establishment and growth exists."

What makes a good working climate is the combination of the concrete building blocks of business—training programs for employees, available land for location or expansion of facilities, easy access to markets, a good economic standard of living, and the amenities important to the individuals employed by businesses— entertainment, recreational, and educational opportunities.

Montgomery provides both the concrete for solid business foundations and the amenities that make doing business here so appealing.

TRAINING

Employee training programs available in Montgomery cover all the bases, from job skills necessary for workers in large industrial plants, to high-tech training for those on the edge of the information technology age.

In 1990 the Montgomery Area Chamber of Commerce developed COSBE, the Council of Small Business Enterprises, to help meet the financial, educational, and practical needs of small-business owners. Photo by Robert Fouts.

The Alabama TechnaCenter Research Park provides a centrally-located training facility, land where computer and software companies can locate their businesses, and a residential community. The park is an ideal asset for the growth of Montgomery business. Photo by Robert Fouts.

Visible from I-85 is the heart of information technology training available to Montgomery businesses, the Alabama TechnaCenter Research Park. The TechnaCenter, a project of Ballard Companies, Development and Commercial Real Estate, is a privately-owned 400-acre park comprised of a 49-acre research park, with 200 acres for residential usage, commercial acreage, and an adjacent country club with golf course.

This combination of a centrally-located training facility, land where computer and software companies can locate their businesses, and a residential community, makes the Alabama TechnaCenter Research Park an ideal asset for the growth of Montgomery business.

An important function of the TechnaCenter park is employee training for Montgomery area companies.

Located on the grounds of the TechnaCenter park is the Institute for Advanced Information Systems. The goal of IAIS is "to develop a facility for the advancement of training, education, research, and development capabilities in the fields of computer software and information systems engineering," according to M. Robert Taffet, training manager for the Advanced Technology Group located in the Institute.

A little more than three years ago, the TechnaCenter was developed in response to an anticipated $1 to $2 million in estimated contract work over a period of 5 to 10 years that would be brought into the state by the Standard Systems Group, located at Gunter Annex of Maxwell Air Force Base.

"The question from the local community was, 'To attract the businesses, what is needed?' " Taffet said. The answer from the software companies polled by TechnaCenter developers included a place to train employees, the support of an educational institution, and the development of software.

The Montgomery City Council approved the formation of the Montgomery Public Educational Building Authority, which authorized a $2.7-million public education bond to build the IAIS. The five acres of land for the IAIS was donated by W. S. Newell. The facility is comprised of 33,300 square feet.

Huntsville, which is home to one of the three largest research parks in the United States, was used as a model for the TechnaCenter Research Park.

Currently, the IAIS is operated by Auburn University at Montgomery and Auburn University, main campus. "The whole idea behind it is when the bond issue is paid, [IAIS] will become an Auburn University facility," Taffet explained.

Training programs at the IAIS are ongoing, and keep growing to meet the increased need. The estimated $1 to $2 million in contracts has blossomed into more than $10 billion, and the number of software companies in Montgomery has grown from 2 to 61 in the little more than five years the facility has been in operation.

The IAIS offers training to a variety of groups and individuals. There are four main operations of the facility.

The Alabama Industrial Development Training provides a trained workforce for industries expanding or coming into Alabama. AIDT has trained workforces for General Electric, Singapore Aerospace (located in Mobile), and is currently training employees for Mercedes Benz, whose new plant will be located just outside Tuscaloosa. AIDT's Montgomery center was established to support training for Montgomery's information technology industries.

Training in this area includes expertise in Ada, a programming language. Training also includes teaching employees how to use a specific computer system, UNIX training (an operating system, like DOS), and networking. Thousands of employees have been trained through the AIDT program.

"Montgomery now has more Ada-qualified programmers per capita than anywhere else in the world," Taffet said.

In addition to its software training operations at the TechnaCenter, the Alabama Industrial Development Training Institute offers a total training system for the manufacturing industry throughout the state.

AIDT is a state agency, created in 1971 and incorporated into the secondary education system. According to its mission statement, "The mission of Alabama Industrial Development Training is to provide quality workforce development for Alabama's new and existing industries, and to expand the opportunities of its citizens through the jobs these industries create."

Basically, AIDT provides all the help a company could need. "If a company wants to locate here from somewhere else, or expand its existing operation, we will train their employees to go to work, at no cost to the company," said Phyllis Wesley, media coordinator for AIDT.

The training program actually begins with a needs assessment, in which an AIDT representative meets with the company management to find out exactly what skills and qualities they need in a workforce. AIDT then develops a training program, recruits trainees who meet the

The Gunter Industrial Park houses major corporations, such as Smith Industries, Thermalex, Giles Enterprises, Rheem Manufacturing, American Sterilizer Company, EDS, and others. Photo by Robert Fouts.

The Lewis Library, located in west Montgomery, is equipped with state-of-the-art computer equipment to aid in conducting research. This is just one of the many amenities Montgomery has to offer. Photo by Robert Fouts.

*T*raining is available not only for large corporations, but for small businesses as well. In 1990 the Montgomery Area Chamber of Commerce developed COSBE, the Council of Small Business Enterprises. The goal of COSBE is to help meet the financial, educational, and practical needs of small-business owners. Small businesses, employing less than 100, now make up about 92 percent of Chamber membership.

Small businesses make a large financial contribution to the Montgomery economy. Photos by Robert Fouts.

needs requirement, and implements a training program.

Often, the training program incorporates staff from the company itself, because they are most familiar with the operations of the business. Also, AIDT instructors will help with training and assist company personnel in teaching the trainees.

After training, the company is under no obligation to hire the trainees, and the trainee is not obligated to accept a job from the company. However, the idea is to train specific people for specific jobs that a particular company needs. "We don't train unless there is a job waiting," Wesley said.

If the company does not yet have facilities where employees may receive training, or if there is no nearby facility for this purpose, AIDT has Mobile Training Units (MTUs), which are large portable classrooms that can be brought on-site even while the business is being constructed.

Last year, AIDT trained 1,003 people in Montgomery for companies including Jefferson Smurfit, Kershaw Manufacturing, Liz Claiborne, Dow-UTC, and Thermal Components, among others.

In addition to its training center in Montgomery at the TechnaCenter Research Park, AIDT has facilities adjacent to John Patterson Technical School and has training centers in Huntsville and Mobile.

"Some people question that these services are offered 'free,'" Wesley said. "But if you pay taxes, you paid for it. Even businesses that aren't located here yet contribute by deciding to move here—if we can get people in this state better jobs, that's the return on our investment," she said.

Auburn University at Montgomery's Continuing Education program offers open enrollment for businesses and the general public in software courses. Students may take classes from the beginner to advanced levels.

AUM's Advanced Technology Group at the IAIS provides contractual software training for state and federal employees, as well as central Alabama businesses and industries.

The State of Alabama Department of Finance, Data Systems Management Division, Information Technology Group controls the vast majority of computer software training for the state. Development work also is done by this group. The Financial Resource Management Systems (FRMS) fully integrated all state agencies in the areas of payroll, purchasing, personnel, and procurement. Whereas each state office used to keep track of separate bookkeeping, the system has now integrated all offices.

"Every day at 6:00 A.M., the state knows exactly where it stands fiscally," Taffet said. "This is the only fully integrated system of its kind."

Government leaders from nearly every state in the nation have visited the IAIS to see this system in action and to study the possibilities of integrating their own state systems in the future, he said.

The IAIS houses 10 computer labs equipped with the latest PC and Sun workstations, with most of those networked to the Alabama Supercomputer Network. The facility also contains office space, classrooms, and conference areas.

The IAIS is a cooperative effort between community, business, and education, Taffet believes. "This is a conduit from software companies to Auburn University to AUM, to contractors—to let each other know what is needed," he said.

Auburn University offers a master's degree in computer science and engineering, with needed courses offered at IAIS. Also, IAIS lets the AUM and AU campuses know what high-intensity undergraduate math classes need to be offered to students interested in pursuing the computer science and engineering master's degree.

"The Institute for Advanced Information Systems, and the TechnaCenter as a whole, is an example of a community effort to attract companies, to attract business, to the state. And it is a successful effort," Taffet said.

Additional training and educational opportunities can be found through degree and continuing education programs offered by Troy State University at Montgomery, Huntingdon College, Alabama State University, John Patterson Technical College, and Trenholm State Technical College.

Training is available not only for large corporations, but for small businesses as well. In 1990 the Montgomery Area Chamber of Commerce developed COSBE, the Council of Small Business Enterprises. The goal of COSBE is to help meet the financial, educational, and practical needs of small-business owners. Small businesses, employing less than 100, now make up about 92 percent of Chamber membership.

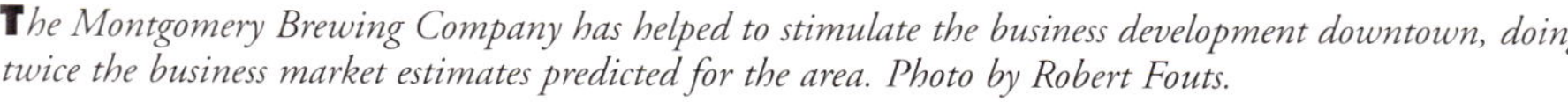

The Montgomery Brewing Company has helped to stimulate the business development downtown, doing twice the business market estimates predicted for the area. Photo by Robert Fouts.

First Alabama
UNION
COURT SQUARE

As the name suggests, Commerce Street is a center for Montgomery business, as the location of banks, broadcasting studios, central offices, shops, and restaurants. Photo by Robert Fouts.

COSBE was the idea of small-business owner Margaret Carpenter, president of Compos-It, and Montgomery Mayor Emory Folmar, working with the Chamber of Commerce.

As a woman in business by herself (after the death of her husband in 1963), Carpenter found businessmen and bankers would not take her seriously.

So she joined the Chamber of Commerce. "It's a proving ground," she said of the Chamber. "You can build your credibility by working with the Chamber, because everything they do is good for the area," she said.

Carpenter began volunteering, and launched Jubilee CityFest, which now draws thousands of visitors to Montgomery every year. She was the first woman to serve on the Chamber's executive committee, and served as the Chamber's first woman chairman in 1995.

Being a small-business owner herself, she recognized the financial contribution small businesses make to the economy and also realized their need for extra help and attention in order to succeed.

After attending a small-business workshop in Oklahoma, she worked to develop the COSBE program. COSBE offers free small-business counseling in a number of areas, including accounting, advertising, business management, financial planning, insurance, and more.

Special seminars and educational programs also help small-business owners find the help they need. Counseling is available from successful businessmen and women in the same or similar field as a struggling new small-business owner. These experienced business people can provide helpful insight and tips.

Beyond educational support, COSBE has spawned the development of the Montgomery Area Community Development Corporation (MACDC), a nonprofit corporation which provides alternative financing for small business. Through MACDC, anyone who might not have access to conventional financing resources can apply for a loan, totaling up to $75,000. The MACDC is made up of eight area banks: AmSouth Bank of Alabama, Colonial Bank, Compass Bank, First Alabama Bank, First Montgomery Bank, First Tuskegee Bank, SouthTrust Bank, N.A., and Sterling Bank.

The Chamber also launched in 1995 ChamberChoice—an affordable health insurance plan for business owners and their employees. The idea is for small businesses to form a group-purchasing alliance, allowing them to receive group-rate health insurance for their employees.

Finally, COSBE provides that needed "pat on the back," recognizing outstanding small businesses for their achievements, and provides a

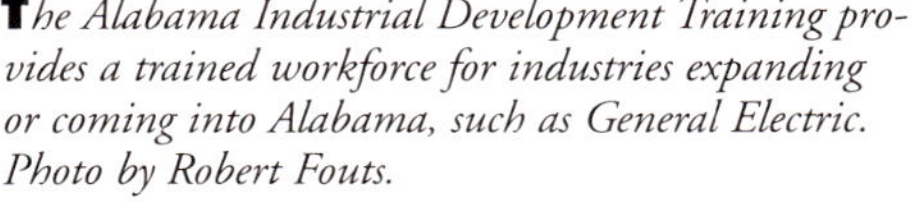

The Alabama Industrial Development Training provides a trained workforce for industries expanding or coming into Alabama, such as General Electric. Photo by Robert Fouts.

networking system for small-business owners to get to know each other. Other benefits offered through COSBE include a free counseling program conducted by retired executives providing advice to new business owners, drawing on the wisdom of their experiences. This program is called SCORE, the Service Corps of Retired Executives. Additionally, COSBE provides a valuable networking system that allows small-business owners to meet and get to know one another. Final plans are currently underway to open a small-business incubator in Montgomery, where 20 to 30 new companies a year are expected to launch.

LOCATION

Now that training is taken care of, business owners need to know they will be able to find a good location for their business, and one that will allow for growth.

The South is one of the fastest-growing business markets, and the Montgomery area offers plenty of opportunity for business location and expansion.

The Gunter Industrial Park houses such corporations as American Sterilizer Company, Rheem Manufacturing, EDS, and others. The Alabama TechnaCenter Research Park is home to GTE, Alabama Rural Electric Cooperative Association, and the Institute for Advanced Information Systems, with other properties in development.

Liz Claiborne, Blue Bell Ice Cream, and Flowers Bakery were able to establish large industrial facilities in Montgomery, and General Electric located its plastics plant in nearby Lowndes County.

This economic growth has spread through the metro-Montgomery area. Arkay Plastics and Wright Plastics recently located in Prattville, while Russell Corp. has expanded with new facilities in Elmore County.

Development in the city also includes a revitalization of the downtown area, with new construction including the Embassy Suites Hotel and Conference Center, a $22.5-million project; The Advertiser Company production facility, a $15-million undertaking; and the Retirement Systems of Alabama Tower, Alabama Activities Center, and other RSA projects totalling an estimated $125 million.

The next big project on the horizon is the construction of a new Federal Courthouse building. Construction costs for the 271,000-square-foot project are estimated at $41 million. Construction is set to begin in July of 1996, and

An international corporate giant, KinderCare operates from headquarters inside Montgomery's Executive Park. Photo courtesy of KinderCare.

the project will take approximately 30 to 36 months to complete.

Downtown construction is expected to keep growing, with the addition of a new Capital City Club and planned riverfront developments.

TRANSPORTATION

Once settled in Montgomery, businesses will find it easy to get products, services, and employees where they need to go from the city's central location. Whether moving people or goods is the objective, Montgomery's planes, trains, and automobiles—not to mention the Alabama River— will get the job done.

Dannelly Field is an air carrier airport located within the Montgomery city limits, southwest of the central business district. Activities at the airport include air carrier operations, such as passenger, mail, and air cargo service; military operations by the Alabama Air and Army National Guard; general aviation operations; corporate aircraft operations; and flight base operation activities (aircraft sales, charter, cargo, agricultural operations, major and minor airframe, power plant repairs, and flight instructing).

Four airlines transport passengers to destinations including Atlanta, Memphis, Charlotte, and many others. About 220,000 people are enplaned per year, and approximately 1 million people visit the Montgomery Airport each year.

The interstate system will quickly get cars and trucks to where they are going. I-85 and I-65 lead to Atlanta, Birmingham, Mobile, Huntsville, and Nashville, and provide quick and easy interchange routes for connecting with other major highways. Atlanta is a straight-shot, two-and-a-half-hour trip northeast; Birmingham is about an hour and 30 minutes away, and Mobile can be reached in about three hours.

A system of rail travel is available for cargo transport both in and out of Montgomery, and passenger travel is available from stations in nearby Birmingham. Industrial routes run on a varied cycle to assure businesses of quick transport opportunities.

"Rail is a key factor for certain types of industry," said Al Cook, senior vice president of corporate development for the Montgomery Area Chamber of Commerce. Rail transport is particularly useful for chemical industries as a safe, efficient method of ground transport for resins and plastics. Jefferson Smurfit and General Electric are two of the Montgomery companies that make use of rail service.

The Alabama State Docks provide port of entry for cargo traveling along the Alabama River. Barges transport large loads to major ports. "The Alabama River is navigable all the way to the port of Mobile, so you can essentially get to anywhere in the world from here," Cook said.

The river is used primarily for the transport of sand and gravel, and occasionally grain and some chemicals. During the summer, some ports are not navigable due to low water levels, but the river is fully navigable about 60 to 70 percent of the time, Cook said.

THE AMENITIES

Of course, it takes more than concrete to make a business run. The best location, training, and transport routes in the world will not make a company successful if its employees are unhappy with their quality of life.

Montgomery can give businesses the best of both worlds. "We're not a huge metropolitan area, but I think we're a real optimum-size city. You don't want for anything, but there's not too much of it, either," said Tom Somerville, district manager for BellSouth.

He, along with his wife and children, moved to Montgomery from Birmingham in 1975. "When we came here in 1975 from Birmingham, it was a little different culture, but if you're willing to go out and meet people and get involved with them, you'll find they respond in kind," he said. "No matter what you're interested in—arts, sports, community service, youth activities—you can find it here. You can find your niche."

"We have an unusual quality of life that companies and their executives are just amazed by," agreed Carpenter. "This is a town where one person can make a difference if they want to," she said.

Recognizing that executives often get to see Montgomery's charms before moving here, but their spouses often do not, Carpenter helped create a "Reluctant Spouse Committee" to allay spouses' fears of moving to the "redneck South."

"We really take a bum rap on our image," Carpenter explained. "People make jokes about

Schlumberger is an example of a worldwide corporation that recognizes the business value of a central Alabama location. Photo by Robert Fouts.

Two regional malls provide the citizens of central Alabama a unique shopping experience. Photo by Robert Fouts.

A *system of rail travel is available for cargo transport both in and out of Montgomery. Photo by Robert Fouts.*

F*rom Montgomery's Dannelly Field, four airlines transport passengers to destinations including Atlanta, Memphis, Charlotte, and many others. Photo by Robert Fouts.*

the South being slow or backward. This is a cultural committee to show people apprehensive about moving here what we really have to offer."

Through the Reluctant Spouse Committee, Montgomery newcomers can find out about cultural attractions such as the Montgomery Museum of Fine Arts, Montgomery Symphony Orchestra, the Alabama Shakespeare Festival, Montgomery Ballet, and Alabama Dance Theatre.

They learn about educational opportunities, volunteer groups, civic clubs, and organizations—everything Montgomery has to offer. "We've got everything in the world—everything is a plus for us," Carpenter said.

"There has to be a reason so many people choose to locate a business in the Montgomery area, and, more important, why they choose to stay here even after retiring or changing careers," said Chamber President Randy George.

"Generally, you could stick a dart in the map anywhere in the Southeast and operate a business fairly the same," he said. "The things that really make the difference in the final analysis have to do with people, and the personality of the town, and the attitude of the people who live here."

Like many towns in the South, Montgomery offers good weather, excellent transportation, and a good business climate in general. "But its greatest resource is its people. It's true," George said. "It has more to do with chivalry, kindness, a willingness to do what's right, even when no one's looking." **m**

Gates 1 to 5 →
Restaurant / Gifts
Waiting / Vending
Waiting / Vending
Lounge
Ticketing / Check-in
USAir
EXPRESS

A MILITARY SALUTE

Everywhere you go in Montgomery, you see them. In the workplace, at the local PTA meeting, or rolling up their sleeves to volunteer wherever help is needed. They are the members of the military community in Montgomery.

The area's military population includes officers and enlisted personnel at Maxwell Air Force Base (MAFB) and Gunter Annex; students at the many schools on MAFB, including the Air War College, Officer Training School, and Air Command and Staff College; and numerous people who serve in the National Guard and military reserve programs throughout the tri-county area of Montgomery, Autauga, and Elmore Counties.

Maxwell Air Force Base and Gunter Annex bring in top military leaders from throughout the world to Montgomery. When members of the military leave Montgomery, they take a bit of the city with them in their hearts. And we, their hosts, are left with a broader picture of the world. Photo by Robert Fouts.

Additionally, there are some 10,000 military retirees who have selected Montgomery above anywhere else in the world to make their home.

"The relationship between members of the military and Montgomerians is long-standing and one of the best anywhere in the nation," said Captain Robert Gonzales, chief of public affairs for the 42nd Air Base Wing. "Maxwell-Gunter has one of the best community relationships in the entire Air Force," Gonzales said. "A relationship like this doesn't just happen. It takes a lot of work, from people in the city and people on the base."

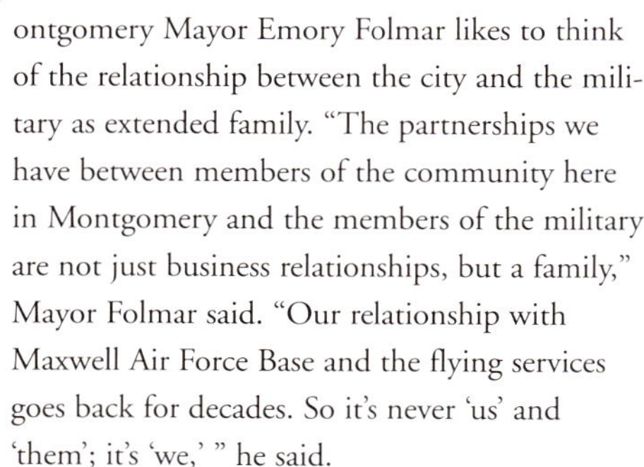

ontgomery Mayor Emory Folmar likes to think of the relationship between the city and the military as extended family. "The partnerships we have between members of the community here in Montgomery and the members of the military are not just business relationships, but a family," Mayor Folmar said. "Our relationship with Maxwell Air Force Base and the flying services goes back for decades. So it's never 'us' and 'them'; it's 'we,' " he said.

The area where Maxwell Air Force Base now stands was first used for flight by Orville and Wilbur Wright, who established a civilian pilot training school in Montgomery in 1910. A hangar located in the general area where base operations now stands served as the Wright brothers' first airplane hangar in those early years.

In years to follow, the airstrip was developed and expanded and became a site for Army Air Force pilot training. The Air Corps Tactical School was established in the years between World War I and World War II, and pilots from throughout the United States came to Montgomery to receive the best training available.

The site was originally called Maxwell Field in 1922, in honor of Lieutenant William Calvin Maxwell, a United States Army pilot who died when his plane crashed in Manilla, Philippines, in 1920. Lieutenant Maxwell died while steering his plummeting aircraft away from a plantation filled with children at play, sparing their lives with the sacrifice of his own. With the development of the United States Air Force, the site was designated Maxwell Air Force Base in January 1948.

From the early tactical school rose the idea for an Air University, a direct recognition of the importance of professional education to the new service's future.

The concept of an Air University was devised in 1946, under the direction of General Muir S. Fairchild, who was the university's first commander. It is Air University's mission to conduct professional military education, graduate education, and professional continuing education for officers, enlisted personnel, and civilians to prepare them for command, staff, leadership, and management responsibilities. Its students come from all over the world.

Air University is recognized as the nation's center for aerospace education, providing specialized education to meet Air Force requirements in scientific, technological, managerial, and other professional areas. The university is also responsible for research in many areas of aerospace and flight technology.

There are several schools under the direction of Air University.

Squadron Officer School is the first level of the professional military education for an Air Force officer. The school provides professional development for Air Force captains, and covers subjects on officership, communication skills, leadership in the Air Force, and force employment. This is a seven-week program.

The Air Command and Staff College provides intermediate professional military education to prepare selected officers for command and staff responsibilities. The student body of the resident course is composed of mid-career officers from the Air Force, other services, selected Department of Defense civilians, and international officers.

The curriculum includes command studies, combat support, space, nuclear and theater war-

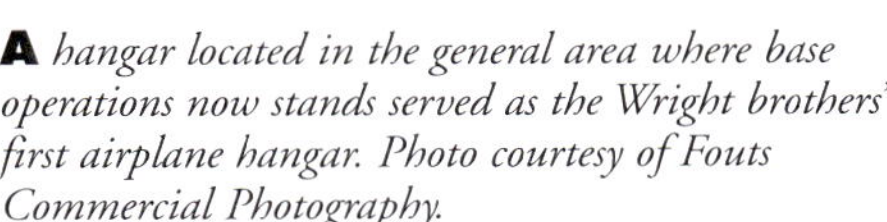

A *hangar located in the general area where base operations now stands served as the Wright brothers' first airplane hangar. Photo courtesy of Fouts Commercial Photography.*

T *he area where Maxwell Air Force Base now stands was first used for flight by Orville and Wilbur Wright, who established a civilian pilot training school in Montgomery in 1910. Photo by Robert Fouts.*

fare, low intensity conflict, military history and doctrine, national security affairs, quality concepts, staff communications, and the profession of arms.

Officers are stationed in Montgomery for about one year while completing the ACSC program. About 550 students attend the course in residence, while more than 7,464 enroll in the associate programs (group-study program or correspondence course) each year.

The Air War College is the Air Force's senior professional military education school. It prepares selected colonels and lieutenant colonels for key command and staff assignments. The core curriculum provides a strong focus on the study of military strategy.

Officer Training School includes Basic Officer Training and Commissioned Officer Training. In Basic Officer Training, a 13-and-one-half-week program, officer candidates are prepared for the professional, physical, and technical challenges of commissioned service through a rigorous curriculum focusing on communicative skills, leadership studies, professional knowledge, and defense studies. One of the highlights of the program is the Leadership Reaction course, a field exercise in which small groups of students test their ability to reason quickly and lead effectively to get the group through a specialized obstacle course.

The Commissioned Officer Training program provides military orientation and indoctrination to commissioned, nonline officers to include doctors, nurses, lawyers, and those in similar fields. There are three courses designed to suit specific needs. All of the courses reflect

the basic OTS curriculum. The length of these courses varies from two to three weeks.

Other educational programs under the Air University include the Air Force Institute of Technology; Civil Air Patrol; College for Enlisted Professional Military Education; College of Aerospace Doctrine, Research, and Education; Community College of the Air Force; Ira C. Eaker College for Professional Development; Air Force ROTC; and the Air Force Quality Institute.

Additionally, the Air University Library, called the Fairchild Library in honor of General Muir S. Fairchild, holds comprehensive collections covering issues of military affairs, international relations, aerospace operation, higher education, leadership and management, and social sciences. Holdings include 380,000 books and bound periodical volumes, more than 512,000 military-specific documents, and more than 850,000 maps and charts. Also, the library subscribes to nearly 1,900 journals and newspapers from throughout the world.

Just as Maxwell Air Force Base's Air University plays an important role worldwide in air and space power education, Gunter Annex's Headquarters Standard Systems Group (SSG)

takes center stage in information technology and communications computer systems for major commands and Air Force bases around the world.

Currently the SSG is assigned to the Air Force Material Command, specifically the Electronic Systems Center, headquartered in Hanscom Air Force Base, Massachusetts. The mission of the SSG is to provide specified standard information and telecommunications systems to major commands and Air Force bases. The Standard Systems Group designs, develops, acquires, produces, maintains, and manages, for their life cycles, computer systems for the Air Force, Department of Defense, and other federal agencies worldwide.

The Standard Systems Group has its origins in the establishment of the Air Force Data Systems Design Center, created in 1967 to design, develop, program, test, implement, and maintain all assigned automated data processing systems. The Data Systems Design Center was located at Bolling Air Force Base in Maryland. In 1971 the unit was relocated to Gunter Air Force Base in Montgomery.

In 1985 the Headquarters Air Force Teleprocessing Center, activated at Gunter in 1984, was redesignated the Standard Information Systems Center. This unit was renamed the Standard Systems Center (SSC) in late 1986. In 1989 the Computer Systems Division was activated at Gunter, and the SSC became its largest subordinate unit. After merging the functions of the SSC with those of a few other computer systems and services operations, the organization was redesignated as Headquarters Standard Systems Group in 1995.

The current organizational structure of the SSG consists of approximately 2,500 people, including military, civilian, and contractors. The center has more than 1,800 manpower authorizations, about 40 percent of that civilian.

The blend in the business world of civilian and military personnel at Gunter Annex and Maxwell Air Force Base, working side by side to meet a common goal and purpose, is exemplary of the military-civilian interaction in the community as well.

"The relationship between the Montgomery community and Maxwell-Gunter has always been good," said Rod Payne, vice president of military and international affairs for the Montgomery Area Chamber of Commerce, and a retired vice commander of Air University.

"We are now working to continue to improve that relationship. It's important because the

Maxwell Air Force Base was named in honor of Lieutenant William Calvin Maxwell, a United States Army pilot who died when his plane crashed in Manilla, Philippines, in 1920. Photo by Robert Fouts.

The area's military population includes officers and enlisted personnel at Maxwell Air Force Base and Gunter Annex, students at the many schools on MAFB, and numerous people who serve in the National Guard and military reserve programs throughout the tri-county area. Photo by Robert Fouts.

EXIT

HEADQUARTERS
STANDARD SYSTEMS GROUP

military community—active duty, guard, and reserves—is very important to the community as a whole," he said. From a financial standpoint, the military, including guard and reserves, brings over $1.1 billion to Montgomery annually, Payne said.

The population of Maxwell-Gunter, which includes Air University, Wing, and Associated Units (such as the Standard Systems Group), is about 9,700, according to the 42nd ABW Public Affairs Office. Counting active duty, dependents, retirees, and other factors, the military population is estimated at 40,000.

Additionally, the bases provide approximately 6,000 secondary jobs, and military personnel donate more than 130,000 volunteer man-hours to the community on an annual basis.

In 1994 the Maxwell-Gunter volunteers, comprised of about 2,355 members of the Maxwell-Gunter family, were recognized by the Montgomery community as Volunteers of the Year. In addition to the man-hours spent in a variety of programs, the military community raised and distributed almost $1 million to directly benefit the Montgomery community.

Members of the military offer their services in a wide variety of areas. As Partners In Education to local schools, they provide guest speakers, tutor students, sponsor leadership programs, organize base tours for students, participate in work days to refurbish school buildings, and even treat exceptional students to flights aboard Aero Club planes.

Additionally, they serve as volunteers in community and national service agencies and are active members of their local churches, schools, and neighborhoods.

In order to help foster the relationship between military and community, the Montgomery Area Chamber of Commerce has developed four programs specifically to build closeness between business and military leaders, as well as individuals.

"We want the citizenry of the Montgomery area to realize what these people do for the community and also the economy," said Tom Albrecht, chairman of the Military Affairs Committee, a branch of the Chamber's Military Affairs Council.

The Maxwell/Gunter/Montgomery Partners (MGM Partners) program pairs key individuals, one from the business community and the other from the military. These partners attend social and business functions together, spend time in each other's work areas, and see how the other functions for one year. This is to foster understanding and closeness.

"Our effort is for the community and the military to see how the other half lives," Albrecht said.

The Air War College (AWC) Project Interface assigns a couple from the community to act as a liaison to a seminar group from the AWC. The couple ensures that the seminar members are aware of activities going on in the community and act as "buddies" to help them learn what is available to them in the city.

Interface partners host special get-togethers and parties for their seminar groups, arrange tours of the city and help AWC students find out what activities are available in Montgomery to suit their interests. Many Project Interface participants develop close bonds and continue to correspond with their military friends after their tour of duty in Montgomery is over.

Jean Hackman has been involved with Project Interface since it began three years ago, and has served as a program coordinator. Each year she hosts a party for the entire seminar group, including students and their spouses, plus the directors of the Air War College, host families involved in the Interface program, and Chamber leaders.

The party provides an opportunity for everybody to get to know each other, Hackman said. "It's important for members of the military to have contacts—liaisons—in the community. Otherwise, they really don't get a chance to know Montgomery. They can be kind of isolated on the base," she said. Students at the Air War College are stationed in Montgomery for one year, and are from all branches of military service. They generally range in age from about 35 to 45 Hackman estimates.

Prior to the beginning of each new AWC session, volunteers who wish to be Interface hosts fill out a questionnaire to determine their interests. Students at AWC also fill out a questionnaire and are matched as closely as possible with host couples or families who share similar interests.

Throughout the year that the students are in Montgomery, host couples get together with their military friends at least once a month, and often help out on a regular basis with day-to-day problems or questions.

"They [students] have a multitude of problems and questions," Hackman said. "It's nice for them to have somebody to call here, who knows the community. I helped with questions ranging from how their children could get involved in the community, to recommending doctors, or just helping them over being lonesome." Hackman sees Project Interface as a win-win situation for all involved.

The Air University Library holds comprehensive collections covering issues of military affairs, international relations, aerospace operation, higher education, leadership and management, and social sciences. Photo by Robert Fouts.

Gunter Annex's Headquarters Standard Systems Group takes center stage in information technology and communications computer systems for major commands and Air Force bases around the world. Photo courtesy of U.S. Air Force.

A strong relationship with the community is obvious in the number of military personnel who choose to retire in the Montgomery area, selecting it above anywhere else in the world. Photo by Robert Fouts. (left)

The military operations of the Alabama Air and Army National Guard are headquartered at Montgomery's Dannelly Field. Photo by Robert Fouts. (top)

Air Force firefighters on Maxwell-Gunter are ready to respond to any contingency from structural fires to aircraft incidents. Photo courtesy of U.S. Air Force. (below)

1LT KARL W. RICHTER
KIA JULY 28, 1967, NORTH VIETNAM
-OF THE WARRIOR BREED-

Members of the military offer their services to the community in a wide variety of areas. Photo by Robert Fouts.

From the early tactical school rose the idea for an Air University, a direct recognition of the importance of professional education to the new service's future. Photo by Robert Fouts. (left)

The Standard Systems Group designs, develops, acquires, produces, maintains, and manages computer systems for the Air Force, Department of Defense, and other federal agencies worldwide. Photo by Robert Fouts.

"For the military, it's an opportunity to learn about the community and form friendships. There isn't a whole lot they don't get to know about Montgomery after being a part of Interface—from the Alabama Shakespeare Festival to the zoo," she said.

"For hosts, I think they really learn what Maxwell is all about here in Montgomery," she said. Participants in Project Interface attend many special programs and events at Maxwell Air Force Base, allowing them to become more familiar with military life, she explained.

"Also, they get a chance to know people who will be our future leaders. These are our military leaders, and they will be our future generals and leaders," Hackman said.

"We've celebrated our daughters' weddings, the births of our two grandsons, and major holidays with them," said program participant Dottye Hannan of her experience with the officers she and her husband, Jim, have entertained. "We are still close with many of the people we have hosted."

A similar program, OTS (Officers Training School) Operation Classmate, pairs an individual or family from the community with an OTS class. Students at OTS are usually young, college-aged people, and their hosts can help them learn how to get involved in whatever community they are stationed, so the students not only have a pleasant experience in Montgomery, but also feel more at ease reaching out to a new community when they are transferred.

"Social interaction between people in the city and members of the military adds an extra dimension to the relationship, outside of business," Mayor Folmar said. "I enjoy our friends here in the military. They are good folks, interesting people, and, more importantly, they defend this country. Military leaders have spoken favorably about our relationship with the military being one of the best anywhere in the world," he said. "We work hard at it, but it's a labor of love."

The good relationship is obvious in the number of military personnel who choose to retire in Montgomery, selecting our area above anywhere else in the world.

"I have no doubt I made the right decision to stay in Montgomery," Payne said. "I like the way people approach life here. They are always ready to step forward and make good things happen," he said.

During his service in the Air Force, Payne was stationed many different places, both in the United States and overseas. He was an integral part of Air University, retiring as vice commander of Air University in 1994.

"In my mind, this is the only place I've ever lived where local government leaders, key community and business leaders, the Chamber, and key civic, social, and nonprofit agencies are all in the same boat, paddling in the same direction," he said. "They all want to work to make the right thing happen. I have never seen that to the same extent anywhere else. It's exciting, and it's what made me want to make this my home." **77**

The senior officers' quarters at Maxwell were built between 1932 and 1935 and are among the most elegant found on any U.S. Air Force base. The 99 houses are set in a park-like setting with open grassy areas, winding streets, sidewalks, and shade trees. These houses are listed on the National Historic Register. Photo courtesy of U.S. Air Force.

The population of Maxwell-Gunter, which includes Air University, Wing, and Associated Units (such as the Standard Systems Group), is about 9,700, according to the 42nd ABW Public Affairs Office. Counting active duty, dependents, retirees, and other factors, the military population is estimated at 40,000.

The Air War College Project Interface assigns a couple from the community to act as a liaison to a seminar group from the AWC. Interface partners host special get-togethers and parties for their seminar groups, arrange tours of the city, and help AWC students find out what activities are available in Montgomery. Photo by Robert Fouts.

GOVERNMENT IN PROGRESS

Standing at the foot of the State Capitol building, at the base of the massive marble staircase, looking upward as the sun warms the majestic white dome and glints off marble columns as big around as large tree trunks, one begins to feel the awesome power of government, politics, and tradition that make Montgomery unique as the Capital City of Alabama.

Montgomery has been the state capital since 1846, and has rarely relinquished her proud position of power since that time. Photo by Robert Fouts. Archival photo courtesy of Fouts Commercial Photography.

Montgomery has been the state capital since 1846, and has rarely relinquished her proud position of power since that time. Even when Alabama seceded from the Union during the Civil War, Montgomery retained her leadership status for three months, becoming the Capital of the Confederacy under its president, Jefferson Davis, before the newly formed governmental seat was moved to Richmond, Virginia.

The first Capitol building was constructed in the Greek Revival style in 1847, from designs created by Philadelphia architect Stephen Button. Tragically, the structure burned in 1849. When it came time to rebuild, the Greek Revival style was kept, and the new structure, constructed in 1850-1851, still stands today as the center section of the present Capitol building. In this section visitors can still view the original governor's suite, house chamber, and senate chamber, restored and decorated to authentically replicate the way the rooms looked when originally used.

The rear wing of the Capitol building was added in 1885, and the two side wings were added between 1906 and 1912. The most modern addition to the building is a rear portico, designed in a neoclassical style to match the original west front portico, added in 1992. The newest addition allows for an underground tunnel linking the Capitol building with the State House, where the new senate and house chambers are located, along with other offices of state government.

The beautiful domed Capitol building has watched over many significant changes in Montgomery's history. The house chamber was the site of the Alabama Legislature's decision to secede from the Union. The inauguration of Confederate President Jefferson Davis in February of 1861 was held on the grand front porch of the building, and a bronze star marks the approximate location where he pledged to lead the fledgling nation.

A decade later, when freedom from slavery had been gained and freedom from discrimination was sought, the Capitol steps welcomed participants of the Selma-to-Montgomery civil rights march, led by Dr. Martin Luther King Jr., as they culminated their symbolic trek on the Capitol steps March 25, 1965.

In recognition of the significant role the State Capitol has played in the history of the state and the nation, the building was designated a National Historic Landmark in 1960.

A massive $60-million renovation project begun in the 1970s and finished in 1992 restored

The rotunda, beneath the dome of the Capitol building, features colorful murals depicting Alabama's historic heritage. Photo by Robert Fouts. (left)

Alabama governors have lived in this 1906 mansion since its purchase by the State of Alabama in the 1950s. Designed by architect Weatherly Carter for Robert Ligon, the house reflects the neo-classical influence so in demand in the early years of the twentieth century. Photo by Robert Fouts. (right)

the Capitol to its former glory. Experts stripped away years of paint and plaster to reveal the original wallpapers, paint, and design of the building, with every aspect painstakingly researched and restored. Murals originally painted in 1930 around the interior circumference of the dome depict scenes from Alabama history. From the carpeting on the floors to the chandeliers in the ceilings, and even to the artwork decorating the walls to the tip-top of the Capitol dome, the Alabama State Capitol building is an authentic trip into state history.

Throughout the downtown area, the architecture that houses state government echoes the white-marbled elegance of the Capitol building. From the State of Alabama Archives and History Building, which not only houses history but is also a bit of architectural history in its own right, to the still-new Gordon Persons Building, the classic columned architecture is a reflection of the grandeur of days past, and a reminder of the presence of government in the day-to-day life of Montgomery's citizens.

Indeed, the federal, state, and local governments provide 25 percent of the total jobs in Montgomery, employing approximately 37,400 people, according to figures calculated by the State Department of Industrial Relations in June of 1995. The federal government accounts for 6,900 of that number, while the State of Alabama, city, and county governments provide 30,500 jobs in Montgomery County.

"The federal, state, and local governments obviously play a significant role in the Montgomery area economy," said Al Cook, senior vice president of corporate development for the Montgomery Area Chamber of Commerce. "The government is a large part of the bedrock of the economy, making up a quarter of the workforce, which lends a great deal of stability to our area."

Operating in the shadow of such grandeur, many local governments could get overshadowed by the workings of the state. However, Montgomery's city and county governments stand as firm examples of good government and sound fiscal leadership.

Led by Montgomery Mayor Emory Folmar, the city government has consistently provided top-quality services to the citizens of Montgomery, while also consistently operating on a budget always in the black.

A top priority for Mayor Folmar is the protection of Montgomery citizens by the city police and fire departments. According to a survey conducted by the FBI in 1994, Montgomery was ranked 18th on the list of safest cities its size in the United States, out of close to 200 cities of comparable size. There are more police officers per capita in Montgomery than most cities the same size, according to Lieutenant Cindy Reynolds, crime prevention officer for the Montgomery Police Department.

"Overall, our report card compared to cities of comparable size is very good," said Police Chief John Wilson III. "Of course, we're not immune to social ills, but overall we've been able to get out in front of problems other cities are facing, and have tried to learn from their experiences and develop programs to prevent those problems before they happen here," he said.

Programs have included the development of a school security bureau; a strong DARE (Drug Abuse Resistance Education) program; and a community services bureau, which administers crime prevention programs such as Neighborhood Watch. Other programs developed with an eye toward prevention include police security at sporting events, which has been in place since the 1970s. Also, the Montgomery Police Department developed an active security program for the South Alabama State Fair, including a gang watch initiative started recently, in which police are posted at fair entrances to collect hats, jackets, or other items that might be considered gang "uniform." This helps prevent conflicts between rival factions.

"I am proud to say that we have not experienced a major event at the fair in its history," Wilson said. "We are not going to wait for a situation to happen before we make a plan of response. Our philosophy is to deter the problem," he said. "Montgomery's city government and its citizens have provided the positive support to allow the police department to send a message that crime will not be tolerated in the city," Wilson said.

"It is a well-known fact you can have the best police department in the world, but we can be no more effective than the support we get from the community, from the mayor, and from the city government," he said. "And it's a fact that Mayor Folmar and the city council have been 100 percent, dyed-in-the-wool public safety

*T*hroughout the downtown area, the architecture that houses state government echoes the white-marbled elegance of the Capitol building. Photo by Robert Fouts.

The Gordon Persons Building is a reflection of the grandeur of days past, and a reminder of the presence of government in the day-to-day life of Montgomery's citizens. Photo by Robert Fouts.

Montgomery's skyline seems to change almost daily, as a wealth of new construction is springing to life downtown. At the heart of the downtown renaissance is the Retirement Systems of Alabama. Photo by Robert Fouts.

The federal, state, and local governments play a significant role in the Montgomery area economy, making up a quarter of the workforce, which lends a great deal of economic stability. Photos by Robert Fouts.

Public safety always has and always will be my number one priority," Mayor Folmar said. "The ability to go about in peace and safety assures civilization in my mind."

W*hile the Montgomery Fire Department may answer about 24,000 fire and rescue calls each year, firefighters always have time to teach children about fire safety. Photo by Robert Fouts. (left)*

T*he goal of the Montgomery Police Department is crime prevention. Community interaction with programs such as McGruff the Crime Dog help teach children the importance of personal safety. Photo by Robert Fouts. (right)*

Led by Mayor Emory Folmar, the city government has consistently provided top-quality services to the citizens of Montgomery, while also consistently operating on a budget always in the black. Photo by Robert Fouts.

According to a 1994 FBI survey, Montgomery ranked in the top 20 percent of safest cities its size in the United States. There are more police officers per capita in Montgomery than most cities of comparable size. Photo by Robert Fouts.

The Department of Human Resources and the Montgomery County Health Department recently moved into new buildings in west Montgomery. The move accomplished two goals: it was a step in the effort to renovate and re-energize west Montgomery, and it provided a more efficient system of operation for these agencies by allowing them to consolidate many smaller offices into a central location. Photo by Robert Fouts.

supporters for as long as I've been here, which is about 20 years."

The goal of the Montgomery Police Department is to continue its program of crime prevention, and it will focus on two main areas to accomplish that goal in the future.

Internally, the department plans to improve every aspect of department technology, using a 10-year plan for improvement to include an electronic booking system, an electronic reporting system in the field, and computers in the police cars, among others. "Everyone sees police work as toting guns and sticks and riding in cars," Wilson said. "Well, we don't want to get left behind in technology. We want to have the best equipment available to help us fight crime, so it's our goal to become a technology-intensive department."

The other main goal is external—the treatment and, eventually, prevention of juvenile crime. "Juvenile crime is the single largest problem faced not only by this state, but in the nation as well, because those kids are our future," Wilson said. "We will continue to explore every way we can to bring those kids back, to help them become productive members of the community and of society."

One program under this initiative has already gotten underway. The Community Services Program gives youths who are nonviolent offenders the opportunity to work, placing them in jobs in city departments including maintenance, sanitation, and landfills.

"Juvenile crime prevention is our number one priority," Wilson said. "If you stop crime there, you don't have adults who commit crimes."

The Montgomery Fire Department excels in its service to the community as well, earning the city a Class 2 rating from the Insurance Service Organization. The rating is based on how well the department meets a wide variety of standards, including ability to fight a "normal" fire (as opposed to a disaster situation), equipment in place to handle emergency calls, facilities, and personnel, among others, according to Deputy Chief James Fulmer. The rating also takes into account the city's water distribution system and fire hydrants.

"There are very few cities—not more than a handful—that have earned a Class 2 rating," Fulmer said. "We set a high standard for our department, and we have the full backing of our city officials," he said. "The mayor and the city council put a lot of emphasis on public safety. We have outstanding equipment, and the mayor makes sure we have the funds we need to operate." There are currently 424 people employed by the fire department, including 7 civilians. There

are more than 700 people on a waiting list seeking employment with the department. "That's the key—personnel," Fulmer said. "You can have a million-dollar piece of equipment, but if you don't have someone qualified to operate it, it does you no good."

The fire department answers about 24,000 calls each year, with calls including both fire and rescue situations. There are 15 fire stations in the city.

The fire department has two primary goals, Fulmer said—providing fire protection and providing pre-hospital emergency care. Fire protection involves prevention through education and enforcement of the fire code standards, as well as suppression, or putting out the flames. Pre-hospital emergency care is administered by the fire department's paramedics, also called "firemedics." Additionally, there are support units and personnel to help meet both the department's goals.

Having a Class 2 rating assures Montgomery citizens excellent rates on homeowner insurance premiums, which is based primarily on the city fire department protection available, Fulmer said.

"Public safety always has and always will be my number one priority," Mayor Folmar said. "The ability to go about in peace and safety assures civilization in my mind."

In addition to keeping its residents safe, Montgomery government places priority on keeping the city beautiful. Sanitation and maintenance crews provide regular services throughout Montgomery to assure neighborhoods, parks, and public property are kept in tip-top shape.

And the city government is willing to go that extra mile to ensure a cleaner planet for tomorrow. The Montgomery Clean City Commission, in cooperation with the City of Montgomery Sanitation Department and the McInnis Recycling Center, provides a free citywide curbside recycling program. The program serves almost 64,000 homes and provides pick-up of paper, aluminum, and glass recyclable items.

"The curbside pick-up of recyclable items began as a pilot program in 1988, as a part of the annual citywide GLAD Bag-A-Thon city beautification program," said Susan Carmichael, program coordinator for the Montgomery Clean City Commission. The first program was operated through the McInnis Recycling Center.

The recycling plan was so popular, another pilot program was developed, this time for a city-sponsored municipal curbside recycling program, which began in 1989. Again, the citizens of Montgomery responded with enthusiasm, and the program was gradually expanded to include more homes each year until it became a citywide program in 1995. "It was an expensive project, but it would be more expensive not to do it," said Mayor Folmar of the program.

It is estimated that every person throws away about four pounds of trash every day. Some items take 500 years or longer to break down or decompose. Less land is available for landfills and fewer are being built each year, Carmichael explained. "People have the perception when you throw something into a landfill and throw dirt on it, it will go away in a couple of days. It just doesn't work like that," she said.

While the city recycling program does not service apartments or businesses, which contract with private waste disposal companies for trash pick-up, the Clean City Commission is working to establish alternative recycling programs in these areas.

Some businesses are able to work with their waste disposal companies to include a recycling program, and recycling drop-off points are available at many locations throughout the city to serve businesses and apartment residents.

Items collected for recycling are delivered to the McInnis Recycling Center, where they are sorted and recycled. The McInnis Recycling Center provides jobs for about 14 people with mental and/or physical challenges.

Currently, the curbside recycling program is only accepting paper (newspaper, white paper), glass, and aluminum, which can be processed by McInnis, but separate recycling areas are set up throughout the city that can accept plastic and magazines.

"I think it takes every citizen, in their work field as well as their homes, supporting this program to make it work," Carmichael said. "This is a program that should unite the city in an effort that doesn't cost them a dime and is for the betterment of the city and community."

Another area of life receiving constant attention and renovation in Montgomery is its roadways. City streets, including the busy Eastern Bypass, formerly crowded Dalraida Road, Bell Street, Perry Street, Day Street, and the Atlanta Highway, have all recently received the attentions of city maintenance crews, which worked diligently and often at night to make necessary repairs and improvements with as little interruption of the daily routine for citizens as possible.

The quality of life in Montgomery also falls high on the priority list for city government. Recently, two new libraries were constructed to serve citizens, the Lowder Library to serve east Montgomery, and the Lewis Library located in west Montgomery. Both libraries are equipped with state-of-the-art computer equipment to aid in conducting research at the libraries.

Additionally, the main branch of the Montgomery Public Library, located downtown, underwent extensive renovation in 1988, when the Montgomery Museum of Fine Arts, which had previously shared the facilities in which the library is currently located, was relocated to the Wynton M. Blount Cultural Park. The renovation allowed the library to expand, adding a children's reading area, an auditorium, and increasing the library's capacity for adding to its collection.

Above all, Mayor Folmar hopes to meet the needs of the citizens of Montgomery by listening to what they have to say. "I try to work with every citizen who has problems and concerns," Mayor Folmar said. "Our department heads on down to the people who answer the phones are instructed the only reason they have a job is to serve the people who call—to serve the citizens." He hopes this attitude is communicated to the citizens, and that this creates a climate of accessibility.

"The openness of the city is something that's very important, and something that I value. I want people to feel free to walk up to me and ask questions about why we're doing what we're doing, or to tell me what they'd like to see happen," the mayor said.

"For the future, I think the city's role is to provide the environment and the climate for business to grow," Mayor Folmar said. "It's not the city's business to be in business, but to provide a climate for businesses to want to come to Montgomery," he said. "I want to recruit businesses to come here that pay fair wages and treat people and the community well."

The mayor would like to see the city take an active role in revitalization of the downtown area as well, a project already well underway with the construction of the Retirement Systems of Alabama buildings; the expansion of established Montgomery companies into the downtown area, such as the Advertiser Company's new production facility; and new businesses such as the Embassy Suites Hotel. Also, the downtown and riverfront area gained a new city park, Overlook Park.

"The revitalization of downtown is evident," Mayor Folmar said. "And there are even more opportunities ahead of us."

PORTRAIT OF OUR PEOPLE

More than bricks and mortar, a city is built by the people that make up her community. In each city, there are certain individuals who reach out to give that little extra something. While some of these con-tributions are marked with great fanfare, and celebrated for their remarkable nature, others go almost unnoticed, except for the very fact that Montgomery just wouldn't be what she is today if these people did not do what they do.

Emory Folmar has served as Mayor of Montgomery since 1977, and through the years his wife, Anita, has been by his side, working in her own way to make the city a better place to live. Mrs. Folmar is active in many areas through her efforts as a volunteer. Some of her activities include the Montgomery Ballet, Alabama Dance Theatre, Montgomery Symphony Orchestra and Symphony League, the United Way Residential Campaign, CCPAC, the Highland Games, and the Montgomery Children's Center. Photo by Robert Fouts.

Whether or not they receive praise, whether or not their actions are lauded by others, these special people will persevere. For them, there is no other road. They work, not to hear applause for their deeds ringing in their ears, but straining, ever anxious, to see even the faintest hint of a smile from a newcomer or a visitor upon discovering what they have always known—Montgomery is a treasure.

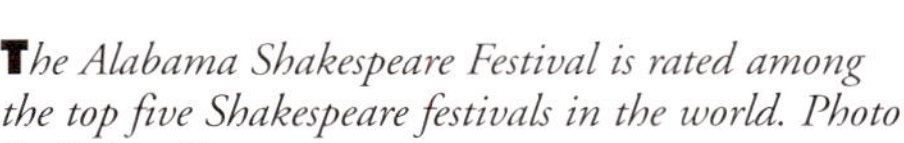

*T*he Alabama Shakespeare Festival is rated among the top five Shakespeare festivals in the world. Photo by Robert Fouts.

*W*inton "Red" Blount's generous donation of land and financial support has infused the city's cultural landscape with new lifeblood. Photo by Robert Fouts.

WINTON MALCOLM "RED" BLOUNT

When speaking of the arts in Montgomery, it will not be long into the conversation before Winton "Red" Blount's name is mentioned. With his generous donation of land and financial support, Blount has infused the city's cultural landscape with new lifeblood.

Blount's most obvious contribution to the arts in Montgomery is the Wynton M. Blount Cultural Park, which contains the Alabama Shakespeare Festival, "the joy of Blount's life," and the Montgomery Museum of Fine Arts on its grounds.

In 1995 the Alabama Shakespeare Festival, rated among the top five Shakespeare festivals in the world, celebrated its 25th anniversary, and its 10th year in Montgomery.

Blount was instrumental in saving the festival from near-certain extinction in 1982. Based north of Montgomery in Anniston, Alabama, the Alabama Shakespeare Festival was limited to a six-week season, with performances held in a high school auditorium. The short season was not enough to sustain the company, and it faced bankruptcy.

Winton Blount's wife, Carolyn, had been active in supporting the Alabama Shakespeare Festival for many years, so the company's directors decided to approach Mr. Blount to ask for his help and financial support.

"I told them if they were willing to move to Montgomery, I would provide them a top-quality theater, and they took me up on it before they left their seats," Blount recalls, laughing. "I knew I was in trouble then," he joked.

The undertaking was dubbed "Red's Folly" early on by skeptics who doubted the city's ability or desire to support a Shakespeare theater, Blount said. "Now, people come from all over the world to visit the theater," he said. "It's wonderful to see the response of the people. It was

my view people were hungry for it. Particularly in the South, we are storytellers. This answers that need."

Blount, along with a development committee, traveled to see 10 noted Shakespeare theaters throughout the world to gather ideas for the design of the new theater in Montgomery.

The $21.5-million theater opened its doors in 1985. Blount named it the Carolyn Blount Theatre in honor of his wife.

"All I know about Shakespeare I learned from my wife," he said. "Nothing we could have done could have been more happy and joyful for Carolyn and myself. It's just been a joy and delight," he said.

Also located in the Blount Cultural Park is the Montgomery Museum of Fine Arts. The museum was relocated from its previous cramped quarters, shared with the Montgomery Public Library, to the beautiful park in 1988. The anchor of the museum's permanent collection is the Blount Collection, 41 paintings by major American artists, valued at $15 to $20 million.

Blount began collecting works by American artists in the late 1970s, as an idea for celebrating the nation's bicentennial, he said. The collection was called "Arts, Inc." and traveled throughout the country and to several countries in South America.

"It's a passion," Blount said of the arts. "And you have to get it, and once you get it, it's never-ending. The arts are important to all of us, and I think it's just imbedded in us."

Mr. Blount hopes to continue to add to the Cultural Park, with talk of including facilities for the Montgomery Ballet, and perhaps an amphitheater.

"I think [the park] contributes to the life here in Montgomery and changes the image not only of Montgomery but of Alabama. I like to think as a result every arts group in the city has grown," Blount said.

MORRIS S. DEES JR.

People either love him or hate him. When you don't allow others to ride the fence, forcing them instead to face their conscience about what is right and what is wrong, you tend to inspire extreme reactions. Morris S. Dees Jr., through his work as chief trial counsel at the Southern Poverty Law Center, which he founded in 1971 with Joseph J. Levin Jr., has grown used to causing a stir. The center is a nonprofit organization that works to protect and advance the legal rights of people of all races, with a special compassion for those who are too poor to pay for legal services.

Dees grew up in Montgomery and became a successful businessman while still a student at the University of Alabama. He and longtime friend and fellow student Millard Fuller ran a profitable mail-order catalog business and became publishers before completing their law degrees. After graduation, the two established a private practice law firm. But the events of the time, the early 1960s, forced Dees to examine his stand on the issue of civil rights, and he felt drawn to take a more active role. He began to participate in and support civil rights actions, and began to feel the sting of criticism. His cases included lawsuits on behalf of the American Civil Liberties Union, and he won a case ending policies of racial segregation within the Montgomery YMCA.

In 1969 Dees sold his successful mail-order business, and he and Levin established a law partnership, agreeing to bill only those clients who could afford to pay. This was the foundation on which today's Southern Poverty Law Center was built. Along with Levin, Dees successfully defended a teacher who had been fired for assigning an "unacceptable" novel to her students as a reading assignment; argued a case that would lead to a landmark Supreme Court decision forcing the United States military to provide equal benefits for women; and he even attacked the local *Montgomery Advertiser* newspaper, forcing it to change its policy of printing segregated social announcements.

"Montgomery is a very traditional town," Dees said. "People were irritated with me for upsetting the status quo. They had seen me go from the son of a local farmer to become a person who challenged a lot of things they held sacred and dear," he said.

It was not his intention, Dees said, to go about making folks angry, but he refused to compromise his conscience to avoid stepping on any toes.

"I always consider my local community first, because this is where I grew up, and I'm happy here. I love this town. But then I have to consider a larger community, of the United States," Dees said.

In the years since its establishment, the mission of the SPLC has grown to include many new branches of service. Klanwatch is a task force that monitors the activities not only of the Ku Klux Klan and other white supremacist groups, but of antigovernment militia groups and other extremist organizations as well. The services of the Klanwatch organization were called upon to assist in the investigation of the recent tragic bombing of the Alfred P. Murrah Federal Building in Oklahoma City, Oklahoma.

The SPLC also oversees a publishing company that produces a series of literature and video materials entitled Teaching Tolerance, designed to "help teachers promote interracial and intercultural understanding in the classroom," according to SPLC literature. The educational magazine is sent free to 500,000 educators, and recently won the top award given by the Educational Press Association of America, the Golden Lamp Award for Excellence in Educational Journalism.

The SPLC's Teaching Tolerance branch also recently created a film, *A Time For Justice: America's Civil Rights Movement*, which won an Academy Award for excellence in documentary filmmaking.

The work of the Southern Poverty Law Center literally "goes from the courtroom to the classroom," Dees said. "On the classroom level, it's a fight to have tolerance, to develop tolerance. In court, it's the fight against intolerance," he explained.

While the work of the Southern Poverty Law Center still draws fire from its critics, sometimes literally—the original SPLC building was destroyed by a bomb in 1983, to be replaced by the shiny modern facility that features an extensive security system and armed guards to screen visitors—the city has come a long way since the days of violence in the battle for civil rights.

"We, the South, have changed a lot," Dees said. "In the beginning, people fought hard to keep the trappings of an old way of life. But blacks and whites have grown up together. People have known each other, worked together, side by side. Now, it's not uncommon to see blacks and whites sit at a table together, sharing a meal. In 1966 that would have been unheard of. I'm not saying the South is free of prejudice—on either side—but we've taken major steps," he said.

To remind Montgomerians, and visitors to the city, of the value of that journey, the SPLC commissioned architect Maya Lin to create the Civil Rights Memorial in 1989. The names of 40 people who lost their lives in the fight for equal justice are inscribed on the black granite monument.

"I think it's important for people to deal with problems, even if they are controversial," Dees said. "It's important, as a part of a community, to support it—in business, in the arts, in government. But it's also important to recognize and say, 'Here's this person who is not getting justice because of something that is wrong.' And to do something about it."

"I always consider my local community first, because this is where I grew up, and I'm happy here. I love this town. But then I have to consider a larger community, of the United States," Dees said.

Morris Dees helped found the Southern Poverty Law Center, a nonprofit organization that works to protect and advance the legal rights of people of all races, with a special compassion for those who are financially unable to pay for legal services. Photo by Robert Fouts.

RIGHTEOUSNESS LIKE A MIGHTY STREAM

MOSE T.

His house is unassuming, resting on the corner of one of Montgomery's oldest streets, Sayre Street. It seems appropriate that Mose Tolliver, better known throughout the art world as folk artist Mose T., should live on this street, named after Zelda Sayre Fitzgerald, wife of famed author of the Jazz Age, F. Scott Fitzgerald, and an accomplished artist in her own right.

Although Tolliver is renowned in art circles for his work, it is rare that a person has to call ahead to make an appointment to visit with the artist, who will turn 80 years old on July 4, 1996. Folks just walk up on his porch and rap on the screen door, asking whoever opens it for a visit with Mose T.

If he's in the mood, you're more than welcome to come on in. It's almost certain you'll find him perched on the edge of his bed, painting.

As he lays the brush down on the bedspread, speckled with the many colors of past works, you have the feeling Tolliver is timeless—you could return in another 80 years to find him still sitting here, surrounded by cans of paint and boxes of brushes, committing the fanciful birds and flowers and people of his imagination to his wooden canvas.

By painting houses and decorating porches in his spare time, Mose T. began creating his unique folk art about 67 years ago. His only medium to this day is house paint, and he prefers a simple piece of wood for his "canvas."

He began seriously concentrating on his art in the 1960s, when he was injured on his job at a furniture factory. A load of marble crushed his feet, leaving him unable to walk without the assistance of crutches.

His first painting was a bird, and he spent four or five weeks on it, getting every detail just right, he recalls.

He sold his first painting for two quarts of wine and two boxes of snuff, he said. He still recalls his first big sale, several paintings bought for $3,000. And it still fills him with wonder.

When you ask Mose T. how he feels about being famous, he just laughs. He's not famous, he insists.

When in the mood, he paints like a man possessed. Two partially completed paintings lie drying at his feet, waiting for their final touches, while he begins a third. His brush dips into the can of black paint at his elbow as he begins to form the perfect circle that will be the head of the figure he is creating. All the works on this day depict a person, who Mose says is himself. In the works, he includes his crutches.

"I paint myself a lot," he said. "I like to paint everything, though."

Usually, he will paint one subject continuously until he has "too many" of that thing; then he will switch to something new, he said. Usually, he paints about 15 pictures of the same subject— each unique in its color and composition— before he changes subjects, he said. Flowers, birds, crosses, watermelons, and even dinosaurs are some of his favorite subjects. He has painted images of cars and buses, and often creates creatures from his imagination, giving them life in the framework of his art. Also, he paints things people request, usually portraits done from photographs, and he sometimes paints on furniture.

Although the images are simple, art critics have heralded Tolliver's knack for mixing colors not only for a beautiful effect, but also to lend a particular mood to his creations—humor, eroticism, reverence, eeriness. The creatures that come to life at the end of his brush are complex at their heart, conveying Tolliver's own unique view of the world.

Despite the popularity of his work, and his self-disputed fame, Mose T. is a simple man, easily pleased with the company of good friends. His only need is a constant supply of paint and brushes.

"When I first started painting, I said I couldn't do this because I needed more paint. So they gave me paint," he said, still grinning with wonderment at that good fortune. "They said, 'There. Now can you paint for us?' So I said, 'I need some brushes,'" he recalls, laughing wickedly at this good trick. "And they gave me brushes."

Thank heaven.

Folk artists such as Mose T. are respected for their primitive style of painting. Although the images he paints are simple, critics have heralded Mose Tolliver's knack for mixing colors. The creatures that come to life at the end of his brush are complex at their heart, conveying Tolliver's own unique view of the world. Photo by Robert Fouts.

LACK DOG ANTIQUES
West Barrington Massachusetts

JIM WILSON JR.

You don't have to look far in the city of Montgomery to see where Jim Wilson Jr. has left his mark. His philanthropic efforts touch areas of art, education, and the community.

He is a major sponsor of the Montgomery Ballet, supporting its fund-raising efforts by bringing an acclaimed guest company to the city each year for a special performance and reception. He donated funds for the construction of an auditorium at the Montgomery Museum of Fine Arts, which bears his name, and regularly supports local and regional artists through the purchase of their work and by commissioning them to provide artwork for his many real estate ventures. Wilson also sponsors the Blue-Gray College Tennis Tournament, funded the renovation of Montgomery's historic Union Station, and sponsored the construction of a new gymnasium at the Bell Road YMCA.

In the area of education, Wilson is actively involved with Montgomery's Huntingdon College as a trustee. He recently raised funds for the construction of a 21,000-square-foot School of Business building on the Huntingdon campus, which was named for his father, James Winfrey Wilson Sr. Additionally, he provides the Wilson Scholarship to enable students to attend Huntingdon College. He is a sponsor of the Huntingdon golf team, providing them the use of the course at the Wynlakes Golf and Country Club, just one of the many successful properties Wilson has developed to enrich his hometown of Montgomery. To assure Montgomery's scholars receive the recognition they deserve, and to assure the success of Huntingdon College well into the future, Wilson initiated the Huntingdon Scholars' Night, a fund-raiser that brings such celebrity guest speakers as Bob Hope, Henry Kissinger, and Art Buchwald to the city.

Wilson also is a patron of local Trinity Presbyterian School and The Montgomery Academy; and he is a staunch supporter of his own alma mater, Tulane University. Recently, Wilson was responsible for the construction of the James W. Wilson Intercollegiate Athletic Center, a 75,000-square-foot athletic training facility at Tulane. The center houses coaches' offices, training areas, a Hall of Fame museum, and reception areas.

Kelly-Springfield, a tire manufacturer, became the sponsor of the Blue-Gray Football Classic through an introduction by Jim Wilson, who owns Big Ten Tire stores. The Blue-Gray Football Classic, one of the most prestigious college tournaments, entertains Montgomerians as a part of the Christmas holiday tradition and presents the city in a positive light as host of a game showcasing the best college football players from throughout the nation. "That's good for Montgomery," says Wilson.

In the business arena, Wilson has made a city, regional, and state impact. Jim Wilson & Associates helps improve the standard of living in many communities with its visionary developments—shopping malls, office buildings, hotels, tire stores, and residential properties. It was Wilson's hope that the Wynlakes residential community and adjoining Wynlakes Golf and Country Club would provide Montgomery with an extraordinary environment where families and friends could be and play together.

These accomplishments are just the tip of the iceberg. Wilson supports his community in small ways each day, whether through sponsoring a local artist's exhibition or providing a helping hand, financially, to a school or community organization. Recently, he was honored for his accomplishments by the Alabama Humanities Foundation, which selected him as the Corporate Citizen in the Humanities for 1995.

But you couldn't convince Wilson that what he does is anything out of the ordinary. To him, it's all a part of being a good, active citizen. "We believe in tithing," he said matter-of-factly. "I just want Montgomery to be a great place to live."

Jim Wilson's philanthropic efforts touch areas of art, education, and the community. Photo courtesy of Jim Wilson & Associates.

Jim Wilson's Wynlakes residential community and adjoining Wynlakes Golf and Country Club provide Montgomery with an extraordinary environment where families and friends can play and be together. Photo by Robert Fouts.

SPEED
LIMIT
25

"Camp Sunshine gives these youngsters role models, or mentors, they can look up to, who provide structure and firmness, but also love and acceptance," Sawyer said. "Knowing that someone is there as a volunteer, just because they care, really gives these children a sense of how valuable they are."

Laurie Weil and Kathy Sawyer developed Camp Sunshine, a program that mixes fun with serious messages about such topics as the importance of staying in school, the dangers of drug and alcohol abuse, and information about the prevention of pregnancy and sexually transmitted diseases. Photo by Robert Fouts.

From the desire to restore the hope, faith, and optimism of inner-city children, a simple idea was born—Camp Sunshine. Photo courtesy of Camp Sunshine.

LAURIE WEIL AND KATHY SAWYER

Everyone has heard the expression, "When opportunity knocks. . . ." But what do you do when it seems opportunity doesn't even know where your neighborhood is, much less where to find your door?

This question had bothered Laurie Weil for awhile. As a college student, she took a sociology class, and her eyes were opened to the problems faced by inner-city children. At the root of the poverty, the despair, the crime, the vicious circles of violence, Weil saw a common thread—a lack of opportunities.

From the desire to restore hope, faith, and optimism, a simple, but beautiful, idea was born—Camp Sunshine.

During the school year, youngsters in the inner city had teachers for inspiration and schoolwork to occupy their minds. But what about those long, empty summer months? It was here that Weil saw a void that needed to be filled, to keep these young people going, and to give them a little something extra, something special they could feel was just for them.

She especially concentrated her efforts on designing a program for young girls. At the time, the YMCA was much more one-gendered than it is now, with the emphasis being on boys, she explained. She enlisted the help of the Girl Scouts and community volunteers and held the first Camp Sunshine in 1970.

The day camp program was a mixture of fun and enrichment, with girls from area housing communities invited to participate. Camp Sunshine continued for three years.

"Then, I got married, and got a job, and Camp Sunshine just sort of fell away," Weil said. But it was never far from her mind.

"I kept wondering about the camp, and wondering how I could get it going again. I knew it was something that could be positive for those girls," she said.

In 1986 she met Kathy Sawyer at a Leadership Montgomery class (a program that gets people in the community involved in different areas of service). "It was a friendship I believe was meant to be," Weil said.

One evening after class, Sawyer mentioned she was concerned about girls living in the neighborhoods of west Montgomery who had nothing to do during the summer, Weil said. Weil immediately told Sawyer about Camp Sunshine, and they both knew they had to resurrect the idea.

Once again, they enlisted the help of the Girl Scouts, and recruited volunteers to be day camp counselors.

They devised a program that would once again mix fun with serious messages about such topics as health and nutrition, the importance of staying in school, the dangers of drug and alcohol abuse, and, for the older girls, information about the prevention of pregnancy and sexually transmitted diseases.

Alabama State University generously donated its campus as home base for the program, and Weil and Sawyer began to gather campers.

In the beginning, the two women went to the housing communities on foot and looked for youngsters to invite to camp. They then asked to speak to the youngsters' parents or parent, and asked that parent for the names of other children who might like to go to day camp.

Because many of the campers would have trouble getting to the day camp site, Sawyer and Weil enlisted the help of the Montgomery County Board of Education, which provides buses for the program.

Through the years since its inception, the community has embraced Camp Sunshine. The program has grown to include field trips to such Montgomery attractions as the Montgomery Zoo, the Alabama Shakespeare Festival, and the Montgomery Museum of Fine Arts. The week wraps up with a day of outdoor fun and learning at the Girl Scouts' Camp Kiwanis. Hundreds of volunteers work to make Camp Sunshine a success, including individuals, community organizations, and businesses.

"People have rarely told us no. It's really been a heartening experience," Weil said.

Four years ago, Camp Sunshine was expanded to include a program for boys, conducted in cooperation with the Boy Scouts' Tukabatchee Area Council. The boys' program is based at Camp Tukabatchee and features such activities as hiking, canoeing, archery, and other sports.

While youngsters have fun and learn interesting and important things, the main purpose of Camp Sunshine is to provide encouragement and a healthy sense of self-worth, Weil and Sawyer are quick to point out.

"People who grow up with limited opportunities lose hope," Weil said. "They don't know that they can dream. Camp Sunshine wanted to make a difference in that regard. We hope that if we as a society will increase opportunities for these youths, they will respond accordingly," she said.

"People tend to think of Camp Sunshine as just fun for kids in the summertime," Sawyer added. "It is, but for us it's bigger than that. Even though we can't measure it, we believe that we can provide hope where before there was no hope. For so many of these kids, it's hard to imagine a future. They don't see tomorrow; they don't expect anything," she said. "We want them to realize there is strength and ability in self—to overcome obstacles and achieve what you want to do."

An average of 90 girls ages 7 to 12 attend Camp Sunshine each year, and about 65 boys ages 7 to 10 attend Camp Sunshine. In order to keep youths involved, a junior aide program has been added to the girls' program, in which six girls who have attended Camp Sunshine in the past, but who have grown too old for the program, are selected to be junior counselors. The girls must interview for the junior aide positions, teaching them job skills such as how to fill out an application, and how to dress for and conduct themselves in an interview. Girls selected for the junior aide positions are paid a stipend of up to $100 for the week, giving them a feeling of pride in their work and accomplishment, Weil said.

Another way the Camp Sunshine program works to keep the youngsters involved in positive activities is the establishment of year-round Girl Scout and Boy Scout troops in the housing projects. A part-time employee has been hired to act as troop leader for these programs, providing consistency.

While they know that camping and scouting cannot provide all the answers for youngsters faced with difficult situations, Camp Sunshine is a good start, Weil and Sawyer believe.

"A number of factors have to come together to help a healthy child make it," Weil said. "I know that some of the things these kids face can be overpowering, but I think Camp Sunshine and its year-round program can come in as one positive factor and if combined with just a few others—a supportive teacher, a close relationship with a parent or relative—a child can make it."

"Camp Sunshine gives these youngsters role models, or mentors, they can look up to, who provide structure and firmness, but also love and acceptance," Sawyer said. "Knowing that someone is there as a volunteer, just because they care, really gives these children a sense of how valuable they are."

CORNERSTONES OF THE COMMUNITY

Montgomery is a big city wrapped in small-town charm. Newcomers are often surprised by the many amenities Montgomery has to offer, including top-notch colleges and universities and world-renowned cultural attractions.

Vaughn Road Park is a great place for an enjoyable walk. Photo by Robert Fouts.

Yet, with all this, Montgomery manages to remain a sweet, friendly town, with all the charming feel of Andy Griffith's Mayberry. People take the time to say, "hello," and neighbors really do care.

"I didn't know where I was going, but when I got here I was very surprised," recalled Nellie Gerreald, who moved to Montgomery five years ago when her husband, Tull, relocated here for a job. The couple moved from New York City.

"I got a lot of jokes from my friends about moving to the 'deep South,' " she said. "They asked if we had electricity and running water," she said, laughing. "I said, yes, we had all that, and much more."

After spending most of her life in the hustle and bustle of New York City, Gerreald feared she would be bored in Montgomery. Her fears were soon laid to rest.

"It's quite a growing community," she said of Montgomery. "I was impressed with the Alabama Shakespeare Festival, and loved the museum. It was great to find these things here."

Another thing that impressed Gerreald was the countryside. "I really like to see nature—horses and cows. Here, you feel like you're in the country, right in the city."

Now, she wars between her desire to see Montgomery continue to grow with business and other developments, and wanting it always to keep that small-town charm.

"People here are so friendly," she said. "In New York, I lived among seven million people. There, you're anonymous. Here, it's always, 'Hi, how are you doing?' even from strangers. I'm saying 'hi' to Stan the Terminix man now," she joked.

"When I first moved here, I didn't know how I'd live outside the big city. Now, I like it. And I don't want to live anywhere else."

"This is a very good place to raise a family," said Tom Somerville, district manager for BellSouth. He moved here with his wife and two children (he now has four children) in 1975.

He grew up in the South, in Memphis, and attended college at the University of Alabama before working in Birmingham and eventually transferring with BellSouth to Montgomery.

Somerville is pleased with the growth he has seen in Montgomery, particularly in the areas of arts and education.

"There are countless opportunities here. No matter what you are interested in—arts, sports, volunteer work—you're bound to find something you enjoy here," he said.

EDUCATION

Education is a high priority in Montgomery, particularly in the area of the Montgomery Public School (MPS) system. School system administrators and educators are looking for ways to bring the Montgomery Public School system into the twenty-first century, providing Montgomery children with the best education possible.

Already, they have reached their first goal, to increase measurable academic student achievement. According to information compiled in the 1995 MPS Annual Report, the Montgomery Public School system posted gains in system-wide Stanford Achievement Test scores for the first time in five years. Fourth-graders' scores increased in 14 of 19 areas tested. Eighth-graders' scores increased in nine areas.

Other success stories include:

☐ The 1995 graduating class of the MPS received a record $9.4 million in college scholarship offers.

☐ Students from Bellingrath Junior High placed second in the world in the International Manufacturing Engineering Competition for their creation of a solar-powered car.

☐ Johnson Elementary students won the National Auto Design Challenge for designing a futuristic car.

☐ Lanier High School's Scholar's Bowl team placed 12th in the United States at the American Scholastic Competition.

☐ Crump kindergarten teacher Nancy McGinty is Alabama's 1994 Presidential Award Winner for Excellence in Science Teaching.

☐ *Redbook* magazine designated the Carver Creative and Performing Arts Center as one of the best schools in the country as part of its annual "Best Schools in America Contest."

☐ Catoma Elementary School received the

The Carver Creative and Performing Arts Center magnet school program focuses on developing the artistic talents of its students. Photo by Robert Fouts.

Alabama Power Company's intriguing Alabama Science Center in Montgomery is a favorite field trip site, featuring interactive science exhibits designed for students in the fourth through ninth grades. Photo by Robert Fouts. (right)

LEAD
CORK
STEEL
ALUMINUM
CONDUCTIVITY

MS. COOKE - 2D GRADE
SADDLE UP!

National Coalition for Equality in Schools' "Equality School Award."

□ Dance instructor Gary Moore and his students at the Carver Creative and Performing Arts Center magnet school program were featured on the 1995 program "The Disney Channel Salutes the American Teacher." Moore was nominated for the Disney Channel American Teacher of the Year award in 1995. In 1993 another CCPAC dance instructor, Kathy Hess Wright, was nominated for the award, and she and her students were featured on the program. Hess Wright also was featured in 1995 in *Mirabella* magazine's "America's 1,000 Outstanding Women of the Nineties."

And these are just to name a few of the many accomplishments made by the Montgomery Public School system.

"There is plenty of evidence from students' achievements that a child can go through the Montgomery Public Schools and get a top-notch education and stand tall with any student in the country," said Dr. John A. "Pete" Eberhart, superintendent of Montgomery County Public Schools.

Building on this foundation of proven successes, efforts are underway to improve public education.

"There is a growing groundswell of support for the schools and making the schools better," Eberhart said.

This is being done by evaluating the needs of each individual school and making plans to address that school's specific needs and strengths, he said.

The focus of immediate school improvement is fundamental and follows a three-pronged approach: making schools safe and well-ordered, improving student achievement in the basic areas of academics, as well as incorporating more use of modern technology, and getting parents and the community involved as partners in the educational process.

"I think education is important to everybody, not just the children or the people who have children," Eberhart said. "We need to remember the children we are educating today will be our business and community leaders of tomorrow."

Many local businesses are already involved with the students of the Montgomery Public School system through the Partners In Education program. PIE participants help schools by donating volunteers, supplies, and funds to their partner school or schools to meet needs and provide enrichment. In 1995 there were 261 businesses involved in the Partners In Education program.

Education administrators are currently looking into more ways to improve the school system, with plans including the expansion of the

vocational education system to include more technology and hands-on work opportunities. A partnership is being developed with area community colleges as well as businesses and industry to give young people vocational educational training in a cooperative environment, providing them a combination of "thinking and working" skills, Eberhart said.

Another idea on the drawing board to take Montgomery Public Schools into the future is the expansion of the magnet school program. Currently, Montgomery is served by five magnet schools—two arts magnet programs, at Carver Elementary School and Carver High School (the Carver Creative and Performing Arts Center); two academic magnet programs, at Forest Avenue Elementary and Lanier High School (the Lanier Academic Motivational Program, or LAMP); and one combined arts-academic magnet program, at Baldwin Junior High School.

The expansion of the magnet school program in Montgomery will help meet the changing needs of education in areas of advanced technology and the arts, Eberhart said.

"At the very least, [magnet programs] offer a lot more flexibility, and a lot more options about how children get an education," he said. "The school system is moving to meet different needs, and exploring more routes to becoming educated." This does not mean the basic tenants of education, the three R's, will be neglected. Students will still learn the math, writing, and communication skills they will need to perform in whatever field they choose for their future," Eberhart said.

"We are in the process of literally reorganizing and rebuilding the public school system to serve the students into the twenty-first century."

In addition to the Montgomery Public School system, Montgomery is served by many fine private schools, including Green Gate School, The Montgomery Academy, Trinity Presbyterian School, Saint James School, Alabama Christian Academy, and Montgomery Catholic High School, among others.

Private education is an option that allows parents and students to tailor their educational opportunities and environment to meet specific needs and goals. Private education opportunities are available at all levels of study, from preschool through high school, and continuing into higher education.

Green Gate School has offered a rich program of private education in Montgomery since 1971, when it was established as an American Primary School. It began as a preschool facility, and has grown through the years to include elementary education as a staple of its curriculum. Currently,

A well-rounded student's education extends beyond the boundaries of academics. Photo by Robert Fouts.

Education is a high priority in Montgomery, and the Montgomery Public School system provides children with the best education possible. Photo by Robert Fouts.

An academic magnet program at Forest Avenue Elementary provides students with unique hands-on learning opportunities. Photo by Robert Fouts. (above)

Montgomery's educational options allow parents and students to tailor their learning opportunities and environment to meet specific needs and goals. Photo by Robert Fouts. (right)

the school serves students aged 18 months through sixth grade. Two campuses are available in the city.

"The most important thing we can do—that we can teach—is a love of learning," said Yvonna Richardson, administrator of the school. "If you love to learn, your door is open. The worst thing you can do to a child is to take the imagination out of him," she said.

In addition to daily school activities, Green Gate School offers an extensive after-school child care program. In fact, Green Gate was the first school in Montgomery to offer an on-site after-school child care program, Richardson said.

The after-school program includes on-site activities, such as music lessons, Girl Scout and Boy Scout troop meetings, and a shuttle service to take youngsters to activities elsewhere, such as a dance class.

Because many parents work outside the home, and therefore are unable to pick their children up until after 5 P.M., it was important to offer them the opportunity to allow their children to participate in extracurricular activities without the worry of how to get them to and from the activity, Richardson explained.

Another reason many Montgomerians choose private schools for their children's education is the opportunity to reinforce Christian values in an academic environment. This is the reason many parents choose Trinity Presbyterian School, said Brian Willett, principal.

"At Trinity, we integrate a Christian viewpoint into an academic climate. At no time is scholastic integrity compromised, but students are challenged to make their faith a part of their daily life," he said.

Students at Trinity have the opportunity to become involved in a variety of scholastic and extracurricular activities, including academic competitions, arts activities, and athletics.

The school has recently completed a $4-million expansion and renovation, doubling the acreage of the campus and increasing the school's student capacity by almost 40 percent.

Lanier High School offers an academic motivational program, as well as ROTC for students preparing for military careers. Photo by Robert Fouts.

The curriculum also has been expanded in the area of arts education with the addition of speech, drama, and choral music programs. Future plans include the construction of a fine arts facility to further these opportunities.

Additionally, the school is working in cooperation with other Montgomery private schools to address the issue of expanding technological opportunities for students.

"We are working with the other private schools for a kind of consortium, a formal network of cooperation to facilitate the maximum incorporation of technology into our programs at a minimum of expense to each school," Willett explained.

The Montgomery Academy offers students in surrounding communities a unique educational environment in a small school atmosphere, which educators and administrators at the facility believe nurtures personal relationships with students as well as families of the school. An overall 12-to-1 student-teacher ratio creates an educational setting focused on meeting individual needs in the classroom.

Despite the smaller school setting, The Montgomery Academy offers a diverse course selection, after-school activities, athletic programs, and fine art opportunities to support the many demands of today's student.

Faculty commitment reaches far beyond the classroom. Extracurricular activities offered are supported by the school's teachers, who serve as faculty advisors for school service and fine art clubs, sponsors of academic teams, coaches of numerous athletic teams, and as chaperones and guides for cultural trips to major United States cities and foreign countries. The Montgomery Academy's faculty members also have a commitment to their own educational advancement, earning graduate and doctorate degrees. Two are Fulbright scholars and one is an IDEA fellow. According to Headmaster A. Emerson Johnson III, "One need only look cursorily at the re-engineering of American industry to know that today's students need very sophisticated skills to participate in the emerging global work force. The Montgomery Academy proceeds from the assumption that this 'race of the swiftest' will go to those who speak a second language; have powerful skills in the use of technology; can work in teams; are masters of communication, both oral and written; and have studied mathematics and science beyond required levels. The traditional liberal arts—history, literature, art, and philosophy—have never been more important than now."

The school's motto, "The Pursuit of Excellence," is evident in its programs. Eleven AP courses are offered to high school students, the most offered in area schools. Each division of the school, kindergarten through 12, has its own science lab. The Lower School (kindergarten through 4) has complete coordination among all disciplines.

Private education opportunities are available at all levels of study, from preschool through high school, and continuing into higher education. Photo by Lyn Bonham, courtesy of The Montgomery Academy. (left)

Auburn University at Montgomery has a reputation for providing a challenging, enriching educational opportunity. Photo by Frank Williams, courtesy of AUM. (right)

FORDISC
Computerized Forensic Discriminant Functions

AUM *offers something for everyone, with programs designed to meet the needs of traditional, adult, and returning students. Photo by Frank Williams, courtesy of AUM.*

Saint James School, founded in Montgomery in 1955, serves the city from two campus locations, providing educational opportunities for children in kindergarten through 12th grade.

"I think Saint James is unique in that we provide a close, family atmosphere for students, while also offering a wide variety of outstanding academic programs," said Ray Furlong, headmaster for the school.

This close-knit school community provides students with ready access to assistance from teachers and advisors, who will be able to help them with their studies and also help them to plan their future.

Recently, the school has broken ground for a major new expansion, touted by Furlong as the "beginning of the most ambitious and comprehensive program ever undertaken by Saint James," that will "transform Saint James School and enhance the educational opportunities of Saint James students for years to come."

The $8-million construction plan, scheduled for completion for use in the 1997-1998 school year, includes four new buildings along with supporting facilities, parking, landscaping, and site development.

The centerpiece of the new construction will be a fine arts building. This facility will include an auditorium for an audience of more than 500 and a professional quality stage. The building also will be used as a lunchroom for the middle and high school students. There will be two classrooms in the building, a large band room, and an art lab.

Saint James School also is in the developmental stages of creating a discipline-based arts education program. The program will provide a consortium to provide arts education resources for both private and public school teachers in the city of Montgomery, Furlong said.

Montgomery also is rich in opportunity for those seeking opportunities for higher education. Montgomery's colleges and universities offer programs to suit every need, from a traditional full-time college experience to adult and continuing education programs.

HIGHER EDUCATION

Auburn University at Montgomery

In the years since its establishment in 1967 as a metropolitan campus of Auburn University, Auburn University at Montgomery has come into its own.

Its reputation for providing a challenging, enriching educational opportunity; its outstanding development of community outreach branches in the AUM Center for Government and Public Affairs and The Center for Business and Economic Development, among others; and its renowned faculty qualify AUM as a first class educational facility in its own right.

It has been a constant goal of the university to focus on the future, always striving to meet the changing needs of the community and its student body.

AUM offers something for everyone, with programs designed to meet the needs of traditional, adult, and returning students. People of all ages attend classes and participate in campus organizations and activities.

"AUM is on the move, and from where I stand, the future looks very exciting," said Dr. Roy H. Saigo, chancellor of AUM. Expansions are being made in the areas of technology, internship opportunities, research, and community involvement.

Continuing its ongoing relationship with the Alabama TechnaCenter's Institute for Advanced Information Systems, AUM's Advanced Technology Group works to provide consultation, design, and training services to the public, as well as privately contracted businesses.

Additionally, all AUM students carry an information systems course requirement, assuring they are properly equipped to enter today's high-tech job market.

Internship programs give AUM graduates valuable experience, which is attractive to employers. Internships are available in a wide range of areas, including partnerships with businesses, governmental agencies, and other organizations, with areas of study ranging from writing and editing to nursing, biology, and administrative assistantships.

In the area of research, AUM offers opportunities including named professorships with stipends, and opportunities for students to conduct research, present papers at academic and professional forums, and to publish their research results.

"Given its short history, AUM has experienced phenomenal success in accomplishing its three-fold mission of education, research, and service," Dr. Saigo said. "By working together, we can make AUM an even greater resource for Montgomery and Alabama."

Alabama State University

Alabama State University is a historically black institution of higher learning, a direct descendant of the Lincoln Normal School, established in 1867 as one of the first educational institutions for blacks. This makes Alabama State University one of the oldest historically black universities in the United States.

On that foundation, the Alabama State University of today strives to serve people of all races, providing an environment of diversity rooted in its rich educational heritage.

"Although ASU was founded as a predominantly black university, the hand of education is extended to all who will accept it," said Robert Forbus, news services director for ASU. "It's important to remember that ASU is a predominantly black university, not an exclusively black university."

"This is a fine, first-rate university to provide an education to anyone in the state who wishes to come. We want to communicate that, and make it well-known that everyone is welcome at ASU," said Dr. William Hamilton Harris, president of Alabama State University.

"This university is one that has a history of black education, and we're proud of what we've done. The challenge now is to find a way to honor the tradition and history of the people who made the university, while making a commitment to build a future that is different from the past," he said. "As a university evolves, it meets the needs of a changing society."

Harris has developed a theme of "Transforming the university through high quality and diversity" as his motto for the future of Alabama State University.

As ASU enters the twenty-first century, strides are being made to increase the educational opportunities offered at the school. These improvements will come in the areas of facilities as well as coursework.

Recent additions already in place include a new, 11-story residence hall and the new,

Internship programs give AUM graduates valuable job experience. Internships are available in a wide range of areas, including nursing. Photo by Frank Williams, courtesy of AUM.

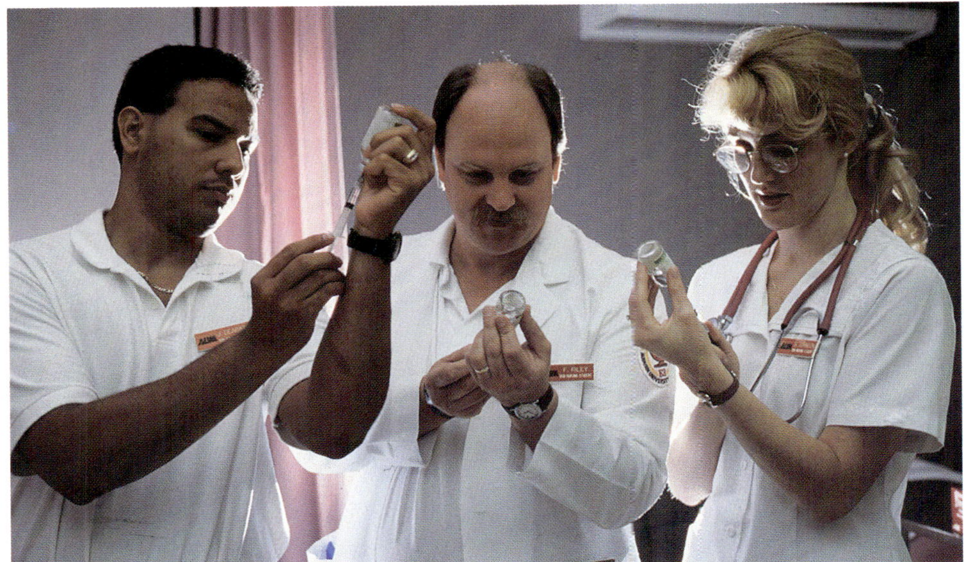

$20-million Joe L. Reed Acadome, which houses a 7,400-seat basketball arena, classrooms, and administrative facilities.

Academic plans include a Ph.D. program in the area of education, a master's degree program in accounting, and an allied health curriculum. New facilities, including a state-of-the-art laboratory, are planned in conjunction with the Allied Health program. Also, this new program of study will involve a cooperative effort between the university and the business and health care community, according to Forbus.

"There will be community involvement in that the university will reach out to the health care community for the development of curriculum and research programs. Health care professionals will be utilized to serve on an advisory board so the program can best serve both the students and the health care industry in Montgomery," he said.

Involvement in the community is a high priority on the agenda for ASU's future, Dr. Harris stressed.

"Alabama State University is a significant institution in the city that has not yet been appreciated for all it can do in the community," he said. "Because of past racial issues, this great body of resources has been overlooked, and we have overlooked the resources the city of Montgomery has to offer. We should work to build a mutual relationship."

"The university isn't just here; it lives here, because the university is people. This is not an enclave. We are looking forward to a long-term involvement, to build on making the relationship between the university and the city based on looking forward to the future rather than memorializing the past."

Troy State University Montgomery

Billing itself as "the evening university" of Montgomery, Troy State University Montgomery places special emphasis on meeting the needs of adult students, who work during the day. A wide range of courses are offered in the evening, allowing a TSUM student to earn his or her degree while attending school exclusively at night.

"Our mission at TSUM is unique. We exist solely to serve the needs of the nontraditional student—men and women who work during the day and yet seek to improve their lives and careers by earning a college degree," said Dr. Glenda McGaha Curry, president of TSUM. "Not only does TSUM make that possible, we make it convenient, by offering a wide range of associate, undergraduate, and graduate degrees that can be completed exclusively through evening and weekend courses at several locations throughout the city."

Additionally, Troy State University Students can "attend" classes in their own homes, with lectures from TSUM and guest professors transmitted over satellite to be broadcast on a local cable television channel.

TSUM also strives to play an active role in the Montgomery community. The university manages the Davis Theatre, a historic landmark in downtown Montgomery which is home to the Montgomery Ballet and the Alabama Dance Theatre, the Montgomery Symphony Orchestra, and plays host to many visiting musical and performing arts groups.

Also, the W. A. Gayle Planetarium, which provides a unique educational experience in the area of space exploration, is operated cooperatively by TSUM and the City of Montgomery.

Plans for the coming years at TSUM include

The Marching Hornets, a nationally acclaimed high-stepping marching band, is open to all students at Alabama State University through audition, and always provides entertainment for crowds at football games, parades, and other events. Photo courtesy of ASU. (above)

Alabama State University strives to serve people of all races, providing an environment of diversity rooted in its rich educational heritage. Photo by Billy Brown, courtesy of ASU. (right)

being an active part of the downtown renaissance that is underway in the Capital City.

"TSUM will continue its commitment to be a full partner in the economic development of downtown Montgomery," Curry said. "Our goal is to transform TSUM into the symbol for higher educational opportunities for the citizens of Montgomery and the surrounding communities while improving the attractiveness of the downtown area," she said.

Plans include the renovation of the university and surrounding areas, and the library facilities will be enhanced to provide automated user services and increased holdings.

"TSUM will truly be a model for the metropolitan community university of the twenty-first century," Curry said.

Huntingdon College

"Enter to grow in wisdom; go forth to apply wisdom in service." The Huntingdon College motto captures the mission and goal of the school: to provide its students not only with the best education they can obtain, but to help them grow into caring, productive citizens of the world as well.

Huntingdon College has been rated as one of the top liberal arts colleges in the country, and has been included in Templeton's Honor Roll of Character-Building Colleges. It is this mixture of academia and social awareness that sets Huntingdon apart, believes college President Dr. Wanda Bigham.

"We value not only the career, but the quality of life our students will have," she said. "We try to have an emphasis on the development of the whole student, not just academically, but in character-building and learning values."

With this goal in mind, Huntingdon College launches "The Huntingdon Plan" in the fall of 1996. The plan strives to maximize the educational experience of Huntingdon students by addressing a mixture of needs in five main areas—technology, world-mindedness, learning by doing, preparation for life after Huntingdon, and an outstanding liberal arts education.

The Huntingdon Plan strives to go the extra mile for students, featuring such amenities as a personal computer provided for each freshman student, which will be his or hers to keep after graduation; financial assistance for a travel/study experience, making it possible for each student to study abroad at little or no personal cost during the student's junior or senior year; and the opportunity to participate in a variety of hands-on learning experiences including internships and cooperative education.

Additionally, freshman students will decide on a service project, for which they will be responsible throughout their years at Huntingdon.

In the past, students have been involved in such service activities as raising funds and helping build houses for Habitat for Humanity (Linda Fuller, cofounder of Habitat for Humanity, is an alumna of Huntingdon College); tutoring at-risk young people from Montgomery's inner-city neighborhoods; and conducting a bicycle safety program for youths, among many other projects.

"It's so important that each of us give something back to the community, and we feel if we don't instill that idea in our students while they are in college, it may be too late," Bigham said. "Our students will be the leaders of tomorrow, and we feel it's important to instill that obligation to others in them," she said.

Bachelor's degrees are available in a wide range of programs of study, including such arts

Huntingdon College has been rated as one of the top liberal arts colleges in the country. Photo by Beth Maynor Young, courtesy of Huntingdon College. (top)

Settled into the lush landscape of Montgomery's historic Old Cloverdale district, Huntingdon College couldn't be more picturesque. Photo by Beth Maynor Young, courtesy of Huntingdon College. (bottom)

programs as dance, drama, music, and musical theater. Pre-professional programs prepare students for graduate study in the areas of dentistry, law, medicine, optometry, pharmacy, physical therapy, theology, and veterinary medicine.

More than one third of Huntingdon College students choose to continue their education with graduate studies.

"A liberal arts education, in my mind, is the continuing education for the future," Bigham said. "It provides the basis to receive information, analyze that information, and utilize it. It prepares students for the challenges they will face in their future, whether that future includes graduate school or entering the career field."

Settled into the lush landscape of Montgomery's historic Old Cloverdale district, Huntingdon College couldn't be more picturesque, with its red brick, ivy-covered buildings. Founded in Tuskegee in 1854 as a coeducational liberal arts college related to the United Methodist Church, the school was relocated to Montgomery in 1909.

Enrollment includes more than 700 students, representing 24 states and 13 countries, with a student/faculty ratio of 12 to 1.

Student activities include the Student Government Association, two national fraternities, two national sororities, a student newspaper, literary magazine, yearbook, intercollegiate, intramural, and club sports, more than 50 clubs, organizations, and honorary societies.

Intercollegiate athletic programs (NAIA) include men's baseball, golf, soccer, and tennis; and women's soccer, softball, tennis, and volleyball.

Faulkner University

"Our obvious difference from other schools in Montgomery is the fact that we are a Christian school, and primarily what we mean by that is we teach the Bible as an integral part of our curriculum," said Dr. Billy Hilyer, president of Faulkner University. "We try to maintain an atmosphere more conducive to better values. I think that's something missing from our society."

Faulkner University's programs include the Alabama Christian College of Arts and Sciences, the Harris School of Business, Adult Education, and the Jones School of Law. Plans are underway to begin a master's degree program in business by 1997.

Another new program at Faulkner University reflects the university's strong emphasis on family values. The Ph.D. program in the study of family life has been established under the banner of Institute for Family Life. This program has a

three-part approach of academic study with emphasis on counseling, research, and service/outreach. "The program is designed to extend beyond the university setting to be a positive influence on the community," Hilyer said.

"The family life program will offer outreach workshops, seminars, and counseling to the community to accomplish that goal. I believe strongly that education needs to leave its ivory tower to some extent. It should never abdicate its role as an educator, but in addition to that it should get involved with the community to offer something to everyone. We have knowledge that can be useful, and it should be shared," he said.

All students at Faulkner University are required to take one course in the family life studies curriculum.

Another area of emphasis for Faulkner University is adult education. There are four adult education centers, and the Montgomery campus recently added special programs designed specifically to suit the needs of adult students.

One of these is the "executive" bachelor's degree in business administration. This one-year completion program allows adult students who have some previous college study to complete their degree at an accelerated rate. The rigorous program offers unconventional class schedules and independent study work to better suit the schedules of students already in the workplace.

Many of Faulkner University's adult study programs incorporate "modular" schedules for course completion, rather than following a standard quarter or semester schedule. The length of study is set to suit the topic, so that information doesn't have to be compressed or stretched to meet a standard time slot, Hilyer explained.

Of course, there are many people who wish to further their education, but feel a nontraditional academic institution of higher learning would serve them better.

John M. Patterson State Technical College

John M. Patterson State Technical College offers a variety of programs designed to provide the necessary skills and instruction to help its graduates find good jobs in technical, industrial, and service professions. Flexible class schedules make J. P. Tech's classes accessible for both "traditional," full-time students, and for those trying to fit in an education around a full- or part-time job.

Established in 1961, Patterson began offering classes in the fall of 1962 as a "trade school." Since that time, the curriculum has expanded to offer the latest in trade and technical instruction for its students, said Larry Taunton, president of John M. Patterson State Technical College.

In addition to offering courses of instruction for those interested in entering a particular career field, J. P. Tech offers training to update the skills of those already employed by particular industries. The school works in partnership with industry to secure the training materials and equipment necessary for this important instruction.

"Our biggest challenge is to stay abreast of the latest, changing technologies," Taunton said. "We found the best way to do this was to get industry involved with us in education," he said.

For example, an automobile manufacturer may need to train its employees in how to use a new piece of equipment. The manufacturer makes an agreement with J. P. Tech to provide the equipment to the school, which then provides the facilities for training and the instructors to teach employees how to use the equipment.

Through the partnership agreement, J. P. Tech is allowed to keep the equipment after the employee training is completed, providing a resource for any future student or employee training in that particular area of technology.

"By utilizing this [partnership], it enables us to stay abreast of what industry is doing and what skills our students will need to be competitive in that market," Taunton said. "And, that kind of working relationship with business and industry allows us to provide not only what they need for their current personnel, but also for our students, who may be their future personnel."

This idea is carried over in another partnership idea in the works at John Patterson Technical College, which involves providing training for students of the Montgomery Public School System.

"We've arrived now at a time in education where more emphasis in the public school system is being placed on technical education. General education is disappearing, being replaced by more of a choice for students, with either an academic or a career emphasis," Taunton explained. "We are working on a partnership with the public school system to ensure those students who choose to pursue a career are getting up-to-date training," he said.

The partnership also is practical, eliminating the need for public schools to duplicate the training facilities and equipment already available at J. P. Tech.

Recently, John M. Patterson State Technical College has established certification standards for its various technical fields, based on national standards. This will assure that students who graduate from J. P. Tech will be able to perform in their chosen career field on a par with those in that field in any area of the United States.

Faulkner University provides higher education in a Christian setting and maintains an atmosphere conducive to building strong moral values. Photo by Robert Fouts.

"It's a win-win situation," Taunton said. "We are a part of this community as an industry in our own right. Our product is just a little different—a people product."

Trenholm State Technical College

Billed as "the college that cares about your future," Trenholm State Technical College is a two-year public institution that provides practical career training to its students.

Trenholm serves more than 850 students from throughout the central Alabama region, ranging in age from 17 to 67.

"We really serve a wide variety of students, from those right out of high school who are seeking some job training, to people who are currently working and want to upgrade their skills in a particular area," said Beverly D. Ross, director of public relations for the college.

Courses are offered on a full-time, part-time, or three-quarter-time basis, with classes scheduled for most courses of study in both the daytime and in the evening. Students receive both classroom instruction and hands-on training in the career field of their choice.

Programs offered by Trenholm include automotive body repair, broadcasting technology, child care and development, commercial food service/culinary arts, dental assisting, dental laboratory technology, emergency medical technology/paramedic, horticulture, medical assisting, medical record technology, nursing assistant/home health aide, office systems technology (including course work in such areas of study as accounting, word/information processing, legal stenography, medical secretary, and executive secretary), plumbing and pipe fitting, and practical nursing.

One of the major benefits of course work at Trenholm Tech is the opportunity students have for internships or "clinicals." After completing a specified number of course hours, students are placed in positions that allow them to get on-the-job training. During the internship period, students receive a letter grade rather than a paycheck. However, many students find full-time jobs as a result of their internships, Ross said.

Nowhere is this success more evident than in Trenholm's culinary arts program, which trains its students for a career as a chef. Trenholm graduates can be found employed as staff, sous chefs, and executive chefs in the kitchens of nearly every fine restaurant in Montgomery, and many of the city's country clubs as well.

The culinary school trains students in every aspect of food preparation, from sanitation and safety to nutrition, to restaurant management, food presentation, and, of course, food preparation. The school's kitchen features both gas and electric appliances, giving students a good range of experience.

In addition to classroom and kitchen lessons, students regularly put their knowledge to the test by preparing and presenting meals for special groups. The Culinary Arts Center hosts groups for educational seminars, and students also cater for special events.

"We feel we do a good job in theory and hands-on practice, but it's important that students have a chance to actually prepare a meal for a group and present it," Ward said. "That way, they learn how to keep to a schedule and the practical aspects of serving diners."

In addition to its regular course of study for adult students, Trenholm works in cooperation with the Montgomery Public Schools system to provide equipment and facilities for high school students involved in the MPS vocational education programs. High school students are bused to the Trenholm campus each school day to attend classes. In this way, Trenholm can share its available resources of facilities and equipment with the school system, while educating young people not only in the practical skills they learn each day in

John M. Patterson State Technical College offers a variety of programs designed to provide the necessary skills and instruction to help its graduates find good jobs in technical, industrial, and service professions. Photo by Robert Fouts.

class, but also to the fact they have a choice for their educational futures.

"It is our goal to provide a quality education and a wholesome environment so that our students are not only academically prepared to compete in the job market, but socially prepared to compete as well. We want our graduates to become productive members of society," Ross said.

CHURCHES

For those seeking spiritual enrichment, Montgomery has a welcoming community of church families, offering a variety of worship services and outreach programs to meet many needs. The city welcomes people of all denominations, with churches to serve the spiritual needs of many faiths.

In addition to traditional worship services, most area churches are involved in a variety of programs designed to educate and meet needs within the community.

Several of the Churches of Christ in Montgomery have combined their efforts to provide an Inner City Ministry program. Area churches supply a combination of volunteers and funding to support the program, which ministers to both the spiritual and physical needs of families "at risk."

The program is modeled after a successful inner city ministry program already in place in Nashville, Murfreesboro, and Chattanooga, Tennessee; and Mobile, Alabama. About 200 volunteers participate in the Montgomery program, which currently serves families in the Trenholm Court housing community.

Future plans include gradually expanding the ministry program, with the help of all city Churches of Christ, to minister to all of the housing communities in the city, which includes 16,000 to 18,000 people, said Ken Kilpatrick, minister at Landmark Church of Christ.

"We're not trying to make a political statement, and we're not using these people to make a

statement," Kilpatrick said. "A lot of these people really don't have any help, and they don't have any hope. If hopelessness is not dealt with, it turns to hurt. That in turn becomes anger, which turns to rage, which eventually causes violence," he said. "We want to help these people break out of that chain reaction to realize they can succeed."

The ministry program addresses the physical needs of those living in the housing communities by providing clothing, food, and helping residents find work.

Spiritual needs are met with a weekly Bible study program and individual counseling programs.

To make the Bible study accessible, seven busses are brought into the housing community to pick up children and adults interested in participating in the Bible study. The participants are then taken to area churches for services, and returned to their homes afterward.

Children enjoy a Bible Theatre program and "Sunday School" type classes. Adults join in Bible study groups, and can receive counseling about such topics as nutrition and job skills.

"The bottom line is we're ministering to children, but also reaching out to their parents to help strengthen the family," Kilpatrick said. "God is the focal point, who can put families back together again."

By helping those in despair find spiritual salvation, the Churches of Christ hope to provide those in need with a core of strength that comes from their belief in God, Kilpatrick explained.

"When God is in proper focus, then no matter what happens around you, you will find strength to stand up under it. It gives you dignity," he said.

To help foster understanding among people of different faiths, members of First United Methodist Church and Temple Beth Or Jewish synagogue have participated in a worship exchange program each Thanksgiving for about 14 years.

A joint service is held for members of First United Methodist and Temple Beth Or, with the place of worship alternating between the church and the synagogue each year.

When the program, which is a nondenominational praise of God as creator of all, is held at First United Methodist Church, the Rabbi Glenn Jacob leads the service. When held at Temple Beth Or, First United Methodist's senior minister, Dr. Karl Stegall, leads the worship service.

"We feel this program helps enrich our own Christian traditions because Christianity flows from Judaism," said Ed Glaize, a minister at First United Methodist Church.

Members at First United Methodist Church also have the opportunity to participate in an ongoing educational program throughout the year, attending Jewish services at Temple Beth Or to learn about the traditional Jewish worship. Also, former Rabbi David Baylinson from Temple Beth Or has taught classes at First United Methodist Church about the Jewish faith, Jewish traditions, and Old Testament Law.

"It works because we share a high level of mutual respect and tolerance for each other—we share the realization that we do worship the same God," Glaize said. "We both try to live out our faith in the best way possible, to try to benefit humanity and show God's love to those around us."

People throughout the nation are enriched each week by the services of Montgomery's Frazer Memorial United Methodist Church, one of the largest congregations in the city.

The church reaches thousands through its nationwide media ministry. The messages of Dr. John Ed Mathison, the senior minister at Frazer, are seen and heard on ACTS and FamilyNet cable along with broadcast television services of the SBC Radio and Television commission. The church owns its own television station that broadcasts in the Montgomery area on TCI of Alabama and Montgomery Cablevision services.

"The media ministry has actually progressed in several phases," said Rusty Taylor, church administrator. The process started with Frazer's Sunday morning worship services being broadcast by local television station WHOA-TV 32. Eventually, Frazer was able to install its own control room, while borrowing broadcast equipment from Channel 32, until finally it was able to purchase its own equipment, Taylor said.

As the media ministry expanded its programming goals, Frazer expanded to acquire its own UHF channel locally, on Channel 13.

Today, the church has full broadcast capabilities, having recently completed construction of a state-of-the-art facility housing studios and production studios.

Frazer church services and other inspirational programs are broadcast on both the ACTS network and the Inspiration Television Network, both national networks.

"It's our inspiration affiliate," Taylor said of the relationship with the networks.

The church also is currently exploring ways to minister using the Internet.

Concerned about the difficulty churches today have in reaching young people, The Dexter Avenue United Methodist Church, located in

***S**tarted in 1905 and occupied in 1908, the First Baptist Church, housing an important and active downtown congregation, reflects Byzantine influences in its design. Photo by Robert Fouts. (left)*

***B**uilt on the site of an earlier structure, Saint Peter's Catholic Church, illustrating its era's interest in Romanesque architectural design, dates from the mid 1850s. Photo by Robert Fouts. (below)*

The First United Methodist congregation moved from an earlier location in downtown Montgomery to this site in Cloverdale Park in the 1930s. Designed by George Aswumb, the building emulates cathedrals of medieval Europe. Photo by Robert Fouts. (previous page)

Frazer Memorial United Methodist Church conducts a media ministry through its own UHF channel. Photo by Robert Fouts.

downtown Montgomery, began "Club 301" on New Year's Eve of 1994. The club features all the fun of a traditional night club scene—music, food, and fellowship—without the alcohol.

The idea for the club actually existed long before it became a reality, said Dr. Gwen Pearson, a counselor with the Dexter Avenue Counseling Center and chairperson for the development of Club 301. She remembers a similar idea first being presented in 1949 by then-pastor Dr. Andrew Turnipseed.

"There were a lot of servicemen here, and [Pastor Turnipseed] had the idea to have square dances in the fellowship hall," she recalled. "It caused a furor back then, and some people even left the church," she said.

The square dance program ended up infusing new life in the church, and energizing the young people of the congregation, Pearson said.

An idea for an actual nightclub at the church was first envisioned in 1965, under the direction of pastor Eugene Peacock, but didn't come to fruition at the time. Peacock did create the name "Club 301," taken both from the address of the church, at 301 McDonough Street, and from the idea of the Christian Trinity— "three in one— Father, Son, and Holy Ghost," Pearson explained.

The idea materialized after Pearson had done extensive counseling with recovering alcoholics. It became apparent they needed a place to have fun, but away from the influence of alcohol.

"Alcoholics are used to going to bars for fellowship. Once they can't do that, they don't really know where to meet people," she said.

The idea for the club was greeted enthusiastically by church administration, and Rick Wooley came on staff to direct the program. It had long been his dream to create a night spot for young people that was alcohol-free.

"We want people to have a good time, and realize they're having a good time, and realize they're having a good time without alcohol," Wooley said.

Eventually, the church hopes to expand the club idea to add a nontraditional worship service, which will welcome people of all faiths.

These are just a few of the many outreach efforts of local congregations. Ministries include the traditional, such as food and clothing drives, vacation Bible study programs and service projects; to the innovative, including puppet shows and musical entertainment directed toward ministering to inner-city youth, tent revivals, and mission trips to foreign lands for every kind of project from building homes to providing health care.

Temple Beth Or dates from the 1950s, but the Jewish congregation built their first edifice in 1862 in downtown Montgomery. Photo by Robert Fouts.

There are many ways to worship, and Montgomery offers choices for people of every faith.

NEIGHBORHOODS

The development of Montgomery's neighborhoods reflects the advancement of methods of transportation, said Mary Ann Neeley, executive director of the Landmarks Foundation and Old Alabama Town.

Some of Montgomery's oldest neighborhoods include the historic district—streets such as South Hull and South Perry, where homes surround the Governor's mansion—the garden district of Cottage Hill, which features homes built around 1904 and reflecting Victorian-style architecture; and Centennial Hill, the first really prosperous black community, established at the turn of the century.

These areas are all located in the downtown area, close to what was once the center of all commerce and social activity, Neeley said.

These homes are not found in what we think of today as "neighborhoods," a concept which did not truly develop until after the invention of the electric streetcar, which allowed people to live further out from the center of business, she explained.

In the 1830s and 1840s, the town moved southward, uphill from the river, but still close enough for people to walk into town, Neeley said. Gradually, city services such as a water works, fire department, gas and electric lighting, and street paving were developed.

"All these are part and parcel of a developing community," she said.

Some of the first true suburban neighborhoods still a part of Montgomery are Old Cloverdale, with architectue dating from the early 1900s, and Capitol Heights, with much of its 1940s architecture intact.

Much of the historic architecture and the traditional neighborhoods faced eradication in the early 1960s, when the interstate system was built.

"The Interstate was a massive destructive force, as far as it destroyed the coherence of Montgomery neighborhoods," Neeley said. "Many old homes were torn down to accommodate the interstate construction, and former neighborhoods were torn in two."

This was not a situation unique to Montgomery, but something that was happening throughout the country as the interstates crossed America.

Finally, in 1965, the Federal government passed the National Historic Preservation Act, which helped draw attention to the destruction

going on, and raise awareness of the importance of preserving the architectural heritage present in the older neighborhoods, Neeley said.

"We became aware that we were throwing away who and what we were," she said.

In the period of the late 1960s and early 1970s, Montgomery's Old Cloverdale and Capitol Heights neighborhoods enjoyed a period of revival and renovation.

"In the early days of this restoration, it was financially attractive to buy an older house of 1920s and 1930s vintage for very little, then fix it up. Then, later, the historic district property values went up because of all the restoration, so the property was worth more," Neeley said.

A little later, the Cottage Hill district, overlooking the city and the Alabama River, benefitted from the same kind of revival. Nowdays, many quaint bed-and-breakfast inns, a restaurant and many antique shops find their homes among the private residences of Cottage Hill, making it a unique, historically influenced community.

In recent years, Montgomery has grown in an eastward direction, a fact made necessary by the Alabama River, which limits development to the west.

Neighborhoods in east Montgomery include apartment and single-family dwellings, in sizes and price ranges to suit a variety of needs.

In the past two to three years, Montgomery has enjoyed a boom in new construction, facilitated by low interest rates and an influx of people brought to the area by new industry.

Many of the newer neighborhoods enjoy amenities ranging from a community pool and clubhouse to full golf course and country club facilities.

Perhaps the crown jewel of Montgomery's newer neighborhoods is Wynlakes. Dubbed the "residential masterpiece," Wynlakes sets the standard for fine living in the city. The neighborhood features estates, executive homes, and garden homes to suit every need.

Each aspect of the design is meticulously planned, from the wooded landscapes to the sparkling lakes and the sprawling golf course, which is rated one of the finest championship courses in the South.

There is a full-service country club located at the heart of the neighborhood, with tennis courts, a refreshing swimming pool, pro shops, and dressing/locker rooms. Also on site at the country club is a fine restaurant and several meeting rooms.

From the peace and quiet of country living to the convenience of a location in the heart of the city, Montgomery offers a wealth of selection.

Those who long to be away from the hustle and bustle of city life even more may choose to call nearby Autauga and Elmore Counties home. Many people who work in Montgomery live in Prattville, just 13 miles north of Montgomery by Interstate-65, or Wetumpka, a short 15-mile stretch northeast of Montgomery on Highway 231. Prattville and Wetumpka offer many of the conveniences of modern life, but in a quiet, country setting.

Prattville is one of the fastest growing cities in the state, with population tripling in the past two decades. Current population for the Prattville area is approximately 37,000.

"We've still got the small, friendly town atmosphere, with a lot of the metropolitan advantages," said Deborah McGill, director of economic development for the Prattville Area Chamber of Commerce.

A strong base for growth in Prattville is a healthy climate for industry. Early on, Prattville earned a reputation as the "birthplace of industry in Alabama," as its founding father, Daniel Pratt, established one of the first and largest cotton gin manufacturing companies in the world on Autauga Creek in 1832.

Building on that history, Prattville is now home to such industries as Union Camp Paper Company, a more than $300-million operation located on the Alabama River, Molded Industrial Friction Company, Montgomery Packaging Corporation, Cavnar-Johnson Cordage Company, Card Lock Company, Crystal Lake Manufacturing Company, Bednar, Inc., and Renewed Resources, among others.

During the 1995-1996 business year, Prattville had three major industrial announcements, including a new, state-of-the-art medical facility, the Baptist Medical Park, which will be under the direction of Baptist Health Services in Montgomery. The park, which will complement

The Episcopal congregation of Saint John's retained the services of the New York architectural firm of Wills and Dudley to design a church for them in the 1850s, soon after Montgomery became the state capital. Both the interior and exterior reflect strong Gothic Revival influences. Photo by Robert Fouts. (previous page)

The garden district of Cottage Hill features homes built around 1904 and reflects Victorian-style architecture. Photo by Robert Fouts. (right)

A unique charm. infuses the architecture of the city. Photos by Robert Fouts. (previous page)

In the late 1960s and early 1970s, Montgomery's Old Cloverdale neighborhood enjoyed a period of revival and renovation. A sense of community pride and involvement makes it a great place to raise a family. Photos by Robert Fouts.

the services of the existing Autauga Medical Center, will be developed on 50 acres. Phase I will be a three-story 50,000-square-foot medical office building able to accommodate approximately 25 physicians. An adjacent 25,000-square-foot ambulatory services facility is planned to include diagnostic testing and imaging, outpatient rehabilitation, and other ambulatory services.

Phase I is scheduled for completion in late summer of 1996. Future phases of development include an acute care hospital, recovery care center, nursing home, and birthing center.

The presence of a strong industrial community assures jobs for Prattville's citizens and a healthy economic environment for the city, reflected in its strong local shopping facilities, schools, and parks.

Homes are available in a wide variety of sizes and price ranges, with real estate prices and taxes tending to be lower than in other areas of the country, making it an attractive choice for families and retirees.

Prattville offers a variety of recreational opportunities as well, including eight parks, the world's only flag museum, a branch of the Montgomery Ballet School of Dance, historic Prattvillage, local arts festivals, the Prattville Community Chorus, and Emerald Falls Adventure Golf, which includes go-kart tracks, batting cages, and "Wet n' Wild" bumper boats. There is a water park under construction at Emerald Falls as well.

Prattville also is proud of its historic sites, including Buena Vista, a grand mansion built in 1822 by Major William Montgomery. Buena Vista is the only structure in Autauga County listed on the National Register of Historic Places. It is reported that General Andrew Jackson, upon visiting the mansion, was so impressed with the special circular staircase which spirals 24 feet upward to the third floor banquet hall, he had it duplicated for his home in Nashville, Tennessee. Many brides from throughout the Southeast choose stately Buena Vista as a romantic site for their wedding and reception.

From the peace and quiet of country living to the convenience of a location in the heart of the city, Montgomery offers a wealth of selection.

One of the first true suburban neighborhoods still a part of Montgomery is Capitol Heights, with much of its 1940s architecture intact. Photo by Robert Fouts. (left)

In the past few years, Montgomery has enjoyed a boom in new construction, especially in east Montgomery. Photo by Robert Fouts. (right)

Many of the newer neighborhoods in east Montgomery, such as Wynlakes, enjoy amenities such as a tennis club and golf course. Photo by Robert Fouts.

"Even with all the new business development, and real estate development, Prattville is able to hold on to its history," McGill said. "We offer the luxury of country living, with the conveniences of modern life close at hand in the community, and the amenities of Montgomery just a short drive away."

Dubbed the "City of Natural Beauty," Wetumpka, the county seat of Elmore County, offers a lush, hilly terrain; a historic downtown district; and the rolling waters of the Coosa River, a paradise for fishing, swimming, water skiing, and even kayaking. Wetumpka boasts "affordable leisure living outside the busy city atmosphere and gives the convenience of small town closeness and attitude." A selection of restaurants, shops, and offices are a cozy complement to the larger nearby shopping malls of Montgomery.

The Elmore County School system offers a wide range of programs and curriculum for students in grades kindergarten through 12, serving more than 3,000 students with public and private school choices.

Housing choices are affordable and varied. The new Emerald Mountain residential development offers a wide range of floor plans nestled into spectacular views in the hillside of Wetumpka, plus a full-service clubhouse open to all neighborhood residents, and community tennis courts.

Recreational activities abound, with the Wetumpka area offering two large lakes, two major rivers, and smaller bodies of water. The Coosa River cuts through the center of the city and has a public boat launch. The river is pollution free and is ideal for a variety of water sports.

Outdoorsmen and hunters will find plenty of places to roam, and woods rich with deer, turkey, dove, quail, and squirrel.

The Wetumpka YMCA offers programs for both adults and youths, including organized sports leagues, athletic instructional clinics and workshops, a competitive gymnastics team, after school child care programs, and Hi-Y and Tri-Hi-Y youth leadership programs. Also, the YMCA offers adult fitness programs including aerobics and weight training. The facility offers members access to tennis courts, a swimming pool, athletic

Prattville is one of the fastest growing cities in the state, yet it retains its small, friendly town atmosphere. Photo by Robert Fouts. (left)

Wetumpka boasts affordable leisure living outside the city and gives the convenience of small town closeness and attitude. The Wetumpka Christmas Parade is a favorite community event. Photo by Robert Fouts. (above)

fields, a gymnasium, and meeting rooms. Programs are available especially for families, such as cookouts and special trips including canoeing and camping.

Additionally, Quail Walk Country Club is available to Wetumpka residents, offering swimming, tennis, and an 18-hole golf course, driving range, and clubhouse facilities for meetings and banquets.

The City of Wetumpka provides such recreational amenities as two tennis courts and seven ball fields, with organized youth and adult baseball leagues.

For those with an interest in history, a visit to nearby Fort Toulouse/Jackson Park is a must. The 165-acre National Historic Landmark park boasts a partially restored French fort and an American fort, and Living History Programs are presented regularly, giving visitors a glimpse into the past as volunteers dress, work, and play as settlers would have done in the early 1700s. Re-enactment activities include demonstrations of cooking, tanning, blacksmithing, and battles. Other amenities of the park include nature trails, the William Bartrum Arboretum, picnic areas, a boat launch, a museum, and a campground.

Just outside Wetumpka's city limits is Jasmine Hill Gardens, "where ancient Greece comes alive."

The gardens feature the world's only full-scale replica of the Temple of Hera, where the Olympic flame begins its journey, in Greece. In 1996 the Olympic torch will come to Jasmine Hill on its way to the games in Atlanta, for a celebration at Montgomery's own "Temple of Hera."

Throughout the Jasmine Hill Gardens, more than 30 sculptures, fountains, and artwork honor Olympic heroes and the mythical gods of ancient Greece, all surrounded by 17 acres of exotic and beautiful flowering plants.

Throughout the year, Wetumpka residents enjoy a variety of festivals and recreational activities including the nationally-acclaimed "Christmas on the Coosa," a spectacular floating parade of lights.

Wetumpka is the choice for singles, families, and retirees who enjoy the benefits of a peaceful, nostalgic small town atmosphere, close to jobs, shopping, and entertainment in Montgomery. *n*

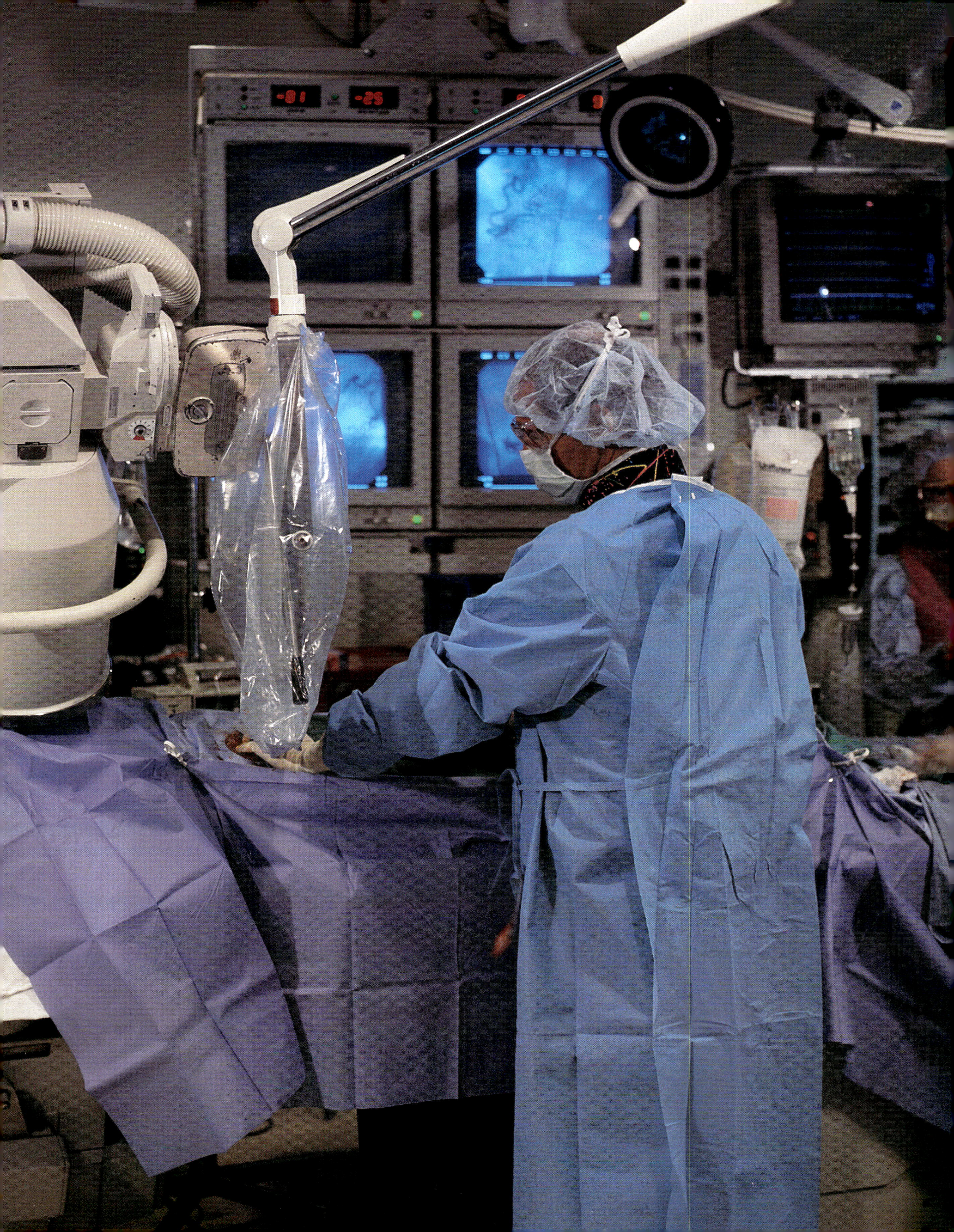

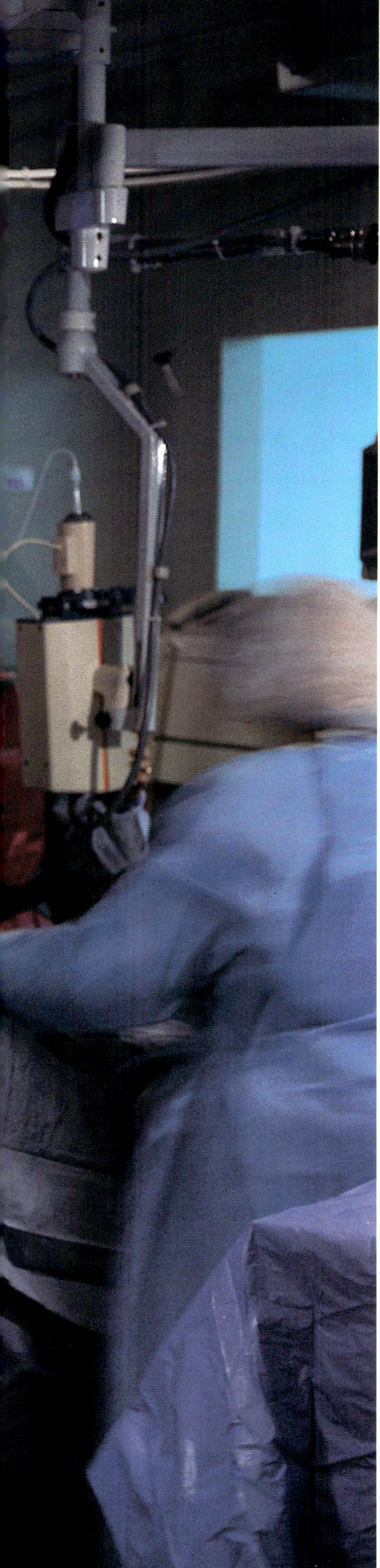

A HEALTHY ATTITUDE

Montgomery offers an extensive health care system, with four full-service hospitals and numerous specialized care facilities located in the Capital City. From receiving care for the common cold to undergoing advanced medical procedures including open-heart surgery, Montgomery residents feel secure in the knowledge that their needs can be met by dedicated physicians and health care professionals.

From the birth of a baby to undergoing advanced surgery, Montgomery residents' needs are met by the dedicated physicians and health care professionals in the city. Photos by Robert Fouts.

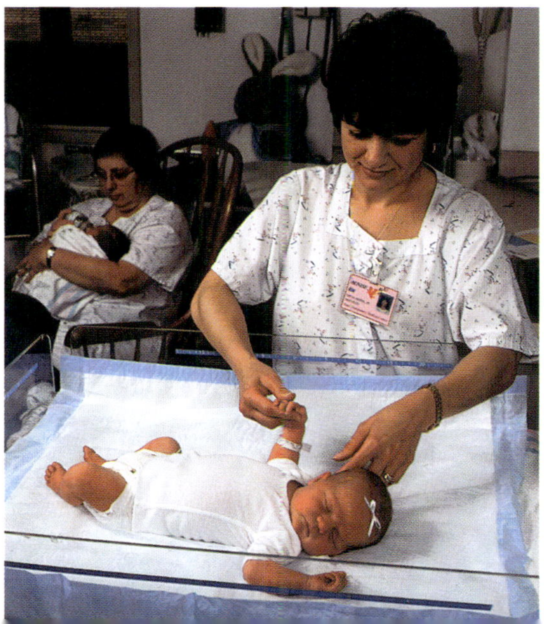

Whenever a need arises, whenever the cry for help is issued, Montgomery's medical community is ready to respond. From a case of the sniffles to open-heart surgery, residents can rest assured they are in capable and caring hands.

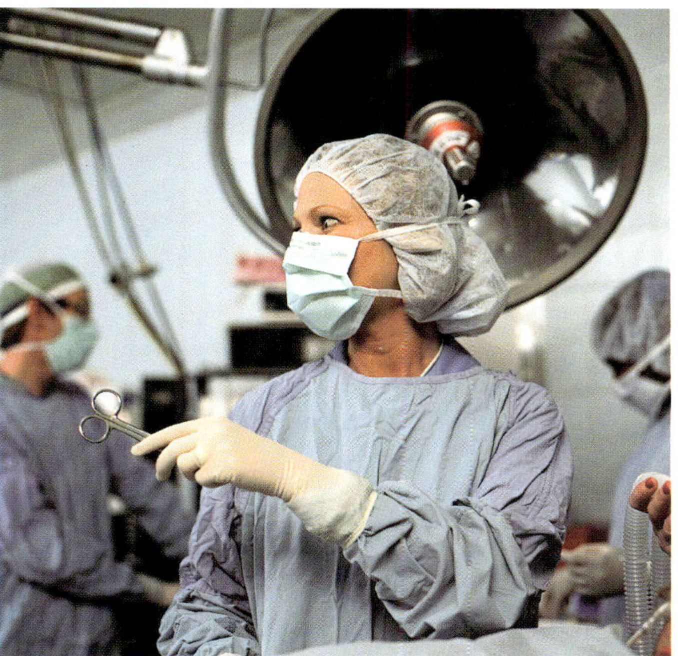

Montgomery's medical community is ready to respond to any situation. Photo courtesy of Baptist Medical Center. (above)

Montgomery offers an extensive health care system, with four full-service hospitals and numerous specialized care facilities located in the Capital City. Photo by Robert Fouts. (left)

BAPTIST MEDICAL CENTER

From the first germ of an idea conceived in 1955, to the first construction of the 124-bed Baptist Hospital in 1963, Baptist Medical Center has grown steadily to become a cornerstone of the Montgomery health care community. Currently, the medical center is a 454-bed facility employing 1,700 people. The hospital is part of Baptist Health Services Corporation, which includes eight subsidiaries, including Pri-Med walk-in medical treatment clinics, a surgical center, pharmacy, and assisted-living retirement community among them. Also, the foundation manages Meadhaven, an emotional health and addictive disease treatment center.

Baptist also has recently begun construction on the Baptist Medical Park in nearby Prattville. The 82,000-square-foot facility will include outpatient services and medical offices, with additions to be made as the needs of the Prattville community become more clear.

New additions in Montgomery include the Parker Women's Pavilion, which offers a full range of women's health services, including obstetrical and gynecological services, a breast health clinic, and a full range of educational services such as the Stork Club, for expectant parents.

The Baptist Chest Pain Center, a specialized care center for the early diagnosis and treatment of heart disease and heart attacks, also is a new service of Baptist. It is designed to educate people about the importance of seeking an early diagnosis for chest pains, assuring early treatment if a serious heart problem exists.

"The basic purpose of the Chest Pain Center is to reduce deaths from heart attack," said Rick Derrick, director of public relations for BMC. "Sometimes, people will put off coming into the emergency room with chest pains because they're afraid it will turn out to be something minor, and then they'll be embarrassed. The Chest Pain Center provides a place where they can come and feel comfortable to find out and not take chances, because that's what the doctors are there for—specifically to find out what is causing the chest pain, whether it's something minor or something serious," he said. The Chest Pain Center is the only one of its kind in the Montgomery area, Derrick said. Construction of the Cardiovascular Institute, which will house the Montgomery Cardiology Associates, among other services, is underway. The institute will

further the heart care services offered by the hospital, including those of the new Chest Pain Center. Recently, Baptist Medical Center has also added open-heart surgery capabilities to its range of services in this area.

An important service offered by Baptist Medical Center is its Neonatal Intensive Care Unit, which serves 21 counties. The NICU treats premature and severely ill newborn babies. Infants weighing as little as a pound and a half have been successfully treated by Baptist's NICU services.

"It's miraculous to see it," Derrick said of the work done by the NICU staff.

Additionally, Baptist offers all the services you would expect from a health care leader, and then some. Unique features include a sleep studies lab and a robotic arm for surgery.

In addition to health care treatment services, Baptist Medical Center places high emphasis on the prevention of health problems through education, called the Wellness program.

"The responsibility for good health doesn't just lie with the medical profession, but also with individuals to take advantage of the programs available for them to take care of themselves," said Linda Lee, assistant director of public relations for BMC. "It's a partnership."

Educational efforts begin with Baptist Medical Center's partnership with the Montgomery Public Schools system. They act as Partners In Education with Harrison Elementary School and Davis Elementary School, and also provide health care assistance to all Montgomery Public Schools by providing medical supplies such as bandages and first aid kits for school nurses, and each year they work to provide medical equipment such as exam tables, lights, and blood pressure equipment to a public school.

"This is sometimes the only medical exam these kids get, when they go to see the school nurse," Derrick explained. "We are fortunate to have been able to help diagnose several children with medical problems through this service in the schools," he said.

An additional educational program in place in the public schools is a cooperative effort between Baptist Medical Center and the American Heart Association. Called "Heart Smart," the program features educational information about the dangers of smoking and about how to care for the heart through healthy eating and exercise. The educational materials are designed specifically to

Baptist Medical Center has grown steadily to become a cornerstone of the Montgomery health care community. Currently, the medical center is a 454-bed facility employing 1,700 people. Photo by Robert Fouts.

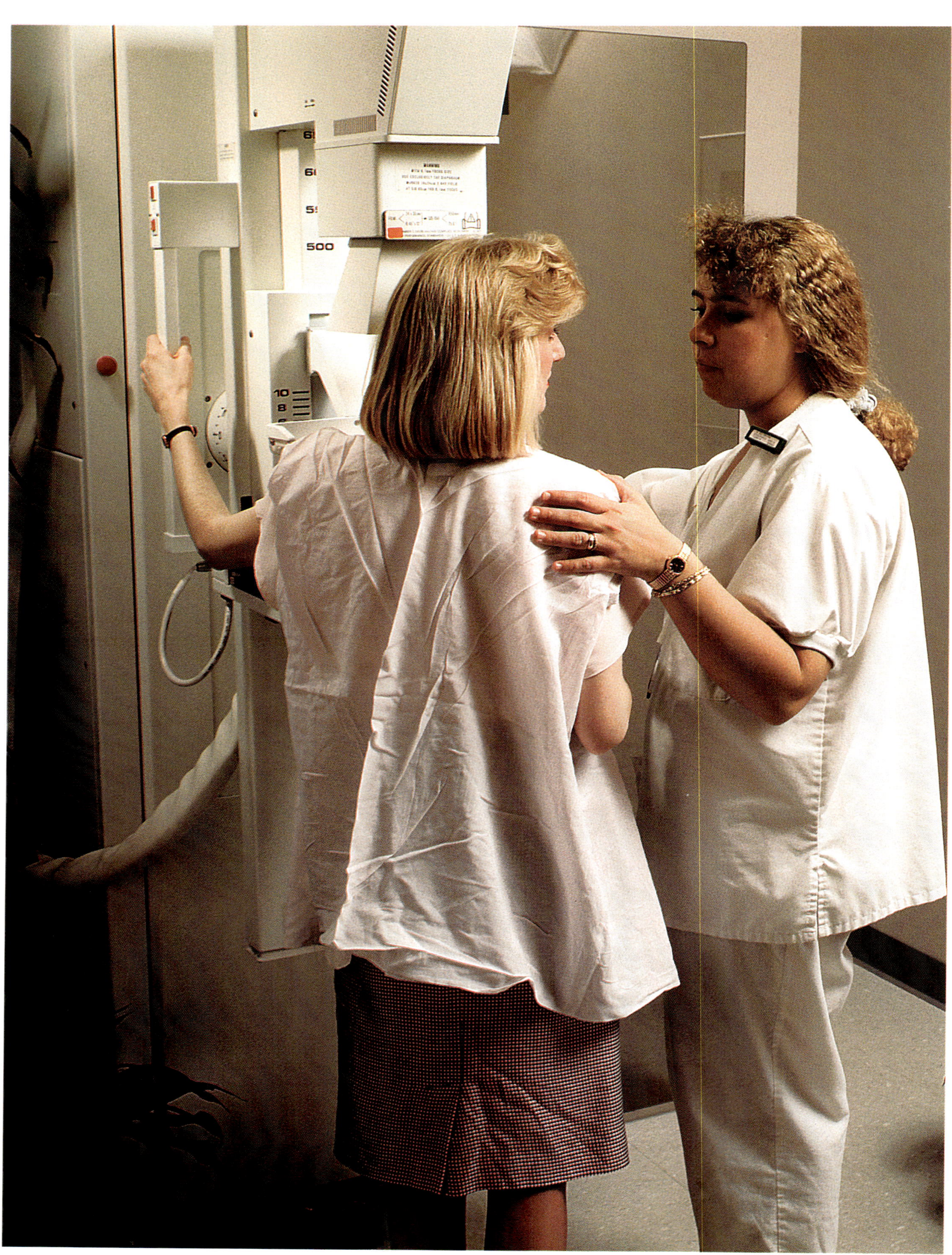

Specialized diagnostic laboratories provide Montgomery doctors and patients with state-of-the-art equipment for such procedures as mammography, among others. Photo by Robert Fouts.

suit the needs of youngsters in different age groups. Baptist has donated $40,000 to the program, which will be an ongoing effort to include every school in the Montgomery Public Schools system.

Derrick is proud of Baptist Medical Center's commitment to "wellness," considering it a crucial ingredient in the mission of the hospital.

"We want to be here for people when they need us in times of illness, but we also feel it is most important to keep them healthy," Derrick said. "We are striving to do this through a variety of methods including education and community involvement."

JACKSON HOSPITAL

For 50 years, Jackson Hospital has been a health care leader in Montgomery. In 1946 the hospital was founded—with a grand total of 36 beds—by a group of physicians led by Dr. Frank Jackson; his brother, Dr. Truett Jackson; and their father, Dr. B. F. Jackson. The original hospital was housed in three wooden frame houses on the corner of Forest Avenue and Pine Street, very

near the location where the modern Jackson Hospital facility stands today.

"It was the dream of Dr. Frank Jackson to provide medical service for the people of Montgomery, to serve the people of Montgomery as his neighbors," said Victoria W. Jones, executive director of the Jackson Hospital Foundation. "Jackson is the only hospital in Montgomery that was created through the vision of a few local people with a great deal of local support. That same commitment to the community continues today," she said.

Jackson Hospital is currently licensed for 400 beds and employs a total of 1,350 people.

The year 1996 marks the golden anniversary of Jackson Hospital, with the hospital's rich history being celebrated by a huge step forward into the future. In April of 1996, officials at Jackson Hospital broke ground for a new, state-of-the-art hospital facility, designed to replace the old East Wing and West Wing that date back to the original construction of the hospital in the 1950s. The modern facility will be constructed in two phases, with a completion date

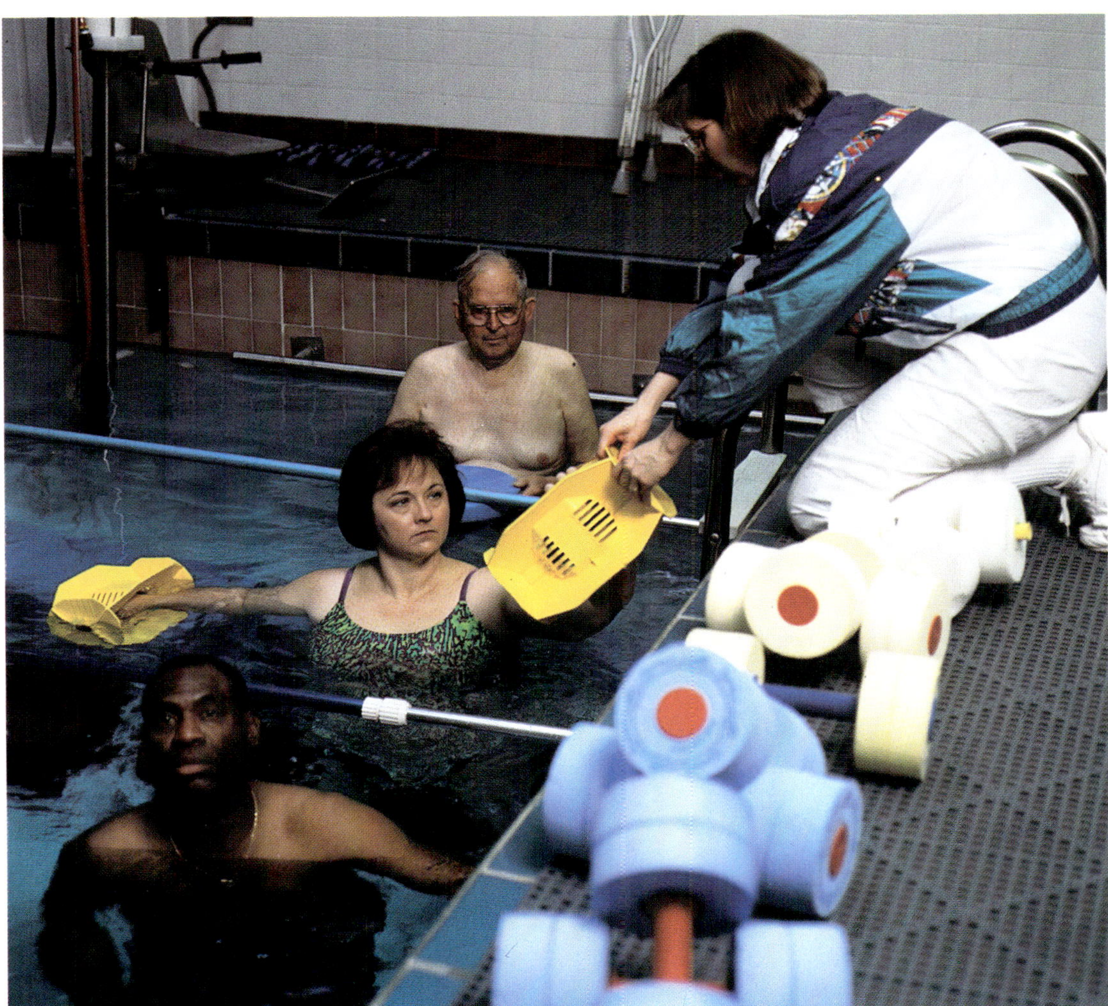

For those patients needing specialized care, Montgomery offers rehabilitative therapy. Photo by Robert Fouts.

JACKSON HOSPITAL
REDUCED SPEED AHEAD
REDU SPE AHE

of 1999, "just in time for the new century," according to Jones.

The new facility will feature a new design with the goal of providing the most technologically-advanced medical care available, and the capacity to continue to grow to meet the demands of the future, Jones said.

The multistory medical complex will house a large, expanded emergency room facility and will provide all radiology services for the convenience of not only the ER, but also the high volume of outpatient traffic that is the mark of the future of health care, as outpatient treatment and shorter hospital stays are the trend in health care services.

Patient floors also have a state-of-the-art design, with a modern nursing station located at the nucleus of the plan, with patient rooms arranged in a circular fashion around the station. This will allow nurses on duty a view of each patient. "Because less severe medical problems are being treated on an outpatient basis more and more, people who stay in the hospital will be more severe cases, and the elderly with multiple problems," Jones explained. "They will need a higher degree of care, and more constant monitoring."

The new building also will be capable of supporting a cutting-edge information systems network, creating a communications network that will allow almost instant access to whatever medical services are needed.

All these innovations will allow Jackson Hospital to keep providing the top-quality service Montgomerians have come to expect, Jones said.

"Things we are known for the most are the very strong contingent of neurologists and neurosurgeons on staff, a very strong orthopedic contingent, and we are the only hospital in our area with an inpatient oncology/cancer unit," Jones said.

Jackson also is the only hospital in Montgomery with LDRP facilities—suites with the capacity of handling labor, delivery, recovery, and postpartum services in one room.

In addition to providing service at their hospital facility, Jackson Hospital is involved in reaching out to the community. Jackson supports athletes in Montgomery through a cooperative agreement with Rehabilitation Associates, with physicians and nurses providing preparticipation physical examinations for all athletes preparing to play school sports.

In addition, Jackson hosts various citywide health screenings, is a Partner in Education with Forest Avenue Elementary School, and hosts Community Challenge, an annual event designed to promote physical fitness and well-being while raising funds for the hospital.

"The tradition of being a partner in the community goes back to the very beginning of the creation of this hospital," Jones said. "And it is a priority to keep those bonds strong."

COLUMBIA REGIONAL MEDICAL CENTER

Columbia Regional Medical Center, formerly known as Montgomery Regional Medical Center, offers all the services you expect from a top-notch national hospital corporation, and then a little something more. They prove every day they are the hospital "with heart."

Founded in 1902 by the Daughters of Charity as Saint Margaret's Hospital, the health care facility was purchased in 1989 by Humana Healthcare Corporation, which later merged with Columbia HCA. Columbia also owns Columbia East Montgomery Medical Center, the Montgomery Surgery Center, and CareOne Home Health in Montgomery, and the company recently purchased the Autauga Medical Center and owns the Four Rivers Medical Center in Selma.

Also, Columbia has recently added the Montgomery Wound Care Center to its family of health care services, providing Montgomerians with specialized care for wounds that are difficult to heal, such as diabetic ulcerations.

A unique program sponsored through Columbia Regional Medical Center is the Gift of Life, which provides obstetrical care for indigent mothers. Care includes prenatal counseling, birth preparation classes, childcare classes, and medical services for delivery.

In 1995 a partnership was developed between the hospital and Telephone Pioneers of America's Montgomery chapter. The Telephone Pioneers sponsored "baby showers" to collect needed items for the expectant mothers, purchased "Little Golden Books" to encourage literacy by helping mothers read to their children, and volunteered their time to the program in many other areas.

"This cooperative effort really shows how a hospital and a business can work together to make a difference," said Margaret Mahearg, public relations director for Columbia Regional Medical Center.

But what Columbia Regional Medical Center does best is heart care, said Anthony Eubanks, R.N., director of cardiac services for the hospital. "We are the most experienced in heart care—any and all types of treatments," Eubanks said.

Columbia Regional Medical Center has led the way in providing state-of-the-art diagnostic and treatment procedures for the care of the

For 50 years, Jackson Hospital has been a health care leader in Montgomery. Photo by Robert Fouts. (previous page)

Education can often be the best prevention to illness. Montgomery's health care community takes the time to educate its patients. Photo by Robert Fouts. (top)

What Columbia Regional Medical Center does best is heart care, leading the way in providing state-of-the-art diagnostic and treatment procedures for the care of the heart. Not only is the patient cared for, but also the waiting family. Photo by Robert Fouts. (bottom)

heart. Cardiac catheterization was first offered in Montgomery at the hospital in 1972. Open-heart surgery was offered to Montgomerians in 1978. Balloon angioplasty procedures, which help clear blocked heart passages, were added in 1983.

Currently, the medical center offers all noninvasive heart treatment procedures medically available for people of all ages. There are three open-heart suites, two fully-staffed cardiac cath labs, and an electrophysiology lab available at Columbia Regional Medical Center to serve the community.

And Columbia Regional Medical Center is still leading the way in innovations for heart care.

"In the past year and a half, we have been implanting coronary stints, which is the next wave in heart health care," Eubanks said. After angioplasty, there is a chance of blockages coming back, he explained. The heart stint helps reduce that risk by keeping passages open.

Perhaps one of the most significant steps Columbia Regional Medical Center has taken to ensure heart health takes place outside of the hospital. The medical center donated five portable electrocardiograph machines to the Montgomery Firemedics, with a goal of decreasing the time it takes for a patient with a heart attack or suspected heart attack to get proper treatment.

The firemedics are the first to respond to any 911 emergency call received anywhere in the city and to provide medical treatment. The portable electrocardiograph system actually has three different parts—a 12-lead EKG system, the same technology a patient would have access to in a hospital, that monitors the patient's heart signals; a cellular modem that allows paramedics to transmit the data they receive from the patient to the hospital while still en route to the emergency room; and a receiver located in the Columbia Regional Medical Center emergency room that can monitor the signals instantly.

Physicians specifically on call to answer heart needs are able to interpret the EKG data sent from the ambulance and have proper treatment ready and waiting for the patient upon his arrival at the hospital. Because the heart muscle does not regenerate itself, time is of the essence in treatment of heart patients. Treatment must begin as soon as possible, before too much of the heart muscle is damaged.

"This system decreases the amount of time spent because a diagnosis can be made while the patient is still en route to the hospital," Eubanks said. "That's the thing I'm most proud of,

because I feel it's the next step in heart treatment. I feel this will be the next big impact to decrease morbidity and mortality in the heart patient," he said.

Columbia Regional Medical Center doesn't stop care for its heart patients once they have been treated and released. The "Open House for Open-Heart and Angioplasty Patients" is a reunion held each year to bring together those who have shared the experience of open-heart surgery or angioplasty procedures.

Also, the medical center offers the bimonthly "Heart of Montgomery Club," open to anyone with an interest in the health of the heart, or who has had a problem with his or her heart. The club features expert guest speakers to address such topics as coronary risk factors, the symptoms and treatment of depression after a serious illness, and proper exercise programs to suit specific ages and needs, among many others.

COLUMBIA EAST MONTGOMERY MEDICAL CENTER

Columbia East Montgomery Medical Center (formerly known as East Montgomery Medical Center) is the newest hospital in Montgomery, established as University Medical Center in 1977. The hospital was purchased in 1983 by Humana, Inc., which later merged with Columbia HCA, Inc., the world's largest hospital company. Located in the heart of east Montgomery, the fastest-growing area in the city, Columbia East Montgomery Medical Center has grown into a fine full-service hospital capable of providing treatment for a variety of illnesses and injuries, including diagnostic services, outpatient services, emergency medical care, and surgery.

But perhaps Columbia East Montgomery Medical Center's proudest accomplishment is its emphasis on obstetrics, from prepregnancy and prenatal care to delivery, and even beyond.

For the expectant parent, Columbia East Montgomery Medical Center offers programs to answer just about any question, all under the umbrella of the Family Matters program. It all begins with a celebration of the pregnancy with the Baby Shower program, which invites expectant couples to Columbia East Montgomery for an orientation and tour of the obstetrical unit. The one-hour program provides information to help couples make an informed decision when choosing a hospital for this momentous occasion in their lives.

A variety of classes offered through Family Matters prepares parents for the coming baby. Courses include baby care, breast feeding,

pregnancy 101, Lamaze, prepared childbirth, and sibling preparation. Classes are designed to answer questions on a wide range of topics, addressing both physical and emotional issues that result from pregnancy.

Expectant parents also are invited to join the Cradle Club. As a member, they will receive a monthly newsletter (corresponding to the month of pregnancy, including 10th month, or postnatal) and coupons for baby products.

Obstetrical facilities at Columbia East Montgomery Medical Center include five LDR (labor/delivery/recovery) rooms and two LDRP (labor/delivery/recovery/postpartum) rooms. Expectant parents are encouraged to discuss various options for labor and delivery with their physician, and to work with their doctor to make an active choice about their baby's delivery.

But obstetrical care doesn't end after the delivery at Columbia East Montgomery. A unique service offered by the hospital is the Momnibus program. This is a complimentary home-visitation program. At the parents' request, a nurse educator will come to the new parents' home to refresh the skills they learned in prenatal education classes and answer any questions the new parents might have.

Also, if the baby goes home before its PKU blood work (a standard series of blood tests for newborns) has been done, it can be done by the Momnibus nurse in the family's home, eliminating the need for another trip to the hospital.

"A lot of young couples are interested in knowing everything they can about the coming baby," said Pat Garrison, director of the Cradle Club program. "They are used to having things scheduled, and they want to have a plan for having a baby, too," she said.

ADDITIONAL SERVICES

Aside from the comprehensive facilities and services offered by Montgomery's four hospitals, specialized medical care is available to meet the growing and changing needs of a busy community.

Private practice physicians offer treatment in areas from family practice to internal medicine, sports medicine to ophthalmology, neurology to orthodontics, and anything in between.

Special "walk-in" medical treatment centers, including American Family Care Medical Centers, Med-One, and Pri-Med, are open hours beyond the normal doctor's office schedule, often seven days a week, to provide care for minor emergencies, family medicine, industrial

Columbia East Montgomery Medical Center's unique service offered to new parents is the Momnibus. At the parents' request, a nurse educator will come to the new parents' home to answer any questions the new parents might have. Photo courtesy of Columbia East Montgomery Medical Center.

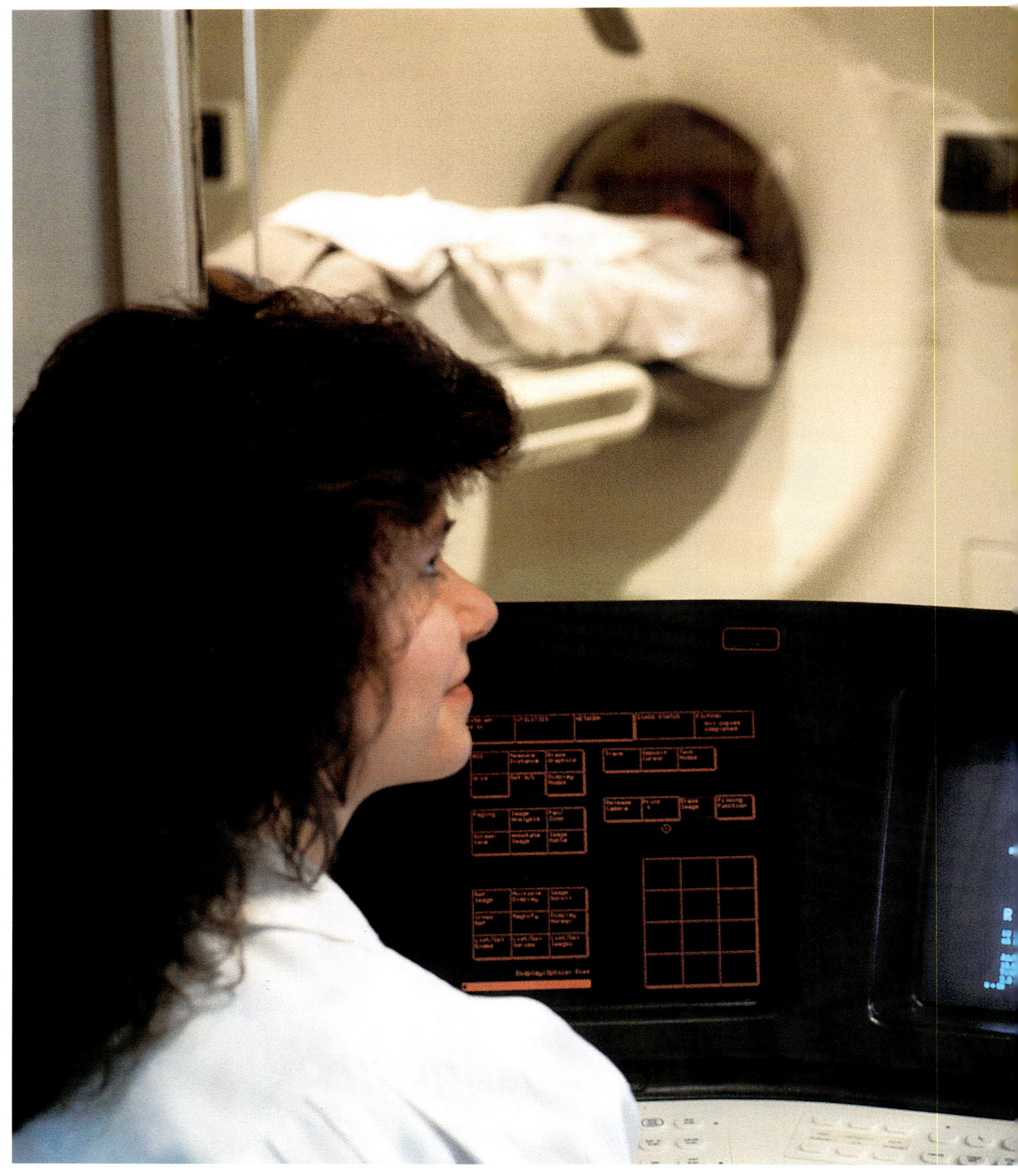

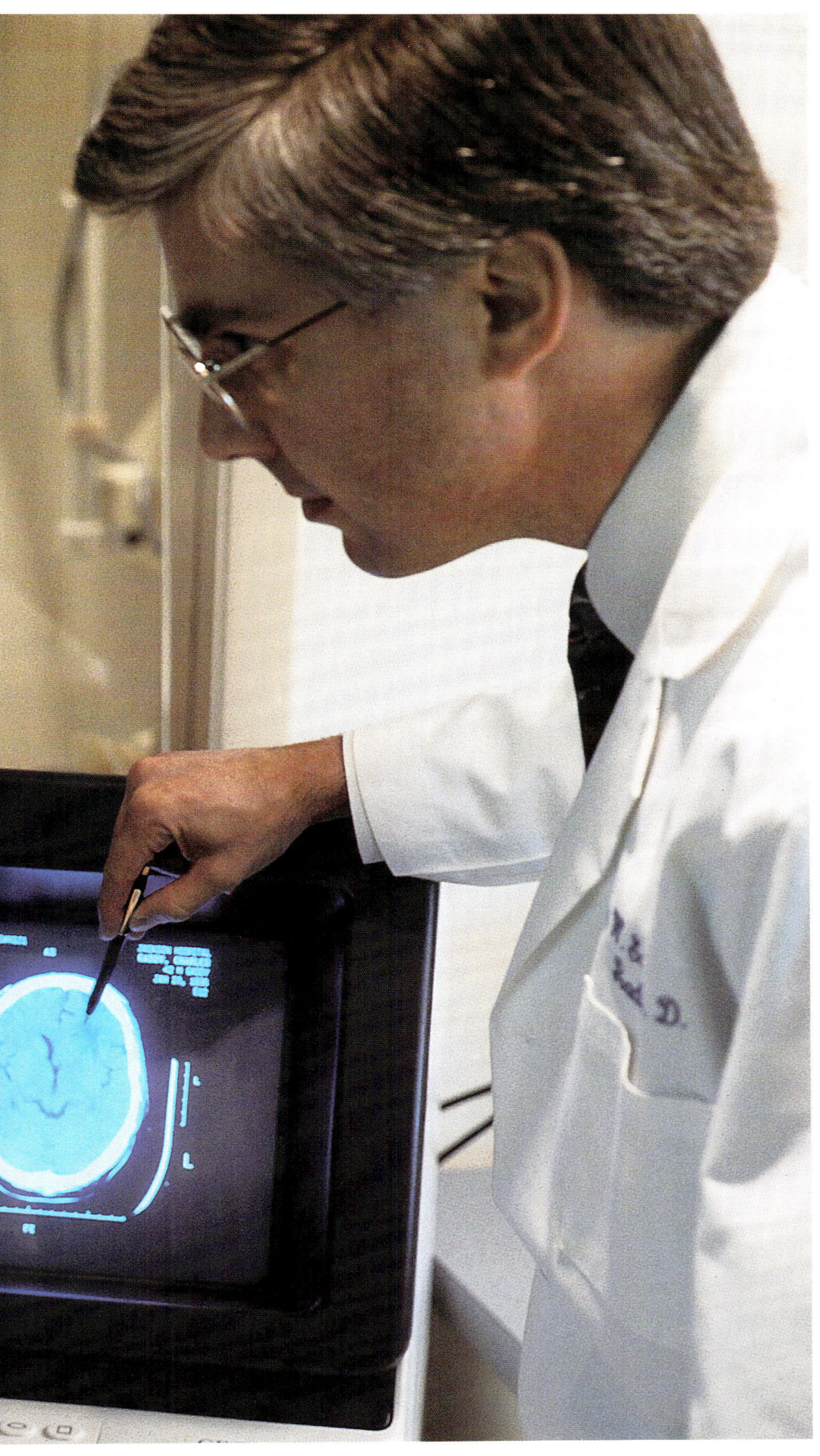

State-of-the-art equipment helps physicians make accurate diagnoses. Photo by Robert Fouts.

medicine, and minor injuries. Most of these centers also provide on-site prescription services.

Diagnostic laboratories provide Montgomery doctors and patients with state-of-the-art equipment for such exploratory and preventative procedures as blood work and analysis, CT, mammography, ultrasound, fluoroscopy, nuclear medicine, MRI, and general radiology, among others. These services can be the key to early detection and treatment of medical problems.

Medical groups, including several doctors specializing in a particular field, provide patients with a setting in which they can receive specific treatment for their illness, drawing on a base of expertise and research in areas including cardio-vascular disease, cancer, orthopedic medicine, pediatrics, kidney disease, and more.

Montgomery's veterans can take advantage of medical care facilities at the Veterans' Administration Hospital, offering outpatient treatment, emergency medical care, and patient admission for medical and surgical services.

For those patients needing long-term care, Montgomery offers home health care services including skilled nursing, medical social services, physical and speech therapy, cardiac rehabilitation, occupational therapy, IV therapy, aides and orderlies, and live-in companions.

Also, there are many assisted-living and nursing homes available in Montgomery, providing such services as 24-hour assistance, meals, planned activities, nurse on duty and on-call, and emergency call systems.

Two Montgomery hospice programs, Baptist Hospice and Hospice of Montgomery, provide specialized in-home care and counseling for terminally ill patients and their families.

In addition to its offering of treatments for physical ailments, Montgomery offers a wide range of services to meet the mental and emotional needs of its citizens, including psychological evaluation and treatment, including the areas of adult, adolescent, and child psychology, family therapy, marriage and sexual counseling, eating disorders, depression, and panic disorders; addictive disease counseling, with both outpatient and inpatient services; and long-term psychiatric care facilities.

Whenever a need arises, whenever the cry for help is issued, Montgomery's medical community is ready to respond. From a case of the sniffles to open-heart surgery, residents can rest assured they are in capable and caring hands. *m*

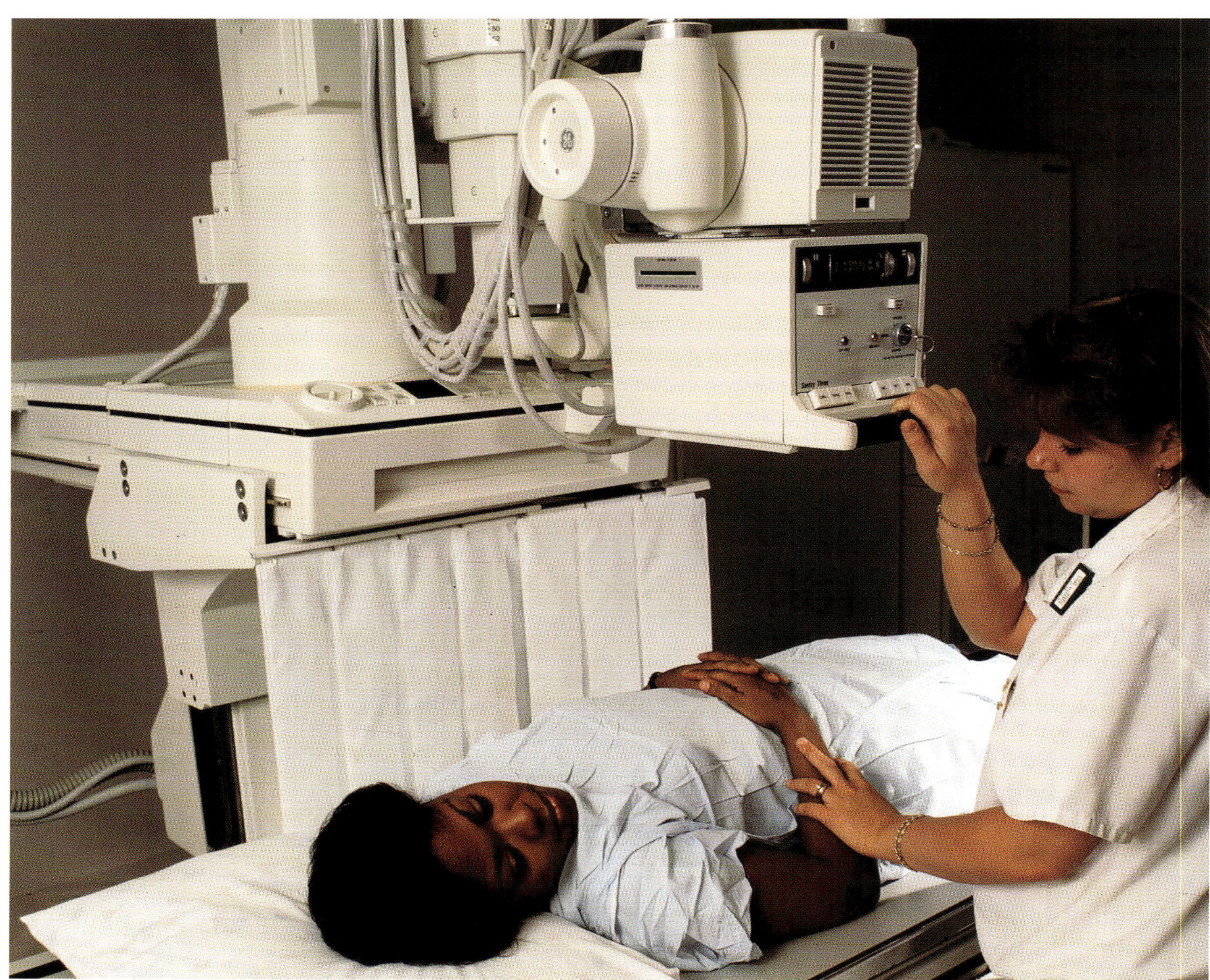

Montgomery's residents feel secure in the knowledge that their needs can be met by dedicated physicians and health care professionals.

Compassionate care is key to a healthy community. Photo by Robert Fouts. (above)

Private practice physicians offer treatment in areas from family practice to internal medicine, sports medicine to ophthalmology, neurology to orthodontics, and anything in between. Photo by Robert Fouts. (right)

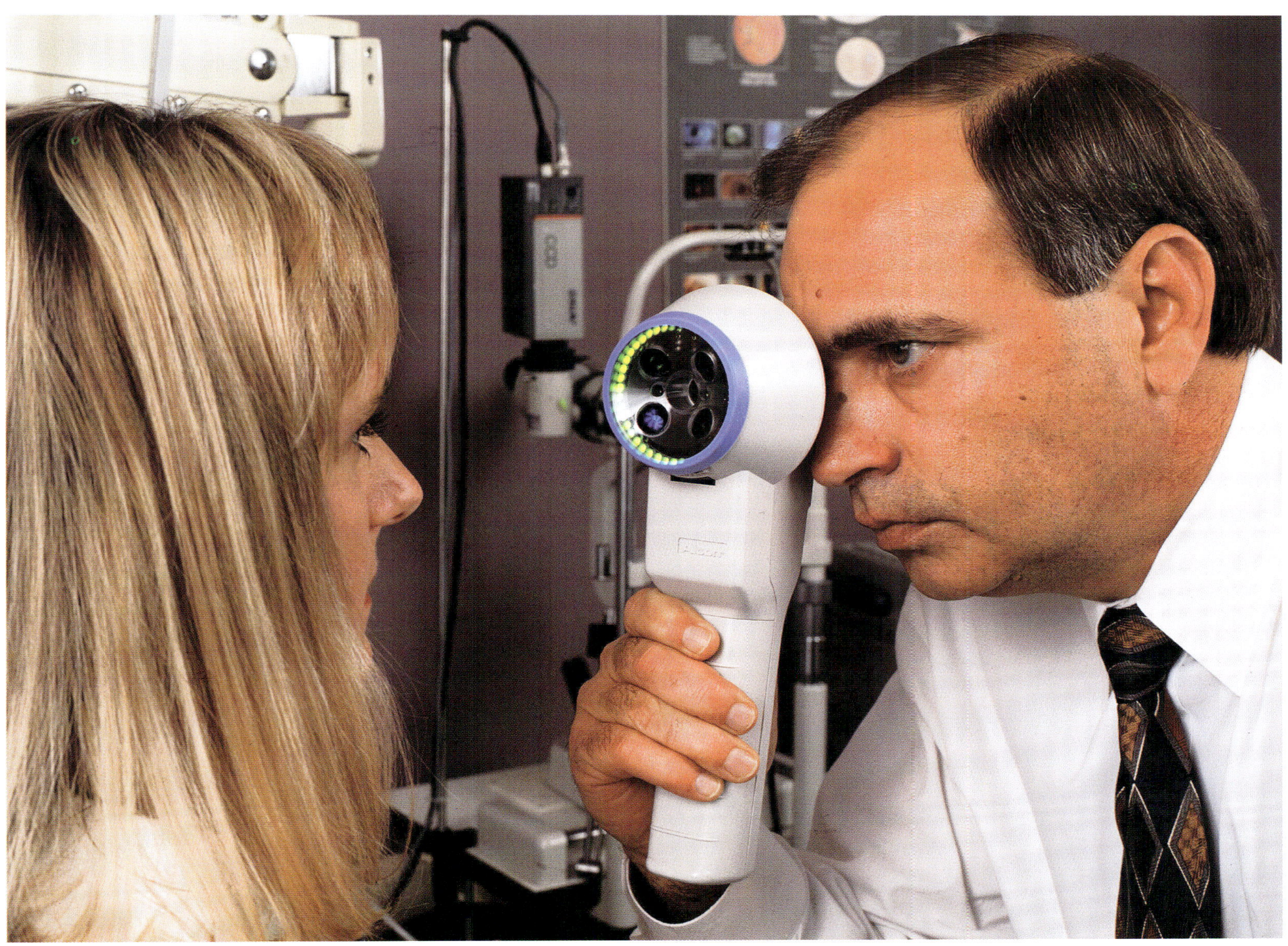

DOWNTOWN RENAISSANCE

As we head into the year 2000, Montgomery is poised on the brink of the new century and moving forward into the future. Many changes are taking place in the Capital City, with a strong emphasis being placed on the revitalization of the downtown area and the development of the riverfront.

Every Memorial Day weekend, downtown Montgomery comes alive with the music, entertainment, food, and family fun that make up the Jubilee CityFest celebration. The Jubilee Pops Concert, a performance held on the lawn of the Alabama Archives and History Building, is just one of the popular events. Photo by Robert Fouts.

Montgomery's skyline seems to change almost daily, as a wealth of new construction is springing to life downtown. At the heart of the downtown renaissance is the Retirement Systems of Alabama, headed by Dr. David Bronner. Under Bronner's direction, the RSA has added six modern new office buildings, a multipurpose activity center, and a child care center to the downtown makeup. Additionally, there are five new parking decks and a splendid park, complete with a reflecting pool modeled after the one that lies in front of the Washington Monument in Washington, D.C.

A major component of Montgomery's ongoing downtown revitalization has been the construction of many new state office buildings through the Retirement Systems of Alabama, under the direction of Dr. David Bronner. This effort has beautified downtown with the addition of fountains, like this one located outside the RSA Activity Center, and parks. Photo by Robert Fouts.

Many changes are taking place in the Capital City, with a strong emphasis being placed on the revitalization of the downtown area. Photo by Robert Fouts.

*T*he RSA construction projects have positively affected 14 to 15 city blocks so far. "Studies show you can't have a meaningful impact on a downtown unless you do at least four or five blocks," Bronner explained. "With our 14 to 15 blocks, we have made a significant impact."

The RSA construction project began in 1977 with the development of the building that now houses the retirement system offices, among others. While Bronner never announced his intention to create a new network of state office buildings, all located downtown, the plan was always in the back of his mind.

"It didn't come about as a 'plan,' because if I had suggested a plan, it never would have gotten done," Bronner said. Suggesting such a huge undertaking would have left room for others to second-guess the plan, to doubt, and to come up with too many reasons why it just couldn't be done, he explained. So, he decided to go at it one building at a time, announcing his plans only for what was currently on the drawing board.

The purpose behind Bronner's idea for a network of office complexes located centrally in downtown Montgomery is a simple one—to achieve a greater degree of efficiency in state government.

"State agencies were spread all over the city, with more than 14 separate offices. It was impossible to manage," Bronner said. "With everyone spread out like that, it was very inefficient and there was poor communication. Just to have a meeting among several different departments you had to allow about 30 minutes for people to travel from all over town. You could kill three to four hours just for a 15-minute meeting."

*T*he new Embassy Suites Hotel is convenient to business travelers and convention-goers attending events at the Civic Center. Photo by Robert Fouts.

*T*he modern, multipurpose Montgomery Civic Center is appropriate for meetings, catered functions, and product exhibitions. Photo by Robert Fouts.

Built in 1896, the glorious Union Station has undergone major renovation. Photo by Robert Fouts.

A new addition to the waterfront is Overlook Park, located high on a bluff overlooking the river. Historic markers are located along a scenic walkway, providing information about the history of the river and of Montgomery. Photo by Robert Fouts.

CITY OF MONTGOMERY
OVERLOOK PARK
1995
EMORY FOLMAR, MAYOR
MONTGOMERY CITY COUNCIL
JOSEPH DICKERSON, PRESIDENT
MRS. ALICE REYNOLDS,
PRES. PRO-TEM
E. T. (BUD) CHAMBERS
MARK GILMORE, JR.
LEO HAMMONDS
RICK McBRIDE
RICHARD VONCUS
JOE L. REED
BILLY TURNER
DESIGNED AND CONSTRUCTED
BY THE CITY OF MONTGOMERY

***T**wice each year, in the spring and fall, the Montgomery Symphony League takes advantage of the weather and the beautiful view from Court Square to host the Brown Bag Concerts. The concerts are open to the public and feature the music of different local bands each week. The Symphony League raises money at the events by selling donated pizza and drinks. The proceeds are used to sponsor special performances of the symphony for area sixth-grade students. Photo by Robert Fouts.*

***E**rected by the City of Montgomery in 1885 in the Artesian Basin, Court Square Fountain is one of Montgomery's favorite structures, symbolizing the town's history, aesthetic interests, and civic concern for beauty in the marketplace. Photo by Robert Fouts.*

"The revitalization of downtown is evident," said Mayor Emory Folmar. "Opportunities in Montgomery are continuing to grow, and we are working to make sure that there will always be growth."

THOMPSON MANSION C. 1850
MONTGOMERY VISITORS CENTER
CONVENTION AND VISITORS DIVISION
MONTGOMERY AREA CHAMBER OF COMMERCE
401 MADISON AVENUE

Creating an office complex network downtown solved several problems at once—it located offices that need to interact near one another, it placed state agencies nearer the Capitol and State House where they could work together more effectively, and it brought a new life to downtown.

"Montgomery is a pretty neat little town, with the historic State Capitol building and park, but it was getting a little run-down after 100-plus years," Bronner said.

He saw the effect individual construction projects had on downtown, as they revitalized the area just around them. "But one project is like a lonely flower in the desert," he said. He longed to make all of downtown an oasis.

The long-term construction plan can be seen in each individual RSA building. While each is a unique structure, common elements add a touch of consistency to the development. Gray-silver brick work, lots of glass, gold paint, and dusty green roofs link each project. The buildings were designed to complement the stately white marble columned structures that were already present, Bronner said.

The new buildings also incorporate elements of other classic architecture—for example, the reflecting pool in the park, which was itself modeled after Bryant Park in New York City. The RSA Plaza restaurant was designed to duplicate the Tavern on the Green restaurant, also located in New York City.

Bronner feels it was the responsibility of the state government to take the first step in revitalizing downtown with new construction. "If the state had decided to move its offices out east, downtown would have died," he said. "If the state started to bail out, no private businessman would want to put his money downtown either. But if the state makes a commitment and brings in 2,000 to 6,000 new employees downtown, it provides a new infrastructure."

It is estimated that the RSA construction effort is a quarter-of-a-billion-dollar project. Bronner estimates the money spent on RSA construction projects alone will turn over five to seven times in the local economy, taking into account the jobs the construction projects create and the new employees in downtown Montgomery.

"For every $100 million spent, we will have generated $500 to 700 million for the economy," he said. "All it does is help the state over time."

Bronner hopes the RSA construction projects will inspire others to make the move into downtown. Already, this idea is bearing fruit, as new construction includes a renovated Alabama Cattlemen's Association building and a new State Judicial Center.

New businesses include several new, small cafes and restaurants, and two major additions, the Embassy Suites Hotel and the Montgomery Brewing Company.

The Embassy Suites, a John Q. Hammonds hotel, offers 237 suites, 15,000 square feet of meeting space with seating for up to 1,200 people, a ballroom, 12 meeting rooms, and 2 board rooms. The hotel also offers a full-service restaurant, catering capabilities, and a banquet room that seats 900.

Conveniently located next to the Montgomery Civic Center, the Embassy Suites Hotel is convenient to business travelers and convention-goers attending events at the Civic Center. Also, the hotel is located next to historic Union Station and the riverfront.

"We hope to tie in with the *Betsy Ann* riverboat, the Davis Theatre, the Brew Pub, the Civic Center, and the beautiful facility next door— Union Station—so we can act as a kind of catalyst to bring some of those activities together," said Kenneth E. Cunningham, CHA, general manager of the new hotel. "I think we'll bring additional attractions, additional stability, and, in general, add additional activity to the downtown area," he said.

Montgomery Mayor Emory Folmar was instrumental in making the location of Embassy Suites downtown a reality.

The new Montgomery Brewing Company has certainly served up a barrel of fun since its opening in late 1995, providing fine food, national and local musical acts, and, of course, freshly brewed beer on tap.

Brewpubs such as the Montgomery Brewing Company have been popular throughout the nation for as many as 10 years, but there had not been a brewing company in Montgomery since the late 1800s, when the original Montgomery Brewing Company was located at North Hull Street.

The Alabama Brewpub Act of 1992 made it possible for brewpubs to be located in historically significant buildings, and requiring them to serve beer "directly from serving vessels," or on tap— draught (or draft) beer.

The Montgomery Area Chamber of Commerce's Visitor Information Center on Madison Avenue provides maps and attraction information for new residents and visitors. Photo by Robert Fouts.

In 1851, cotton merchant and railroad entrepreneur John Murphy built this house incorporating many Greek Revival elements in grand design. It is quite appropriate that it is now home of the Montgomery Water Works and Sewer Board, as Murphy was one of the incorporators of Montgomery's first efforts at establishing a city water system. Photo by Robert Fouts. (above)

Downtown Montgomery presents a mix of nineteenth and early twentieth-century structures. Photo by Robert Fouts. (right)

The Montgomery Brewing Company is located at 12 West Jefferson Street in downtown Montgomery, in a building constructed in 1913 by the GM&O Railroad. The brewpub joins the continuing move toward a downtown renaissance, started with the RSA office network construction, and furthered with the building of the new Embassy Suites Hotel and the Overlook Park facility.

"It was the intent of the [brewpub] law to restore historically significant buildings and to have a renaissance downtown," said Barry Morton, proprietor of the Montgomery Brewing Company brewpub. "And nothing succeeds like success. We're stimulating the business development down here, which is what we hoped to do."

Morton hopes to see the area develop to become another "Five Points South," a popular center for entertainment in Birmingham. The Montgomery Brewing Company is off to a good start, doing twice the business market estimates predicted for the area, Morton said. Projections show the brewing company has the potential to produce $2 million in revenue in its first year.

The brewpub hosts average crowds of between 200 to 400 people each night, consuming an average of 10 kegs of beer per night. "The brewing process takes 14 days, and we're still working out how much to brew to meet the demand," he said.

There are three venues available at the brewpub—a cafe for fine dining; a pub with a more casual atmosphere and with a large stage for hosting local, regional, and national bands; and a sports lounge on the second floor of the building featuring television sets for watching games, pool tables, and dart boards. Plans also include a banquet facility on the second floor.

Morton also hopes to see the Montgomery Brewing Company take an active role in the community, with plans in the works to sponsor an entertainment stage at Jubilee CityFest.

In addition to the emphasis on construction in downtown Montgomery is the importance of one of the city's best natural resources—the Alabama River.

Currently, Montgomerians enjoy Riverfront Park, a picturesque picnic area on the banks of the Alabama River, and the *Betsy Ann* riverboat is anchored at the riverfront docks, offering

The Civil Rights Memorial, located appropriately in front of the Southern Poverty Law Center in downtown Montgomery, was created by architect Maya Lin. The names of 40 people who lost their lives in the fight for equal justice are inscribed on the black granite monument. Photo by Robert Fouts.

...UNTIL JUSTICE ROLLS DOWN LIKE WATERS
AND RIGHTEOUSNESS LIKE A MIGHTY STREAM
MARTIN LUTHER KING

excursions in traditional old-style fashion down the river. The *Betsy Ann* also hosts many special cruises throughout the year, with music, food, and dancing.

A new addition to the waterfront is Overlook Park, thanks to the leadership of Mayor Emory Folmar. This facility is located high on a bluff overlooking the river and features covered picnic facilities where once abandoned car lots stood. Historic markers placed by the Landmarks Foundation are located along a scenic walkway, providing park visitors with bits of information about the history of the river and of Montgomery.

Overlook Park is the first step in a plan to extensively renovate the riverfront area. Montgomery Area Chamber of Commerce officials are currently working with consultants who designed stunning river walk developments in such places as Chattanooga, Tennessee, and Savannah, Georgia.

"We want to showcase one of the city's major resources—the river," said Randy George, president of the Montgomery Area Chamber of Commerce. "It is the crown of the overall quality of life for the area, and it should be developed as such," he said. The riverfront revitalization initiative had been discussed at length by Montgomery's leaders, and was of particular interest to local businessman Will Hill Tankersley. An avid Montgomery history buff, Tankersley was concerned the riverfront might be forgotten in the crush of the modern world. He feels its importance can be highlighted in a way that not only preserves its role as a part of history, but also in such a way that Montgomerians can get more enjoyment from the river.

"There are all kinds of things that can be done down here," he said of the river. "People can keep boats here on a marina, water ski, fish, and shop."

Tankersley hopes to see the development of apartments overlooking the river as well, encouraging more people to move into the downtown area to take advantage of the spectacular view.

Talk finally turned to action, and the plans for the riverfront were set in motion by Margaret Carpenter, who was chairman of the "Committee of 100," an organization of business leaders dedicated to the improvement of the city. In the spring of 1995, Carpenter was approached by Tankersley, Bowen Ballard, and Clyde Wood, who suggested to her the

Committee should take a more active, hands-on role in the community, she remembers.

"At the same time, there was talk that something ought to happen to move on the riverfront development idea, which had been discussed for some time but not pursued to any real end," Carpenter said. "To me, the two seemed to go hand in hand."

In order to inspire members of the Committee of 100 to pursue the riverfront development idea, Carpenter enlisted the help of Montgomery judges to stage a "mock trial," with the Committee as defendant, accused of inactivity.

"I just wanted to do something different, to get them interested and motivated in the project, rather than just standing up there reading off facts and figures," Carpenter said, laughing.

The performance was a hit, and the Committee secured a consultant to study the Montgomery downtown and riverfront area to determine what changes and additions would best benefit the city.

"When you think of developing the riverfront, you can't just think of going through the tunnel and there you are at the water; you have to think of starting at the Capitol and working from there to include all the surrounding area," Carpenter said. "It's all a part of the greater plan." Eight members of the Committee of 100 traveled to cities such as Chattanooga, Augusta, and Columbus to study riverfront revitalizations those cities had undertaken.

Possibilities for the new riverfront construction include a riverwalk to extend from Maxwell Air Force Base to the Northern Bypass, a distance of about two and a half miles; a civil rights museum; and an Indian history museum, among other ideas.

"One of the greatest things has been [Mayor Emory Folmar's] doing the Overlook Park," Carpenter said. "That really got people excited and interested in what was going on with the riverfront."

Dr. Bronner also supports the idea of incorporating more upscale housing into the downtown area, seeing it as the final step toward fortifying and strengthening the downtown area.

"The revitalization of downtown is evident," said Mayor Emory Folmar. "Opportunities in Montgomery are continuing to grow, and we are working to make sure that there will always be growth. The downtown area and the riverfront are the next steps for Montgomery's development. There are some exciting things happening for Montgomery's future." *M*

The New South Art Gallery and Shop features the work of local, regional, and national artists, with an emphasis on the South and Southeast regions. The gallery, located upstairs at the downtown business, features monthly or bimonthly shows of original artwork, while the shop sells one-of-a-kind art and art pieces, including jewelry, furniture, and sculpture. Photo by Robert Fouts. (top)

Interesting new restaurants as well as old favorites contribute to the economic viability of downtown. Photo by Robert Fouts. (bottom left & right)

TIME OUT

"Mom, I'm bored! I want something to do!" For many parents, this is a familiar song, as children go on a continuous quest for fun and excitement. But Montgomery makes it easy for children and adults alike to find plenty of answers to the puzzle of what to do with the time on their hands. Through the combined efforts of the City of Montgomery Parks and Recreation Department, the Montgomery YMCA, and private businesses, Montgomery contains a wealth of activities to meet any need. We've got sporting events to thrill the serious athlete, the weekend enthusiast, and the armchair quarterback; our area parks and attractions provide countless hours of fun for the whole family; and Montgomery is host to some of the best special events in the region.

The South Alabama State Fair is a widely anticipated event. Annually, the event draws a crowd of more than 200,000 during its week-long run. Photo by Robert Fouts.

Providing quality sports and recreation opportunities is of utmost importance to Mayor Emory Folmar, who believes sports not only provide physical exercise, but also give youngsters something to do to help occupy their time and keep them out of trouble, while teaching them the lessons of life.

"As the scripture says, 'Train up a child in the way he should go, and when he grows older, he will not depart from it.' Young people can learn the lessons of life on the playing field—lessons of responsibility, individual accomplishment, team play, how to win and lose gracefully. And those are lessons they can use throughout their lives," Folmar said. "It means so much to me to see so many young people involved in the things they should be."

Tennis enthusiasts will enjoy the O'Connor Tennis Center, the Lagoon Park tennis courts, or any of the many other courts available for play in city parks. Photo by Robert Fouts.

MONTGOMERY PARKS AND RECREATION DEPARTMENT

The City of Montgomery Parks and Recreation Department is responsible for a variety of events and activities offered to the people of the city. Duties of the department include upkeep of the city's more than 1,600 acres of parks, including maintenance of equipment and facilities; supervision of the city's 22 community centers and their activities; direction of amateur athletic programs; direction of the city's junior high school athletics for both boys and girls; and operation of special facilities and services, as well as special events—quite an undertaking.

There are more than 72 parks in the Montgomery area, providing such amenities as walking and jogging trails, exercise stations, playground equipment, swimming pools, picnic tables and shelters, tennis courts, ballparks and courts, barbecue grills, and more. Whether your interest is getting in shape, playing a game with friends, or just lazing the day away lying in the sunshine, Montgomery offers a park to suit your need—and, in most cases, right in "your own backyard."

One of the most recent additions to the city's network of parks is Overlook Park, dedicated in June of 1995. Overlook Park is a two-and-a-half-acre scenic park located on a bluff of the Alabama River. It features three scenic overlooks, a large gazebo, walking paths, and park benches. There are historic markers placed at intervals along the walkway, providing educational information about the Alabama River, the Creek Indians who made their home along its banks, and the first settlers of Montgomery. The markers were provided by the Landmarks Foundation, which is dedicated to preserving Montgomery history.

While reminding Montgomerians of the city's history, the Overlook Park also is a first step in Montgomery's plan for the future, which includes the revitalization of the downtown area and the riverfront, all of which are visible from Overlook Park.

Additionally, Montgomery is home to large, specialized parks designed specifically to meet the needs of the serious sports enthusiast.

Lagoon Park is a 410-acre facility built in 1976 and is the largest recreational complex in Montgomery. It boasts a 5-field softball complex, 17 fully lighted tennis courts, a driving range, and an 18-hole championship golf course, which has been rated as one of the nation's top 50 courses.

The softball complex is ideal for tournament play, with a central control tower allowing visibility for all five fields. The Lagoon complex has earned Montgomery the title of "Softball Capital of the South." Lagoon Park regularly hosts various tournaments, including the Men's Class C Slow Pitch National Softball Tournament.

Additionally, 40-acre Dean Fain Park, located in east Montgomery, offers four lighted softball fields and a central control tower. Together, Lagoon and Fain Parks provide Montgomery the ability to serve up to 420 teams, with a tournament capacity of 140 teams. Recently, the city was host to the Air National Guard 30th Annual National Softball Tournament, which brought 127 teams and more than 3,000 people into Montgomery from 39 states.

More than 8,000 adults in Montgomery participate in softball leagues during the summer

Lagoon Park is the largest recreational complex in Montgomery. It boasts a 5-field softball complex, ideal for tournament play. Photo by Robert Fouts. (above)

Numerous private and public golf courses are available for play in Montgomery. Photo by Robert Fouts. (left)

and fall, and more than 6,000 young people take part in the summer Dixie Youth Baseball program, which includes both boys' baseball and girls' softball programs for youths of all ages. As many as 420 adult teams play in the summer league, and up to 140 teams play in the fall league.

Buddy Watson Park, a new 30-acre facility, features four baseball fields and related buildings. The baseball fields include three Dixie Youth fields with 200-foot radius (one lighted), and one lighted 290-foot radius field for Dixie Boys. The park also offers a jogging trail, picnic shelters, playground equipment, and an open play area.

Tennis enthusiasts will enjoy the O'Connor Tennis Center, which boasts 11 laykold tennis courts, plus four outdoor handball courts, shuffleboard, locker rooms, and a pro shop. The 17 Lagoon Park tennis courts are lighted, and one is stadium-complete, with seating for 2,500 spectators.

Montgomery also boasts two primary sports arenas, Cramton Bowl and Paterson Field. Centrally located in downtown Montgomery, these two athletic facilities are home to high school and college-level football and baseball, as well as special events and activities.

Cramton Bowl is a 24,000-seat arena that regularly plays host to high school football matchups and the occasional college game. The bowl is also the site of big dreams for the city's junior high school football teams, as it plays host to the annual Junior High City Championship football battle. The top four finishers in junior high football action get their first taste of playing in Cramton Bowl each year as they meet to fight for the city consolation and champion titles. No doubt many a junior high athlete has left the event dreaming of one day donning the uniform of one of Montgomery's high school teams and returning to that field of honor.

In addition to city and regional football action, Cramton Bowl is home each year to the Blue-Gray All-Star Football Classic, a Christmas day tradition that brings the top college athletes from throughout the country to Montgomery for a spectacular battle.

Paterson Field, which can accommodate 6,400 spectators, is home to Montgomery's baseball action, hosting area high school competition, college play, and Dixie baseball competitions. In 1995 Paterson Field was filled to capacity for a grudge match between intrastate rivals Auburn University and the University of Alabama.

A highlight of Montgomery baseball action each year is the NCAA Division II National Baseball Championship, which brings in the best of the best from colleges throughout the country. The eight-day event involves approximately 300 players and coaches, and draws an average of 45,000 spectators.

Providing prime parks and sports facilities benefits not only the people who enjoy the facilities and play the games, but also Montgomery businesses and the city economy. Montgomery regularly hosts such tournaments as the Senior Series Golf Tournament, the Blue-Gray Tennis Classic, and the Blue-Gray Junior Tennis Classic, among others.

"The average softball tournament will bring in approximately $1 million in one weekend," said Dawn Railey, manager of marketing and public relations for the Montgomery Parks and Recreation Department. "Not only do those people play ball here at our parks, but they also stay in hotels, eat at restaurants, shop, visit attractions—it's good for the economy of the city all the way around," she said. "Tournaments bring money into the community that stays here and works here for the good of the city."

"The commitment to providing quality recreational facilities is of primary importance to the mayor and this department, because it enhances the quality of life," Railey said. "People come here and say, 'What wonderful facilities you have here.'"

But the Montgomery Parks and Recreation Department not only assures first-class facilities for "the games people play," but also oversees the various sports and recreational activities offered in the community.

There are 22 community centers located throughout the city, offering a wide range of athletic, social, and educational opportunities for the people in surrounding neighborhoods. The City Parks and Recreation Department coordinates the activities of each center, with the help of dedicated volunteers from each community. Programs are designed to appeal to people of all ages, with activities ranging from martial arts to arts and crafts, basketball to bingo. Community centers also are used by the city junior high schools as sites for school athletic programs.

Montgomery is unique in that the City Parks and Recreation Department also is responsible for coordinating the junior high athletics program, in cooperation with the Montgomery

Paterson Field, which can accommodate 6,400 spectators, was filled to capacity in 1995 for a grudge match between intrastate rivals Auburn University and the University of Alabama. Photo by Robert Fouts.

Cramton Bowl is a 24,000-seat arena that regularly plays host to high school football matchups and the occasional college game, such as the Alabama State University Turkey Day Classic. Photo courtesy of ASU.

County Board of Education. Montgomery is the only city in the United States which fully administers its junior high athletic programs through this type of relationship. The program includes more than 3,000 young people, participating in sports including boys' football, basketball, golf, wrestling, track, soccer, and tennis; and girls' volleyball, bowling, basketball, track, softball, tennis, cheerleading, and dance. This system of administration allows junior high school athletic programs to call upon the vast resources of the City of Montgomery to assure their professional development and success.

The Montgomery Parks and Recreation Department also reaches beyond the boundaries of the traditional recreational activity to meet the special needs of area residents. Perhaps one of the proudest accomplishments of the department is the Montgomery Therapeutic Recreation Center, a recreational center designed specifically to meet the needs of the city's physically and mentally challenged citizens.

Regular programs of the center include swimming, weight training, bowling, gymnastics, arts and crafts, team sports, and games. Also, the center hosts meetings such as Cub Scouts and Girl Scouts, with troops especially for those with physical or mental challenges. Several day camps are held each year, featuring special workshops and field trips.

The center also is home to the Montgomery Wheelchair Sports Club, a new program sponsored through funding from the Kiwanis Club of Montgomery. Through the league, people who use wheelchairs are learning to participate in sports including tennis, scuba diving, fishing, and rugby.

The Montgomery Therapeutic Recreation Center also trains athletes for the Special Olympics and hosts some of the games. The TRC is a 26,000-square-foot barrier-free facility featuring a gymnasium, indoor and outdoor pools, weight room, game room, meeting rooms, locker rooms, a kitchen, four tennis courts, and a playground area. The services of the TRC are free

to Montgomery residents who have a physical or mental disability.

The Armory Learning Arts Center provides art, drama, music, gymnastic, and dance programs to nearly 1,500 children and adults in Montgomery. The facility features two dance studios, four studios for art, acting, and music workshops, a gallery for displaying the works of local and regional artists, the city's only public photo lab, and a new, state-of-the art gymnastics facility.

Additionally, the Armory Learning Arts Center is home to the Alabama Dance Theatre, a local company performing classical and repertory dance, and providing dance instruction from beginner through intermediate levels.

An educational facility jointly operated by the City of Montgomery Parks and Recreation Department and Troy State University in Montgomery is the W. A. Gayle Planetarium. Located in Oak Park and established in 1968, the planetarium is one of the major facilities of its kind in the United States. It features an auditorium designed specifically for simulating the

natural sky by projecting images of the sun, moon, planets, stars, and other celestial objects onto a 50-foot domed ceiling.

The planetarium is visited each year by more than 23,000 people, many of them school children. The facility offers special educational programs designed especially to meet the needs of a variety of age groups.

One of Montgomery's most breathtaking attractions is the Montgomery Zoo. What began in 1972 as a 6-acre children's zoo housing less than 75 species of animals was renovated in 1990 to cover 40 acres, and is home to more than 700 animals representing about 200 different species, many of which are endangered. The renovation was an ambitious effort by Montgomery Mayor Emory Folmar, in cooperation with community leaders, citizens, and the Montgomery Zoo Friends support group.

The Montgomery Zoo places high emphasis on wildlife conservation and education, providing a number of programs, activities, and events to teach zoo visitors and the community about

Top college athletes from throughout the country compete in the Blue-Gray Football Classic, one of the most prestigious college tournaments. Photo by Robert Fouts.

*S*ome of the finest college football in the nation is played just a short drive from Montgomery. Photo courtesy of Auburn University.

*S*ports enthusiasts can enjoy a variety of college athletics in Montgomery. Photo by Frank Williams courtesy of AUM.

*T*he Montgomery Therapeutic Recreation Center, a recreational center designed specifically to meet the needs of the city's physically and mentally challenged citizens, is home to the Montgomery Wheelchair Sports Club. Photo by Robert Fouts.

Rawlings
Lady
13
Senators
BERRY
00
COLLEGE
3

the importance of preserving our natural resources, including the habitats these animals need to survive in the wild. Education staff and trained volunteers provide programs, tours, live animal demonstrations, and answer visitor questions about the collection.

"This [education] activity is an important part of the City of Montgomery Zoo's commitment to preserving wildlife and fostering a greater understanding of nature and environmental awareness among our visitors," said zoo Director Bill Fiore.

The zoo also is involved in species repopulation programs, and its bald eagle program has released more than 17 eagles into the wild in Alabama and surrounding states. The zoo's professional management team of administrators, curators, zookeepers, full-time veterinary staff, and educators has positioned the new zoo as a center of wildlife conservation and education. It is one of fewer than 175 zoos nationwide that is accredited by the American Association of Zoos and Aquariums.

A unique feature of the Montgomery Zoo is its spacious, natural environments that not only provide spectacular views of the animals for zoo visitors, but also ensure the health and well-being of the animals. Gone are the traditional "cages" so often associated with zoos. Natural and hidden man-made barriers using the latest state-of-the-art features of modern zoo design eliminate the need for "concrete and bars."

The barrier-free concept also allows zoo visitors to get a better idea of what animals would be found together naturally in the wild by grouping them together. Predators are separated from other animals by natural and hidden barriers. Tigers enjoy a cool dip in a pool fed by a waterfall in their exhibit, teaching visitors that these big cats enjoy the water. Lions and cheetahs watch their prey from rock outcroppings, and give curious zoo visitors the eye as well. Large mixed species areas for hoofstock and birds from five continents display the intricate relationships among species as they would be viewed in their native homes of Africa, Asia, Australia, South America, or North America.

Highlights of the Montgomery Zoo include a rare white Bengal tiger, the newly-renovated monkey island, cheetahs, a new bald eagle exhibit, and a reptile house, allowing visitors to get an up-close and personal view of the slithering, slinking members of the wild kingdom.

The Montgomery Zoo also features an Overlook Cafe, providing a shady respite where visitors can enjoy a meal and a refreshing drink, and the McMonty-102 Express, a miniature train that takes visitors on a rolling tour around the perimeter of the zoo.

The zoo also hosts a number of fun-filled family events throughout the year, with the goal of bringing more people to the zoo to

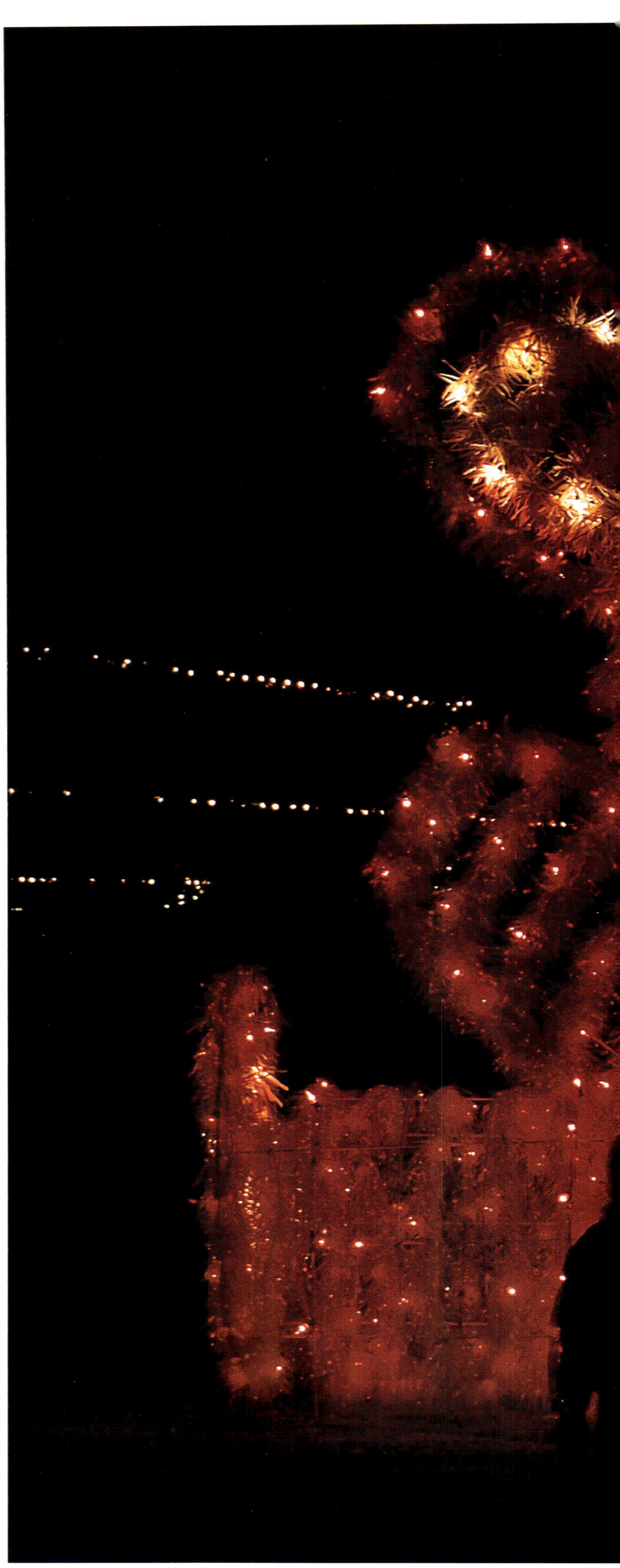

*T*he zoo also hosts a number of fun-filled family events throughout the year, with the goal of bringing more people to the zoo to learn about wildlife. Funds from special events are put back into the zoo to continue its education and conservation programs.

One of Montgomery's finest attractions is the Montgomery Zoo, home to more than 700 animals representing about 200 different species, many of which are endangered. The zoo ushers in the holiday season in grand style each year with its Festival of Lights. The festival sets the zoo a-sparkle with spectacular lighted displays of animals. Photos by Robert Fouts.

learn about wildlife. Funds from special events are put back into the zoo to continue its education and conservation programs.

Zoo Weekend, held in early spring each year, features musical entertainment, demonstrations from the Montgomery Zoo's own education department, plus games and more. The weekend is a fund-raiser for the zoo, with proceeds going toward renovations of current exhibits or for bringing new animals to the zoo. In the fall, the zoo hosts Zoo Boo, a weekend of scary fun including a haunted train ride, goodie stations, and entertainment. Proceeds from Zoo Boo go to benefit the educational programs of the Montgomery Zoo.

The zoo ushers in the holiday season in grand style each year with its Festival of Lights. The festival sets the zoo a-sparkle with spectacular lighted displays of animals, including bears, giraffes, and big cats, plus holiday characters like Santa Claus and Frosty the Snowman. Some of the displays even "come to life" with movement—dinosaurs created of strand upon strand of lights appear to turn and reach for zoo visitors, while a slithery lighted snake flicks his tongue in welcome. The light displays are sponsored by area businesses.

More than 300,000 people visit the Montgomery Zoo each year, making it one of the most popular attractions in the city.

For the future, the Montgomery Zoo will continue its long-term commitment to growth and excellence in zoo operations for the local community. The quality of life of the animals in the Montgomery Zoo is viewed as a benchmark of the caring and compassionate spirit of the City of Montgomery and its citizens, Fiore

believes. "The superb Montgomery Zoo is an oasis in our increasingly urbanized world and a reflection of the overall quality of life and excellence in the Montgomery community," he said.

MONTGOMERY AREA YMCA

The Montgomery Area YMCA has been held up as a model throughout the nation for what a YMCA program should be. Programs run the gamut from organized youth and adult sports to junior high and high school leadership programs, to camps and child care.

The Montgomery Area YMCA soccer program is the largest in the state, under the direction of the Soccer Branch YMCA. It involves more than 2,500 youngsters in programs including boys' and girls' recreational outdoor soccer, indoor soccer, and premiere soccer. Premiere soccer is open to boys and girls on a try-out basis, and is for the advanced, more competitive soccer player.

The City of Montgomery Parks and Recreation Department, in cooperation with the YMCA, constructed a 10-field soccer complex for the program, dubbed the Emory Folmar Soccer Complex. The city plans to construct a three-story control tower on the site, housing concession areas, restrooms, and a press box providing a view of all fields. This will allow Montgomery to host larger soccer tournaments in the future.

In addition to the strong soccer program, Montgomery is home to the Montgomery YMCA Barracudas swim program. The program provides both summer recreational and a year-round competitive swim team. The more than 80 youngsters in the year-round program compete on the local, state, regional, and national

The Montgomery Area YMCA soccer program is the largest in the state, involving more than 2,500 youngsters in various programs. Photo by Robert Fouts. (above)

The Montgomery YMCA Barracudas swim program provides both summer recreational and a year-round competitive swim team. More than 80 youngsters in the year-round program compete on the local, state, regional, and national level each year. Photo by Robert Fouts. (right)

HOOKER HEADERS
GUMOUT
Jim Pe
JEGS
UNDERCOVER
Chassis
RACE CARS
VP Racing Fuels
CRANE ROCKERS
'THE WHEEL' BY IW
CRANE Cams
ATI TREEMASTER CONVERTERS
K-MOTION
WELD
FELPRO
EARLS

level each year. The program is open to youths ages 6 to 20. Each year, approximately 1,665 young people participate in the recreational and competitive programs of the Montgomery YMCA Barracudas.

Additionally, the YMCA is active in developing programs to target the special needs of at-risk youngsters. Success by Six, Head Start child care, and TimeOut are a few of the programs developed by the YMCA in conjunction with community supporters to aid in the development and growth of young people placed "at risk" by such factors as poverty and crime.

Bill Chandler, general director for the Montgomery Area YMCA, believes the success of the YMCA in the city is due to two factors: dedicated volunteers and the ability to change to meet current needs. "It's the volunteers that make the Montgomery YMCA a success. We as professionals can't do the job without the support of laymen," Chandler said.

Because of the strong relationship between YMCA staff and volunteers, the YMCA's Metro Board of Directors "can open any door in the city—they have that much leadership in the city," Chandler said. Once those doors are opened, YMCA officials and volunteers must not be afraid to step through them, he said.

"I think we've done a good job of adjusting to change. We have been willing to take on new challenges and establish new programs to meet needs," Chandler said.

The Montgomery Area YMCA has served as a leader in teen work among all YMCAs in the country with the development of such programs as Youth In Government, which gives teens hands-on experience in leading city and state government in mock sessions; International Youth Camp (in cooperation with the Montgomery Lions Club), which brings young people from all over the world to Montgomery and allows Montgomery youths to travel to other countries; YMCA Conference on National Affairs, which is a leadership conference held in Washington, D.C.; Blue Ridge High School Christian Values Conference, and many more.

"I like to say we're in the children business," Chandler said. "If you tell a child he can't do it, he can't. We're here to say, 'I love you; you can do it,'" he said. That kind of unconditional support is needed by young people now more than ever, Chandler believes.

"The challenge for us right now is to make the changes to effectively serve young people. We have to learn to be more effective in dealing with children in low-income communities," he said. "Adults have created an environment that is not good for children—not intentionally, but we didn't stop it until it was already built up. Now we have to undo it a little bit at a time."

Programs in the works for the YMCA in the near future include the development of a computer training program for young people at the Kershaw Branch YMCA to serve west Montgomery; participation in Project Upward, a program of the Montgomery Public Schools system for young people in an alternative school situation; and the expansion of the TimeOut program, which helps provide positive activities and role model situations for troubled youngsters.

Additionally, the YMCA hopes to expand the soccer program and construct an indoor soccer facility, which would be the only one of its kind in the state.

The Montgomery Motor Sports Park, a quarter-mile drag strip, hosts NHRA class races in the professional sportsmen racing classes, top-alcohol dragster, and top-alcohol funny car. Photo by Robert Fouts. (previous page)

Each year, the Alabama Cattlemen's Association is host to the Southeastern Livestock Exposition and PRCA (Professional Rodeo Cowboys Association) Championship Rodeo at the Garrett Coliseum. The rodeo brings in some of the top cowboys from throughout the country, while the Southeastern Livestock Exposition brings adults and youth from throughout the Southeast to compete in livestock shows and judging events, junior rodeo activities, and educational programs. Photo by Robert Fouts.

The South Alabama State Fair is sponsored by the Kiwanis Club of Montgomery, with proceeds from admission going to benefit youth, charitable, and educational organizations throughout the Montgomery area. Photo by Robert Fouts.

RACING

"Central Alabama is racing fan country." Allen Daniels, owner of the Montgomery Motor Speedway, knows of what he speaks. The track draws close to 1,000 spectators on an average racing night, and many more when special events like the Southern All Stars and Coca-Cola Classic are held.

Montgomery's oval track has been offering the tops in speedway action since 1953, making the Montgomery Motor Speedway the oldest paved stock car track in Alabama.

The half-mile of banked asphalt hosts four classes of racing: cadet, pure stock, street stock, and late model, with classes ranging from 10 to 50 laps around the track. And plans are in the works to add an additional racing class next season, Daniels said. "Our goal is to build a stepping stone format of racing to allow a racer to enter at the cadet class and progress from there."

Currently, there are about 60 cars in the pits every racing night, with top class late model making up 17 to 20 cars of that number. The Montgomery Motor Speedway boasts cars from Florida, Georgia, and Mississippi in addition to Alabama racers. The season begins in mid-March, kicking off with the Coca-Cola Classic, and ends the last week of October with the Alabama 200, with races generally held every other weekend.

"The heart of short track stock car racing in the South is probably Alabama," Daniels said. "All the big names that everyone is so familiar with in racing ran this track and speak fondly of it." And you don't have to be a racing regular to recognize some of the greats Daniels mentions: Bobby and Davey Allison, Richard Petty, Neal Bonnet, and Hut Strickland all have run their laps on the Montgomery Motor Speedway track, he said. "In fact, Neal Bonnet won his first late model race in Montgomery," Daniels said.

The Montgomery Motor Speedway is "an ideal layout," according to Daniels, long enough to provide lots of excitement. "This is not a follow-the-leader track—racing skills on the part of the driver determine the outcome more than just raw horsepower," he said.

And the Montgomery Motor Speedway's location in central Alabama is also a plus, giving it the ability to draw race drivers from tracks in nearby Birmingham, Mobile, Atlanta, and Pensacola, all big racing cities.

"If you build it, they will come." Like his counterpart in the movie *Field of Dreams*, Charlie Neil, owner of the Montgomery Motor Sports Park, seemed to hear this message in his head as he dreamed of a drag racing park in Montgomery. That dream became a reality in June of 1995 as the first cars went screaming down the track in competition at the new Motor

Sports Park with the Mayor's Cup race, a National Hot Rod Association stop on the SuperQuick tour.

"There's a long history of drag racing here in Montgomery," Neil said. The original Capitol City Dragway hosted such racing greats as Tommy Ivo and Shirley Muldowney in its heyday, before moving to Montgomery's west side. After a few years, it relocated off the Old Selma Highway and was renamed the Montgomery International Dragway. After a couple years, it changed its name again, back to the Capitol City Dragway, where races are still run on Friday nights.

Neil looked at locating his dream there, but realized he needed more land to accomplish his vision. In October of 1993, he purchased the land off the Northern Bypass and began building the Montgomery Motor Sports Park, a 335-acre facility. From the control tower to the sand trap is a distance of 4,200 feet.

The quarter-mile drag strip hosts NHRA class races in the professional sportsmen racing classes, top-alcohol dragster, and top-alcohol funny car; plus class cars in the super comp, comp, super street, super stock, stock, and super gas categories. The track also hosts sportsmen bracket racing and junior dragsters.

In addition to the NHRA quarter-mile shows, every Saturday night features a run on a one-eight-mile track, and each Wednesday night is a "Test and Tune," at which time the racetrack is open to the general public for racing their own automobiles.

"A lot of people come out who did this years ago as youngsters and want to do it again, and they have a ball," Neil said. "That's what Wednesday nights are for. It's just fun; there's lots of folks in the pits, hanging over fenders and talking shop. They get in line, go down the track, and do it again," he said.

Saturday night are the sportsmen races, featuring local and nonlocal race drivers who compete for a $1,000 first place purse and modified street races for a $300 purse.

Already the track is showing success, and recently the Montgomery Motor Sports Park hosted the Winston Weekend, bringing 400 race teams from 17 states and one province of Canada into the city.

The idea for building a drag strip in Montgomery came to Neil when he realized there were drag strips throughout the Southeast, but none in Alabama. He called the NHRA to find out about starting up a strip here and built his track to NHRA specifications. "Already, this track has a reputation nationally for being flat, long, and smooth. It's a very quick racetrack," Neil said.

His long-term goal, he said, is to host an NHRA national event.

While the track is showing early promise, Neil said he plans to keep it that way by keeping a family atmosphere at the park. "This is an opportunity for dads to build a bridge with their kids. I'm here to tell you, a hot rod can be a bridge. There are a lot of people who were kind of involved with drag racing or hot rods when they were younger, and they enjoy sharing that knowledge with their children," Neil said.

Neil plans to add go-cart racing for the kids and "not so kids" on Sunday afternoons. Also, he has started a high school eliminator category to run on Saturday nights just for high school-age youngsters.

In addition to races, Neil hopes to host car shows and swap meets at the Motor Sports Park. "I'm very optimistic for what the future may hold for Montgomery Motor Sports Park," he said.

SPECIAL EVENTS

As if that weren't enough to fill your calendar, save room for the many special events and festivals that Montgomery is host to every year.

Probably the biggest event on tap all year is Jubilee CityFest, held every Memorial Day weekend. This street festival of grand proportions draws visitors not only from within the city, but from throughout the region as well. Fun-seekers crowd the streets of downtown Montgomery each year to enjoy the music, entertainment, food, and family fun that make up the Jubilee CityFest celebration.

Jubilee started in 1976 as a bicentennial project of Landmarks Foundation. It had a modest beginning as a weekend tour of historic houses and churches in downtown Montgomery. In the next two years, Jubilee became a tradition under the direction of the Council of Jewish Women, and its scope was expanded to include more activities. Rides aboard the *General Richard Montgomery* riverboat (now replaced at the riverfront dock by the *Betsy Ann*), music and entertainment at Court Square, children's pony rides, and tea at the Governor's Mansion hosted by then First Lady Cornelia Wallace filled out the schedule of events.

In 1979 the Council of Jewish Women approached the Montgomery Area Chamber of Commerce about incorporating the event into its program of work. The Chamber agreed to

*In 1995 Jubilee CityFest attracted a record 90,000 people from throughout the Southeast. The event has been featured in **Southern Living** magazine as one of the top 10 festivals in the region. Photo by Robert Fouts.*

manage the event for one year, and again expanded the goals of Jubilee, this time to make it a family event with more children's activities and musical entertainment. A long-term goal was to draw attention to the historical, cultural, and recreational activities available in the city and create renewed interest in the downtown area.

As it turned out, the Chamber's one-year commitment lasted more than 15 years, under the direction of volunteer Margaret Carpenter. In that time, the festival's attendance grew from 1,500 to more than 50,000. The event draws on the resources of the City of Montgomery and the Montgomery Area Chamber of Commerce to continue its success.

Each year, Jubilee CityFest has grown and now includes four stages of musical entertainment, including jazz and blues, classic rock, alternative, and country styles. There also is a special children's festival, featuring a variety of entertaining and educational activities for little ones, including puppet shows, magic, arts and crafts, and more. Also included in Jubilee CityFest weekend is a "pops" performance by the

Montgomery Symphony Orchestra, and the NCAA Division II World Series baseball tournament.

In 1995 Jubilee CityFest attracted a record 90,000 people from throughout the Southeast, and required the assistance of some 1,400 volunteers. The event has been featured in *Southern Living* magazine as one of the top 10 festivals in the region. "Jubilee represents what we consider the best of Montgomery," said Marianne Thompson, executive director of Jubilee CityFest. "It's a very eclectic blend of musical entertainment, arts, and more—there's something for everyone."

The South Alabama State Fair is another event that is widely anticipated in Montgomery and the surrounding area each fall. The flashing, sparkling lights of the midway, the smell of sizzling Polish sausage and grilled onions, the excited squeals and screams of youngsters as they get their first glimpse of the excitement unfolding before them—all are a part of the tradition of the fair.

The South Alabama State Fair began in 1954. Annually, the event draws a crowd of more than

Montgomerians enjoy "getting away from it all" at nearby Lake Martin or Lake Jordan. These two recreational sites offer a wealth of activities for the outdoor enthusiast, from swimming to boating to waterskiing. Both lakes feature picnic and camping areas close by, so fun-seekers can easily make a weekend or week-long excursion. Photo by Robert Fouts.

The State Farmers Market, located on the corner of Federal Drive and Coliseum Boulevard, features a wide array of seasonal produce. Photo by Robert Fouts.

200,000 during its week-long run. The South Alabama State Fair is sponsored by the Kiwanis Club of Montgomery, with proceeds from admission going to benefit youth, charitable, and educational organizations throughout the Montgomery area. Annually, the fair raises more than $2 million in outright donations and presents more than $1 million in premiums and prizes in the many competitions held throughout the week.

"The fair is oriented to the family, and we try to have something to appeal to all ages," said Hazel Ashmore, general manager for the South Alabama State Fair. "It's an opportunity to showcase Alabama and its people—that's what fairs are all about. Plus, people feel they are contributing to the community because all of the proceeds go right back into the community," she said.

An always-popular aspect of the fair is the many shows and contests held throughout the week. From flower shows to photographs, artwork, crafts and food, and even livestock, the fair brings out the very best from Montgomery and the surrounding area. Ribbons and cash prizes are awarded to the top finishers in each category.

"We have categories of interest to all ages, men, women, and children," said Evielean Howell, director of the Creative Living Center. Last year a new 'awesome sandwich' category was added just for young people, with the event judged live on "school day," when area public schools allow children a holiday to attend the fair. A new sewing contest also is designed for the younger fair-goer.

In addition to the competitions, demonstrations including cooking, spinning and weaving, sewing, basket-making, quilting, and painting will be going on at the Creative Living Center throughout the week.

The fair also offers something special for music lovers, with top musical entertainers visiting Montgomery each year as part of the fair festivities.

"Shoppers, start your engines!" Festival in the Park is an arts and crafts spectacular that draws more than 30,000 people annually to Oak Park in Montgomery and features handwork from some of the top artisans in the country. This is a juried show, indicating that everyone wishing to participate in the festival has to first submit slides or samples of his or her work, which are then judged and selected as acceptable for Festival in the Park. Each judge is an artist in his or her own right, with extensive credentials in showing his work and/or teaching art.

Judges select works for display at Festival in the Park to represent a variety of art and craft styles. Artwork will feature items in many mediums, including sculpture, pottery, painting, fabric, jewelry, and more. Crafts will include such mediums as basket weaving, dried flowers, dolls, clothes, toys, and more.

"You're going to find the best of each category here, and a lot of variety. The people selected to participate in Festival in the Park are very talented," said Dawn Railey, manager of marketing and public relations for the City of Montgomery Parks and Recreation Department.

In addition to the fine selection of arts and crafts goods, visitors to Festival in the Park will find continuous entertainment on three stages and in the park's arena area, provided largely by local groups including cheer and dance teams, cloggers, musicians, acting troupes, and other talented folks. Also, the Montgomery Fire Department and the Montgomery Police Department provide educational displays each year, with programs designed for both children and adults. Area community centers provide concessions and baked goods, with proceeds from sales going to benefit their programs. A children's area provides activities and games especially for youngsters, including face painting and macaroni art.

"This is a fun family day," Railey said. "It gives people a chance to get out and mingle with people in the community and it showcases the talent here in Montgomery. It's something we're real proud of." Festival in the Park was selected as one of America's 100 best traditional/folk craft events by *Sunshine Artist Magazine.*

Montgomerians can "travel" to Scotland each fall without leaving their own backyards, as the city is home to the annual Alabama Highland Games. Held on the grounds of the beautiful Wynton M. Blount Cultural Park, the games are a celebration of Montgomery's Scottish heritage. "A Scotsman founded Montgomery, so most people who are native Montgomerians have some Scottish heritage," said Kathy Beattie, executive director of the Alabama Highland Games. "Not everyone can afford to visit Scotland, but they can come out to the Shakespeare Festival for a day and experience a little piece of Scottish culture," she said.

The day features traditional Scottish sports, such as "tossing of the caber" and sheaf putting (throwing a 56-pound weight). Also, visitors to the Highland Games will enjoy the sights and sounds of the bagpipe bands, can taste traditional Scottish foods, and research their own family trees. Another popular event of the games is the sheep shearing and shepherding demonstrations.

The Scottish festival began when members of Montgomery's Saint Andrew's Society decided they wanted to have a special gathering to display the talents that are unique to their heritage. Eventually, the Alabama Highland Games office was formed to administrate the festival. The Blount Foundation is the largest single sponsor of the games, and other local corporations also sponsor the annual event.

"Up, up and away . . . ." For more than 10 years, the Montgomery Hot Air Balloon Spectacular has been filling the skies over the city with the colorful sight of hot air balloons. In 1995 the spectacular was expanded to include a music festival, featuring both classic rock and roll and country music to provide a little something for everyone.

The Balloon Spectacular features tethered and distance balloon rides and brings an average of more than 40 balloonists to the Capital City. Proceeds raised from event admission and concession sales go to benefit the Center for the Prevention of Child Abuse.

"This is a wonderful event, and there is something for everyone—kids, adults, people of all ages," said 1995 event chairman Dan McKay. "And, best of all, coming out to the Balloon Spectacular means you are helping those in need." *M*

CHAPTER TEN

LET US ENTERTAIN YOU

You catch your breath in anticipation as the house lights dim and a faint glow lights the stage before you. There is a moment of dark silence as the audience hovers in that instant of calm before the action suddenly bursts into view like a whirlwind of color and sound, erasing time until the last line is spoken, the last pirouette executed in perfect form, the last note falls.

T*he Alabama Shakespeare Festival is currently the fifth largest Shakespeare festival in the world, and attracts more than 300,000 visitors to Montgomery from all 50 states and more than 60 foreign countries each year. Photos by Robert Fouts.*

Put down that luggage! You don't have to travel to New York to experience the wonder of the arts. It's all right here in Montgomery. Many newcomers to the city are surprised by the wealth of cultural diversity offered in the Capital City. World-class theater, symphony, ballet, art—all find a home in Montgomery.

ALABAMA SHAKESPEARE FESTIVAL

*I*t's hard to believe a theater company that opened its first play, *Hamlet*, to an audience of two—a play reviewer and his wife—would become the world-renowned attraction that now holds center stage in the Wynton M. Blount Cultural Park. The Alabama Shakespeare Festival is currently the fifth largest Shakespeare festival in the world, and attracts more than 300,000 visitors to Montgomery from all 50 states and more than 60 foreign countries each year. The Alabama Shakespeare Festival was created in Anniston, Alabama, where it had its humble beginnings in 1972 as a summer stock theater project housed in the Anniston High School auditorium. Eventually, the Shakespeare Festival grew to garner critical acclaim, but still lacked the financial support to keep it afloat.

Facing bankruptcy in the early 1980s in Anniston, ASF organizers, led by Carolyn Blount, who served on the ASF Board of Directors in Anniston, approached Mrs. Blount's husband, Winton Blount, about funding the theater in its search for a new home. He agreed, but only if the theater would relocate to Montgomery.

In December of 1985, the Alabama Shakespeare Festival moved to Montgomery, as the result of Mr. And Mrs. Winton Blount's $21.5-million gift of a performing arts complex set in a 250-acre park, the Wynton M. Blount Cultural Park.

The Alabama Shakespeare Festival's new home was dubbed the Carolyn Blount Theatre, in honor of Mrs. Blount, and the complex became the largest single gift in the history of American arts giving. The theater houses two separate theaters, the 750-seat Festival Stage and the 225-seat Octagon Theatre. Additional facilities include production shops, administrative work spaces, reception rooms, ticket sales area, and concession area. The complex contains more than 100,000 square feet of space.

The Wynton M. Blount Cultural Park was designed by landscape architect the late Russell Page, and is modeled after traditional English countryside.

A statue of William Shakespeare stands in the theater lobby. It was done by John Quincy Adams Ward and is considered to be the premiere American statue of the Bard, according to ASF information.

From its original six-week summer season in Anniston, ASF has been able to expand in its

*T*he Alabama Shakespeare Festival generally produces at least three works by William Shakespeare each season, plus works by classic authors, as well as musicals and contemporary plays. Photo courtesy of the Alabama Shakespeare Festival.

1500
1900
1500

new home to produce an almost year-round schedule. Alabama Shakespeare Festival generally produces at least three works by William Shakespeare each season, plus works by classic authors such as Moliere, George Bernard Shaw, and Anton Chekhov, as well as musicals and contemporary plays. The season includes 10 to 14 plays.

Theater Artistic Director Kent Thompson hopes eventually to expand the theater's programming to a full year-round schedule.

ASF also operates student and adult educational programs, including a Master of Fine Arts program. MFA students produce one play each season. Camp Shakespeare, held each summer, is open to young people and features a week-long study of the many varied aspects that make up a theater production, including acting, costuming, lighting, and music.

Other educational programs include "Theatre in the Mind," a free program featuring author talks, lectures, and actor discussions designed to help audiences learn more about the plays; and Children's Theatre and "SchoolFest," special productions for school children throughout the state and region designed to give young people early exposure to theater and answer their questions about the art form.

The Alabama Shakespeare Festival also has developed a Southern Writers' Project, begun in 1991, to showcase the talent of Southern writers and to examine Southern issues. *Grover* was the project's debut production in 1993, and *Lizard* was performed in 1994. Both plays received critical acclaim, and *Lizard* was selected for inclusion in the 1996 Olympic Arts Festival in Atlanta.

MONTGOMERY MUSEUM OF FINE ARTS

The Montgomery Museum of Fine Arts, founded in 1930, is the oldest fine arts museum in Alabama. It began in a small abandoned schoolhouse, where it remained until 1959, when it moved into quarters it shared with the Montgomery Public Library downtown. In 1980, on the museum's 50th anniversary, supporters realized it needed room to grow and began a campaign to relocate to larger quarters. And what grand quarters they are! In September of 1988 the museum opened the doors of its new home in the Wynton M. Blount Cultural Park.

The permanent collection that serves as the cornerstone of the museum's exhibits is the Blount Collection, 41 paintings donated by local businessman and philanthropist Winton Blount. The collection includes works by noted American artists John Singer Sargent and Edward Hopper, and spans 200 years of American art.

Additionally, the museum boasts a fine collection of European prints, including works by Rembrandt, Caneletto, and Goya; and regional works by such Southern artists as Anne Goldthwaite, Walter Anderson, and Montgomery's own Zelda Sayre Fitzgerald.

In the fall of 1993, the museum was able to expand with the addition of the Young Gallery, a more than 5,000-square-foot space made possible through a gift of $500,000 from Montgomerian Ida Belle Young. The Young Gallery houses contemporary American art as well as the Southern regional art from the museum's permanent collection.

Also within the museum, 3,000 feet of gallery space is dedicated to ARTWORKS, an educational gallery featuring exhibits that museum patrons can explore through touch, sight, and sound to learn about works in the permanent collection, and art in general. Although ARTWORKS was designed primarily for children, many adults enjoy getting lost in its interactive spaces, participating in such kinetic artworks as a tilting canvas, onto which the guest artist can arrange soft sculptures in whatever design pleases the eye; a six-foot Tannenbaum screen that creates a "shadow" of rainbow colors and vibrating textures; or a kaleidoscope into which you can step and watch the colors dance overhead. ARTWORKS also offers a variety of workshops for children and adults.

The museum hosts a variety of traveling exhibits, which have covered such venues as art found in everyday culture, architecture, and printmaking.

"A museum is like a library, or a visual reference," said Mark Johnson, museum director. "This is where the community can come to be educated about history and man's cultural achievements right up to the present time. How artists respond to events and ideas helps other people understand themselves better," he said.

In addition to the permanent and traveling collections, the museum also hosts many educational programs, lectures, and tours. The museum's outreach into the community is capped off each year with the Flimp Festival, or "Art in the Park," a weekend festival of music, art, and entertainment. Flimp Festival features a variety of hands-on art activities for people of all ages, including chalk drawings, finger painting, paper-making, and painting.

"In the course of a year, we hope to provide opportunities for everyone in the community to

ARTWORKS is an educational art gallery. While designed primarily for children, many adults enjoy getting lost in its interactive spaces. Photo by Robert Fouts. (left)

The Montgomery Museum of Fine Arts, founded in 1930, is the oldest fine arts museum in Alabama. Photo by Robert Fouts. (below)

The museum boasts a fine collection of European prints, including works by Rembrandt, Caneletto, and Goya; and regional works by such Southern artists as Anne Goldthwaite, Walter Anderson, and Montgomery's own Zelda Sayre Fitzgerald. Photo by Robert Fouts. (right)

The Flimp Festival highlights a variety of hands-on art activities for people of all ages, including chalk drawings, finger painting, paper-making, and painting. A Do-Dah Parade, featuring family pets in their best attire, is a favorite activity of the Flimp Festival. Colorful balloons contribute to the weekend festival of music, art, and entertainment. Photos by Robert Fouts. (above)

be challenged, educated, and entertained," Johnson said. "Sometimes those efforts are large-reaching, like Flimp Festival; sometimes they are more intimate, like a collection of prints. Some we yell about; some are a surprise as you turn a corner."

"Having a museum is nice, but the real satisfaction is when you see someone respond to it. That's the product—the enjoyment the public receives in response to what we do," he said.

MONTGOMERY SYMPHONY ORCHESTRA

A volunteer community orchestra of about 75 players, the Montgomery Symphony Orchestra is made up of people of all ages, all skill levels, and all backgrounds. But they have one thing in common. They love to play classical music. "And we do it with gusto—gusto and relish," said Helen Steineker, administrative manager of the MSO, with a smile.

The Montgomery Symphony Orchestra performs a Symphony Season of six concerts (two are duplicate performances of the Holiday Pops concert), plus two free outdoor concerts, two free concerts for sixth-graders, and one out-of-town performance. The outdoor concerts are Broadway Under the Stars, a collection of show tunes from popular Broadway musicals, held each summer at the Wynton M. Blount Cultural Park, and the Jubilee Pops Concert, a performance held on the lawn of the Alabama Archives and History Building in downtown Montgomery and included in the festivities of Jubilee CityFest held Memorial Day weekend.

"It's not as busy a schedule as a professional orchestra, but it's very ambitious and busy for a

volunteer orchestra. We love to play and that's what we're here for," Steineker said.

The MSO really is the community orchestra for the city. It welcomes musicians of all calibers, from professionally skilled to those who pick up an instrument for sheer enjoyment at the end of a busy day at another career. A scholarship fund is available through the symphony for any of its members who wants to continue his or her instruction to improve musical ability.

"Most cities cannot afford to have a professional symphony. It's labor intensive, taking 80-90 people full time. But, at the same time, most towns can't afford to be without a source of music," Steineker said. The Montgomery Symphony Orchestra answers the problem perfectly.

The organization had simple beginnings, with groups of musicians gathering at local community centers to play together simply for the love of the music.

"Through the years, we've developed and matured, but that's really who we are—a group of people who share and support a hobby," she said. "We're very fortunate that the people in the Montgomery community have been so generous in their support of us. And that also is a confirmation to us that what we're doing is good and right."

The Montgomery Symphony Orchestra depends not only on the support of the community, but also on business and corporate sponsorship to keep it going. "All of our concerts are sponsored by businesses here in the community," Steineker said. "Most other symphonies would be envious of the relationship we have with the business community. We have formed a very successful long-term relationship with many of the companies in

We have formed a very successful long-term relationship with many of the companies in Montgomery, and were it not for these corporate friendships, the symphony would not enjoy being able to perform on such a regular basis.

A *volunteer community orchestra of about 75 players, the Montgomery Symphony Orchestra is made up of people who love to play classical music. Photo by Robert Fouts. (top left)*

The Montgomery Youth Orchestra provides a social and educational outlet for young musicians, while giving them the opportunity to learn and perform classical music. Photo by Robert Fouts. (above)*

The Montgomery Symphony Orchestra performs Broadway Under the Stars, a collection of show tunes from popular Broadway musicals, held each summer at the Wynton M. Blount Cultural Park. Photo by Robert Fouts. (right)*

Montgomery, and were it not for these corporate friendships, the symphony would not enjoy being able to perform on such a regular basis," she said.

In addition to the Montgomery Symphony Orchestra's concert schedule, the Montgomery Symphony League sponsors the Montgomery Youth Orchestra, open to young people in junior high and high school, by audition. The MYO provides a social and educational outlet for young musicians, while giving them the opportunity to learn and perform classical music. The youngsters do not necessarily have to be interested in pursuing a career in music to benefit from the experience, Steineker stressed.

"One of our philosophies is we feel skills children learn when they play an instrument and are part of an orchestra serve them well in whatever career they choose to pursue. We don't support the youth orchestra to grow musicians, but just to help develop good people."

It is for the same reason the Symphony League sponsors free concerts for area sixth-grade students—to expose them to a musical form they might not otherwise allow themselves to experience. "The Symphony League is unique in that it has become the educational arm of the symphony," Steineker said.

Another educational program of the symphony is the Young Artists Concerto Competition. This program welcomes junior and senior high school students from Alabama and the four contiguous states to compete for the prize of a cash award and the opportunity to perform with the Montgomery Symphony Orchestra in one major performance. Sponsored by the Blount Foundation, the concerto competition boasts a purse of nearly $8,000, with $5,000 to go to the first place finisher, the largest purse in the Southeast for a competition of this level.

The Montgomery Symphony Orchestra also hosts the MSO Fellow program, a competition that brings a violinist of the highest caliber to Montgomery to play with the orchestra for two years. The Fellow position allows the guest musician to devote his or her energies to playing his instrument and growing as an artist for the duration of the program. The MSO has expanded the program to include a "Cello Fellow" search in alternate years.

"We're here to meet the needs of Montgomery, but we also exist for selfish reasons," Steineker summed it up. "There are at least 70 people in Montgomery who just love to play, and we're here to serve them."

Thomas Hinds is the conductor of the Montgomery Symphony Orchestra.

ALABAMA DANCE THEATRE

Founded in 1986 by its current artistic director, Kitty Seale, the Alabama Dance Theatre is a dance company focusing primarily on training and education in dance. Based at the Armory Learning Arts Center, the dance training program is conducted through the Montgomery Parks and Recreation Department.

"We train from young ages all the way up to the professional level," Seale said. "Many of our dancers continue on to well-known companies, colleges, and universities."

The Alabama Dance Theatre exposes its students to an "eclectic" repertoire to include classical, contemporary, and neoclassical styles of dance. "Since we are trying to create dancers here, we want to give them exposure to all that we can. And I think it makes an interesting program for the audience," Seale said of the mix of styles.

The Alabama Dance Theatre's company performs two major productions each year. *Mistletoe* is a holiday performance with a classical repertoire. In this performance, the company produces a well-known classical piece. Recently, the Alabama Dance Theatre performed *Cinderella*. The spring concert includes a mixture of performances, including something from the classical repertoire and one mixed-repertoire piece.

Additionally, the Alabama Dance Theatre welcomes guest teachers each year for an intensive three-week summer workshop for its students, followed by a free performance for the community, entitled "Late Day of Late Summer." Guest instructors have included Sonia Arova, Eldar Aliev, Larissa Sklyanskaya, Wes Chapman, and Francesca Corkle.

Both Seale and ballet master Haynes Owens have a background in Montgomery, giving them a special sense of dedication to what they do, Seale believes.

"So many people have come back to Montgomery to work in their art form. They are committed to the community," she said. "And there is strong support of the arts by Montgomery business and city leaders, like Red [Winton] Blount and Mayor Emory Folmar. That business and city support of the

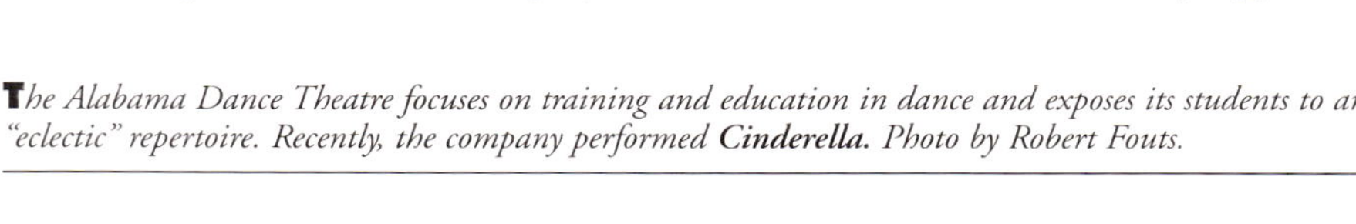

The Alabama Dance Theatre focuses on training and education in dance and exposes its students to an "eclectic" repertoire. Recently, the company performed **Cinderella**. Photo by Robert Fouts.

The Montgomery Ballet has the distinct honor of being the only professional ballet company in Montgomery, boasting seven professional dancers in its ranks. Photo by Robert Fouts.

arts means a lot—they set the standard. If we didn't have that support, we couldn't do nearly as well as we do. We couldn't exist, really."

Whether or not the students of the Alabama Dance Theatre continue in the art as professional dancers, they have gained valuable "life lessons" of discipline, hard work, and commitment, Seale believes. And the people of Montgomery gain something beautiful, and something of which they can be proud.

"We give back to the city a company of really polished, talented young people they can be proud of. We're proud to be part of the reason people are attracted to Montgomery, why they should want to come here to live. And we're in very good company."

The Alabama Dance Theatre company travels within the Southeast to perform at regional festivals, and ADT is a member of the South Eastern Regional Ballet Association (SERBA) and an affiliate of Regional Dance America.

THE MONTGOMERY BALLET

The Montgomery Ballet has the distinct honor of being the only professional ballet company in Montgomery, boasting seven professional dancers in its ranks. Additionally, the Montgomery Ballet School trains dancers from age three-and-a-half to adult, drawing on the resources of its professional company to provide expert instruction. There is a performing wing of the Montgomery Ballet School as well, called the Montgomery Youth Ballet.

The Montgomery Ballet has marked several turning points in recent years, with the most important being the transition from a civic ballet company to a professional ballet company in 1986. The Montgomery Ballet began as the Montgomery Civic Ballet in 1958, supported entirely by community volunteers. Drawing dancers from area schools, the civic ballet company performed relying on guest artists to fill main roles, and guest companies to perform larger productions. It was selected for membership in the South Eastern Regional Ballet Association (SERBA) in 1964, and presented its first performance at the South Alabama State Fair in 1967. The first Performance on the Green, an annual tradition to this day, was performed at Huntingdon College in 1974.

Under the guidance of Director Duane Dishion, the ballet performed *The Nutcracker*, which has become an annual Montgomery Christmas tradition, for the first time in Montgomery in December of 1976.

The ballet continued to grow under the direction of Gary Moore, who became artistic director in 1980. In his four years at the helm, Moore created at least 20 ballets for the Civic. In 1984 Don Steffey became artistic director. His wife took over the direction of the Montgomery School of Ballet. Their vision was to turn the Montgomery Civic Ballet into a professional company—the Montgomery Ballet, as it is today.

In 1987 the Montgomery Ballet earned the honor of being designated "The Official Performing Ballet Company of the City of Montgomery."

In 1995 the Montgomery Ballet named David Anderson as artistic director and Priscilla Crommelin-Ball as associate artistic director. Anderson performed with the San Francisco Ballet and the American Ballet Theatre. He also appeared in the Broadway production of *Applause*.

Crommelin-Ball served previously as ballet mistress of the Montgomery Ballet and as principal classical ballet teacher in the school. She has been associated with the Montgomery Ballet for many years, having attended classes at the school while growing up, when she visited her cousin Lucy Leak Stone, who taught dance in the city. Stone would take Crommelin-Ball to auditions at the then Montgomery Civic Ballet.

"At the time, people went to independent ballet schools. The best students from those schools auditioned for the civic ballet, to be in performances of the Montgomery Civic Ballet," Crommelin-Ball explained. "It was a real honor to be a part of the Montgomery Civic Ballet."

Crommelin-Ball danced as the first Sugarplum Fairy in the Montgomery Civic Ballet's first production of *The Nutcracker*. Crommelin-Ball performed as a professional ballerina for many years, and was a member of the original Harkness Ballet of New York in residency in Monte Carlo, Ballets Felix Blaska in Grenoble, France, and as principal dancer of the Maryland Ballet and the Birmingham Ballet, among others.

Another recent turning point for the Montgomery Ballet was its selection for membership in Dance USA, a national association of dance companies that includes such renowned members as the American Ballet Theatre, the New York City Ballet, and the San Francisco Ballet. "Even though we're a small professional ballet company, we're in the most noteworthy association of ballet companies," Crommelin-Ball said. "It's like a promotion from SERBA."

Montgomery Ballet School students present the Performance on the Green at the Wynton M. Blount Cultural Park. Photos by Robert Fouts.

The Montgomery Ballet professional company and Montgomery Ballet School recently moved into new, larger quarters to accommodate the needs of its growing program.

"What is important about this school is that all the teachers are currently or have been professional dancers, so students are getting the very best training they could possibly receive. Students are exposed every day to professional dancers. It's an inspiration to them to learn from their role models," Crommelin-Ball said.

Each summer, the Montgomery Ballet hosts an Intensive Summer Seminar, featuring a guest master instructor/choreographer for a 10-day period. In 1995 the instructor was Ron Guidi, director of the Oakland Ballet. Following the summer seminar, Montgomery Ballet School students present the Performance on the Green, a free performance held at the Wynton M. Blount Cultural Park as a kind of "thank you" to the citizens of Montgomery for their support throughout the regular season.

The season for the Montgomery Ballet includes a spring concert, at which the company debuts a full-length ballet developed by the resident choreographer; and Ballet and the Beasts, a free performance at the Montgomery Zoo. Each Christmas, the Montgomery Ballet presents *The Nutcracker.*

Additionally, each year the Montgomery Ballet hosts a guest professional dance company for "The Wilson Project." Funded by Jim Wilson Jr. & Associates, the program brings a guest company to the city to put on a benefit performance to raise funds for the Montgomery Ballet. In 1995 the Montgomery Ballet hosted the Oakland Ballet's performance of *Romeo and Juliet,* and in 1996 plans to host the Ballet Hispanico of New York.

"Traditionally, ballet and the arts in general have relied completely on the support of individuals. Now, the support of the city and government is very important too. But we need audiences to exist," Crommelin-Ball said.

"The ballet is a cultural enrichment, and the fact that Montgomery has a professional ballet company here is an asset to the community. Montgomery is a very cultural city—it always has been," Crommelin-Ball said.

The Davis Theatre for the Performing Arts is a center for arts culture as home to the Montgomery Symphony Orchestra, the Montgomery Ballet, and the Alabama Dance Theatre. Photo by Robert Fouts.

THE DAVIS THEATRE FOR THE PERFORMING ARTS

Long-time Montgomery residents can still remember movie matinees on Saturday afternoons, Friday night date-nights in the balcony, and film debuts at the historic Davis Theatre. Constructed in 1929, the Davis Theatre was considered a "Movie Palace" designed to show the new "talking pictures," as well as the occasional live show.

Today, the theater is a center for arts culture as home to the Montgomery Symphony Orchestra, the Montgomery Ballet, and the Alabama Dance Theatre. Also, the theater hosts special events such as the annual "Glitz, Glamour, and Gourmet" fund-raising project of the Montgomery Autauga Elmore Medical Auxiliary, and such traveling performances as *42nd Street*. The 1,200-seat theater also can be rented for performances from interested organizations.

"Our focus is for this theater to continue to provide the people of the region, and those who come here to visit, with a place to enjoy quality entertainment in a lavish, nostalgic setting," said Paul McNeeley, executive director of the Davis Theatre.

Plans are in the works to establish a formal season of shows to be performed at the Davis Theatre, with the primary focus to be musicals, McNeeley said. "We are more readily designed for musicals, with a full orchestra pit. We are not in competition with the Alabama Shakespeare Festival. I think they are recognized for their classic performances and strong dramatic performances. We want to be primarily a venue for musicals, to help offer to this region a wide variety of quality entertainment," he said.

As a downtown landmark, the Davis Theatre remains one of only a handful of theaters of its kind in the South. It offers excellent acoustics, a state-of-the art sound and lighting system, and, of course, its full-size orchestra pit, an amenity not often found in modern theaters. Many of the restorations are due largely to the generosity of the late Tine W. Davis and his wife, Eunice Davis McNeill. Most recently, Mrs. McNeill donated funds used to enclose the alley between the theater and Whitley Hall. The area serves as an entertainment area and opens into a redecorated Civic Room at the Whitley.

The Davis Theatre is operated through Troy State University in Montgomery.

THE F. SCOTT AND ZELDA FITZGERALD MUSEUM

When Julian and Leslie McPhillips purchased the vintage home at 831 Felder Avenue, they never expected to cause such a stir. They simply hoped to save a historic old home from the wrecking ball—a historic old home once inhabited by F. Scott Fitzgerald, author and eventually symbol of the Jazz Age, who penned such classics as *The Great Gatsby* and *The Beautiful and the Damned;* and his wife, Zelda Sayre Fitzgerald, an artist in her own right as a painter (some of her works hang in the Montgomery Museum of Fine Arts) and author of the novel *Save Me the Waltz*.

"In December of 1986 we bought the house, and almost immediately an article appeared in the paper [*the Montgomery Advertiser*] saying that we might make it into a museum," says a

Montgomery native Zelda Sayre (seated at piano) was the belle of society. It was in Montgomery that Scott Fitzgerald first met Zelda, at a dance at the Montgomery Country Club in 1918. The F. Scott and Zelda Fitzgerald Museum is the only museum dedicated to the life and works of the Fitzgeralds in the world. Archival photo courtesy Fouts Commercial Photography. Photo by Robert Fouts.

bemused Mr. McPhillips. "I never called anyone or made any announcements about it, but somehow everyone just found out about it," he said, laughing.

And it didn't sound like a bad idea, at that. "I guess I always had it in the back of my mind to make it a museum," he admits.

Zelda Sayre Fitzgerald was a Montgomery native, and the belle of society. It was in Montgomery that Scott first met Zelda, at a dance at the Montgomery Country Club in July of 1918. While he was instantly smitten, Scott wooed Zelda ardently to persuade the debutante darling to be his bride. Worried about how he would support her, Zelda broke their first engagement in 1919, but the pair finally married April 3, 1920, after Scott published *This Side of Paradise*. The couple rented the house at 819 Felder Avenue from September of 1931 until the spring of 1932. Zelda was hospitalized for a nervous breakdown in February of 1932 and did not return to live in the house afterward.

"The house is the only place left in Montgomery where Scott and Zelda lived together as a married couple," McPhillips said. The house where Zelda grew up was torn down many years ago.

"I felt it was an incredible shortcoming and void not to have a museum for Scott and Zelda," McPhillips said. "This will be by far the greatest thing done to commemorate their memory, and I hope perhaps to make something positive for the future, to preserve their legacy."

Currently, the F. Scott and Zelda Fitzgerald Museum is the only museum dedicated to the life and works of the Fitzgeralds in the world. It houses an extensive collection of photographs; original correspondence between Zelda and Scott; prints of Zelda's paintings; copies of Scott's novels, including original editions and foreign language translations; newspaper clippings; furniture from Zelda's childhood home; and other memorabilia and artifacts. Visitors to the museum also can watch a videotape detailing the life and works of F. Scott and Zelda Fitzgerald.

Because the restoration and upkeep of a museum-quality home is a large job for just one family, the Museum Association was incorporated in 1987 to aid in fund-raising efforts, and to work to add to the collection. Currently, only a main section of the downstairs of the home is open for viewing. In time, McPhillips hopes to restore the entire home. A major fund-raising event, featuring a silent and live auction, is held each year to benefit the museum. Guests dress festively in "Roaring 20s" garb, and a Scott and

The Alabama State Council on the Arts houses the Alabama Artist Gallery in Montgomery, which displays a wide range of art by Alabama artists, including folk art, contemporary work, and traditional pieces. Photo by Robert Fouts.

Zelda look-alike contest is the highlight of the evening.

Thousands of people from throughout the world visit the F. Scott and Zelda Fitzgerald Museum each year. "Just as Scott and Zelda belonged to the world, and not just Montgomery, we would hope the museum would be something for everyone, for people everywhere, not just Montgomery," McPhillips said.

ALABAMA STATE COUNCIL ON THE ARTS

Although the council is a state agency whose duty it is to administer a grants program to non-profit arts organizations statewide, the Alabama State Council on the Arts' Montgomery location makes it a ready resource for Montgomery artists and arts supporters.

The council uses a combination of one-third state and two-thirds federal monies to fund arts programs, and it also administers the development of special projects and partnerships, such as the Alabama Center for Traditional Culture, Design Alabama, the Alabama Writers Forum, Alabama Alliance for Arts and Education, and the Alabama African-American Arts Alliance, among others.

In addition to providing outright grants, the State Council on the Arts works to promote the arts and artists statewide. Most recently, the council began a billboard campaign featuring the works of Alabama artists and encouraging Alabamians to support the arts. This campaign is repeated annually, featuring a variety of new artwork each year.

The Alabama State Council on the Arts also houses the Alabama Artists Gallery in Montgomery. The gallery displays a wide range of art by Alabama artists, including folk art, contemporary works, and traditional pieces. The collection changes periodically to feature new works.

"Although we are here to serve artists from all over the state, people in Montgomery especially have the opportunity to make use of our resources," said Al Head, executive director for the Alabama State Council on the Arts. "We have a council staff on hand to provide a wide range of assistance to individuals and groups in the city."

The council also offers a resource library available for use by the public, and it keeps an active file of Alabama artists. "If a business wants to buy a painting, commission a sculpture, or find craftsmen, we can help them locate and utilize Alabama artists," Head said.

A current initiative of the arts council is emphasis on art in education. The council is working to develop model programs throughout the country that involve or incorporate the arts into the basic curriculum. Montgomery's own Carver Creative and Performing Arts Center magnet school program is a model for this project, Head said.

Above all, Head hopes that Montgomerians will view the Alabama State Council on the Arts as an approachable, valuable resource for the continued development of arts in the city.

"I think Montgomery, being the Capital City, sometimes views state government as an entity unto itself," he said. "I would hope that the community at large would utilize the resources of state government—the Alabama State Council on the Arts, the state universities in the city. There's a lot going on and a lot here, if people just take a look around."

MONTGOMERY BUSINESS COMMITTEE FOR THE ARTS

"Arts are good for business, and business is good for the arts." Working under this theory and motto, the Montgomery Business Committee for the Arts was established in 1980, with the ultimate goal of strengthening the arts in Montgomery through the support of local businesses.

MBCA business members believe business investments in the arts enable the arts to contribute to the quality of life and economic vitality of our communities, in addition to improving the academic performance of youngsters and adding to the success of business.

The MBCA, which is a charter member of the National Business Committee for the Arts regional affiliate program, headquartered in New York City, was founded by community and business leaders Winton M. Blount, Robert S. Weil, and Frank A. Plummer.

In its early days, the MBCA, in cooperation with Blount, Inc., undertook a fact-finding mission called Arts Explorations to determine the city's existing arts resources and its needs in the many areas of the arts. Also, it examined how businesses, cultural organizations, clubs, and governmental entities were already involved with the arts, and how those ties could be strengthened.

Once the MBCA had a clear idea of the needs of the community in the area of the arts, the Arts Action Task Force was formed, cosponsored by Mayor Emory Folmar, the MBCA, and Blount, Inc. Made up of about 50 community leaders, the task force set as its goal "the establishment of the Montgomery area as a center for the arts in Alabama," and developed a 10-year plan to meet this goal, according to MBCA history.

An essential part of strengthening the arts is the involvement and continued support of local businesses, which are essential sponsors for concerts, exhibitions, and commissioned artwork.

It is the responsibility of the Montgomery Business Committee for the Arts to work as a liaison between businesses and arts organizations in the city to build bonds that benefit both parties, said Elmore DeMott, executive director of the MBCA.

"We are not designed to be a fund-raising entity in ourselves, but to establish ties between businesses and the arts," she said. "We like businesses to become directly involved with projects, and we want to form lasting partnerships, so we try to match compatible interests and goals to meet what both are looking for."

DeMott has found that the most successful partnerships are those that directly involve a company's employees in support of the arts. This gives them a reason to feel attached to the arts in Montgomery, and to feel a personal responsibility for supporting arts programs, she explained.

In order to foster the bonds between businesses and the arts, MBCA takes a three-pronged approach, including the areas of recognition, involvement, and education.

Annually, the MBCA presents the Business in the Arts Awards, a "pat on the back" for businesses that have shown outstanding support for the arts consistently. Winners are recognized at a special luncheon, and are presented with original artwork in place of a standard plaque or trophy.

In an effort to directly involve and recognize the achievements of employees, the MBCA sponsors the "On My Own Time" art exhibition. Employees of participating businesses are encouraged to submit original artwork in a variety of different categories. Judges from the arts and business communities award prizes for the top artwork in each category.

Educational efforts include the Metropolitan Opera Workshop, held each year on the campus of Auburn University at Montgomery. This outstanding event brings together teachers from throughout the Montgomery Public Schools system with opera performers, producers, and technicians from the New York Metropolitan Opera for a week-long workshop, during which the educators learn how to teach opera to their students.

Business involvement in the arts has grown steadily since the inception of the MBCA, with membership growing from a mere handful of businesses. Future plans are to involve more small businesses in sponsorship of the arts through financial and volunteer contributions; to involve more younger people in support of and participation in arts programs; and to make things happen in the Montgomery area arts world that would not be possible without the support of the MBCA.

Currently, an MBCA task force is evaluating the mission of the organization and setting both long-and short-term goals in an effort to ensure the MBCA continues to have significant value to its business members and the community.

"We hope to serve as a catalyst for strengthening the arts in Montgomery," said Fran Jones, who was involved in MBCA when it was initially established, and has been a longtime supporter of the arts in Montgomery. "Our goal is helping all of the arts organizations to be strong so that Montgomery will be recognized as a good cultural city. We want Montgomery to be a place where people want to live," she said. "And that, in turn, is good for the businesses. It's a wonderful partnership in which everybody benefits." **M**

Part Two
MONTGOMERY'S
ENTERPRISES

of COMMERCE

C H A P T E R   E L E V E N

NETWORKS

The area's transportation, communications, and energy firms keep people, information, and power circulating inside and outside the Montgomery area. Photo by Robert Fouts.

ALABAMA POWER COMPANY

*I*n the electric energy business, quality is measured by service reliability, price, and customer satisfaction. The good news for Alabama Power customers is that their energy supplier is a high quality company and is still seeking improvements. Its drive for success motivates Alabama Power to provide its customers with the best service.

The company's ability to provide a high degree of energy reliability is attributable to a variety of factors, from innovative maintenance programs to high-tech transmission line monitoring equipment. But in addition to its service reliability, and of equal importance to its customers, has been Alabama Power's success in maintaining electric prices that are counted among the lowest in the country.

The entity that would become Alabama Power Company came into existence in 1902 when steamboat Captain William Patrick Lay filed incorporation papers with dreams of harnessing the water power of Alabama's river system to produce electricity. In 1907 congress approved Lay's plan to build a dam and power plant on the Coosa River, but it was not until 1912, when Lay met the ambitious hydroelectric pioneer James Mitchell, that the dream became a reality.

Montgomery attorney Thomas Martin joined the two and worked to consolidate separate groups with individual claims along the Alabama rivers. With the help of willing English and American investors, the three men were able to underwrite Mitchell's ambitious 20-year master plan for hydroelectric development in Alabama. Within two years, the young company was generating electricity from Lay Dam and from a coal-fired steam plant in Gadsden. Montgomery's first power generator was known as Montgomery Light and Water Power Company.

Today, the company operates 14 hydroelectric plants, 7 fossil fuel plants, and 1 nuclear electric generating plant in Alabama. The utility employs 7,500 Alabamians and provides electric service to 1,018 communities in 56 counties in the southern two-thirds of Alabama.

Montgomery County is included in the company's Southern Division, which stretches south to Greenville, north to Clanton, east to Auburn, and west to Marion. Approximately 250 Montgomery area employees serve more than 95,000 homes, businesses, and industries in and around the Capital City.

Alabama Power is one of five utilities owned by The Southern Company—one of America's largest investor-owned electric utility groups. The Southern Company supplies energy to customers in Alabama, Georgia, the Florida panhandle, and southeastern Mississippi and operates other companies, including Southern Communications Services, Southern Company Services, Southern Electric International, Southern Development and Investment Group, and Southern Nuclear. In 1994 the holding company was cited in *Fortune Magazine's* 13th annual corporate reputation survey as the most well-managed electric utility in the nation.

Visionary and progressive management has created in Alabama Power Company an organization recognized as much for the quality of its product as for its contributions to the quality of life in Alabama. Most obviously, the company provides an essential service that not only contributes to higher standards of living for its customers, but also creates stable jobs and other economic opportunity.

To better serve its customers and to stimulate economic development, Alabama Power gives priority to cost containment, continuously seeking innovative ways to reduce expenses and keep rates stable. The company has implemented improved technology to reduce costly maintenance, standardized engineering practices and materials for more cost-effective procurement, and developed employee incentive programs to encourage creative thinking and cost-cutting strategies at every level of the organization. Because of these efforts and more, the residential

*N*o company recognizes better than Alabama Power the value of affordable energy in bringing new business and industry to the state.

*T*he company's Alabama Science Center in Montgomery is a favorite field trip site, featuring interactive science exhibits and unique displays designed for students in the fourth through ninth grades.

price for electricity in Alabama has risen less than 5 percent in the past decade, while inflation has risen more than 44 percent during the same period.

No company recognizes better than Alabama Power the value of affordable energy in bringing new business and industry to the state. In the 1920s the company became the first to actively recruit industry to Alabama and remains at the forefront of economic development today.

The high-tech Alabama Resource Centers located in Birmingham and Montgomery represent the company's commitment to progress. The centers provide a one-stop information data bank where business executives can glean detailed information on industrial parks, demographics, labor, taxes, utility services, education, industrial training, and transportation. Impressive computer and multimedia programming offers the most accurate economic information available and goes a long way in promoting Alabama as an attractive business and industrial location.

Alabama Power also recognizes the crucial importance of quality education to the state's continued growth and offers generous statewide support, including adopt-a-school programs, a Teacher Corps made up of more than 900 employees who volunteer to take educational programs into the state's classrooms, and a grant program that contributed more than $1.4 million toward proven and innovative learning programs in 1994. The company's intriguing Alabama Science Center in Montgomery has become a favorite field trip site, featuring interactive science exhibits and unique displays designed for students in the fourth through ninth grades.

With generating facilities on Alabama's waterways and timberlands, Alabama Power equally recognizes its responsibility to environmental protection. The company has invested money and manpower into programs ranging from researching new technologies for cleaner air emissions to implementing enhanced living conditions for endangered species found on company properties.

The key for Alabama Power is to protect the delicate balance between meeting the vital electric needs of its customers and preserving the environments that surround its facilities. Among its contributions, the company joined with the State of Alabama to implement a nesting program designed to increase the state's bald eagle population, created a wildlife refuge at the 1,850-acre Farley Nuclear plant near Dothan, and joined with the Alabama Conservancy and Brunos grocery stores to keep discarded Christmas trees out of landfills. To minimize the effect on the environment from coal-burning, Alabama Power has invested more than $750 million in facilities to clean the air. The company is also working on ways to develop markets for coal ash from coal-fired plants, and employs non-emission electric vehicles in its corporate fleet.

These actions are indicative of Alabama Power's tradition as a solid corporate citizen, willingly supporting the various needs of the communities it serves. The Alabama Power Foundation was established in 1989 as a central entity to efficiently handle the company's charitable giving and to encourage others in the business community to give. In 1994 the foundation contributed gifts totaling more than $3 million to worthy, tax-exempt organizations in the categories of health and human services, public and private education, civic activities, and arts and culture.

In addition to the vast resources of the foundation, Alabama Power encourages its employees to give of themselves in their home communities. It is common to find Alabama Power employees at work as loaned executives to local United Way campaigns, as Red Cross volunteers, or as leaders in civic organizations. The company leads by example, implementing programs like Project Share, which provides an avenue for donated dollars to help meet the emergency heating or cooling needs of the sick and elderly.

Every day the employees of Alabama Power Company handle complex and multifaceted tasks ranging from high-tech power production and distribution to responsive customer service, from economic development to environmental protection. But despite the complexities of the business, Alabama Power stays focused on a single goal: to do whatever it takes to ensure the people of Alabama a powerful future.

A drive for success motivates Alabama Power to provide its customers with the best service.

ALABAMA ELECTRIC COOPERATIVE

*I*n 1941, when most of rural America was still without electricity, 11 electric cooperatives joined forces to form Alabama Electric Cooperative. That unity has served as AEC's foundation from its early struggling days until today, when AEC is recognized as a leader among generation and transmission cooperatives nationwide.

member systems, but the local community as well, AEC emphasizes area development by promoting employment opportunities through industrial recruitment. The AEC membership realizes the economic benefits of industrial customers who seek to expand their operations. As competitive energy providers to prominent United States and international corporations and industries, AEC and its member-owners are providing more than just electricity—they are spurring economic growth and marketing a way of life for area residents.

AEC and its member-owners are active in a number of industrial and community development projects directed to revitalize America. Through an aggressive economic development program, AEC helps access funding for rural infrastructure available through state and federal programs. Focusing on specific projects that promote customer density and sales volume, AEC is committed to working with its distribution power systems to develop more efficient and economic business opportunities.

AEC has distinguished itself in the utility industry by investing in the latest operational systems and processes, ranging from state-of-the-art generation technology to infrared thermal imaging equipment. The cooperative promotes the efficient use of electric energy and is committed to the increased application of electric

technologies that improve the quality of life while preserving our natural resources.

AEC's generating plants includes the Charles R. Lowman Power Plant in Leroy, Alabama; the nation's first compressed air energy storage unit in McIntosh, Alabama; the McWilliams Power Plant near Andalusia, Alabama; two hydroelectric plants on the Conecuh River in Alabama; and the Portland Gas Turbine in Walton County, Florida. In addition, AEC has an ownership interest in the James H. Miller Jr. Electric Generating Plant near Birmingham, Alabama.

Competitive rates, a strong financial position, and reliable service have moved AEC to the forefront of the utility industry. On the threshold of the twenty-first century, AEC, its Montgomery area member distributors, and more than 500 employees are guiding the consumer-owned utility industry into a new era. *n*

A*n aggressive maintenance program ensures AEC is equipped to offer reliable electrical service at the lowest possible cost.*

Headquartered in Andalusia, Alabama, AEC is a generation and transmission cooperative that provides wholesale power to 12 Alabama distribution cooperatives, four Florida distribution cooperatives, four Alabama municipal systems, and one industrial distributor. These 21 member-owners meet the energy needs of more than 280,000 member-consumers in 39 Alabama counties and 10 counties in the Florida panhandle. The AEC power system encompasses approximately 24,500 square miles in Alabama and 7,500 square miles in Florida. District service centers strategically located in south Alabama and northwest Florida enable AEC to reliably meet the energy needs of its member-owners.

The member systems located near metropolitan areas realize the economic benefits of progressive urban centers that are gradually expanding into non-urban areas. Dixie Electric Cooperative, Central Alabama Electric Cooperative, Pioneer Electric Cooperative, Tallapoosa River Electric Cooperative, and South Alabama Electric Cooperative are Montgomery area cooperatives experiencing power system development due to residential, commercial, and industrial growth.

Recognizing that economic development benefits not only AEC and its consumer-owned

T*he Charles R. Lowman Power Plant is located on the banks of the Tombigbee River near Leroy, Alabama.*

DIXIE ELECTRIC COOPERATIVE

Dixie Electric Cooperative, headquartered in Union Springs, Alabama, is one of more than 1,000 rural electric systems across the country and one of 22 electric cooperatives in Alabama.

For more than 50 years, Dixie has worked to provide its member-consumers the best possible service at the lowest possible cost. State-of-the-art equipment enables the cooperative to provide quality electrical service, while an in-house computer system and electronic metering assure high-quality customer service.

Today, Dixie Electric Cooperative leads with technology—an indication of the challenges the company has overcome. When the cooperative incorporated in 1938, bringing the countryside to life was an overwhelming task for Dixie's pioneers. To ensure a reliable supply of power, Dixie joined other cooperatives in central and south Alabama and northwest Florida as a member-owner of Alabama Electric Cooperative, a generation and transmission cooperative that provides wholesale power for member distribution.

To better serve its member-consumers, Dixie Electric Cooperative has undergone many expansions during its years of service. Locations in Montgomery and Union Springs employ more than 70 workers, each committed to improving the quality of life for area residents.

As expectations of cooperative members evolve, Dixie continues to provide the amenities of comfortable living by offering services to improve energy efficiency. Along with providing basic electric service and power-quality consulting, Dixie also markets Good Cents energy-efficiency standards for new, improved, and manufactured homes and offers power quality consulting.

In 1976 Dixie began managing the South Bullock County Water Authority. The system began with 508 customers and now serves more than 2,400. The cooperative and water authority partnership continues to upgrade the existing water system to ensure a dependable and reliable water supply in the years ahead.

In recent years, Dixie's service area has experienced significant growth and now extends into more urban areas. Dixie meets the energy needs of many exclusive residential communities in east Montgomery. However, the versatility of Dixie's power distribution system also allows the cooperative to provide reliable and economical energy to major industrial customers, including the Alabama TechnaCenter Research Park, a progressive computer research center located in east Montgomery.

Dixie Electric Cooperative is active in a number of industrial and community development projects. Recognizing that new and expanding industry stimulates growth, attracts additional businesses, and creates job opportunities, Dixie is active in the Montgomery Area Chamber of Commerce, as well as a number of other service and economic development organizations.

Based on recent studies, Dixie Electric Cooperative's electricity sales are expected to increase annually through the year 2014, and total consumers are expected to increase by approximately 10,000 during the same period.

Dixie provides reliable and responsive service to member-consumers in Bullock, Montgomery, Macon, Lee, Lowndes, Pike, Barbour, and Tallapoosa Counties. The cooperative's board of directors, management, and employees realize success is measured not in miles of line or kilowatt hours sold, but rather in member satisfaction.

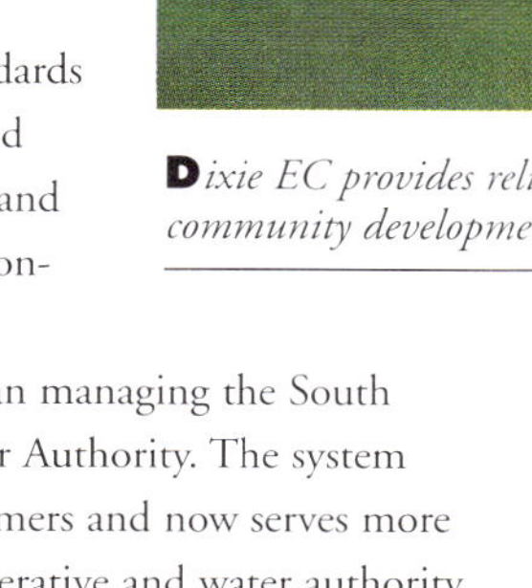

Dixie EC provides reliable electric service to many prestigious residential community developments.

The versatility of Dixie EC's power distribution system enables it to meet the energy needs of large industrial customers, including the Alabama TechnaCenter.

Dixie EC is continuously upgrading its power lines, both overhead and underground, to meet the increasing needs of its rapidly growing service territory.

WSFA TELEVISION

The 40-plus-year history of WSFA-TV is full of "firsts" and inspiring success stories, but it has been the station's progressive approach to serving the community and meeting the information needs of its audience that has made it a central Alabama entertainment icon.

It is impossible to compile a story about the station recognized throughout central Alabama as "Alabama's News Source" without referencing its rich and compelling historical impact. After all, WSFA was the news outlet to the world during the turbulent 1950s and '60s, was the first in Alabama to own commercial film processing equipment, the first to put cameras on the floor of the Alabama Legislature, the first Alabama station to hire a black reporter, and the first to produce a regularly scheduled hour-long newscast. But it has been foresight and a willingness to take calculated risks that sets the station apart.

"From day one there has been a firm commitment to provide the finest in local news coverage," said Operations Manager Carl Stephens. "Our news is, and always has been, at the very heart of our programming."

WSFA was founded as Alabama's fourth radio station in 1930 by Gordon Persons, who later went on to become governor of Alabama. In December 1954, Montgomery Broadcasting Company added WSFA-TV to the radio property. At 7 A.M. on Christmas morning the official program test began, followed by the first real program, Charles Dickens' *A Christmas Carol,* that evening.

*W*SFA News 12 Managing Editor and Anchor Bob Howell takes his experience, knowledge, and understanding of Alabama politics into the field and reports from the Capitol. Photo by Floyd Dozier.

*W*SFA News 12 Storm Team's Rich Thomas (far right), Bill Taylor, and Jennifer Schram keep a constant watch on central and south Alabama's weather. When severe weather threatens, state-of-the-art weather equipment helps them keep Channel 12 viewers instantly informed. Photo by Floyd Dozier.

In February 1955, Oklahoma Publishing Company purchased both the radio and television stations. A staff of 35 manned the young station from new facilities on East Delano Avenue, with a transmitter site 23 miles south of Montgomery at Mount Carmel. WSFA-Radio was later sold and its call letters changed to the familiar WHHY. The television station was purchased by its current owner, Cosmos Broadcasting Company, in 1959.

Although expansions and renovations have altered the appearance of the station's south Montgomery headquarters, WSFA still operates from its original location. Massive satellite dishes and live broadcast trucks are a familiar sight and community landmarks. Recent interior renovations and a plan to renovate the control room indicate a plan to stay.

WSFA's reputation as a highly credible news outlet was in place almost immediately. Frank McGee, the station's first news director, earned great respect for his coverage of the Civil Rights Movement in the mid 1950s. McGee went on to become a nationally prominent anchor with NBC. He covered the nation's space program from Cape Canaveral and later became host of the popular *Today* show.

At the height of the Civil Rights Movement, WSFA became a temporary home to reporters from all three American networks and the Canadian Broadcasting Company, said Stephens. "We were the only station with the equipment to do the job," he said.

McGee is just one of several WSFA news personalities who have gone on to gain prominence in the industry. He was joined on the early news team by anchor Crawford Rice, who later became president of Gaylord Broadcasting Company, sports director Leroy Paul, the first host of the trend-setting *Auburn Football Review,* and weatherman Hines Wolters, who is remembered by many today for his closing salutation, "Take care and fare thee well."

Like McGee, cameraman Laurens Pierce moved to the networks and later, while working for CBS, shot the only footage of the George Wallace assassination attempt.

Although quality newspeople have come and gone, WSFA has a tradition of longevity among its on-air staff. Sports Director Phil Snow has been with the station since 1964 and hosting the *Auburn Football Review* since 1976. Anchor Bob Howell has been with the station for more than 20 years, and the popular Rich Thomas has predicted area weather for more than 14 years.

"In the early days there just weren't many programs you could buy from the networks, so, to better entertain our viewers, we used our capabilities for live broadcasting to offer a variety of local shows," said Stephens. Those programs and their popular hosts are remembered fondly by long-time Montgomerians.

Betsy Plummer hosted the informative *How Do You Do It?,* while Catherine Wright Tennille and later Idelle Brooks hosted the 15-minute talk show *The Guest Room.* Perhaps most popular was Jack Turner's weekly country music show, *Alabama Jubilee,* which often featured his daughter, Dixie, known for her line in the commercial, "Mama, it's the Farm Bureau man."

Stephens smiles a bit when reminded of his four-year stint as *Cartoon Carl,* a popular children's show that brought 18 to 20 children, ages 5 to 10, to the studio daily. "People can remember it and talk about it, but it was live—there was no videotape and no film."

The local shows gave way to syndicated programming, but viewer loyalty has never waned. The station's top-ranked news shows keep its audience tuned in.

"Management knew in the early days we would build our audience loyalty through strong local news coverage, and it's still our priority," said Vice President and General Manager Harold Culver. "Within the last few years we've added two new newscasts, *Live At Five* and *Today In Alabama,* each designed to meet different viewer needs at strategic times. We now have a total of 3 hours and 25 minutes of news a day, and if the need arises, we'll add more."

With a viewership that stretches over 36 counties, WSFA recognizes the need for innovation and diversity to keep interest alive. The station has led the way in news coverage with innovations like the popular "TowerCam 12," which offers a beautiful rooftop view of downtown Montgomery, "First Warning 12," "Lightning Track," and "Doppler Radar" for the most up-to-date weather information, closed captioning for the hearing impaired, and E-mail communication for viewer feedback.

As much as its recognition as an industry leader, WSFA is known for its generous support of community-based programs. Through its popular "Class Act" and "Best of the Class" programs, WSFA has visibly demonstrated its commitment to education. The station works with the American Red Cross each year to promote one of the area's most successful blood drives. WSFA is also known for its generous public service programming and willingness to disseminate important community service items through its news programming.

"We haven't concentrated on a single area, but we have supported diverse areas where we see a real need," said Culver. "We realize how important television can be to a community organization."

WSFA has changed with the industry as broadcast technology has developed from film to videotape to today's hybrid of videotape and digital technology. WSFA is studying the rapidly approaching wave of High Definition TV technology, which will put an entirely new screen quality in every living room.

But for WSFA, the more things change, the more they stay the same. "As more and more channels, the Internet, and all sorts of other entertainment sources compete for our viewers' attention, none of them will be able to serve the need for local news programming better than we will," said Stephens.

The groundwork is laid. For WSFA, the strength of the past is clearly the foundation for the future 🔲

The WSFA News 12 anchor team is recognized throughout central Alabama as "Alabama's News Source." Pictured (left to right, front row) are: Kim Wanous, Carrie Johnson, Kim Hendrix, Rich Thomas, Phil Snow, Bob Howell, (back row) Bill Taylor, Jeff Shearer, Alex Wystrach, Ken Smith, Jennifer Schram, and Barry Ammons. More than 150 years of combined experience helps them bring viewers the most factual, detailed, and complete coverage of the day's news. Photo by Paul Robertson Jr.

BELLSOUTH

There is perhaps no industry more dynamic, more challenging, or more critical than today's competitive world of telecommunications. Montgomerians and citizens worldwide depend upon the reliable transportation of information for their very existences. BellSouth is at the forefront of this changing environment to ensure its customers have access to the finest communications tools available.

Montgomery discovered the conveniences of the telephone on April 5, 1880, when Southern Bell Telephone and Telegraph Company officially opened the state's third telephone exchange.

Since those days of "cord boards" and manual connections, the company has moved aggressively in response to area needs and industry changes. By 1952 Southern Bell serviced about 39,000 telephones in Montgomery. By the mid-'60s, the company had introduced direct long distance, or "1-plus" dialing. The next two decades brought state-of-the-art switching systems and Custom Calling Services such as Call Forwarding and Call Waiting.

The mid-'80s ushered in the breakup of the Bell System, creating a new era for the telecommunications industry. And, as a new millennium approaches, the company is preparing to compete in an even more wide-open business environment. In 1995 the BellSouth companies, including Montgomery's South Central Bell, took on the single BellSouth name, offering a streamlined and focused single source for its customers' communications needs.

In Montgomery, BellSouth leads in the deployment of digital switching and fiber-optic technology. At the beginning of 1996, the company is serving more than 155,000 area customer lines in the Montgomery and has more than 10,500 strand miles of fiber-optic cable in service. The entire network offers customers the most efficient, reliable, and comprehensive communications link available.

Montgomery's advanced network can provide everything from basic telephone to full-motion video services with Integrated Services Digital Network, a digital freeway that moves voice, data, telemetry, video, and facsimile separately or simultaneously over one telephone line.

These kinds of options are made available through BellSouth's strategic capital investment, expended not only for new and improved services, but also for infrastructure enhancements that will refine the network's long-term efficiency and reliability.

"We believe we are a strategic industry," said Ty Fondren, manager of corporate and external affairs. "No business or community can grow if it is hamstrung by inadequate communication. We do everything we can to keep our network in line with community need."

With the future at its doorstep, BellSouth is moving into Synchronous Optical Network, or SONET, which represents the newest generation of telecommunications transport, multiplexing, and cross-connect products. Asynchronous Transmission Mode, a digital technology that provides for transmission of high speed data, voice, and imaging services is also in the works.

But high-tech communications is not the only critical service BellSouth provides. The company has long been at the heart of community service in Montgomery. BellSouth Pioneers spearhead the company's giving efforts and have generously shared more than 2 million service hours in Alabama. BellSouth was one of Montgomery's first Partners In Education and today partners with three local schools. In addition, BellSouth employees take on leadership roles in many civic and service organizations in the community.

Leadership translates into every aspect of business at BellSouth. In a marketplace of increasing telecommunications choices, BellSouth is combining cutting-edge technologies and dedicated people to ensure it remains the best connection today and into the next century.

BellSouth Pioneers provide hearing screening programs for local youth. Montgomery's Pioneers donate thousands of dollars and hours to area causes every year.

BellSouth leads the way in the deployment of fiber-optic technology. Technician Doug Thomas splices strands in an east Montgomery fiber facility.

ALAGASCO
AN ENERGEN COMPANY

The story behind the development of Alagasco, America's 35th largest natural gas distribution company, began in 1852 when the Montgomery Gas Light Company was chartered to provide manufactured gas for the town's street lamps. Today with more than 1,300 employees serving some 450,000 customers in 180 Alabama towns and cities, Alagasco is the state's largest natural gas distribution company.

More than 100 years after its founding, the company became a public utility in 1953. In 1979 the utility formed a holding company, known as Alagasco, which was renamed Energen in 1985 and is operated under the direction of Chairman and Chief Executive Officer Rex Lysinger.

The mid-1980s brought transition and positive change to Alagasco, including the hiring of President Mike Warren, whose primary goal was to create a progressive organization dedicated to innovation, customer satisfaction, market growth, and employee development.

Alagasco is recognized for a variety of progressive initiatives, including the weatherization of more than 50,000 homes in less than 10 years to help low-income customers reduce their utility bills, the use of thorough cross-training to enhance employee development, the establishment of quality-of-life focus groups to identify work and family issues that affect job performance, and the use of suggestion programs to encourage employee action and innovation. In 1993 Alagasco was listed by authors Robert Levering and Milton Moskowitz as one of the "100 best companies to work for in America."

In addition to internal corporate change, the natural gas distribution business itself is constantly evolving. For years Alagasco purchased natural gas from a single supplier; today the company purchases its product from two major interstate supplier pipelines and more than 20 spot market suppliers. This diversity increases the utility's flexibility and cost efficiency, which is passed on to the customer.

With a commitment to new market growth, Alagasco aggressively pursues opportunities to acquire new service territories and today brings its customer-centered service to more than two-thirds of the state's population.

The utility is also dedicated to supporting the natural growth of its existing service areas. In 1994 Alagasco constructed a nine-mile pipeline to serve a new electric generating plant in Greene County. The company also responded quickly to meet the natural gas energy needs required for

the new Mercedes-Benz automotive assembly plant in Vance, Alabama, and a number of associated satellite facilities.

An ardent supporter of statewide economic development, Alagasco, in cooperation with the Alabama Public Service Commission, implemented an innovative rate-setting procedure in 1983 which has helped attract and maintain business and industry. The Rate Stabilization and Equalization Program simplifies the tariff-setting process and reduces the frequency of rate changes.

Dedication to customer satisfaction has been the driving force behind the company's progressive initiatives. In 1996 Alagasco will implement a state-of-the-art $15-million Customer Automated Technology System which will provide the infrastructure necessary to support innovative customer service programs for the future.

Environmental protection is also high on Alagasco's priority list. Supplying a resource recognized by many as the "environmental protection energy," the utility makes every effort to preserve the environment through programs ranging from environmentally sensitive pipeline development to in-house recycling programs. Forty percent of the vehicles among the company's corporate fleet are now powered by clean-burning natural gas.

Like most industries in today's dynamic business world, natural gas distributors face growing

change and intense competition. While the future is full of challenges and uncertainties, Alagasco's visionary approach to business and customer satisfaction indicates the company is well up to the task. 𝓷

Many Gas Advantage Home communities are under construction throughout Alagasco's service territory

WHATLEY CONTRACT CARRIERS, INC.

Whatley Contract Carriers, Inc., a rapidly growing truckload service company, operates its primary offices out of Montgomery with another office located in the southeast Alabama town of Headland. The company, which today employs 126, was established in 1989 by Joe Whatley. He entered the business with a mission to provide stable, consistent trucking services to the building materials and paper industries.

The company operates in the flatbed and dry van segments of the trucking industry. Whatley Contract Carriers began as a flatbed carrier serving the building supply market by transporting brick, steel, lumber, and masonry products. After completing its first two years in business and establishing a solid track record and customer base, Whatley Contract Carriers opened a second office in Headland in 1993.

The company implemented its dry van division in late 1990 to take advantage of opportunities in serving the general dry commodities market, transporting primarily pulp board and paper. In 1994 the company earned total revenues in excess of $12 million. Of those earnings, approximately 71 percent were realized by the dry van division, which serves customers in New England, the Midwest, and the Southwest, and 29 percent were earned from flatbed operations throughout Alabama and the Southeast.

Whatley Contract Carriers, Inc., a rapidly growing truckload service company, operates its primary offices out of Montgomery.

The associates of Whatley Contract Carriers prides themselves on providing dependable service at economical prices. A testimony to the quality of the company's service is its on-time delivery record of better than 98 percent.

Whatley Contract Carriers prides itself on providing dependable service at economical prices. A testimony to the quality of the company's service is its on-time delivery record of better than 98 percent. Additionally, the company enjoys a loyal base of quality, long-standing clients. Whatley's top 10 customers represent approximately 48 percent of the company's revenue. Notable names among the company's dry van division client list include Jefferson Smurfit/Container Corp., Mead Paper, Georgia Pacific Corp., MacMillan Bloedel, and Wal-Mart Stores. In the flatbed division, leading customers include Bethlehem Steel, Georgia Pacific, Louisiana Pacific, Jenkins Brick, GAF Roofing, and ELK Corp.

Recognized and well-respected in his industry, Joe Whatley is a member of the board of directors of the Alabama Trucking Association, a member of the Interstate Truckload Carriers Conference, American Trucking Association, and a member of the board of trustees of the Alabama Trucking Association's Workers' Compensation Trust Fund.

Whatley stresses the importance of finding qualified, highly skilled drivers who are committed to professional service and delivering goods in a safe and efficient manner. The company's safety director is responsible for training and supervising personnel to keep safety awareness a top priority. An emphasis on safety begins when an individual is hired and continues throughout the career of every Whatley Contract Carriers driver.

Whatley Contract Carriers is also proud of its community involvement. The company is the primary sponsor of the Montgomery YMCA's Barracuda Swim Team and sponsors two Dixie Youth Little League baseball teams. The company received the Montgomery Area Chamber of Commerce's prestigious Emerging 30 Award in 1994, designating Whatley Contract Carriers as one of Montgomery's top 30 small businesses.

On the strength of its current success and expectations for continued growth, Whatley is planning to open a third office in Birmingham in 1996. But a commitment to its Montgomery base will keep the organization's headquarters in the capital city. As the company's founder states, "People are what makes the difference, and the Montgomery area is a great place to find the right kind of dedicated people to do the job." **77**

C H A P T E R   T W E L V E

MANUFACTURING, DISTRIBUTION & TECHNOLOGY

Producing and moving goods for individuals and industry, manufacturing, distribution, and technology firms provide employment for many Montgomery area residents. Photo by Robert Fouts.

SMITH INDUSTRIES, INC.

From the basement of a brownstone on West 94th Street in New York City, to a 195,000-square-foot manufacturing facility on a 33-acre industrial park site in east Montgomery, Smith Industries, Inc. has steadily progressed over time.

In 1926, to supplement his income as a traveling salesman for the National Lead Company, Jay L. Smith, the father of seven, began supplying brass and cast iron fittings from a make-shift basement operation. Today, as it celebrates its 70th anniversary, Smith Industries; Inc., having survived and flourished through the Great Depression and World War II, operates three divisions with facilities in six states and Canada, employing 400 people, and markets many of its products worldwide.

By 1933 Jay L. Smith had moved his steadily growing casting supply business to a plant in Newark, New Jersey. The business grew slowly, but consistently, during the Depression years. World War II brought great opportunity for the manufacture of defense-related materials, and the company continued to grow. But it was not until after the war that Jay R. Smith Manufacturing Company jumped into the plumbing industry with both feet and began to take advantage of the industrial construction boom underway at the time.

Smith Industries, Inc. is a privately owned, third generation company that started literally on a shoestring and became an organization with international impact. Photo by Fouts Commercial Photography.

Jay L. Smith died in 1942, leaving control of the company to his wife and son, Jay R., the father of Bruce and his brother, Jay L. Smith. After many years, Jay R. Smith became the sole owner of the company and was later succeeded by his son, Jay L. Smith, now president and owner.

Continued corporate expansion and two more relocations in the New Jersey area finally led Smith Industries to consider its most significant move, from Piscataway, New Jersey, to Montgomery, Alabama, in January 1979.

"One of the things we are most proud of is that we are a privately owned, third generation company that started literally on a shoestring and became an organization with international impact," said Bruce Smith, vice president for marketing and sales and one of the founder's grandsons.

Jay R. Smith Manufacturing Company, the largest of the company's three divisions, operates from the Montgomery plant. More than 300 employees work to design, manufacture, package, market, and distribute a wide variety of plumbing and drainage products for the commercial and industrial construction industry.

Smith Industries, Inc. also consists of Potter-Roemer, a California-based fire protection equipment manufacturer, and Precision Arc Company, a Bridgeport, Connecticut, manufacturer of the company's water hammer arresters and arc welding systems. "The companies are interdependent; we feed off each other. There is an interdependence that makes the whole greater than the sum of its parts," Smith said.

O. A. Wilkerson, senior vice president for finance and administration, remembers the move. "We had to expand where we could best meet the long-term strategic objectives of the corporation, and Montgomery offered that opportunity. We were able to purchase land for future expansion, in a location that is excellent for distribution, and had an abundant labor pool to select new employees."

The company began moving 34 families to Montgomery in 1978 and hired approximately 225 local people. "We had 7,000 applications for

Smith Industries is a people-oriented organization with proactive communications and low personnel turnover. Photo by Fouts Commercial Photography.

The specification plumbing and draining business is the anchor of Smith Industries, Inc. Photo by Fouts Commerccial Photography.

engineered plumbing specialty items in the world.

Smith Industries recognized the impact and began to take advantage of the global marketplace in the 1970s when the energy crisis stimulated construction and expansion in the Middle East. The company has since increased its international presence in the Middle East and Southeast Asia. In 1993 the Jay R. Smith Manufacturing Company Division entered into a strategic alliance with a German company to market their trench drain products in the North American plumbing markets. "Globalization is ever present . . . sourcing and selling . . . we are certainly not everywhere yet," said Smith.

From its corporate mission statement to the decorative floor mat at the entrance to its offices, Smith Industries emphasizes its motto: "Customer Driven."

"In the past we focused on the quality of our product, and continue to look for ways to improve, but we have established confidence in our products and are now determined more than ever to make our customers' jobs easier," Smith said. "How can we improve our manufacturer representative's selling efforts; how can we make the engineer's job easier when he's writing specifications; how can we help the contractor to spend less time installing Smith products; and how can we facilitate the plumbing wholesaler's purchase of our products?"

Most important, he adds, in today's dynamic business environment is technological competitiveness. "Drainage products are not going to go away, and their design probably won't change much . . . a drain will always be a trough that operates with gravity through a hole in the ground. But the technology that gives us the ability to interact electronically, quickly, and responsively with our customers will change, and we must be on the edge."

Recognizing its role as an industry leader,

Smith Industries created an Environmental Products Group which distributes a product line that separates oil from waste water before the water enters the sewer system. The company also uses recycled plastics in its production process. According to Smith, there is great market growth potential in environmental products, but, just as importantly, there are long-lasting environmental benefits.

Smith Industries exemplifies a responsible approach to business in many ways. It is a people-oriented organization with proactive communications and low personnel turnover. The company strives for good working conditions with a strong safety emphasis while being environmentally responsible. The company's quiet, but consistent, commitment to the Montgomery area is one more example.

The company is sensitive to its community responsibilities and supports a variety of local organizations. "We have never sought the spotlight; we're not a public company," said Smith. "We are committed to Montgomery." ∏

More than 300 employees work to design, manufacture, package, market, and distribute a wide variety of plumbing and drainage products for the commercial and industrial construction industry. Photos by Fouts Commercial Photography.

those 225 jobs," said Wilkerson, "so you could say we had a pretty good selection."

The Montgomery facility, which is located in the Gunter Industrial Park, includes 25,000 square feet of office space. The remainder of the building is a fully integrated manufacturing and warehousing facility. "We do the machining, fabrication, assembling, enameling, and plating right here," said Wilkerson. "All the elements to manufacture our products are under one roof."

The Montgomery facility has recently completed its third expansion, a 15,000-square-foot plant addition. "We continue to grow because we continue to expand our product lines, and we continue to use our core business, the specification plumbing and draining business, as our anchor," said Smith. "In addition, we have streamlined our operations, and the longer we are here, the more solid our foundation becomes."

Smith products are sold primarily through manufacturers' representatives all over the United States and in many foreign countries. The company now produces more than 10,000 different parts, operates 45 service centers nationwide, and has become one of the major producers of

RHEEM MANUFACTURING

As home to the world's most famous and most innovative producer of water heaters, one could say the city of Montgomery is in hot water—and proud of it.

Rheem Manufacturing, the maker and marketer of world-renowned Rheem and Ruud water heaters, has operated a major manufacturing plant in the Capital City since 1972. For nearly a quarter of a century Rheem has been a respected economic contributor and corporate citizen in central Alabama.

But the company's long-term commitment to Alabama became crystal clear in 1989, when Rheem moved its Water Heater Division worldwide headquarters to Montgomery from Chicago and expanded its local manufacturing plant from 440,000 to 700,000 square feet.

The Montgomery facility is one of five Rheem manufacturing plants in North America. Employing a dedicated work force of more than 1,200, the massive Gunter Industrial Park production plant produces more than 7,000 water heaters per day, accounting for nearly two-thirds of Rheem's total water heater production capacity.

The company began humbly in the late 1920s when brothers Dick and Don Rheem started a steel drum galvanizing business. Their efforts later turned to building steel drums and tank components for water heaters; and in 1931, they began producing complete water heaters. The

Rheem Manufacturing's Water Heater Division sells over 2 million water heaters annually.

young company never faltered. In 1959, after significant growth through acquisition, Rheem purchased the well-known Ruud Manufacturing Co., gaining access to a broader line of commercial products and powerful name recognition.

The company has since gained market share through intelligent acquisition and incredible innovation. In fact, the list of Rheem patents reads like a history of the water heater industry.

Today, Rheem Manufacturing's Water Heater Division sells over 2 million water heaters annually. Because the company has maintained a low profile over the years, few realize it is the largest manufacturing operation in Montgomery. In fact, Rheem employees earn an annual payroll of $30 million and fringe benefits in excess of $11 million. In addition, Rheem estimates it spends approximately $24 million each year on in-state purchases, making its direct economic impact even more substantial.

Under the leadership of President Stewart Farwell, Rheem's Water Heater Division designs, develops, manufactures, and markets a broad range of gas and electric water heaters for both the residential and commercial housing markets in the United States and Canada. The company markets its products primarily to plumbing wholesalers and to the residential replacement market, with a major focus on the rapidly growing retail do-it-yourself store. The "Richmond" brand is the company's major retail line of water heater and is available in such stores as Lowe's and Home Quarters.

Rheem has been a leader in technological innovation since its founding, and Farwell attributes its market leadership today to aggressive research and development aimed at bringing more efficient and durable water heaters to the marketplace.

"We are always looking for ways to do things better, cheaper, and faster than the competition," said Farwell. One recent example of the company's product innovation is its Marathon brand nonmetallic water heater, which offers a lifetime warranty because it does not rust. In years past the company has led the industry with countless other innovations, including the Rheem Coppermatic, one of the finest water heaters ever

Shown is Rheem's 50-bay loading dock at the company's 600,000 square foot manufacturing plant.

built featuring a durable copper shell within a conventional steel tank, the screw-in gasketed heating element for electric residential water heaters, and the Rheem Gasmaster burner with super-accurate port alignment for better flame distribution and improved performance.

The Water Heater Division's active R&D group, located in Montgomery along with the company's executive, administrative, advertising, marketing, and human resource staffs, is still integral to Rheem's success. Mandated to stay on the cutting edge of the industry, with an eye focused at least 10 years into the future, Rheem's research group frequently adds to its considerable in-house expertise by employing the services of graduate engineering students from Auburn University and the University of Alabama.

But at Rheem Manufacturing, innovation also takes on forms other than new product development. Progressive management techniques and a concern for employee satisfaction make Rheem one of the area's most respected employers.

"The state of Alabama is blessed with a good, hardworking workforce," said Farwell. "We will do all we can to help the employees who serve us so well."

Progressive policies and programs such as incentive programs encouraging employees to develop new ideas or make cost-cutting recommendations, an on-site medical center that reduces absenteeism and provides a welcomed service, a monthly newsletter written by employees and for employees to build stronger communication, and company-supported educational opportunities ranging from a worksite GED program to computer training are testimony to Rheem's employee commitment.

At Rheem, well-trained, dedicated employees are considered essential to the company's ultimate goal of customer satisfaction. In continual pursuit of that goal, the company employs intensive quality control measures throughout each step of the production process, maintains strategically located factory warehouses and distribution centers nationwide to strengthen the company's ability to move its products quickly to the consumer, and invests in state-of-the art computer technology to ensure responsive service. A newly implemented $17-million computer system, which integrates plant activities nationwide to maximize production capacity and efficiency, is the company's latest commitment to its uncompromising service ethic.

On a quest to ensure its competitiveness in a growing global marketplace, Rheem has in recent years invested nearly $40 million in its Water Heater Division for improved production process equipment and research and development. In 1996 the company will achieve ISO 9000 certification. A series of international quality and management assurance standards, certification will assure companies and consumers worldwide of Rheem's priority attitude toward quality.

Although Rheem Manufacturing can boast a rich and successful past, the company spends little time looking back. Instead, Rheem is intensely focused on the future. With a commitment to quality products, innovative marketing, technological leadership, and employee excellence, Rheem will take advantage of future opportunities to make history in the water heating industry for years to come. **❚❚**

Employing a dedicated work force of more than 1,200, the massive Gunter Industrial Park production plant produces more than 7,000 water heaters per day, accounting for nearly two-thirds of Rheem's total water heater production capacity.

GE PLASTICS

About 20 miles west of Montgomery, amidst a sprawling rural Alabama landscape covered with trees, streams, and wildlife, sits a $900-million GE Plastics plant that manufactures one of the strongest, most technologically-advanced products in the modern world.

The GE Plastics plant, located on 6,300 acres (nearly 10 square miles) in the Lowndes County community of Burkville, is the place where LEXAN® polycarbonate resin is made. LEXAN is a material that has nearly countless uses and is valuable to major global markets, including the automotive, appliance, business equipment, compact disc, and bottled water industries.

GE Plastics, one of 12 businesses in the $60-billion GE Company, is the world's leader in engineering thermoplastics. Its products are used in applications requiring extraordinary strength, impact resistance, and high-temperature stability. The Burkville plant is one of 20 GE Plastics plants on five continents, and one of only four in the world that makes LEXAN.

In 1985, after reviewing 150 locations, screening 9 potential sites, and looking carefully at 4 semifinalists, GE Plastics chose the Alabama site as home for the largest greenfield plant investment in corporate history. Since then, the company's Alabama investment has grown considerably. At startup in 1987, after two and one-half years of construction, the company had invested $325 million and spent almost $380 million in total capital. Today, the expansive plant represents an $800-million investment with capacity to produce 330 million pounds of LEXAN resin annually. A 1996 expansion will increase production to 450 million pounds per year and raise the corporate investment to some $940 million.

Among the criteria that brought GE to Alabama were a site sufficient for the manufacturing facilities with ample buffer area, a trainable workforce with a strong work ethic, a state training program, close access to rivers and highways, railway availability, quality living conditions that would be attractive to transfers and new recruits, easy accessibility, and a favorable environmental climate.

According to GE Plastics' manager of employee and community relations, Al Wollerton, the company found all of that and more. "Alabama had the specifics we needed. But since coming here we have discovered the added value of strong governmental support, cultural and recreational offerings far beyond what one would expect in a community this size, excellent sources of higher education, and cultural diversity brought to this area through our military installations and the internationally renowned Air War College."

The plant, which actually sits on only 350 acres, is composed of six individual plant operations. These are resin production, brine recovery, bisphenol A, finishing, utilities, and waste handling areas. Each area is either a customer of, or supplier to, another operations area.

For an operation of this magnitude, time on-line and in production is money—and lots of it. Some 400 highly trained, technically skilled employees administer and operate the plant. Nearly 350 work directly in operations on four rotating shifts, running the plant 24 hours a day, seven days a week. The Alabama Industrial Development Training office, which Wollerton calls "one of Alabama's finest provisions for economic development," recruits and trains prospective GE employees. Contracting with experienced plant employees for first-hand instruction, AIDT provides a 13-week training program, loaded with environmental regulatory information, chemistry, and mathematics. Those who succeed through the process then proceed through additional interviews before taking their spot in the high-tech, computer-controlled process facility, where continuous learning is an integral part of its work environment.

"Our people are absolutely our most important resource," said Wollerton. "We have a dedicated and loyal group of employees who know they face high expectations and perform up to them every day." One indication of the company's appreciation for its employees is its highly competitive salary scale. Each year GE Plastics boosts the central Alabama economy with its $19-million-plus payroll.

In addition to concern for its employees, GE Plastics is concerned about the environment in which it works, and, in some ways, the two come together. Employee volunteers run the company's wildlife and land management committee, engaging in stewardship programs ranging from forest management to pond management and migratory bird programs. Employees and their families enjoy site ponds and land for recreational hunting and fishing; and, in one year, volunteers planted 100,000 evergreen and hardwood seedlings. In testament to their efforts, the plant has been designated an officially recognized site of the Wildlife Habitat Enhancement Council and was named "Rookie of the Year" in 1996.

Since production began in 1987, GE Plastics has reduced its emissions by 61 percent, while increasing production four-fold, and has twice received the Alabama Water Environmental Association's Award of Excellence for Industrial Wastewater Treatment. This kind of success is

GE Plastics, one of 12 businesses in the $60-billion GE Company, is the world's leader in engineering thermoplastics.

About 20 miles west of Montgomery, amidst a sprawling rural Alabama landscape, sits a $900-million GE Plastics plant that manufactures one of the strongest, most technologically-advanced products in the modern world.

directly related to the company's financial commitment to environmental protection. When the plant opened in 1987, more than 25 percent of the total investment went into environmental and safety systems, which are continuously upgraded and improved.

Community responsibility is still another area of intense interest for GE Plastics. Recognizing its role as a corporate leader and major employer, the company expresses its concern for quality education in several ways. The GE fund awarded Lowndes County Public Schools a $1-million grant used during five years to improve math, science, and English skills and double the number of students who attended college. The program was a success, and GE Plastics continues to financially support the Lowndes County schools. A mentoring program carried out by GE employees for Lowndes County High School students has also been very successful. In

Montgomery County, GE awarded $50,000 for the establishment of an alternative school that has provided a new and productive dimension to the public school system.

Experienced now in its role as a major Alabama industry, GE Plastics actively supports economic development by serving as a member of the Alabama Economic Development Partnership and the Montgomery Area Chamber of Commerce. GE employees are some of the most visible leaders on many volunteer boards, including the YMCA and the United Way of Montgomery.

In virtually every way, the GE Plastics plant in Burkville, Alabama, is a world-class operation. But its significance is every bit as local as it is global. For, while the world benefits from the strength and quality of the product it produces, central Alabama benefits from the strength and quality of the company itself. *n*

ALABAMA MACHINERY AND SUPPLY COMPANY

*I*n many ways, the evolution of the Alabama Machinery and Supply Company parallels the historical development of Montgomery. Founded just after the turn of the century as the state entered an era of industrial progress, the company has recorded a rich corporate history.

Alabama Machinery and Supply Company was established April 1, 1902. Brothers Arthur and William K. Pelzer foresaw a need for a supplier to the state's growing number of industrial, lumber, and mechanized farming concerns. By 1906 the company had outgrown its original space and purchased two adjacent buildings on Coosa Street, comprising almost 100,000 square feet of warehouse space. The company grew and prospered at that landmark location, which is today listed on the National Register of Historic Places.

In 1922 Alabama Machinery and Supply Company acquired the G. W. Barnett Hardware Company and began distributing hardware to dealers across Alabama. In 1926 the company opened the Daylight Machine Shop and Bama Foundry on North Court Street. The machine shop was so named because of its innovative steel construction with extensive use of glass windows, providing much improved interior lighting over brick constructed buildings. These two new operations were to supply parts and do repair work for the local mills. As Alabama became an important lumber-producing state, the company decided to manufacture its own sawmills. The popular Bama Saw Mill was the first in the South to have its carriages and mandrels equipped with roller bearings.

In 1966 Alabama Machinery and Supply Company was purchased by F. G. "Micky" Reinehr. After 20 years of experience in the management of wholesale hardware, industrial supply, and steel fabricating companies, Mr. Reinehr recognized the changing trends in merchandising. In response to the area's building boom, he discontinued the company's wholesale hardware line and opened, instead, building products and construction supply divisions to serve home builders and heavy contractors. In 1974 he established a wholesale metal-working cutting tool specialty division, Cobal-Tru, which markets drill bits, taps, endmills, holesaws, and threading dies nationwide.

Today the company continues to be operated with a progressive eye by C. M. "Mike" Reinehr. After earning a B.S. in mathematics from the Georgia Institute of Technology and an MBA in finance from Georgia State University, Mike Reinehr returned to the family business and learned the ropes under his father's direction.

In 1995, after 93 years, Alabama Machinery and Supply Company moved from its original location into newer, modern facilities on Bibb Street. The move was clearly necessary to prepare the company for doing business in the twenty-first century.

Alabama Machinery and Supply is known throughout the region as a responsive, knowledgeable, and dependable general-line maintenance, repair, and operating supply distributor. With a loyal clientele composed of industrial, construction industry, and other commercial accounts, the company maintains in inventory, or has available through direct shipment, a literal smorgasbord of supplies and equipment.

Alabama Machinery and Supply Company is known and appreciated for its willingness to listen to customer needs, find the supplies they want, and make them available quickly and responsively. "Our only true business is customer service," said Reinehr. "We are here solely to serve Alabama's construction and industrial businesses." As an example, the company has moved quickly in recent years to stock a variety of safety and environmental bioremediation products to help their customers respond successfully to an increasing number of OSHA and EPA mandates.

But perhaps the company's strongest sales tool is its dedicated staff, made up of expert individuals. "We have always been a very people-oriented company," said Reinehr. "We value our employees as individuals, and we try to make this a satisfying place to work." That philosophy has paid major dividends in the form of employee longevity and expertise—two major reasons customers keep coming back.

A diversified approach to business has, over the years, helped soften the blows of temporary economic downturns or the seasonal swings commonly associated with the construction industry. According to Reinehr, business has been on the upswing since the early 1990s, and the potential

*A*labama Machinery and Supply is known throughout the region as a responsive, knowledgeable, and dependable general-line maintenance, repair, and operating supply distributor.

for continued growth is encouraging. "If we are aggressive, innovative, and maintain our market share, our sales will grow as the economy in Alabama grows."

Alabama Machinery and Supply is looking enthusiastically toward the future, preparing for the Information Age. A believer in the value of technology, Reinehr has fully computerized the company and established an E-mail address to more efficiently communicate with customers and suppliers. He plans to produce a company Web page on the Internet and an on-line products catalogue.

To its credit, Alabama Machinery and Supply Company has found a way to balance a great tradition of service with a strong vision for the future. The company stands prepared at the threshold of a promising new century, dedicated to meeting the dynamic and changing needs of Alabama's modern industrial and construction markets.

BAMA FOUNDRY

The Bama Foundry operation of Alabama Machinery and Supply Company continues to operate on North Court Street. Although it no longer produces the Bama Saw Mill, it continues to manufacture both gray iron and aluminum, machinery, construction, paving, and architectural castings. Bama Foundry is known as a general jobbing foundry, producing a variety of work for numerous customers. It is managed by Charles O. "Chuck" Parkinson, a 10-year veteran of the company.

Bama Foundry has the capacity to mold and pour iron castings of up to 7,500 pounds in weight and aluminum castings of up to 450 pounds in weight. Almost every manhole in the city of Montgomery has the name "Bama" cast into its surface.

Architectural castings have become one of Bama Foundry's most popular products. As cities all over the country are rediscovering their heritage and the beauty in classic, older buildings, there has developed a large demand for decorative, and sometimes load-bearing, castings for renovation projects. Parkinson is only too happy to describe the jobs in which his castings have been used— places like Chicago, New York, Atlanta, and New Orleans. Other castings which are produced by Bama Foundry include railroad brake shoes, farm implements, including parts for peanut harvesting equipment, wear plates, muller wheels, plumbing fixtures, counterweights, conveyor chain sprockets, and scale testing weights.

While the concept of the casting process, or founding, is simple, the execution is much more difficult. In fact, founding is still as much an art as a science.

Architectural castings have become one of Bama Foundry's most popular products.

It appears there will always be a need for iron castings, and Bama Foundry is looking to the future, determined to be a part of that future. 🔲

The Bama Foundry operation of Alabama Machinery and Supply Company manufactures both gray iron and aluminum, machinery, construction, paving, and architectural castings.

THERMALEX, INC.

*E*ach month more than 1.6 million pounds of aluminum pass through Montgomery's Thermalex manufacturing plant where it is extruded into precision micro-tubing and shipped to automobile manufacturers worldwide.

*T*hermalex is one of only a handful of manufacturers capable of making multivoid micro extruded tubes that can withstand the extreme pressures and temperatures required by today's environmentally safe refrigeration gases.

Operating out of a $28-million plant in Montgomery's Gunter Industrial Park, Thermalex, Inc. specializes in manufacturing difficult heat exchange shapes used in automobile air conditioning condensers and evaporators, and other high-tech profiles. Although the company is only 10 years old, Thermalex already holds more than 65 percent of the condenser market and serves such major clients as General Motors and foreign automaker Nippondenso.

Thermalex, Inc. was established in 1985 as a joint venture between Thermal Components, Inc. of Montgomery and Mitsubishi Aluminum Company of Japan. The company was formed to meet the increasingly sophisticated need for precision aluminum extrusions used in the automotive, electronic, and other highly technical industries. Thermalex is one of only a handful of manufacturers capable of making multivoid micro extruded tubes that can withstand the extreme pressures and temperatures required by today's environmentally safe refrigeration gases.

In 1993 Chuck Carver was named president of the company and charged with the task of developing Thermalex into a thriving, independent entity, separate of Thermal Components Division. During the past three years, company revenues have increased more than fivefold, from $9 million to $46 million, and markets have expanded beyond the United States into the Far East, Europe, South Africa, Brazil, Argentina, Mexico, and Australia.

On average, the plant turns out between 8 and 10 million tubes per month, and demand continues to grow as more and more manufacturers discover the Thermalex standard for quality and service.

The company's 170,000-square-foot manufacturing plant includes three state-of-the-art extrusion press lines which operate 24 hours a day, 7 days a week. Over 200 employees, many of whom perform highly specialized tasks, work in three shifts.

At Thermalex, managers encourage front-line participation and decision making. Management staffs conduct daily "huddle" meetings with their teammates on the production line, resulting in better teamwork, strong morale, accurate communications, enhanced training, and the sharing of innovative ideas. Employee turnover is low, which contributes to a high level of skill and performance.

Much of the plant's operational success is attributed to the integration of corporate cultures, with the Japanese emphasis on teamwork and the American emphasis on individual initiative. The executive management team includes three Japanese managers in charge of technology and development, quality assurance, and extrusion engineering.

On the plant floor, employees wear company T-shirts espousing the Thermalex commitment to safety, quality, and productivity. The company's Total Productive Maintenance program runs through production, maintenance, engineering, shipping, and customer support to ensure customers get the product they want, when they want it.

This kind of quality and dependability is essential because Thermalex products must conform with the Automobile Industry Action Group's QS-9000 quality standards system, which is a standard international measure for accepted production practices.

The "quality first" attitude seeps through every aspect of the Thermalex operation, from equipment maintenance to product inspection and housekeeping. The company even ships its product via its own dedicated fleet of over-the-road tractor trailers to minimize damage and eliminate logistical problems.

From start to finish, the Thermalex team continues to set a higher standard for aluminum extrusions for its demanding automotive and industrial customers. *n*

*T*he company's 170,000-square-foot manufacturing plant includes three state-of-the-art extrusion press lines which operate 24 hours a day, 7 days a week.

THERMAL COMPONENTS, INC.

Thermal Components, Inc. is recognized for innovative production of heat transfer products. Established in 1971, Thermal Components Division is headquartered in the Montgomery-based Thermal Components Group, which also includes Thermalex, Inc., another Montgomery-based entity; General Thermodynamics; McKenica; and Romac Metals. These divisions strategically combine to provide across-the-board capabilities in engineering, design, machinery and equipment, and production for heat transfer products sold primarily to the automotive, trucking, and recreational vehicle industries.

The 140,000-square-foot Thermal Components plant, located in Gunter Industrial Park, includes a state-of-the-art production facility, along with nearly 10,000 square feet of administrative and engineering space. Recognizing the division's potential, Thermal's parent company, Insilco, has invested approximately $10 million in plant upgrades and expansions during the past five years, and plant employment has increased by 65 percent. Today the company employs some 365 Montgomerians with an annual payroll of approximately $8.5 million.

Thermal Components produces two primary product lines, including small and large diameter thinwall welded tubing in brass and aluminum, as well as steel and aluminum heat exchangers.

These products are sold worldwide by a direct sales force and independent sales representatives.

The company's customer base includes corporate giants like Ford Motor Company, General Motors, John Deere, and Kenworth Trucks, as well as smaller independent and privately owned enterprises such as radiator manufacturers and automobile parts distributors.

Over the years, Thermal Components has produced and sold more than 70 million pounds of high frequency welded brass thinwall tubing, more than 34 million pounds of aluminum thinwall tubing, and more than 3 million pounds of welded steel tubing. Thermal's specialized knowledge of technical processes and its attention to quality allow the company to produce the thinnest gage welded tube in the world.

Through its aggressive engineering and research and development departments, Thermal Components strives to stay on the cutting edge of its industry. Thermal has produced more than a billion feet of welded tubing, which has set a new standard for dependable service. The company also holds several patents issued for the Parallel Flow Condenser, the type used to meet today's stringent environmental regulations for HFC 134 A refrigerant.

In addition to industry-leading innovation, Thermal has an extensive testing facility. With this value-added capability, the company can build prototypes and conduct performance testing at a customer's request.

Thermal Components also operates an aftermarket distribution center that markets its products through a network of wholesale distributors. The operation sells both nationally and internationally. A recent customer survey returned a 100-percent rating for quality.

In fact, the quality first theme runs throughout each plant operation. Thermal Components maintains an aggressive quality department, and is well on its way to meeting all the stringent

requirements mandated under the world's new QS 9000 international quality manufacturing standards. The company lives by a 13-point quality policy and in 1994 earned Ford Motor Company's Q1 Preferred Quality Award.

Thermal Components produces two primary product lines, including small and large diameter thinwall welded tubing in brass and aluminum, as well as steel and aluminum heat exchangers. Photo by Greg Sailor.

In just more than 20 years, Thermal Components has become a leading supplier to the heat transfer and transportation industries. Its progressive work goes a long way in keeping the vehicles of the world on the move. With a nearly 75-percent increase in revenues during the past five years, and tremendous market expectation for its aluminum products, Thermal Components is a company on the move. *m*

Thermal's specialized knowledge of technical processes and its attention to quality allow the company to produce the thinnest gage welded tube in the world. Photo by Greg Sailor.

SABEL INDUSTRIES, INC.

During Reconstruction, when the South was struggling to overcome the devastation of the Civil War, a German immigrant named Marx Sabel combined his extraordinary determination and innovation to create an economic opportunity that has served his family well for five generations.

Sabel Industries, Inc. is the oldest business in Montgomery still run by its founding family. Keith Sabel, president and chief executive officer, is the founder's great-great-grandson. He has worked with the company for more than 20 years.

Sabel Steel was officially founded in 1869 when Marx moved to Montgomery to establish a leather and carriage distribution center. A post-war currency shortage forced him to barter his wares for old iron salvaged from the war, resulting in the birth of his scrap metal business.

As times changed, so did the Sabel enterprise. In the late 1930s, as scrap metal recycling became more lucrative, the company closed its leather works. And in 1949, as America's economy expanded, Sabel entered the new steel distribution business. By 1953 the company had built a warehouse and opened its first steel service center on North Court Street. In the mid-1960s, in answer to a market void, Keith's father, J. L., directed the company into steel reinforcing bar fabrication.

Today Sabel Industries covers 35 acres with 357,000 square feet under roof, with associated operations placed strategically throughout Alabama. In 1995 company revenues exceeded $50 million.

Sabel operates steel service centers in Montgomery, Dothan, Theodore, and Tuscaloosa to provide new steel to clients in Alabama, Georgia, the Mississippi coast, and the Florida panhandle. A member of the Steel Service Center Institute, Sabel processes nearly 90 percent of the steel it sells, including pattern burning, plate shearing, and cutting to order.

Sabel also operates two local scrap metal recycling plants which process and sell scrap metal to mini and integrated mills nationwide. With vision for the future, the company has invested in the most modern, efficient scrap recycling equipment on the market.

The Rebar Fabrication plant fabricates reinforcing steel according to construction specifications. Indicative of its superior service, Sabel labels each bundle to eliminate job site confusion and wasted time.

The Sabel Wholesale Center is a full-service wholesale/retail operation specializing in plumbing, and industrial supplies and hardware. Established in 1956, the wholesale center was the first in central Alabama to stock PVC pipe irrigation systems.

According to Keith Sabel, the company's success is attributable to its workforce of more than 225. "Our employees are our business. We want to make them our business partners and establish long-lasting relationships."

For a business almost entirely dependent on economic prosperity, Sabel Industries has had an extraordinarily successful history. And the Sabel family has shared that success with its community, serving as leaders and philanthropists. The Montgomery Museum of Fine Arts and the Montgomery Zoo are just two of the organizations that have benefited from their generous spirit.

No doubt Marx Sabel would be pleased. After more than 125 years of service, Sabel Industries has become a vital part of the support of Montgomery's strong economic foundation. 𝍖

Sabel Industries, Inc. is the oldest business in Montgomery still run by its founding family. Photo by The Robertsons.

Sabel operates two local scrap metal recycling plants which process and sell scrap metal to mini and integrated mills nationwide. Photo by The Robertsons.

SCHLUMBERGER INDUSTRIES

When Joe Breeding, vice president of personnel for the Gas and Water Division of Schlumberger Industries, talks about the company he works for, his eyes shine as brightly as the polished brass water meters on display in the lobby of Schlumberger's Tallassee, Alabama, manufacturing plant.

A publicly held company based in New York City and traded on the New York Stock Exchange, Schlumberger's interests are worldwide. Its operations are organized into two groups: Oil Field Services and Measurements and Systems. Together the two groups market 11 product lines in 110 countries and employ more than 45,000 people. In 1994 Schlumberger revenues reached nearly $7 billion.

The company, founded 75 years ago, is the world's premiere oil field services provider. "We do everything in the oil business except sell the oil," Breeding said.

Schlumberger operates a 200,000-square-foot water meter manufacturing plant in Tallassee, approximately 25 miles north of Montgomery. Prior to Schlumberger's purchase in 1987, the plant had been operated by Neptune Meter Company.

"In 1987 Schlumberger was the world's leading manufacturer of water meters, but they had no market in the United States," Breeding said. They were one of 30 companies to bid for Neptune. The acquisition was a perfect match, providing Schlumberger with an immediate United States presence and new electronic reading technology. As evidence of its commitment to the Tallassee operation, Schlumberger has invested $32 million in plant upgrades, including an $11.4 million foundry renovation.

The Tallassee plant, which employs 650 people, is one of 18 Schlumberger manufacturing facilities worldwide that makes water meters. The facility is a fully integrated, stand-alone company with its own foundry. The plant not only tools and machines its water meters from scratch, but also produces 90 percent of all the internal components.

In 1994 the plant manufactured 2 million meters, had $100 million in revenues, and pumped a $22-million payroll into the Montgomery area economy. The Tallassee operation is clearly significant. Schlumberger's Water Division worldwide manufactures approximately 7 million meters annually and controls about $500 million in revenues.

The company recently relocated its Water Management Division, under the direction of President Phillip G. Marlar, from Paris to Montgomery. Marlar, a native Montgomerian, said the company elected Montgomery in part because of its close proximity to the Tallassee plant and because "I knew it was a good place to live."

To maintain its competitive edge, Schlumberger is committed to technological development and customer responsiveness. Through aggressive research and development, and in joint venture with Motorola, Schlumberger will soon introduce a Radio Frequency System that will allow two-way radio communication between water, gas, and electric utilities and their meters. The time and cost savings to utilities and utility customers are obvious. "We try to foresee what our customers are going to need and then be the first to make it available," said Breeding.

Schlumberger is a fully integrated, stand-alone plant with its own foundry. The company not only tools and machines its water meters from scratch, but also produces 90 percent of all the internal components such as these electronic ARB registers. Photo by Fouts Commercial Photography.

A high-tech leader in other areas as well, Schlumberger pioneered "Smart Cards," which are used in 60 countries for pay phones, ticket vending machines, retail sales, and medical and banking applications.

Clearly, Schlumberger is one example of a worldwide corporation that recognizes the business value of a central Alabama location. The company is constantly working to recruit top-notch employees, Breeding said. "From this location we can offer employees just about any style of life. From our perspective, the business climate is excellent and the workforce is tremendous." *n*

Schlumberger operates a 200,000-square-foot water meter manufacturing plant in Tallassee, approximately 25 miles north of Montgomery. Photo by Fouts Commercial Photography.

QUALITY NETWORKS, INC.

*I*f experience is the best teacher, it is no wonder Kara Shea Davis and her husband Jim have had such tremendous success with their young and dynamic wiring and cable manufacturing business.

The Davises' comprehensive knowledge of wiring production, combined with their aggressive recognition of the untapped markets, prompted them to enter the wiring assembly business in 1989. They started Quality Networks, Inc. from their living room in 1989 with three partners and a $12,000 investment.

First year sales totalled $30,000, the bulk of which came from a 5,000-piece Diversified Products contract. With little money and no equipment to speak of, Mr. Davis hand-cut, stripped, and terminated the wire himself. Then in 1990, a major contract with Montgomery's Rheem Manufacturing Company propelled QNI forward. The Davises moved their plant to an empty Millbrook drugstore; but within nine months, expansion forced another move into a deserted Wetumpka retail warehouse, where they remained for two more years.

With the help of the Alabama Development Office, Quality Networks obtained a loan to construct a 30,000-square-foot plant in the Wetumpka Industrial Park. In July of 1994, the company moved in but had to build a second 30,000-square-foot plant the next year to keep up with its exponential growth.

Filling a wide-open market niche for second-tier wiring suppliers, Quality Networks grew its revenues from $30,000 in 1989 to $4.9 million in 1994 and nearly $7 million in 1995. About 70 percent of the assemblies manufactured go to the automotive and heavy truck industry, while 30 percent are used in electrical appliances.

Quality Networks, Inc. employs more than 225 employees. The company "builds from paper," which means it manufactures components according to customer specifications. QNI designs the assemblies only when a customer requests design advice or is looking for more cost-effective production processes.

Quality Networks markets and sells its products throughout the United States, Canada, and Mexico. While many of its products are shipped to the Northeast for automotive manufacturers, QNI also produces after-market products used in appliances sold nationwide by retail outlets such as Radio Shack and Wal-Mart.

Clever positioning and marketing savvy have contributed to the company's success. The Davises realized early that to compete successfully they would have to make the smaller assemblies other companies found less profitable and sell to smaller suppliers who serviced the big accounts QNI could not afford to reach. But the company's growth is also inextricably connected to National Industries' long-time success.

Quality people mean quality products, and for Quality Networks, Inc., superior products are essential to survival. All QNI automotive products meet the rigorous QSO 9000 production standards demanded by the automotive industry. Other products are meticulously built to meet the ISO 9000 international quality standard.

To achieve top-rate production, the Davises practice hands-on management, mandate regular employee training, and employ a tough quality assurance/quality control regimen. "Quality has to begin from the time a quote is given until the part is shipped," said Mrs. Davis.

With new customers calling every day and sales increasing literally in leaps and bounds, the possibilities for the future of Quality Networks, Inc. are as endless as the massive bolts of colored wire that feed its busy production lines. *77*

Quality people mean quality products. All Quality Networks, Inc. products are meticulously built to meet the ISO 9000 international quality standard.

THOMPSON TRACTOR COMPANY, INC.

When there is a power outage in an Alabama hospital, chances are those in charge will turn to a generator supplied by Thompson Power Systems. If a commercial fishing vessel on Alabama's Gulf Coast needs a dependable engine for maximum productivity, chances are the captain will select a diesel engine supplied by Thompson Power Systems. If a warehouse manager needs to replace his worn-out forklift, he can look to Thompson Lift Truck Company. And when heavy earthmoving equipment is needed on a construction site anywhere in Alabama, chances are the general contractor will also look to Thompson Tractor Company for help.

In short, Thompson Tractor Company supplies and services more than tractors . . . much more. Founded in north Alabama in 1957 by Hall W. Thompson, Thompson Tractor Company is the exclusive Caterpillar dealer for Alabama and 10 northwest Florida counties. Caterpillar Inc. is the world's largest manufacturer of earthmoving, construction, and materials handling equipment, and a major supplier of diesel and natural gas engines and turbines.

Recognized primarily for its Caterpillar connection, Thompson also supplies and services equipment by other manufacturers, including material handling equipment by Mitsubishi Caterpillar Forklift America, Royal, Teledyne Princeton, K-D Manitou, and Crown; waste recycling and forestry equipment by Morbark; and forestry equipment by Barko and Tigercat.

Under the leadership of Michael D. Thompson, a third generation Caterpillar dealer principal, the company services a diverse market through three business entities. Thompson markets traditional Caterpillar earthmoving and heavy equipment and product support through Thompson Tractor Company. Thompson Lift Truck Company is the source for material handling equipment; and Thompson Power Systems supplies Caterpillar diesel engines and power systems for prime and standby power. The company's far-reaching customer base includes the mining industry, the industrial market, governments, forestry products, building and heavy construction, manufacturing, transportation, warehousing, and the wholesale and retail industries.

One of only 40 authorized Caterpillar dealers in North America, Thompson is based in Birmingham and employs more than 800 people in 12 offices throughout Alabama and the Florida panhandle. The company is divided into four regions, including the southern region which is based in Montgomery and operated under the direction of Philip Lee, southern region manager.

Thompson's Montgomery office building, located on U.S. Highway 80, just off Interstate 85 in east Montgomery, was built in 1977 and originally occupied by the former South Alabama Caterpillar dealer. Thompson acquired that dealership and the 125,000-square-foot facility in 1987, extending its exclusive dealership statewide and into Florida.

Thompson has long been Alabama's market leader among heavy equipment, diesel engine, and lift truck dealers. "We have a strong market share because of the strength of our product and the quality of our service," said Lee. "We are only as good as our people. We work hard to develop and train our people to be the best."

The Thompson Tractor Co. Inc. Montgomery office building, is located on U.S. Highway 80, just off Interstate 85 in east Montgomery.

Indeed, Thompson operates a full-time, in-house training program to ensure all field service technicians are skilled and knowledgeable about all Thompson products. The company concentrates heavily on preventive maintenance, performing diagnostic tests on working equipment to predict and prevent potential maintenance problems before they occur.

In addition to sales and service, Thompson also rents, leases, and finances equipment according to customer need. "We want it to be as easy as possible for our customers to do business with us," said Lee. "Our mission is to be a business partner with each of our customers." *m*

Shown are some of the smiling faces that greet customers at the Thompson Tractor Co., Inc. Montgomery facility.

ALBANY INTERNATIONAL CORPORATION
APPLETON WIRE DIVISION

*I*n 1995 the Appleton Wire Division of Albany International Corporation celebrated its centennial anniversary as one of the world's leading suppliers to the papermaking industry. Since the company's founding as a small family-owned mill in Appleton, Wisconsin, its industry and its products have changed dramatically, and Appleton Wire has consistently been at the forefront of that progress.

Albany International, the world's leading supplier of technologically sophisticated products called paper machine clothing, has 34 plants located in 13 countries.

Albany International is the world's leading supplier of technologically sophisticated products called paper machine "clothing." These products are produced at 34 plants in 13 countries and used on paper machines worldwide to produce all grades of paper from lightweight sanitary tissue to heavyweight container board. These custom-designed, engineered fabrics are manufactured from monofilament and synthetic fiber materials and are essential to paper manufacturing.

While Albany International serves the world with products for all stages of the papermaking process, the company's Appleton Wire Division produces the high-tech plastics used in the critical "forming" process at the front-end of the papermaking process.

Appleton Wire-Montgomery is one of four plants in Albany's Appleton Wire Division. The Montgomery plant is the largest and most versatile synthetic forming fabric manufacturing plant in North America, producing approximately 15 percent of the forming fabrics used in the United States paper industry today.

The plant is located on a 33-acre site on Bell Road near the Troy Highway. When the facility was built in 1952, it encompassed only 15,640 square feet and was located six miles outside the city. But over the years, the city and the plant have grown. Today, the 150,000-square-foot facility employs some 175 employees who together represent more than 3,000 years of experience in the papermaking industry.

An incredibly high percentage of long-time, dedicated employees are at the heart of the successful Montgomery operation. Appleton Wire's impact as a stable employer and vital contributor to the local economy is evidenced by an employee turnover rate of less than one percent.

"There is a combination of things that make us the best at what we do, but I believe the expertise of our people is the real strength behind this operation," said Human Resource Manager Ted Bryant. "Although many of our employees have been in this business all of their lives, they are open to innovation, willing to change, and always looking at opportunities for process improvement."

Appleton Wire's past could well be indicative of what it can do for future developments in the papermaking industry. Paper machine clothing was originally made of metal wire weaving, hence the name Appleton Wire. But in the 1970s the company pioneered the transition to strong, heat-tolerant, high-tech plastic fabrics—an initiative that has forever changed the paper industry. In addition, Appleton Wire has been a leader in developing advanced forming fabrics, especially multilayered fabrics, that are considered today's industry standard.

Among the company's customers benefiting from this uncompromising quest for excellence are Procter & Gamble, Kimberly Clark, International Paper, James River, Union Camp, Georgia-Pacific, Weyerhaeuser, Champion International, Consolidated Papers, S. D. Warren, and Mead Paper. "We have worked hard to earn a fine reputation in a competitive industry; to maintain that position we must keep our customers first," said Bryant.

Positive attitude, innovation, customer service, and the strength of dedicated employees are driving Appleton Wire into a successful second century. *M*

The Montgomery plant, which was built in 1952, employs 175 people and is located on a 33-acre site on Bell Road near the Troy Highway.

GILES ENTERPRISES, INC.

*G*iles Enterprises, Inc. is four related, yet distinct, businesses in one. Operating out of a 100,000-square-foot manufacturing facility in Gunter Industrial Park, Giles serves numerous customers, including restaurants, supermarkets, convenience stores, wholesale distributors, schools, and foodservice management companies.

Giles was founded as a family concern in 1952. It is now a privately held corporation that has achieved its success through dedication to quality and customer service.

The four divisions that make up Giles Enterprises, Inc. are Chester Fried, Chester Fried International, Chester Fried South, and Giles Foodservice Equipment. Each division centers on the products, equipment, and supplies required for the production of Chester Fried Chicken. Although the sales, marketing, and distribution of these products may vary according to division, the end result is great tasting Chester Fried Chicken.

The origin of this product is the manufacturing of the equipment and the blending of breading and spices at the Chester Fried division. As a manufacturer of different size fryers and deli equipment, along with blended products, Chester Fried targets the retail foodservice industry across North America. The brand Chester Fried consists of a marketing program available to those retailers who maintain the standards and guidelines of the Chester Fried registered trademark. This program offers a "branded identity" with the Chester Fried Express supported by a grand opening package, training, point of purchase advertising, packaging, signs, and uniforms.

These products are distributed across the United States and Canada by a network of authorized Chester Fried distributing companies.

Each is assigned a marketing area and is charged with the sales and promotion of Chester Fried to retailers. As with each Chester Fried distributing company, Chester Fried South handles sales, service, training, support, and promotion of Chester Fried across the Southeast.

The third division is Chester Fried International. As a franchise company, Giles has taken its operation expertise and the Chester Fried menu and added several complete store design packages to offer Chester Fried franchises outside of North America. Because Chester Fried has operated successfully within retail operations domestically, international can capitalize on that experience by targeting nontraditional outlets, such as kiosks, express units, and smaller in-line stores. Using this approach, Chester Fried International is able to concentrate on numerous points of distribution with limited investment costs.

Key to the success of smaller, nontraditional marketing is ventless technology. In 1988 Giles patented the ventless hood for foodservice equipment, eliminating the need for outside venting of appliances by cleaning smoke and grease-laden vapor through a series of built-in filters.

This technology has also contributed to the success of Giles Foodservice Equipment. Giles markets a line of predominantly ventless equipment, along with a line of ovens and fryers. Giles'

*G*iles Enterprises depends on quality to maintain continued growth both in North America and abroad for it great tasting Chester Fried Chicken.

equipment allows customers to place operations in areas such as malls and airports that would otherwise be inaccessible. Giles currently supplies Pizza Hut and Chili's, and has installed equipment in locations such as Dodger Stadium, Disney World, the Los Angeles International Airport, and countless others.

The divisions encompassed in Giles Enterprises, Inc. are distinct entities that serve the foodservice industry. By focusing on similar aspects of manufacturing, each division is able to tailor its marketing and industry knowledge to its particular niche and serve its respective customers with an emphasis on quality. Giles Enterprises, Inc. depends on quality to maintain continued growth both in North America and abroad. ▨

*O*perating out of a 100,000-square-foot manufacturing facility in Gunter Industrial Park, Giles serves numerous customers, including restaurants, supermarkets, convenience stores, wholesale distributors, schools, and foodservice management companies.

ALABAMA COMPUTER ASSOCIATES

Five years ago, the entrepreneurial-spirited Rick and Kathy Murchison were looking to change careers and establish a business. Rick, a native Montgomerian, had just completed a 20-year flying career with the Navy. Although the Murchisons considered leaving the Capital City and studied a variety of business options, the challenge and dynamics of the computer business, along with family ties, convinced them to stay and invest here.

"We knew we had something to offer in that we wanted to advise people in an ethical and honorable way. We wanted to develop and cultivate customers for the long haul. We have always been committed to building a business that will grow and stay and not evaporate," said Commander Murchison.

A*labama Computer Associates identifies computer needs, builds to suit, installs, networks, and trains.*

The two opened a retail store on Zelda Road in October 1991. By the spring of 1993, they had to double their floor space and increase staffing. The Murchisons showcase their retail stock, which includes personal computers, peripheral items such as printers, plotters, and scanners, and a variety of educational and productivity-related software on one side of the store. The other side is devoted to "construction and instruction." From that area, the Murchisons construct their own brand of personal computers, repair their computers and other IBM compatible machinery, and offer hands-on technical training.

The full-service operation is, indeed, just that. Alabama Computer Associates identifies computer needs, builds to suit, installs, networks, and trains.

ACA computers are designed and constructed with two key requirements in mind. First, the company carefully assesses what the system must be able to accomplish for the customer. That understanding leads to specific software requirements, which ultimately define hardware specifications. Second, strict adherence to non-proprietary industry standards assures durability, quality, and long-term economical upgrades.

That commitment to cost-effectiveness is at the center of the Murchisons' business philosophy. The staff of experts at Alabama Computer Associates will often recommend minor procedural changes to prevent an unnecessary computer purchase. "We feel if we help you avoid unnecessary expense now, you will come back to us when you really need a computer," said Commander Murchison.

Alabama Computer Associates' customers range from home computer owners to large corporations, state agencies, and schools. Because the company is expert in troubleshooting, networking systems, and providing technical training, more and more businesses are turning to Alabama Computer Associates. Among the company's clients are Weil Brothers Cotton, Troy State University, and the Montgomery Area Mental Health Authority.

At the core of their business is a desire to help others. The company provides pro bono computer repair, cost-free recycled parts, and technical support to their Partner In Education, Dannelly Elementary School, as well as to Dalraida Elementary School. They also assist the Military/Civilian Microcomputer Society in their efforts to provide computer repair to the Montgomery County Public Schools. The company even sponsors a Dixie Gray girls softball team.

I*n October 1991 Rick and Kathy Murchison opened a retail store on Zelda Road. By the spring of 1993, they had to double their floor space and increase staffing.*

For the long term, the Murchisons are exploring possibilities for marketing their computers on a national basis. "We are making plans to move into production and manufacturing in a major way," said Kathy Murchison. "But our 'mom and pop' storefront is not going to go away. We will be here, listening to our customers' needs and doing all we can to meet them, for a long time to come." *n*

KERSHAW MANUFACTURING COMPANY, INC.

In the half-century since Kershaw Manufacturing Company was founded, the railroad industry has changed dramatically; and, to the company's credit, many of the changes are a result of Kershaw's pioneering work.

Kershaw Manufacturing Company is one of the world's leading manufacturers of railway maintenance equipment, offering a diverse product line of more than 50 machines. The company's innovative and effective machinery, which is designed, fabricated, and manufactured at its Montgomery headquarters, has proven useful not just for the railroad industry, but also for utility and forestry industries worldwide. Kershaw's customers include most of the major railroads and many utility companies in more than 40 countries.

Kershaw Manufacturing Company was founded by Royce G. Kershaw Sr., who embarked upon his career in 1924. For more than 20 years, Kershaw supervised the construction or repair of more than 4,000 miles of railroad track across North America. The effort was slow, tedious work and required the labor of massive workforces. In the mid 1940s, to better serve his customers and to increase profits, Kershaw devised a simple piece of machinery which he believed would reduce labor requirements and speed his work. The railroad industry enthusiastically embraced his innovative ballast regulator, demand grew, and in the early 1950s, Kershaw quit the contracting business for full-time manufacturing.

"He was a true pioneer in every sense of the word," said Royce G. Kershaw Jr., who now leads the worldwide company. "At that time there was very little mechanization available for railway maintenance—he realized there were opportunities."

And the elder Mr. Kershaw took advantage of those opportunities. On the heels of the ballast regulator came the ballast cribbing machine and other equipment used to maintain and replace the railway structure, including the steel rails, crossties, and ballasts (stone) below the crossties.

Almost 20 years ago, Kershaw Manufacturing Company moved its operations from West Fairview Avenue to a 250-acre site in Mount Meigs. More than 200 people work at the complex, which includes 150,000 square feet of manufacturing space and administrative offices that house engineering, sales and marketing, customer service, accounting, and general office professionals.

The company recently embarked on a long-term program to develop procedures and documentation for ISO 9000 certification—an international standard of manufacturing excellence necessary for global marketing, and important to Kershaw's future growth.

Kershaw Manufacturing Company is based at a 250-acre site in Mount Meigs and employs more than 225 people.

While the railroad is considered vintage Americana, and the United States boasts the finest railway system in the world, foreign markets today offer some of Kershaw's greatest opportunities. To reach its far and wide markets, Kershaw has enhanced its network of product representatives and is aggressively marketing its goods globally in more than 100 markets. Even more opportunity arises from product obsolescence, and Kershaw continually strives to improve its own products and to find ways to serve its customers more efficiently. "Our engineers want to improve on our products, even to make our own products obsolete, so our customers will have even better choices."

A golden anniversary is usually a time to reflect on past successes, and rightly so, for the Kershaw Manufacturing Company has put a historic stamp on the American railroad. But with a strong product line, global opportunity, and aggressive marketing, it is clear Kershaw is facing forward, with vision for the next 50 years. *M*

Kershaw Manufacturing Company is one of the world's leading manufacturers of railway maintenance equipment.

SIMCALA, INC.

An American flag waves proudly above the site of Simcala Inc.'s Mount Meigs plant site, representative of the facility's stature as the nation's largest United States-owned and operated silicon plant.

Located about 15 miles northeast of Montgomery in rural Mount Meigs, the impressive Simcala manufacturing operation may be one the area's best kept secrets. Built in 1975, the plant is still the newest silicon metal producing plant in the United States. The second largest user of Alabama Power Company-generated electricity in the state, the Simcala plant has three 20,000 kilowatt electric furnaces, each with the capacity to reach 3000 degrees Fahrenheit or higher, and produces an annual capacity of 40,000 net tons of silicon metal and 18,000 net tons of microsilica.

The plant location is ideal for its task as the raw materials used in the manufacturing process, including high purity gravel, metallurgical coal, and woodchips, are in plentiful abundance nearby. In addition, the plant's proximity to Interstate 85 and adjacent railroads makes for convenient distribution.

Simcala employs 170, while its production process creates an additional 510 jobs indirectly related to the operation.

Silicon metal is used in the chemical industry as the basic raw material for the production of silicones. It is also used as an alloying agent in the production of both primary and secondary aluminum. Silicon is also a necessary ingredient in the manufacture of many aluminum castings, die castings, and extrusions. In addition, a small amount of silicon metal serves as the base material for solar and electronic silicons. The microsilica that leaves the plant is used in the refractory, concrete, and minerals industries. Silicon products are sold to a wide variety of customers across the nation, including such notable corporations as GE Silicons, Dow Corning, and Wabash Alloys.

The plant was owned and operated for nearly 20 years by Simetco, Inc. of Canton, Ohio, before being acquired in February 1995 by Simcala, Inc., owned by Capital One Partners, Charter Oak, and the management team. The acquisition not only breathed life back into the operation, but it also moved the company's corporate headquarters from Canton, Ohio, to Montgomery, Alabama.

Under the direction of President and Chief Executive Officer Eddie Boardwine, more than $8 million in upgrades will position the plant to better serve a growing market. "The silicon metal market is exhibiting strong demand growth," said Boardwine. "We intend to take advantage of that demand with efficient facilities operating at capacity and well-trained employees who are equal to the challenge this industry affords."

Simcala recognizes the value of its 170 employees, providing hands-on technical training by instructors from John Patterson State Technical College and the state-supported Alabama Institute of Development and Training. The company also offers other general educational programs and puts each worker through an intensive safety training program.

The Simcala operation maintains a weekly payroll in excess of $120,000 and has an indirect impact on the area's economy, brought about by the effects of wages and material purchases, of some $45 million annually. In addition to its large staff, the Simcala production process creates an additional 510 jobs indirectly related to the operation.

Simcala, Inc. has a proud past and an even more exciting future. It is a thriving business, a vital employer, a valued materials supplier in today's technological world, and a major contributor to the growing central Alabama economy.

Simcala Inc.'s Mount Meigs plant site is the nation's largest United States-owned and operated silicon plant.

DOW-UNITED TECHNOLOGIES COMPOSITE PRODUCTS, INC.

What do you get when you combine the advanced materials experience of Dow Chemical with the design and manufacturing know-how of United Technologies Corporation? A first-rate composites manufacturing facility in central Alabama bringing quality space-age composite products to market.

In late 1989, Dow Chemical and United Technologies initiated a joint venture to establish a commercial composites production facility in neighboring Tallassee, Alabama. The resulting $240-million state-of-the-art plant manufactures polymer-based composites used in the space, aerospace, and automotive industries.

The facility, loaded with the finest composite manufacturing equipment available in the world, encompasses nearly 270,000 square feet, including 64,000 square feet of high-tech clean room space for particle-free production. It runs 24 hours a day under the control of more than 350 technicians skilled in fabricating and assembling composite structures.

Dow-UT has brought more than 30 years of proven defense industry experience to its Alabama plant and is reaching a new level of commercial viability in composite production. Working strenuously to produce the highest quality products at the lowest possible price, Dow-UT is producing a viable product that competes for a wide spectrum of military, commercial, and industrial applications.

Today's composite products have a dimensional accuracy and an extraordinary stability that allows them to replace metal parts traditionally used on airplanes, helicopters, satellites, automobiles, and other products. The composites are lighter and have a higher fatigue tolerance.

In Tallassee, Dow-UT and its dedicated employees are taking every step to earn their market share. "In 30 years of manufacturing, this is the finest workforce I've ever been associated with," Tony Cacace, director of Dow-UT's Alabama operations, said. "These people want to be successful and they are willing to do what it takes."

With 17 process engineers on staff, the company offers full engineering, product design, tool design and fabrication, process planning, and product development services. The design staff utilizes computer-aided design and manufacturing systems to design products and analyze performance. Dow-UT engineers work closely with customer product designers to optimize their efforts; and a fully staffed materials laboratory provides the resources to test potential manufacturing materials.

To further enhance customer service, the company has installed a "visual factory" on the manufacturing floor to encourage management participation and employee ownership. Using bulletin boards, placed strategically at key manufacturing operations throughout the plant, each production team measures output against performance targets in quality, schedule, cost, process, and people. This integrated process encourages innovation, ownership, and continuous process improvement throughout the workforce.

Dow-UT's commitment to production excellence earned the company the 1991 Alabama Senate Productivity Award for achievements in quality and productivity.

Uncompromising excellence has earned Dow-UT a worldwide customer base which includes such corporate giants as Lockheed, McDonnell Douglas, Sikorsky Aircraft, Chrysler Corporation, Boeing, Rohr Aero Services, and Texas Instruments. The plant produces critical components for such intriguing products as the United States Army's Black Hawk helicopter; Sikorsky's 53-E, the free world's largest helicopter; Lockheed satellites; and Chrysler's Viper sports car. With a product four times stronger than steel, market potential is staggering.

From its people, to its processes, to its product, Dow-United Technologies Composite Products, Inc. is a fine example of visionary leadership and corporate excellence at work in central Alabama.

Uncompromising excellence has earned Dow-UT a worldwide customer base which includes such corporate giants as Lockheed, McDonnell Douglas, Sikorsky Aircraft, Chrysler Corporation, Boeing, Rohr Aero Services, and Texas Instruments.

Located in neighboring Tallassee, Dow-United Technologies Composite Products' $240-million state-of-the art plant manufactures polymer-based composites used in the space, aerospace, and automotive industries.

WELLS PRINTING COMPANY

Arthur and Lubie Wells started their printing business with a single small press situated on one side of a cow stall. It had to be a small press to leave ample room for the cow on the other side.

The traditional Wells Printing Company work ethic is enhanced by its attention to equipment and technology.

Today, nearly 50 years later, as Arthur and Lubie's sons carry on the Wells Printing Company legacy, space is not a problem, and the closest thing to farm animals are the humming-birds that flitter at the feeder in the front garden.

After 45 years and all the expansions city zoning would allow at its original Simmons Drive location, Gene and Irvin Wells moved the print shop to its new location at Perimeter Park. The modern 33,000-square-foot facility, equipped with state-of-the-art machinery and amenities, is a far cry from the first shop; but the homespun service and warm smiles that have always been Wells Printing Company still remain.

For years Wells Printing Company made its place by backing up other printers during peak production. Today, other printers look to Wells as an industry leader and an example of customer service at its finest. The reputation that follows Wells is based on a history of honesty, integrity, and hard work. "We try to do everything we say we will do. If it takes 24 hours a day, seven days a week, we will do it on time, if there is any way humanly possible," said Irvin Wells.

The traditional Wells Printing Company work ethic is enhanced by its attention to equipment and technology. The company prides itself in leading the way to take advantage of emerging technologies, for its customers' sakes. Its $4-million facility is loaded with a complete offering of top-of-the-line equipment designed to take a project from conception to distribution. Wells was one of the first printers in the area to move into in-house desktop publishing, and one of the first to buy a four-color short-run press. Recently the company purchased a high-tech $1.4-million five color with coater fully-automated press, so far the only one like it in the state.

But even the finest equipment doesn't run itself. Wells' 37-member staff is one of the most experienced in the business. A family-oriented environment that encourages participation has spawned an extraordinary record of employee longevity and loyalty. And it is the customer who benefits from the know-how. "Our people are the most important asset we have," said Gene Wells. "We listen to them, we keep them informed, and we enjoy our time together."

Although business started small, Wells today serves clients all across America and the world. From Branson, Missouri, to New York and California, clients looking for quality and cost-efficiency call on Wells. Barry Gager, a long-time account executive, explains the success. "In today's world it doesn't matter where you are physically located, as long as you perform—and we perform."

Indeed, the company performs in its community as well, often providing complimentary design and printing for worthy civic, arts, and educational programs. "We don't do it for the hoopla," said Irvin Wells. "It's what we believe in."

With humility amidst great success, Wells Printing Company is well grounded. Its eye is locked on a single goal—to maintain its 50-year tradition of customer service with integrity and trust.

The modern 33,000-square-foot Wells Printing Company is equipped with state-of-the-art machinery and amenities.

MONTGOMERY OFFICE EQUIPMENT

Mike Motley, president of Montgomery Office Equipment, has found that service is the key to selling in the competitive world of office equipment. Founded in 1959 by Motley's father, Max Motley, the company has prospered through the years because of its customer commitment.

Established as Dean and Motley Office Equipment, the company's name soon changed when a third partner, Tom Kelley joined the team. Since opening as a three-man enterprise, Montgomery Office Equipment has grown to staff 35 employees, half of whom make up the firm's respected service staff.

Mike Motley, who took over the reigns of the company from his father in 1983, was raised in the equipment business. As a result, he was prepared to deal with the complexities of the rapidly changing business environment.

Motley first began working in the business during his summer breaks from high school. After graduating from Lee High School in 1961, Motley knew it was the equipment business that held his interest. He initially started his own business in nearby Alexander City, Alabama, but elected in 1967 to sell the business to return to his hometown and Montgomery Office Equipment. In 1995 Motley's Office Equipment

Co. opened in Alexander City. The business is managed by Rusty Motley, Mike's brother.

Motley's business partner, O'Neal Wright, was a vital part of the company from 1983 until his death in 1993. Wright focused on the sales end of the business, growing the company's client base and building loyal customers, while Motley supervised the operational side of the thriving business.

Mike recognized early on that the key to selling effectively was in giving the customer superior service. "If you can't fix what you sell, they aren't going to buy it," said Motley. It is a simple wisdom that has proven profitable as Montgomery Office Equipment has risen to the forefront of office equipment sales and service in the Montgomery area.

In the early days the company was located on Commerce Street and specialized in typewriters, calculators, cash registers, copiers, equipment, and supplies. Today the company specializes in a diverse line of copy machines, fax machines, and related items to meet the needs of the smallest "home office" business to the largest corporate headquarters.

The company's concentration on expedient service and astute salesmanship netted the company some $3.5 million in volume in the past year.

Montgomery Office Equipment has carried the Minolta Copier line for more than 20 years. It also carries Toshiba copiers and Xerox copiers for engineering needs such as blueprint copies.

Mike Motley, president of Montgomery Office Equipment, has found that service is the key to selling in the competitive world of office equipment.

The company's dedication to service even extends to creating innovative service software, which the company has written and sold to other companies throughout the world.

Montgomery Office Equipment's convenient location on the corner of Arba and Hull Streets, just off Interstate 85 near downtown, has proven to be a successful one. The company is in a central location within easy reach of all areas of Montgomery's business community. "We can be anywhere in the city within about 10 minutes or less," said Motley. "This location enhances our ability to serve our customers responsively."

Convenience, excellent service, and quality equipment are all central to the internal workings of this successful home-owned business. As sales and service professionals, the people at Montgomery Office Equipment work hard to ensure their company is running as efficiently and effectively as their customers' machinery. **M**

Today Montgomery Office Equipment specializes in a diverse line of copy machines, fax machines, and related items to meet the needs of the smallest "home office" business to the largest corporate headquarters.

BLOUNT INTERNATIONAL, INC.

The brilliant 50-year history of Blount International, Inc. (NYSE: BLT.A and BLT.B) is a story of business savvy, instinct, courage, statesmanship, generosity, rebound, and commitment to excellence.

Under the leadership of Founder and Chairman of the Board Winton M. "Red" Blount, the company has become a diversified industrial leader dedicated to manufacturing and marketing quality outdoor products, industrial and power equipment, and sporting equipment worldwide.

But prior to earning its place on the international Fortune 500 list of America's largest manufacturers, Blount gained international prominence as one of America's premiere building contractors.

The business upon which Blount International, Inc. was founded began in 1946 when Winton M. "Red" Blount and his brother, Houston, returned to their Union Springs, Alabama, home to run the sand and gravel business their father had built. Fueled by their entrepreneurial spirit, Red Blount led the two headlong into the construction business.

The company's first contracts were to build fish ponds around Union Springs, followed by highway and bridge construction in Alabama and Mississippi. In 1949 Blount Brothers won its first $1 million contract for construction of the First Avenue viaduct in Birmingham.

In the 1950s and '60s, Blount recognized the profitability of high-risk projects and built a reputation for quality work by taking on projects such as the Cape Canaveral launch complex where the first manned space flight to the moon lifted off in 1969.

In 1968, when Red Blount was named United States Postmaster General by President Richard Nixon, the company halted all federal work and successfully developed its private industrial base.

In the late 1970s as domestic construction slowed, Blount turned its attention internationally and earned, among other profitable projects, a joint venture contract to build the $3.5-billion King Saud University in Riyadh, Saudi Arabia, the largest lump sum contract ever awarded.

In the early 1990s, facing economic uncertainties and determined to secure long-term profitability for the company's shareholders, Blount departed from construction and concentrated its resources and management talents on the manufacturing operations, which had been strategically acquired during the '70s and '80s.

Today, under the direction of President and Chief Executive Officer John M. Panettiere, Blount, Inc. has more than 4,600 employees and operates 14 manufacturing facilities in North and South America. It distributes and sells products in more than 130 countries worldwide.

The three-pronged manufacturing operation includes an Outdoor Products Group, which manufactures saw chains, bars, sprockets, maintenance accessories, industrial cutting products, and home and garden products; an Industrial and Power Equipment Group, which manufactures large mechanical timber harvesting equipment, power transmission and hydraulic and gear components; and a Sporting Equipment Group, which makes and markets ammunition, shooting sports accessories, gun care equipment, and a full line of sports optics products.

In 1996 sales increased almost 10 percent to $644.3 million. The company's market leadership is largely attributable to aggressive research and development aimed at product enhancement and innovation, as well as diverse and extensive distribution channels.

While Blount is on a global quest, it has never lost sight of its corporate responsibilities. Blount's corporate contributions and Red Blount's personal generosity in the areas of economic development, educational support, charitable giving, and the arts are considered second to none. The Wynton M. Blount Cultural Park, home to the Montgomery Museum of Fine Arts and the world-class Alabama Shakespeare Festival Complex, is foremost among Mr. Blount's countless contributions.

While the business of Blount has changed substantially, the company has used every endeavor to enhance the quality of life for those it employs and those it serves. The Blount impact in Montgomery, and everywhere it has a business presence, is a sterling example of world-class quality and commitment. 77

Under the leadership (right) Winton M. "Red" Blount, founder and chairman of the board and John M. Panettiere, president and chief executive officer, the company has become a diversified industrial leader dedicated to manufacturing and marketing quality outdoor products, industrial and power equipment, and sporting equipment worldwide.

Blount International, Inc.'s corporate headquarters are located at 4520 Executive Park Drive.

BUSINESS & FINANCE

Montgomery's business, insurance, and financial community offers a strong base for the area's growing economy. Photo by Robert Fouts.

MONTGOMERY AREA CHAMBER OF COMMERCE

As the years go by, the challenges facing the Montgomery Area Chamber of Commerce change in sync with the opportunities that present themselves to a dynamic and progressive community. But the Chamber's mission, targeted at enhancing the area's economic well-being, creating and preserving jobs, and improving the quality of life for all Montgomerians, remains steadfastly the same.

In the early 1870s, when the organization was founded, its first project was to pave Commerce Street, the major business artery running between the center of town and the Alabama River. Today, more than a century-and-a-quarter later, the Chamber is still committed to fundamental economic improvements, but they range in complexity from courting multi-million-dollar high-tech industries to providing business education workshops for aspiring entrepreneurs and small business owners.

Both integral components of the Montgomery community, Maxwell and Gunter are unequivocally among the area's most important socioeconomic contributors. Photo courtesy of Maxwell-Gunter AFB.

and the site of the high-tech Standard Systems Group.

The military recruitment efforts continued after World War I, when the Chamber worked diligently to make Maxwell the center of Air Force professional education and home to the internationally renowned Air University. Both integral components of the Montgomery community, Maxwell and Gunter are unequivocally among the area's most important socioeconomic contributors.

The Chamber has also long held quality educational programming as a priority. Over the years, Chamber officials have worked closely with governmental leaders and educators to help establish and promote strong institutions of higher learning, including Huntingdon College, Alabama State University, Auburn University at Montgomery, Troy State University at Montgomery, Trenholm State Technical College, and John M. Patterson State Technical College.

In recent years, the Chamber established a visionary Education Council, which brought together some of the most innovative minds in the community to research and implement progressive, long-term solutions for strengthening Montgomery's public education system. "The Chamber would like to see a community educating its children to the highest potential," said Margaret Carpenter. "Education is fundamental to our future."

Clearly, strong educational opportunities spawn business and industrial growth, and the Montgomery Area Chamber is well prepared to handle it. The Chamber's economic development initiatives have earned it a ranking among the top five middle market chambers in the United States. In 1995 *Southern Business and Development* magazine named two Montgomery Chamber professionals Southern Economic Development Practitioner Award winners. This national recognition is due largely to the Chamber's successful recruitment of such leading companies as Liz Claiborne, Inc., GE Plastics, Miltope, Blue Bell Ice Cream, and Jefferson Smurfitt to the Montgomery area.

"From an organizational perspective, this

The Chamber established a visionary Education Council, which brought together some of the most innovative minds in the community to research and implement progressive, long-term solutions for strengthening Montgomery's public education system, such as the Chamber's first female chairman, Margaret Carpenter. Photo by Fouts Commercial Photography.

Chamber is held in high esteem by its peers," said Montgomery Area Chamber of Commerce President Randy George. "Many of the professional staff have held leadership positions at the national level and have earned accolades for their work. But if not for the tremendous partnerships that exist among our staff, our community volunteers, our members, and our local government, the level of work we undertake simply would not be accomplished."

Since 1992 the Chamber's work has been focused on achieving the goals outlined in the *Forefront Montgomery* economic development initiative, a five-year strategic plan devised by Chamber volunteers to prepare the Montgomery area for the challenges of the twenty-first century. The plan originally called for the creation of 10,000 new jobs by 1997, but the Chamber significantly surpassed that goal in just three years, and issued a challenge goal calling instead for 20,000 new jobs in the same five-year period. As

Since its founding, the Montgomery Area Chamber has been a significant driving force behind the community's growth and development. With efforts beginning in the 1890s, the organization led the way in securing a navigable channel on the Alabama River between the city of Mobile and Montgomery, a massive project that took some 80 years to complete.

In 1910 the Chamber enticed the Wright brothers to establish a pilot-training airfield on a site that is now part of Maxwell Air Force Base. The organization also encouraged the lease of the city's municipal airport to the Army Air Corps, now the home of the Gunter Annex of Maxwell,

a result of its outstanding success, the Montgomery Area Chamber was named one of the top 10 economic development organizations in the country by *Site Selection* magazine in 1993.

The Montgomery Area Chamber of Commerce has a dedicated membership of more than 1,700 and operates in the capable hands of a 34-member professional staff. The board of directors is composed of 52 business professionals, including the six Chamber officers. Within the Chamber, six councils, made up of members and staff, work to accomplish the goals set out in the *Forefront Montgomery* strategic plan and the annual operational strategy, the Plan of Action.

Recognizing the changing societal trend away from mega-businesses and toward smaller, more efficient business enterprises, the Montgomery Area Chamber of Commerce has used its resources to implement the innovative and popular Council on Small Business Enterprises (COSBE) to strengthen Montgomery's growing small business community. "Small business is not only at the foundation of this organization, but it is also at the foundation of this country," said George. "More than 85 percent of the businesses in this community are small businesses, and it is incumbent upon us to support them to the fullest."

Well-received COSBE programs range from educational seminars and workshops to discounted small group insurance programs and an annual awards program celebrating Montgomery's "Emerging 30," the area's finest new businesses.

Tourism and convention development is also integral to the Chamber's overall economic development strategy. In 1974 the Chamber implemented its Convention and Visitor Development Council and began focusing on building the city's reputation as a convention and tourist destination. A key to the Chamber's success in this market was the establishment of the Montgomery Civic Center in the center of the downtown business district.

Operating from offices in the Chamber's beautiful antebellum Welcome Center in historic Old Alabama Town, the Chamber's Convention and Visitor Development staff promotes the area's widely diverse offering of educational and recreational attractions, including the historic Alabama State Capitol, the First White House of the Confederacy, the famous Dexter Avenue King Memorial Baptist Church, the world-renowned Alabama Shakespeare Festival Theater, the newly expanded Montgomery Zoo, and the annual Jubilee CityFest celebration.

As part of its downtown development strategy, the Chamber added riverfront revitalization to the Forefront Montgomery plan in 1995. Montgomery's picturesque riverfront property is a focal point in the region's development as a center of commerce and tourism. City leadership has already made significant strides toward development of the riverfront with the creation of Overlook Park, high atop a bluff of the Alabama River with a spectacular view of downtown. This is in addition to a $325-million downtown renaissance that includes the beautiful Embassy Suites Hotel, the Blue-Gray Room addition to the Montgomery Civic Center, and luxury office complexes developed by the Retirement Systems of Alabama.

Although the Montgomery Area Chamber of Commerce faces a multitude of challenging tasks,

Montgomery's picturesque riverfront property is a focal point in the region's development as a center of commerce and tourism. Photo by Fouts Commercial Photography.

it has a multitude of impressive resources at its disposal. A skilled and innovative staff, dedicated volunteers, and supportive local governments combine in a partnership that makes the Montgomery Area Chamber one of the finest in America, according to the United States Chamber of Commerce.

It is through these strengths that the Montgomery Area Chamber of Commerce successfully heralds the community's rich heritage, progressive vibrancy, and strong business climate—the characteristics that make Montgomery and the surrounding area a superior location for the enjoyment of both living and working. *m*

The Chamber worked in cooperation with Mayor Emory Folmar and other city leaders to spawn the revitalization of downtown Montgomery. Photo by Fouts Commercial Photography.

SOUTHERN GUARANTY
INSURANCE COMPANY

Since its founding in 1952, Southern Guaranty Insurance Company has combined conservative business practices and sound planning to earn a place among the South's most stable and trusted carriers of property and casualty insurance coverages. A business philosophy based on conservative underwriting and loss reserving has placed the Montgomery-based firm in a position of regional influence.

When Jim L. Ridling joined Southern Guaranty as president and chief executive officer in 1987, one of his main priorities was to establish new company ownership. Foremost among his considerations was to find an owner able to provide long-term stability in return for ownership of a proven, strong, and successful southeastern company. He looked for a parent company that possessed the financial strength to augment Southern Guaranty's stability; one that held a long-term, value-oriented approach to the United States property-liability insurance market; one that had a history of commitment to the insurance industry and a discipline equal to that of Southern Guaranty; and one that would appreciate the value of Southern Guaranty's marketplace, its people, its agents, and its history.

In 1988 Winterthur Swiss Insurance Group, of Winterthur, Switzerland, acquired 100 percent ownership of Southern Guaranty Insurance Company. Winterthur is an international insurance operation with subsidiaries or associated companies in all major worldwide markets.

Southern Guaranty is recognized and respected across the southern United States. In fact, the company has consistently earned an A+ rating from the A. M. Best Company.

In addition to its home office in Montgomery, the company maintains office in Jackson, Mississippi; Atlanta, Georigia; and Raleigh, North Carolina. In 1995 Southern Guaranty purchased Jefferson-Pilot Fire and Casualty Company of Greensboro, North Carolina. The new addition, renamed Southern Pilot Insurance Company, helped expand Southern Guaranty's presence in the Southeast and dramatically enhanced corporate assets.

The company's corporate headquarters are located on Taylor Road in rapidly growing east Montgomery. It is home to more than 120 local employees and a base for another 100 employees who travel frequently from distant locations.

The company is dedicated to Montgomery and plays an active role in civic activities supported through the Montgomery Area Chamber

Southern Guaranty's senior management provides outstanding leadership to its employees and parent company enabling all to enjoy a position of recognition in the Southeast and the United States. Pictured are (left to right) Jim L. Ridling, president and CEO; Guy F. Green Jr., senior vice president, CFO, and secretary/treasurer; William R. Dunn, senior vice president, marketing and underwriting; Henry P. Draughon Jr., senior vice president, claims and general counsel; and Charles L. Keith, senior vice president and CIO.

of Commerce and numerous charitable organizations. For more than 25 consecutive years, 100 percent of Southern Guaranty's employees have contributed to the Montgomery Area United Way campaign, and members of the management team take on campaign leadership responsibilities. The company and its people take pride in the communities where they work and encourage a corporate-wide sense of civic responsibility.

Independent insurance agents who represent Southern Guaranty further the company's important local presence. In selecting representatives, Southern Guaranty looks for professionally managed agencies that are respected in the industry and in their communities.

Committed to serving the interests of its agencies, Southern Guaranty proudly recognizes its Montgomery area representatives:

THE FREDERICK AGENCY

In 1972 Beebe R. Frederick Jr. purchased the Auerbach-Jordan Company and established his own agency. Since its beginning, The Frederick Agency has experienced outstanding growth, both through its internal sales organization and by the acquisition of other agencies.

In just more than two decades, The Frederick Agency has acquired The Heilpern Agency, The Berman Agency, The Bruton Agency, The Wimberly Agency, The Shan Sellers Agency, The Thornell Agency, The Proctor Agency, First Insurors, and Macon-Frederick Agency.

The company operates from offices on South Perry Street in downtown Montgomery and maintains branch offices in Wetumpka, Greenville, and Andalusia.

THE JINRIGHT-TURNER AGENCY

Charles Jinright established an independent insurance agency specializing in life and health plans in 1979. Seven years later he was joined by Randall Turner, who brought his experience in the property and casualty side of the insurance business to the Jinright firm.

After a series of other mergers, Jinright-Turner expanded its lines of service to offer life, health, disability, property, casualty, retirement plans, group benefit plans, personal homewoners, and automobile insurance.

Operating from offices at 4216 Carmichael Road, The Jinright-Turner Agency concentrates on building market share by focusing on personal service.

THE JORDAN-MORGAN AGENCY

Al Jordan and James L. Morgan offer their clients more than 75 years of combined insurance industry experience. Prior to opening his own agency in 1965, Morgan worked for the General Adjustment Bureau, Inc. His early firm, the James L. Morgan Agency, was located on

Mount Meigs Road until he consolidated with the Al Jordan Agency in 1994 and moved to Brewton Street.

Jordan, a native Montgomerian, opened his agency in 1956 after earning an MBA degree from Auburn University and gaining early experience with another Montgomery insurance firm. Both Jordan and Morgan believe their combined volume and staffs have strengthened their offerings. The Jordan-Morgan Agency is committed to maintaining its respected stature in the insurance industry by providing responsive, quality service.

THE STARKE AGENCY, INC.

The Starke Agency, Inc., Montgomery's oldest independent agency, was founded in 1929 and has a pattern of strong growth and profitable associations based upon its community involvement. Located in historic Lower Commerce Street and with a satellite office in Prattville, The Starke Agency's employees are the most highly trained and educated in central Alabama. In 1995 the agency consolidated with Mead & Charles, Inc., and today the company offers total account selling with access to top-rated companies that provide the best in life, disability, personal, homeowners, automobile, and commercial insurance coverages.

Under the leadership of two third-generation insurance professionals, The Starke Agency is committed to long-term relationships. One of Montgomery's most highly automated agencies, Starke professionals review all coverages annually in an effort to make the customers' buying decisions as simple as possible. The company's commitment to service is evidenced by its high customer retention, which exceeds its peers, and an extraordinary doubling of agency premiums within the past five years.

THOMPSON INSURANCE, INC.

The Edward M. Thompson Agency was born in 1962 from a belief that consumers and businesses would benefit from the efforts of a progressive insurance agency. After a stint in the family grocery business and later as a homebuilder, Ed Thompson formed his firm with a strong commitment to professionalism and product knowledge.

Today, Thompson Insurance, Inc. exists as the successor to the original agency with George W. Thompson III as president and Irby J. Thompson as vice president.

Independent insurance agents representing Southern Guaranty in Montgomery are (standing left to right) Charles W. Jinright, Bolling P. Starke III, Irby J. Thompson, Beebe R. Frederick, James L. Morgan, (seated) Randall J. Turner, George W. Thompson III, and Al J. Jordan.

In 1994 Thompson Insurance purchased the Harold Faulkner Agency, another Montgomery firm more than 30 years old. The merger combined two similar business philosophies based on strong customer service.

Located at 2951 Zelda Road, Thompson Insurance is proud to represent some of the nation's best insurance carriers.

STRENGTH, SECURITY, AND STABILITY

The success of Southern Guaranty Insurance Company is based on the strength of its people, the security of strong and supportive ownership, and the stability of its agency relationships. These combined resources continue to elevate the company's stature as a leading insurance company in the southeastern region of the United States. *m*

Southern Guaranty employees produce the products and provide quality service to their customers— policyholders and independent agents.

THE ALFA COMPANIES

"There are no fire departments in the country!" That's the headline that appeared in Alfa Insurance Company's first advertisement in 1946. The ad, targeting rural homeowners and farmers in Alabama, went on to say, "Mr. Farmer, if your house catches fire, there won't be any engines clanging up to pump water into it. You can ring the dinner bell but all the help you're likely to get won't be enough to put it out and you may have to stand by and see everything you have go up in smoke. Then, where will you be? You'll be in a fix unless you have insurance. You can't have a fire department, but you can have insurance."

Thus, Alfa Insurance Company was born. Based upon its growth, profit, and earnings potential, *Forbes Magazine* has ranked the Alfa Corporation one of "The 200 Best Small Companies in America" five times since 1985.

In addition to Alfa's insurance enterprises, the company operates a line of noninsurance businesses engaged in consumer financing, leasing, real estate investments, residential and commercial construction, and real estate sales.

Under the direction of Goodwin L. Myrick, a respected Montgomery business and community leader, Alfa employs a workforce of more than 2,200 people. In Montgomery the company employs 920 individuals, most of whom work from Alfa's 310,000-square-foot office complex on the East South Boulevard.

history of success. Its first property and casualty company began serving farmers in the mid-1940s, and the life insurance company followed in 1972. Today, Alfa insures more than one million policyholders in Alabama, Georgia, and Mississippi.

The company, which has approximately $9 billion of life insurance in force, insures 85 percent of the farms in Alabama and has the second largest share of the state's automobile and homeowners insurance markets. More than 580 professional agents, along with more than 670 certified customer service representatives in 370 service centers, make up the company's customer-focused insurance team.

Alfa's conservative investment philosophy has ensured excellent long-term return, which, over the years, has resulted in higher stockholder dividends and policyholder security. A. M. Best, the leading independent rating service for the insurance industry, gave Alfa's property and casualty group its highest rating, A++, along with an A+ rating for the Alfa Life Insurance Corporation. These superior ratings, awarded to fewer than 10 percent of the nation's insurance companies, are based on soundness, permanence, and financial security.

ALFA REALTY— RESIDENTIAL, COMMERCIAL & CONSTRUCTION

For 40 years, Alfa has been involved in real estate development throughout Alabama and the Southeast. The company has an impressive portfolio of shopping centers, office buildings, residential neighborhoods, apartments, mobile home parks, and a resort hotel. Through

Alfa's home office is located in a recently remodeled and expanded building at *2108 East South Boulevard in Montgomery.*

its real estate investment department, Alfa seeks and undertakes quality commercial and residential development opportunities that have long-term investment potential and the ability to enhance their surrounding communities.

Among its many Montgomery area contributions, Alfa developed the prestigious 450-acre Sturbridge Plantation, a beautiful planned residential community on Vaughn Road, along with the nearby luxurious Sturbridge Commons Apartment Homes and the Sturbridge Village Shopping Center.

Included among Alfa's properties are the Gay Meadows Shopping Center, constructed in 1960 and still home to some of its first tenants, and the Westminster subdivision, which featured Montgomery's first underground utility service. Applebee's Neighborhood Grill on Carter Hill Road opened in 1995 and has become a favorite local eatery. Notably, Alfa's Marriott's Bay Point Resort property in Panama City, Florida, is a favorite panhandle vacation spot.

Although separate business entities, Alfa Builders and Alfa Realty Better Homes and Gardens provide the construction and real estate marketing expertise behind many Alfa developments.

Sturbridge Plantation on Vaughn Road in east Montgomery, offers executive estate homes, traditional and garden homes in elegant styles.

ALFA INSURANCE

Considered among the best capitalized insurance companies in America, Alfa offers the financial strength that guarantees security. The company's stability is founded upon a long

Alfa Builders specializes in construction of distinctive single-family homes, townhomes, and patio homes. In recent years, the company has constructed the Sturbridge developments, the Fox Hollow subdivision off the Atlanta Highway, Vista View near Coliseum Boulevard, Fairfield on Bell Road, and the popular Silver Hills and Greystone neighborhoods in nearby Prattville.

Alfa Realty, an affiliate of the nationwide Better Homes and Gardens network, markets new homes for Alfa Builders, as well as existing homes in the Montgomery metropolitan area. A rapidly growing segment of the Alfa corporate family, the company recently moved its headquarters into offices at 8191 Seaton Place near the Sturbridge community and also maintains offices in Prattville and Wetumpka.

The customer-focused company has more than 50 agents who offer professional resources, including the exclusive Better Homes and Gardens Home Marketing System, Home Buying System, and Home Merchandising System—three proven process-oriented approaches to buying and selling homes.

THE ALABAMA FARMERS FEDERATION

Seventy-five years ago, a handful of farmers, bankers, extension workers, and other business leaders met on the Auburn University campus to establish a group dedicated to protecting Alabama's agricultural interests and to foster the economic, educational, and social well-being of the Alabama farmer.

The Alabama Farmers Federation, the founding entity responsible for Alfa's rich agricultural heritage, carries on that charge today through legislative and public relations activities, as well as educational and promotional efforts provided through various commodity groups within the organization.

As an indication of its astounding growth, the Alabama Farmers Federation claimed 30,826 members in 1936 and more than 384,500 member families in 1996. In addition to the organization's considerable political strength, federation members enjoy a variety of services and benefits made available through the Alfa Services Company. The company's Alfa Health, Alfa Marketing, and AutoSave divisions help federation members acquire group health insurance for the self-employed, discounted automotive and farm supplies, commodities analysis, and commodities marketing services for their farm products. The federation also offers pharmacy discounts, consumer protection advocacy, property protection services, informative membership publications, and even an Alfa MasterCard or Visa.

PROFESSIONAL & COMMUNITY LEADERSHIP

Since its founding, Alfa has been dedicated to the welfare of its customers, its employees, and its community. The company's reputation as a fair and progressive employer has attracted strong, knowledgeable employees to every department. A leader in human resources innovations, Alfa constructed a state-of-the-art daycare facility adjacent to its main office for the preschool children of its employees. The center has been filled to capacity with happy children (and happy parents) since it opened in 1991.

In 1994 the company upgraded its field technology to ensure Alfa agents had access to the

*S*turbridge Village shopping center serves residents in Montgomery's eastern growth corridor.

finest computer equipment available to efficiently meet their clients' needs. The company then donated the used equipment, valued at $750,000, to schools throughout its markets. Each year more than 100 Alfa employees take on leadership roles with the Montgomery Area United Way. Their fund-raising efforts, combined with corporate gifts, account for nearly 25 percent of the resulting contributions.

Clearly, Alfa Insurance Company and Alabama Farmers Federation have changed dramatically over the years, but its loyalty to Alabama, dedication to uncompromising service, and commitment to leadership have not. *m*

*T*he Alabama Farmers Federation speaks out for agriculture and works directly with farmers on important agricultural issues.

MERRILL LYNCH
PRIVATE CLIENT GROUP

From its origins as a brokerage house more than a century ago, Merrill Lynch has grown to become one of the world's leading diversified financial services companies and one of the Montgomery area's most recognized and trusted investment advisors.

Merrill Lynch maintained its local office on Commerce Street in Montgomery's downtown business district for nearly 70 years. As an indication of its continued commitment to the Montgomery area, the company is now located in its beautiful and expansive new offices at Carmichael Center, just off Interstate 85 on the corner of Carmichael and Perry Hill Roads. Its central location and immediate interstate accessibility make the new office convenient both for local clients and those throughout south central Alabama.

Merrill Lynch offers some 200 products and services. The Montgomery office, home to 50 investment professionals, is part of the Merrill Lynch Private Client Group. Merrill Lynch's Private Client Group serves more than 5 million individuals and small- and mid-sized businesses with the goal of achieving planning-based performance over the long term to help clients reach their individual financial objectives. Through the professional skill of highly trained financial consultants, the Private Client Group helps formulate strategies and create financial plans that will carry individuals through their life stages. Merrill Lynch works with younger clients to help them build assets and manage credit; with the more established client to manage their wealth for retirement, estate planning, and charitable giving; and with the business client to manage their cash flow and banking needs, as well as long term planning through the business financial planner. Through its Retirement and Group Employee Benefits Services, Merrill Lynch is a major provider of 401(k) employee savings plans.

Clients also benefit from the Merrill Lynch Trust Company, which seeks to preserve wealth for future generations and enhance its growth potential, the Merrill Lynch Credit Corporation, which supplies clients with secured mortgage, personal credit, and investment financing instruments, and the Merrill Lynch Insurance Group, which helps meet client needs through a network of estate planning and business insurance specialists.

Merrill Lynch Private Client assets worldwide exceed $575 billion, including over $170 billion in mutual funds and private portfolios managed by Merrill Lynch Asset Management.

"We have virtually every financial service available to our clients with the exception of automobile and casualty insurance," said Senior Resident Vice President Marvin Lubin. "But at

Merrill Lynch's Private Client Group serves individuals and small- and mid-sized businesses with the goal of achieving planning-based performance over the long term to help clients reach their individual financial objectives. Photo by Fouts Commerical Photography.

Merrill Lynch's location in the new Carmichael Center offers convenience both for local clients and those throughout south central Alabama. Photo by Fouts Commerical Photography.

the foundation of everything we do is a sincere commitment to integrity and client service. Through financial planning we gain an in-depth understanding of our clients needs and goals. The responsibility for achieving client goals rests with the Merrill Lynch financial consultants whose job it is to assess the clients' long-term financial needs and devise an individual financial plan."

Global investment opportunities and expanding technologies hold new and exciting challenges for Merrill Lynch and its customers. Already the company maintains a global market presence as one of the largest securities broker-dealers and investment banking operations in the world, and, by the year 2005, Merrill Lynch will earn more than half its revenues in foreign markets. This kind of global influence and understanding is critical to clients looking for the broadest financial knowledge base available to them.

The company has the reputation as the leader in economic and financial research. Corporations, policy makers, governmental entities, and educators look to Merrill Lynch as one of the world's foremost financial experts. Because the company does business all over the world, it brings the international perspective so valuable in today's global economy.

After serving the Montgomery area for nearly three-quarters of a century, Merrill Lynch and its employees have become respected community servants. The Merrill Lynch Company espouses the concept of community service and encourages meaningful local participation. The Private Client Group in Montgomery is a friend and supporter of the Montgomery Museum of Fine Arts, Junior League of Montgomery, and United Way. In recent years, Merrill Lynch employees have participated in the city's Christmas in April program, providing the manpower to renovate homes for those in need of assistance.

After more than 100 years of growth and success, Merrill Lynch is ever mindful that service is its first priority. Its recently expanded client commitment is testament to its vision and purpose. With the company's increasing financial strength, a tradition of innovation and customer service, highly trained financial consultants, and a broad product line, Merrill Lynch is positioned for another successful century in Montgomery and worldwide. **M**

FIRST ALABAMA BANK
A REGIONS BANK

First Alabama Bank of Montgomery is a 125-year-old financial institution with a rich and storied history. But it is the bank's commitment to progress—a consistent quest to be on the leading edge of its industry—that has contributed to its stature as central Alabama's largest financial institution.

Founded on April 18, 1871, near the end of Reconstruction, First Alabama Bank played a major role in Montgomery's early economic development, serving as a creditor to the city's thriving cotton industry and supporting new and expanding retail and industrial firms. Since day one, First Alabama has been instrumental in the development of banking in Alabama, spearheading progressive movements in the financial industry that have directly impacted the state's economic expansion.

First Alabama Bank of Montgomery was founded by Dr. William O. Baldwin as the First National Bank of Montgomery. Its early offices were located in the center of downtown on Market Street, or what is today known as Dexter Avenue. Over the years the bank has grown and prospered under strong and stable leadership. Since the turn of the century, First Alabama has had only six other presidents.

First Alabama moved to its present location, a 12-story office complex at the corner of Commerce Street and Court Square, in 1907. Those facilities were further enhanced in 1975 with the addition of a four-story annex and parking garage and an adjacent eight-story headquarters for the bank's holding company. Having established itself by serving the cotton industry early on, First Alabama incorporated the cotton plant as part of its corporate logo. Today the bank remains one of only two Alabama banks with a department specifically designed to assist cotton dealers.

"Among First Alabama's strengths is its ability to draw on its history while never losing sight of the future," said Southeastern Regional President and Executive Board Member Wilbur B. Hufham. "In our view, one of the biggest mistakes any business can make is to fail to look ahead."

Operating with that kind of progressive leadership, First Alabama has always been a driving force in moving banking into the future. In 1955 bank officers worked successfully to pass legislation permitting branch banking in Alabama. The bank opened its first branch in the Cloverdale community and today operates 23 branch offices throughout the metropolitan area, nearly twice as many as any other area bank.

The bank also led the move to allow multi-bank holding companies in Alabama, which dramatically changed the character of banking

Wilbur B. Hufham served as chairman, president, and CEO of First Alabama Bank from 1983 until January 1996.

in the state. In 1971 First Alabama joined with the First National Bank of Huntsville and Birmingham's Exchange Security Bank to form the first such company, First Alabama Bancshares, Inc. Over the years, First Alabama has grown through mergers and acquisitions, its largest and most recent being the 1994 purchase of Montgomery's Union Bank and Trust Company. With that purchase, the bank's local market share grew to nearly 40 percent and First Alabama's assets reached more than $1 billion.

Recognizing its potential for growth through interstate banking, First Alabama Bancshares changed its name to Regions Financial Corporation in 1994. Regions operates offices throughout the southeast in Alabama, Florida, Georgia, Louisiana, and Tennessee and boasts assets in excess of $13.5 billion.

The bank's long-time positioning statement, "Lean on the Green," was derived from its reputation for financial strength and sound management. First Alabama was one of the few banks that stayed open during the Great Depression and never missed a stockholder dividend check. And now, years later, both First Alabama and its holding company are recognized nationally by Thomson BankWatch, Standard and Poor's, and Moody's Investor Services for their consistent earnings records and financial stability.

"We are fortunate to do business in Montgomery," said Ruth Walker, regional marketing officer. "The military and state

First Alabama's Taylor Road branch is one of the bank's newest locations in east Montgomery.

government provide tremendous stability for our economy. We don't experience economic highs and lows; this is a sound banking community."

In addition to leading the way in size, First Alabama has pioneered customer services that have become industry mainstays. The bank was the first to introduce automated teller machines, and today operates more than 20 "Right Place" ATMs locally. The bank was also first with "The Right Call," telephone banking service, and has assigned active task forces to study future banking products such as on-line "virtual banking."

"Our intention is to combine advanced technologies with attention to the old-fashioned basics of listening to the concerns of our customers," said Hufham. "By doing that successfully, we have the financial solutions necessary to meet all of our customers' needs."

*F*irst Alabama sponsors the Montgomery Ballet's Performance on the Green at the Blount Cultural Park.

According to Walker, First Alabama ensures excellent customer service through intensive in-house training programs that concentrate on relationship-building and bank product knowledge. "Customer service is our number one priority and we work hard to make sure the bank staff is prepared to provide uncompromising service," said Walker. "At First Alabama we offer everything from basic checking and savings accounts to loans and trust and investment services. Our corporate services include cash management, industrial development, and commercial loans. It is essential that we are thoroughly skilled and knowledgeable."

First Alabama further ensures service quality by employing local managers and maintaining an independent board of directors made up of local business and civic leaders. "Banking is based on relationships," said Walker. "We can't serve this community without understanding and respect for the specific needs of our customers."

In that vein, First Alabama takes seriously its responsibility as a corporate citizen and cultural contributor to the area it serves. With more than 540 local employees, First Alabama is represented in virtually every civic organization in the city. The bank is one of the primary sponsors of the BEST campaign, a program to raise needed funds for area schools, and participates as a Partner in Education. Bank officers hold key positions in the Montgomery Area United Way and the Montgomery Area Chamber of Commerce. Of all the bank's presidents, each was a leader in the banking community and a strong force in the civic and cultural communities as well. Having led by example, each encouraged company-wide volunteer participation, developing over the years one of Montgomery's finest corporate citizenships.

First Alabama has been instrumental in establishing the flourishing arts culture in Montgomery, sponsoring each year the Montgomery Ballet's Performance on the Green and holding the annual Montgomery Art Guild juried art show which showcases original art work by local artists.

First Alabama's role as a trendsetter in customer service, technologies, product offerings, and community involvement is based on a single pervading philosophy. "Our success in Montgomery is due to our customers," said Wibur Hufham. "We owe the people of Montgomery a great deal, and there are plenty of opportunities for paybacks." *m*

G. *Carlton Barker was elected chairman of the board, president, and chief executive officer of First Alabama Bank on January 8, 1996.*

REGIONS MORTGAGE, INC.

From its inception, the company that would become Regions Mortgage, Inc. has been dedicated to meeting needs and making a difference in the lives of those it services.

Regions Mortgage was founded in 1946 to originate mortgages for returning servicemen. Since then, the company has relied upon its core values of financial strength, product innovation, and long-term relationships to become Alabama's largest mortgage servicing company.

Founders Edward Auerbach and William Jordan established the company as a division of the Auerbach-Jordan Insurance Agency. After serving Montgomery for more than a decade, the company opened its first branch office in Mobile in 1958. Enjoying success in its home state, the company has expanded and today operates 27 offices in Alabama, Florida, Georgia, Louisiana, Mississippi, Tennessee, and South Carolina. Its tremendous growth has moved Regions Mortgage into the ranks of the 50 largest mortgage servicers in the United States.

changed its name to Regions Mortgage in 1995, shortly after First Alabama Bancshares became a member of the Regions Financial Corporation.

The beneficial relationship between First Alabama Bank and Regions Mortgage is testament to both organizations' commitment to quality, progressive service. As a result of the alliance, First Alabama Bank provides full mortgage service in many of its branches, and Regions Mortgage offers its customers the financial backing of Alabama's largest financial institution.

The company's rich history is a story to behold, but the future holds even more promise for Regions Mortgage, Inc. The company has implemented an aggressive growth strategy that is expected to double its servicing portfolio from $10 billion to more than $20 billion by the year 2000. The implementation of innovative marketing techniques, cutting-edge technology enhancements, and responsive product offerings will carry the company into new and expanding markets in Texas, Virginia, and North Carolina by the rapidly approaching turn of the century.

"Our goal is to serve the mortgage needs of each and every borrower and to do what it takes to keep that customer satisfied for life," said Chairman and President John A. Holleman. "We have a strong policy of servicing the loans we originate, because home mortgages are more than just business . . . they're relationships."

Regions Mortgage demonstrates a sincere dedication to building relationships with its customers and the communities it serves. The company has dispatched emergency staff to branches in areas hard-hit by natural disasters to expedite the endorsement of insurance checks, and has created flexible programs for customers whose lives have been disrupted and traumatized.

With more than 500 employees in Montgomery alone, the company's commitment to corporate citizenship reaches deeply into its home community. Its involvement is evidenced by its support for the arts through the Alabama Shakespeare Festival, the Arts Council of Montgomery, and the Montgomery Symphony. Regions Mortgage is equally concerned for the future of Montgomery's children, providing

Regions Mortgage has relied upon its core values of financial strength, product innovation, and long-term relationships to become Alabama's largest mortgage servicing company.

financial resources and volunteer time for efforts such as its role as a Partner in Education with Capitol Heights Junior High School.

As its golden anniversary approaches, Regions Mortgage, Inc. can look ahead with confidence. The strong relationships, professionalism, and dedicated service hallmark the company's brilliant past and are at the very foundation of its promising future. 𝑚

Regions Mortgage's goal is to serve the mortgage needs of each and every borrower and to do what it takes to keep that customer satisfied for life.

In 1972 First Alabama Bank purchased the mortgage company, which by then had become known as Real Estate Financing, Inc. Because of its alliance with the bank, Real Estate Financing

THE BARCLAY AGENCY

The Barclay Agency has built a solid reputation in the insurance industry for its distinctive product innovation, industry expertise, and responsive service. A managing general agency, whose staff has more than 100 years' combined experience, The Barclay Agency is fast becoming a recognized industry leader in the Southeast and beyond.

The Barclay Agency was founded in 1989 by Tom Albrecht, a long-time Montgomery insurance executive, in partnership with insurance executive Med James. The two have combined their industry know-how to offer Barclay's clients a wealth of insight and product options.

The firm's insurance carriers offer a range of insurance coverages from "mom and pop" groceries and taverns, to hard-to-place primary and excess layers, commercial auto, and workers' compensation. The agency has earned a reputation for developing custom programs for niche markets with special insurance needs. Retail insurance agencies turn to The Barclay Agency for help in obtaining coverages that standard markets do not provide.

The Barclay Agency has binding authority with many of the companies it represents and operates as a wholesale Excess and Surplus Lines Broker for those risks not within its binding authority. Over the years, Barclay professionals have researched the marketplace and assembled a group of companies with excellent financial ratings. The firm represents companies from throughout the United States and internationally, including Lloyds of London and other British insurers.

With headquarters on Carmichael Road, and a second office in Birmingham, The Barclay Agency is positioned for easy accessibility not only for its Alabama clients, but also for those in surrounding southeastern states where growth potential abounds.

With a staff of 20 professionals, the agency offers full-service underwriting, quoting, binding, and issuing. These capabilities allow the Barclay Agency to provide a seamless web of service and become the equivalent of a branch office to the companies it represents. "Our most important value-added factor is that we have extensive knowledge of the marketplace because we have been doing business with the same retail agents for years," Albrecht said.

In addition to a full line of property and casualty coverages, the agency provides insurance coverages for professional liability and commercial automobile coverages, including motor truck cargo. The Barclay Agency is noted for its ability to address special insurance needs and has created niche market programs such as an alternative workers' compensation plan and a watercraft insurance program for the nationwide Bass Anglers Sportsman Society.

Albrecht is as determined to make a difference in his community as he is in his profession; and his leadership drives a community-minded spirit within The Barclay Agency. He is actively involved as a director of the Montgomery Area Chamber of Commerce and as chairman of the Chamber's Military Affairs Committee. He

The Barclay Agency has built a solid reputation in the insurance industry for its distinctive product innovation, industry expertise and responsive service.

also serves as a trustee for the Air University Foundation and chairman of the Baptist Health Care Foundation's board of directors, among other worthwhile community contributions.

Albrecht and the staff of The Barclay Agency have built a vast reservoir of professional resources and live by a commitment to those they serve. As a result, the Barclay Agency is positioned to answer the needs of its clients and its community with superior understanding, insight, and dedication. *m*

The firm's insurance carriers offer a range of insurance coverages from "mom and pop" groceries and taverns, to hard-to-place primary and excess layers, commercial auto, and workers' compensation.

COLONIAL BANK OF MONTGOMERY

Colonial Bank has the best of both worlds. Colonial people are recognized as some of the friendliest in the business; Colonial service is personal and uncompromising; and Colonial's reputation as a community bank with a small town flair attracts customers looking for something special. Yet Colonial's multibillion dollar strength is anything but small.

Colonial Bank of Montgomery's parent company, Colonial BancGroup, Inc., is a multistate bank holding company headquartered in downtown Montgomery. It is the fifth largest banking organization in Alabama with assets totaling more than $3.6 billion. It operates more than 100 offices in Alabama, Tennessee, and Georgia.

Colonial Bank of Montgomery, along with its parent company, is based in the striking Colonial Financial Center at One Commerce Street in the heart of Montgomery's downtown business district. Colonial is the only one of Alabama's statewide banks headquartered in Montgomery. "Because we are truly Montgomery's hometown bank in every sense of the word, all the resources we need are right at our fingertips. We can respond quickly to lending requests of any size," according to Colonial Bank of Montgomery President Mac McLeod.

Although its resources are a tremendous asset, something different has been the foundation for Colonial's solid growth since its beginning in 1981. Colonial Bank is operated by local professionals who share local interests and have a personal stake in the welfare of their community.

The same is true for Colonial Banks throughout Alabama and beyond. Each bank has the authority to approve financial transactions of all sizes at the local level. And each bank's board of directors is comprised of hometown men and women who draw from their own experiences to support the local management teams.

Serving its customers from five offices in Montgomery and one in Prattville, Colonial Bank offers an array of services designed to make banking easy and convenient. Colonial provides innovative checking services and a variety of savings and investment options. Whether building or buying a home, purchasing a car, planning a dream vacation, financing a child's education, or starting a new business, Colonial has competitive lending plans for every need. Recognizing the value of their bank as a one-stop financial partner, Colonial bankers live by their motto: "We Can Do."

That same "Can-Do" spirit goes beyond business into the community. Established by Montgomery's prominent Lowder family, Colonial Bank takes its responsibility as a corporate citizen seriously. Colonial employees serve the community on volunteer boards and committees throughout the city. The bank is a major contributor to the Montgomery Area United Way, and executives frequently take on leadership roles with the charity. Colonial Bank is strongly committed to public education, serving as a Partner In Education with a local elementary school and providing volunteer manpower and monetary contributions to improve Montgomery's educational environment.

For Colonial Bank, the future is immense and exciting. The bank already offers the finest in technology and electronic banking.

Meeting customer needs is the top priority at Colonial Bank. Its innovative bank operations staff, its helpful customer service representatives, and its knowledgeable lending officers, are just a few of the reasons why they say, "The Colonial 'Can-Do' spirit is everywhere." *m*

Colonial Bank of Montgomery is based in the Colonial Financial Center at One Commerce Street in the heart of Montgomery's downtown business district.

WEIL BROTHERS-COTTON, INC.

Weil Brothers-Cotton, Inc., nearly 120 years old, merchandises a cornerstone commodity of the international economy. One of the world's leading cotton merchant houses, the company handles the product in nearly every country where the fiber is grown or processed. The worldwide enterprise moves nearly 1.5 million bales in a single year.

The company's founders, Isador and Herman Weil, came to the South from the Bavarian Palatinate as boys, entrusted to the care of their uncles. In 1878 they opened a small country store in Opelika, Alabama. Facing a cash-dry economy, the men accommodated area farmers by accepting raw cotton in payment for merchandise. By the turn of the century, the company's rapid growth prompted its move to the Capital City. Ingenuity and instinct led the Weils to reap a share of the American harvest.

Under the leadership of fourth generation Weils, the company today ranks among the top seven giants in international cotton merchandising. Cousins Bobby Weil Jr. and Andy Weil serve as vice chairman and COO and president, respectively, working from a two-sided antique partners desk, the same as their fathers, Bobby Sr. and Adolph "Bucks" Jr., shared for years.

Much of the company's history originated from simple downtown offices at the corner of Moulton and Montgomery Streets. In 1990 the company moved to its new location in east Montgomery.

Nearly 40 percent of the firm's staff works from the Montgomery office, but Weil's international dealings require offices and agents worldwide. Domestic operations include a Wall Street address and other offices in Memphis, Lubbock, Fresno, Greenville, and Gastonia. Foreign operations are found in Liverpool, Paraguay, Argentina, and Australia. "The company is divisionalized," said Andy Weil. "We entrust a great deal of responsibility to our managers and traders; they are the stewards of their respective divisions, and I would say they are the best in the trade."

With the finest technologies in place and a commitment to continuing development, Weil Brothers-Cotton is on the cutting edge in industry communications. Improved production technologies, such as genetic engineering to enhance product quality and diversity, have increased the options available to the mills Weil Brothers serves. Electronic data interchange makes it possible for Weil Brothers to provide advance information to the mills, meet their stringent fiber specifications, and deliver the cotton just in time for spinning.

A majority of the company's total volume is delivered to United States mills, including Russell, West Point, and Avondale in Alabama.

While Weil Brothers-Cotton is a respected leader in the global marketplace, its commitment to community service has earned the company even greater respect at home. The company staunchly supports area business and economic development efforts, is one of Montgomery's

*The company's founders, Isador and Herman Weil, came to the South and opened their business about the same time artist Winslow Homer painted **Upland Cotton**. Photo by Fouts Commericial Photography.*

leading proponents of the arts, and generously offers resources to widely diverse charities, including the Montgomery Area Food Bank, the American Red Cross, and the Boys' and Girls' Clubs.

Summarizing the family's century-old commitment to service, Weil noted, "Community service returns to the whole of the community many times more than the single effort you put into it. We contribute in that spirit; recognition is not necessary."

Weil Brothers-Cotton goes about its daily business with the same quiet integrity and focus. With the United States staking its claim as the strongest textile producer in the world, the outlook for King Cotton and Weil Brothers is stronger than ever. **𝓂**

One of the world's leading cotton merchant houses, Weil Brothers-Cotton, Inc. handles the product in nearly every country where the fiber is grown or processed. The worldwide enterprise moves nearly 1.5 million bales in a single year. Photo by Fouts Commericial Photography.

COMPASS BANK

The polished marble and sparkling brass inside Compass Bank's headquarters office outwardly reflect the bank's inward commitment to excellence, leadership, and progress.

The financial institution that would become Compass Bank of Montgomery was established in 1957 as People's Bank and Trust Co. In 1964 Central BancShares of the South, Inc. purchased Montgomery's People's Bank. Today, three decades and a name change later, the bank operates eight offices in the Montgomery area and employs approximately 150.

Headquartered in Birmingham, Compass BancShares, Inc. is ranked among the top 100 bank holding companies in America. The corporation operates 188 banks in Alabama, Texas, and Florida, and boasts total assets in excess of $11 billion. "We offer the advantage of strong, far-reaching resources," said Montgomery bank President John Walton. "But we combine those resources with local pride, appreciation for our Montgomery customers, and commitment to this community. It makes for an excellent balance."

A full-service financial institution, Compass provides a complete line of retail banking, corporate banking, mortgage banking, trust, and investment products. The bank prides itself in recognizing its customers' needs and devising the products they want. One example, the "Professional Association," is a popular private banking service offering carefully tailored products, special rates, and bank-sponsored special events, created in appreciation of Montgomery's professional community.

Under Walton's leadership, Compass has forged partnerships with virtually every arts organization in the city. In 1994 the bank received the Montgomery Business Committee for the Arts Award, and Walton was nominated for national recognition. In addition to its cultural commitment, Compass is one of the city's largest United Way contributors, and Walton served as chairman of the organization's 1995 pilot campaign.

Compass Bank is also committed to education. The bank generously provides monetary resources and people-power to Chisholm Elementary School, its partner in education, and supports local colleges and universities through scholarships and endowment funding. A supporting member of the Montgomery Area Chamber of Commerce, Compass joined with other banks to create the Montgomery Area Community Development Corporation, a financing source designed to help minority-owned and undercapitalized businesses succeed.

On the heels of positive change, Compass Bank is prepared to seize additional opportunities ahead. The bank has joined with MicroSoft and Intuit to offer technology that will allow its customers to use home or office personal computers to access their accounts for bill paying, balance review, funds transfer, and other banking transactions. "We are the first in Alabama with this technology, and we will continue to capitalize on technological advances that will enhance our services," Walton said.

For Compass Bank, the future is full of promise. "There is an inherent strength in this community, not just the strength that comes with being a state capital or having a strong military presence. But there is a powerful strength associated with a healthy business climate and a rich cultural environment. We are proud to be both a beneficiary of and a participant in Montgomery." *m*

Under the leadership of board of directors: (left to right) Tranun Fitzpatrick, Franklin Parker, Owen Aronov, Ham Wilson Jr., Chester Mallory, and John Walton, Compass Bank is prepared to seize the opportunities that lie ahead. Not pictured are Goodwin Myrick, Leon Hadley, and Gene Davenport.

In 1993, just months after Central Bank of the South had moved into its Executive Park office, the bank changed its name to Compass. For Compass, the change was timely and opportune. The new name, associated logo, as well as the gray, brilliant red and gold signage provided focus and visibility for a company looking to build its image as a progressive regional financial services organization.

John M. Walton serves as the president of Compass Bank in Montgomery.

MERCHANT CAPITAL

*M*erchant Capital is one of the most noted and respected merchant and investment banking firms in the Southeast. The company, whose corporate headquarters are located in Montgomery, was founded in 1987 by partners who had established careers in the investment banking industry. The firm's responsive reputation has earned Merchant Capital a place as perhaps the most resourceful and service-oriented financial advisory firm in the region.

"We strive to deliver the most creative and reliable service available to corporate and municipal borrowers," said Thomas Ashley Harris, Senior Managing Director. To accomplish that, the firm offers the services of experts skilled in finance, law, real estate development, and economic development. Experienced personnel provide this highly specialized knowledge through offices in Georgia, Mississippi, Florida, and Louisiana.

Merchant Capital's array of services includes municipal bond financing for governmental and public entities, financial advisory services, debt restructuring, and project financing for industrial, commercial, multifamily housing, and health care developments. The firm has invested venture capital for its own account in several operating companies.

The company has been ranked Alabama's number one investment banking firm in municipal bond issues and among the top three nationally in the industrial revenue bond market by Securities Data Company. Principals of Merchant Capital have closed hundreds of tax-exempt bond issues in over 35 states and is consistently ranked number one in the Southeast in industrial revenue bond financings.

As the corporate finance needs of the region have grown, Merchant Capital has become highly regarded for its innovation in public offerings, private placements, mergers and acquisitions, leveraged buyouts, and financial advisory services and evaluations.

Merchant Capital is also experienced in sales and underwriting with experience in both the public and private debt markets. The firm's relationships with institutional and retail investors throughout the United States give Merchant Capital the ability to access the capital market most appropriate for each client.

The company is also a leader in securitized debt financing for income-producing real estate projects. Debt securitization, through tax-exempt or taxable bonds, gives private borrowers access to the public debt markets for a variety of projects including nursing homes, apartment complexes, and manufacturing plants.

The company is known for its willingness to go beyond the traditional role of a securities underwriter, financial advisor, or venture capitalist. As a leader in economic development, Merchant Capital frequently introduces corporate prospects to the communities it represents. Conversely, the firm's knowledge of economic incentives, job training, and governmental services supplements its capital market services.

To grow an investment firm in today's competitive environment requires that the firm consistently provide its clients value. Vice President Daniel Hughes stresses the importance of continuity and relationship-building. "It's important to provide multiple sources of value to the client within a relationship of integrity and trust. I believe we do this better than anyone else."

That kind of attitude, supplemented by hard work, perseverance, and honesty has helped Merchant Capital set the standard for professionalism and reliability in the South's investment banking industry. *M*

*M*erchant Capital is one of the most noted and respected merchant and investment banking firms in the Southeast. Pictured are (seated left to right) Douglas C. Sellers, Thomas Ashley Harris, (standing left to right) W. Daniel Hughes Jr., Robert G. Thomas, Philip W. Fletcher III, Kenneth C. Funderburk, John B. Rucker III, Patrick R. Maloy, and Michael P. Dunn.

FIRST MONTGOMERY BANK

*I*n 1979 First Montgomery Bank opened for business in the lobby of a renovated hotel in downtown Montgomery. By 1995, *Entrepreneur Magazine* had named the bank one of the top small business lenders in the Southeast.

First Montgomery Bank President Bill Richardson has guided the bank's consistent progress since day one. Armed with his experience as a lender to small and mid-sized businesses and a built-in network of business contacts, Richardson set out to carve a profitable niche for his bank. By its second month of operation, the plan was in place and the bank had turned a profit.

In 1986, after seven years of steady growth and with total bank assets of more than $50 million, the bank was ready for another major milestone. To strengthen its growth and improve its ability to make larger loans, First Montgomery Bank formed an alliance with Aliant National Corporation. With the new association came a number of significant changes. Bank resources were enhanced, lending limits grew, bank products improved, and the striking Aliant logo popped up all over town. First Montgomery's central business philosophy, to provide personal service in a warm family atmosphere, has never changed.

With 78 employees and 5 locations in Montgomery, First Montgomery Bank is able to maintain productive, close-knit relationships. "Because of our size, we have great flexibility. We can put out a new product in a week or answer a loan request in substantially less time than it takes other banks. We can move without going through a web of infrastructure," says Richardson.

In 1989 First Montgomery Bank moved its headquarters to an attractive new five-story black granite office building on Zelda Road. The increased visibility and convenient location have contributed to the bank's stable growth. Other offices are strategically located on Bibb Street downtown, the Atlanta Highway, the Southern Boulevard near Montgomery Mall, and Vaughn Road near the Wynlakes subdivision.

First Montgomery's strategy to provide top-rate commercial lending services has paid great dividends, both for the bank and its customers. The bank's popular Prestige 55 program, which offers a variety of personal banking services to the senior market, brings in deposits that are in turn loaned to individuals and businesses.

"We are one of only two Small Business Administration certified lenders in Montgomery.

*F*irst Montgomery Bank's headquarters are located in an attractive black granite office building on Zelda Road. This convenient location has contributed to the bank's stable growth.

We are fortunate that Montgomery has a stable economic climate. For the last five years our economy has supported small business growth, and, as a result, we've seen excellent bank performances in Montgomery," says Richardson. Currently, First Montgomery Bank assets are more than $170 million.

In addition to its commercial lending services, First Montgomery Bank offers a varied and competitive array of personal banking products and services. The bank also provides quality lending services for residential mortgages through its subsidiary, Aliant Mortgage Corporation. For non-traditional banking, including investment and brokerage services and annuities, First Montgomery Bank offers the professional expertise of its affiliate Aliant Financial Services.

ANCHOR MORTGAGE SERVICES, INC.

Family is the key to Anchor Mortgage Services' motivation and success. Motivated by a desire to help families and individuals fulfill their dreams of owning a home, Vicki Williams formed Anchor in 1988 to provide locally owned, independently operated financial expertise in residential lending.

Fueled by Williams' desire to serve others, and her extraordinary financial skills, Anchor Mortgage closed $1 million in loans the first month the company was open and quickly rose to the top of the mortgage industry in production in the Montgomery, Elmore, and Autauga tri-county area. The company earned its record closing month in August 1993, when it reached $13 million in closings. Every year, Anchor has managed to be in the top three mortgage lenders in this area without any bank or real estate company affiliation.

Whether assisting a first-time home buyer, or conducting business with sellers, real estate agents, appraisers, or attorneys, Williams and her staff of 16 are dedicated to providing the most comprehensive service available.

The philosophy that the customer always comes first is central to Anchor's success. By understanding the importance of making her customers feel comfortable as they move through the often trying process of buying a home, Williams creates an atmosphere where her customers feel confident their needs are being met and their interests served. It is this kind of caring attitude that has catapulted Anchor to the top of the mortgage industry in the Capital City.

The company's commitment to maintaining a welcoming, family environment is evident from the first moment a customer steps into Anchor Mortgage's lovely offices. The relaxed, congenial atmosphere is in total contrast to what most people expect from a mortgage firm. But the convivial atmosphere in no way detracts from the first-class professionalism that resounds throughout the company. The firm's expert staff, coupled with a complete array of services which include

Anchor Mortgage Services' expert staff, coupled with a complete array of services, makes the Anchor team a responsive, first-class organization. Photo by Fouts Commercial Photography.

hundreds of loan programs from which to choose, makes the Anchor team a responsive, first-class organization.

Anchor's innovative approach to dealing with people extends to its employees as well, each of whom is treated more like extended family than staff. Flexible working hours, a sick room upstairs for children, and periodic employee retreats are just a few of the caveats that make Anchor an ideal place to work.

Accomplishments have not gone unnoticed. Anchor Mortgage received the Montgomery Area Chamber of Commerce's Corporate Volunteer of the Year Award in 1992, the Council on Small Business Enterprises' Small Business of the Year Award in 1992 and 1994, and the *INC.* magazine Entrepreneur of the Year Award for 1993. Williams, a Montgomery native, was named a Woman of Distinction in 1992 by the *Montgomery Advertiser.*

Williams' goals for her company remain constant—to provide customers with the best service in mortgage lending, while maintaining excellent working conditions and a sense of family for employees.

"Our entire staff exhibits daily the spirit of our mission statement that 'our goal to succeed is anchored by our desire to serve,' " said Williams.

Anchor Mortgage Services' continued and consistent success is testimony to the power of its commitment to excellence. *m*

Anchor Mortgage Services' goal of success is anchored by its desire to serve.

AMSOUTH BANK

Much like its towering headquarters in the heart of the Montgomery downtown business and financial district, AmSouth Bank has long been at the center of activity in the Capital City and on the leading edge of progress in the banking industry.

With total assets exceeding $17 billion, AmSouth Bancorporation is the second largest bank holding company in Alabama and a driving force in the state's financial industry. Since its founding more than a century ago, the organization has led the way with service-enhancing technologies and innovative banking products.

But the professionals at AmSouth believe some things are best left unchanged—like the bank's vital role as a corporate citizen and its long-time commitment to the city of Montgomery. Eagerly embracing community needs, AmSouth bankers commonly take on leadership roles in their community, supporting civic, charitable, educational, religious, and cultural organizations at every level. In 1995, through its Fund for Educational Excellence, AmSouth awarded grants totalling more than $55,000 to 12 schools in and around the Montgomery area. In addition to its philanthropic concerns, AmSouth is committed to enhancing area economic development and led the way with other area banks in establishing the Minority Area Community Development Corporation to help minority business owners pursue their entrepreneurial dreams.

As a result of the combined strengths of unparalleled professionalism and community involvement, the AmSouth organization today includes more than 250 locations in Alabama, Georgia, Florida, and Tennessee and is proudly one of the best capitalized bank holding companies in the United States. In the Montgomery area alone, AmSouth operates 12 locations and employs nearly 200 banking professionals.

AmSouth's tremendous growth has been predicated by the institution's commitment to "quality banking"—an innovative combination of quality products and quality services fundamental to the development of quality lifetime banking relationships.

Offering an array of practical, creative, and convenient banking products, AmSouth is a popular choice for retail banking, corporate banking, trust and investment banking, and mortgage banking. Testament to the bank's commitment to building strong relationships, AmSouth offers its customers valuable discounts, incentives, and benefits for taking advantage of multiple bank services.

Pleasurable banking and customer convenience are central to the AmSouth product line. The first to offer telephone banking in the 1980s and the convenient CheckCard in the 1990s, AmSouth has long been on the dynamic cutting edge of banking technologies. Facing a future destined for considerable technological advancement, AmSouth is preparing to enter the world of "virtual banking." And as interstate banking becomes a reality, AmSouth is investing in the technologies necessary to give its customers full-service banking access across state lines.

Clearly, these efforts toward excellence point to the sincerity behind AmSouth's mission for quality. Quality customer service, quality community service, and quality professional leadership have propelled AmSouth to great heights in Montgomery. The bank is far more than a place of business in Montgomery. It is a vital part of the rich heritage that is Montgomery. **M**

▲ *A 1923 bank teller window is quite different from AmSouth's modern teller windows of today. Though much has changed through the years, one thing remains constant—AmSouth makes certain its customers banking relationships are secure and solid.*

AmSouth will soon move into its new main office, joining in the vibrant renaissance of downtown Montgomery.

KINDERCARE LEARNING CENTERS, INC.

Montgomery-based KinderCare Learning Centers, Inc. serves the nation's smallest in a very big way. The story behind the amazing development of KinderCare is one of vision, innovation, and commitment. A creative concept initiated more than 25 years ago with a single child care center on Montgomery's Sunshine Drive has become America's largest proprietary child care provider and one of Montgomery's finest corporate citizens.

KinderCare's chief executive officer, Dr. Sandra Scarr, is a renowned child psychologist.

KinderCare Learning Centers, Inc. was founded in 1969 on the premise that quality care helps develop children to their full potential. A consistent commitment to quality, concern, and service has resulted in a dynamic corporation that operates nearly 1,140 center-based and corporate child care facilities nationwide on the strength of more than 22,000 dedicated employees.

According to KinderCare's chief executive officer, Dr. Sandra Scarr, a renowned child psychologist, 97 percent of the company's employees serve on its teaching staff—where they are needed most. "Teaching a child how to be a better friend, to be courteous, patient, and kind, is one of the biggest legacies we can give children anywhere," said Dr. Scarr.

The corporate giant, which recorded more than $500 million in revenues in 1995, operates from headquarters inside Montgomery's Executive Park. The Montgomery Support Center provides across- the-board administrative support for KinderCare operations nationwide, including education and training, marketing, purchasing, customer service, accounting, real estate, and facility management. Between the Support Center and area learning centers, KinderCare employs nearly 400 Montgomery area workers.

The company's success has been founded on its commitment to the concept of whole child development, which integrates opportunities to play, learn, think, interact, and understand into each child's every activity. Serving children from ages 6 weeks to 12 years, KinderCare builds into each center a warm and nurturing environment, safe and well-equipped facilities, quality educational programs, licensed and trained care providers, and convenient services such as transportation to and from school.

KinderCare has become the standard for excellence in the growing child care industry. With a 95 percent name recognition rate, the word KinderCare is as synonymous with child care as Xerox is with copiers.

KinderCare continues to propel the industry forward with innovative ideas such as placing "KinderCare at Work" learning centers in workplaces, developing mind-broadening "Playscapes" that extend the learning environment outdoors, encourage learning during playtime, and implement intriguing Macintosh "Play-to-Learn" computer programs.

As testimony to its commitment to growth and accessibility, KinderCare opened 45 new centers in 1995, including its first move into foreign markets with a new center in the United Kingdom. The company plans to develop an additional 50 centers in 1996.

In spite of its growing national and international reach, KinderCare is dedicated to its home base and lends tremendous corporate support to Montgomery area agencies and organizations that touch the lives of children, including the Montgomery Zoo and the Montgomery Area United Way.

From a single center in 1969 to more than 1,000 centers today, KinderCare has changed dramatically, but has never lost sight of its founding mission. For as KinderCare children grow and prosper, the company too will grow and prosper—an exciting prospect for Montgomery and the world. **♏**

Serving children from ages 6 weeks to 12 years, KinderCare provides a warm and nurturing environment, safe and well-equipped facilities, quality educational programs, licensed and trained care providers, and convenient services such as transportation to and from school.

STERLING BANK

*I*n 1989 Montgomery became home to a new kind of bank—an unconventional bank that focuses on extraordinary service provided by a staff of experienced, local bankers committed to the betterment of the community. Sterling Bank was established by a group of Montgomery business and community leaders who recognized that banking as an industry was becoming increasingly centralized. They believed that Montgomery needed a bank that had the ability to make quick decisions for their clients, decisions made right here in Montgomery. This dedication to flexibility and responsiveness has been the key to Sterling's record-breaking success.

From the moment a visitor walks through the door at Sterling Bank, the difference is distinct. There are no tellers blocked by tall counters or long lines of people waiting to be served. Instead, client representatives are seated at desks in the lobby, with the clients and guests relaxing in comfortable chairs while conducting their banking business. This entire concept was new to Montgomery, and has been very well received by the community.

In keeping with the founders' commitment to local leadership, Sterling named Alan Worrell, a Montgomery banker and community leader, as its president and chief executive officer. Worrell and the other hand-picked charter officers had already established successful careers and strong followings at other local banks. The loan officers are experienced professionals who are empowered to meet the needs of their clients.

S*terling Bank is a full-service financial institution offering an array of services, including retail and commercial products and a mortgage department.*

In 1992 Sterling Bank joined Synovus Financial Corp.®, a strong parent company, located in Columbus, Georgia, boasting more than $7.9 billion in assets. The merger enhanced the financial resources available to Sterling Bank, while preserving the local autonomy that has contributed greatly to Sterling's success. In 1994 the bank ranked first among Montgomery banks in asset growth and loan growth, and each year thereafter has proven to be another record-breaking performance for Sterling Bank.

Sterling Bank is a full-service financial institution offering an array of services, including retail and commercial products and a mortgage department. Through its affiliate, Synovus Securities, Inc., Sterling provides discount brokerage services and investment opportunities. The bank's mission is to continue to grow its market share by delivering service beyond what the client expects, while maintaining its reputation for serving the community. Each year, Sterling employees have reached 100 percent participation in the United Way campaign. The bank supports various cultural organizations including the Alabama Shakespeare Festival, the Montgomery Museum of Fine Arts, the Montgomery Ballet, and the Montgomery Symphony.

The distinctive style that sets Sterling Bank apart bodes well for a strong, bright future. As envisioned by its founders, Sterling has earned itself a formidable position in the Montgomery market and is recognized as a leader in business lending. *m*

U*nder the leadership of Senior Vice President Bob Ramsey and President and CEO Alan Worrell, Sterling has earned a formidable position in the Montgomery market.*

JIM WILSON & ASSOCIATES, INC.

Uncompromising quality is the hallmark of every Jim Wilson & Associates' property. The company's flagship property is the extraordinary Riverchase Galleria in Birmingham, Alabama. The Riverchase Galleria is a 2.2-million-square-foot multiuse facility of retail space, an upscale office tower, and The Wynfrey Hotel, a luxury four-star, preferred hotel. Jim Wilson & Associates is also very proud to have developed three of Montgomery's magnificent landmarks—Wynlakes Golf & Country Club, the surrounding Wynlakes community, and the Sterling Centre office building.

Dedication to excellence is the hallmark of Jim Wilson & Associates. Montgomerian Jim Wilson Jr. founded his namesake company in 1975. Since then, Jim Wilson & Associates has developed and managed more than 20 million square feet of successful major retail shopping space in 10 different states. Wilson's company also excels in property expansion and renovation which enhance the profitability of the project while improving customer appeal. Jim Wilson & Associates has also developed and manages a variety of other prospering commercial properties. Wilson is a founder of the Sterling Bank. Wilson and his family own Big 10 Tire Stores, now one of the nation's largest independent tire dealers with over 50 tire stores in Alabama, Florida, and Georgia.

Talent and inspiration are the hallmarks of Jim Wilson Jr. He encourages academics, patronizes the arts, and promotes non-pro athletics in the Southeast. Wilson's vision and investment in his hometown have helped to revitalize the economy and better the quality of life for many Montgomery citizens. His Wynlakes Golf & Country Club is a private club with golf, tennis, dining, pool, and guest villa facilities. The beautiful 18-hole championship golf course, designed by Joe Lee, is a mixture of difficulty and opportunity for all levels of expertise. The brilliantly planned community, also named Wynlakes, takes advantage of golf course views, 18 lakes, fountains, and prismatic landscaping.

The name Jim Wilson is the hallmark of success. *m*

The Riverchase Galleria is a 2.2-million-square-foot multiuse facility of retail space, an upscale office tower, and The Wynfrey Hotel.

Jim Wilson & Associates' flagship property is the extraordinary Riverchase Galleria in Birmingham, Alabama.

Jim Wilson & Associates' Wynlakes Golf & Country Club is a private club surrounded by a brilliantly planned community.

UPREME · COURT · OF
APPELLANT

CHAPTER FOURTEEN

PROFESSIONS

From law to accounting, architecture to public relations, Montgomery's professional firms are recognized as leaders in their fields. Photo by Robert Fouts.

BORDEN, McKEAN AND PAYNE ARCHITECTS

Working under a shared corporate philosophy of mutual respect and dedication to superior work, Borden, McKean and Payne Architects has built one of Montgomery's most accomplished design firms.

Under the direction of partners Robert H. Borden, AIA; Rory L. McKean, AIA; and David H. Payne, AIA; the firm has maintained the highest degree of innovation and service since its beginning in 1982. All three partners hold degrees from Auburn University.

Combining more than 60 years of design experience, the three partners have watched their enterprise grow dramatically. The firm focuses on designing churches, schools, university buildings, and multifamily housing. Included in its impressive portfolio are more than 70 churches of various denominations. The firm has designed over 150 multifamily housing developments and is one of the largest designers of this project type in the Southeast. In 1994 Borden, McKean and Payne ranked ninth in Alabama in volume of work completed.

Borden, McKean and Payne operates at peak proficiency with a 12-member staff. The firm employs six registered architects, three intern architects, a graduate civil engineer who handles construction administration, and two skilled, highly experienced office administrators. "Because of the quality of our people, we believe we have the finest firm in Montgomery," says partner David Payne.

In addition to its personnel strength, Borden, McKean and Payne has invested in technological resources that strengthen its service. The firm was one of the first in Alabama to implement a computerized three-dimensional modeling program that provides a detailed video analysis of a project from every angle, with colors, textures, and landscaping included, long before construction begins. "It's a tremendous thrill for our clients to be able to view their facility very early in the design process," says Rory McKean.

Each project is closely managed by one of the partners to ensure clear, productive communication and to offer clients the greatest degree of professional competence.

To its clients, the firm makes three primary commitments: to create aesthetically pleasing, functional environments at reasonable cost; to listen closely and respond to client needs and desires; and to adhere strictly to project budgets. "Our clients are delighted to find that we listen to their ideas and

The firm is leading the way in educational innovation with its design of the Birmingham Early Learning Center.

program requirements and then translate those ideas into graphic presentations that clearly reflect their vision," says Bobby Borden.

Among the firm's recent educational projects are a $4.4-million addition and renovation of an historically significant intermediate school in Opelika; $3.7-million addition to Trinity Presbyterian School in Montgomery; a $5-million, five-phase project for Alabama Christian School in Montgomery; a $6-million campus for Catholic High School in Montgomery; an $8.8-million middle school in Oxford; and a $3.7-million classroom and media center addition to Auburn High School in Auburn.

The firm is leading the way in educational innovation with its design of the $4.6-million Birmingham Early Learning Center, financed through a unique partnership that includes the City of Birmingham, Auburn University, Alabama Power Company, and other leading corporations. The state-of-the-art center, which serves over 200 preschoolers, is staffed by Auburn University and used for practical, hands-on educational instruction.

Borden, McKean and Payne has also earned a reputation as one of Alabama's foremost church designers, having undertaken design for churches with budgets ranging from $250,000 to $16 million. Perimeter Church, a PCA Presbyterian church and one of the fastest-growing churches in America, is a design masterpiece. The 140,000-square-foot project includes a sanctuary seating 2,400, a school for grades kindergarten through eight, a full-sized gymnasium, a fellowship hall that seats 600, on-site parking for 1,500 cars, and two man-made lakes. The sanctuary features sheer glass walls and a full, working stage, which together create an impressive concert-hall effect.

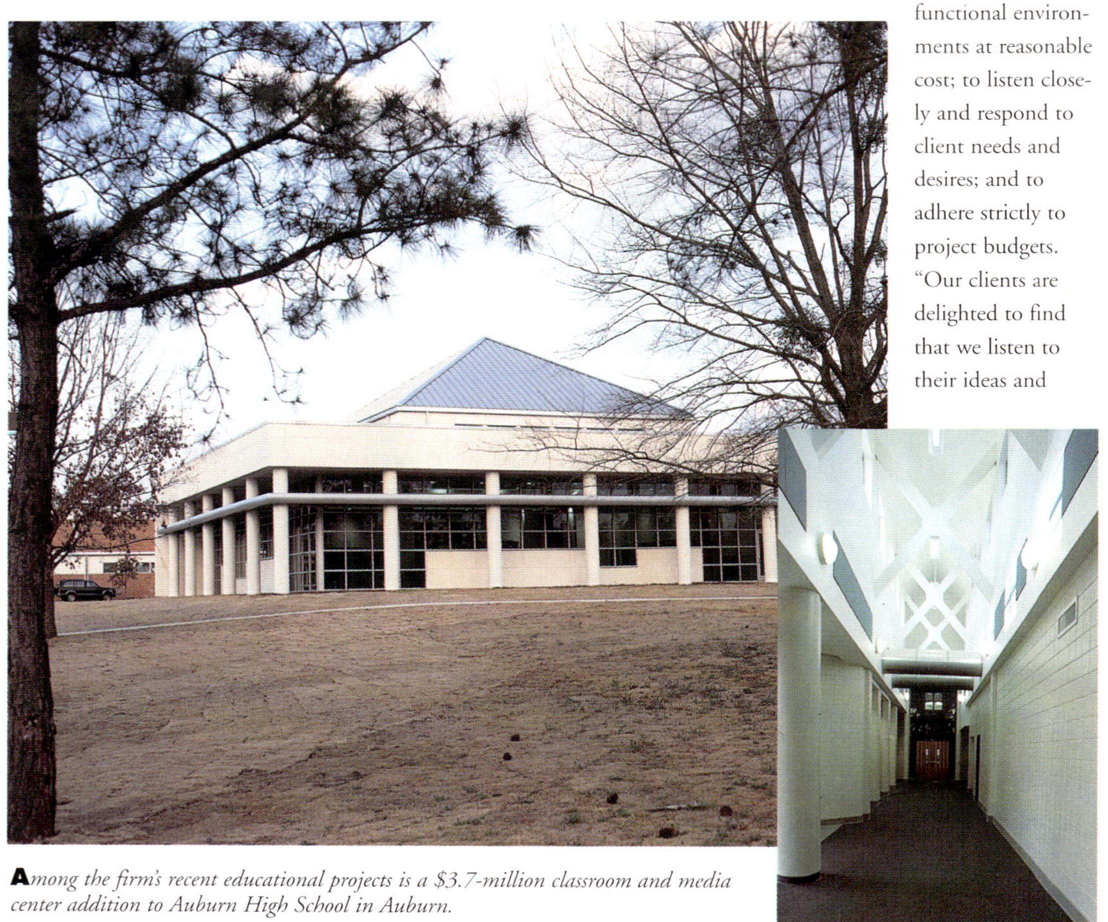

Among the firm's recent educational projects is a $3.7-million classroom and media center addition to Auburn High School in Auburn.

The firm has also designed two new projects as well as a revised master plan for Briarwood Presbyterian Church in Birmingham. Other church projects include additions to East Memorial Baptist, Prattville, and First Baptist, Jacksonville, Alabama, along with several new churches in Montgomery. These include Vaughn Forest Baptist, Saint James Methodist, Bell Road Baptist (formerly Southside Baptist), Lakeview Baptist (formerly Normandale Baptist), Taylor Road Baptist, and Memorial Presbyterian.

One of their most significant office building projects is the $5-million addition and renovation to the Alabama Baptist State Convention building in Montgomery. The firm was selected from over 30 applicants by the United States Department of Labor to design the new $11.5-million Montgomery Job Corps Training Center. This 155,000-square-foot campus includes eight buildings that are skillfully placed on the site to create a pleasant pedestrian mall. Borden, McKean and Payne has also designed facilities for animal research, health care, recreation, performing arts, and industry, as well as libraries and banks.

"We prefer to design projects that will in some way uplift the lives of those served," Payne reflects. The partners and staff put this into action in their community, where they have accepted numerous leadership roles with the Montgomery Area United Way, the Montgomery YMCA, Young Life, and the Jimmy Hitchcock Memorial Award program.

In 1994 the Montgomery Area Chamber of Commerce named the firm to its list of "Emerging 30," Montgomery's most prestigious small-business development award.

Successfully balancing its commitment to professionalism, integrity, service, and innovation, Borden, McKean and Payne Architects has designs on a bright and prosperous future. *m*

An addition and renovation of an historically significant intermediate school in Opelika is another Borden, McKean and Payne project.

The partners prefer to design projects that will in some way uplift the lives of those served, such as the addition to Trinity Presbyterian School in Montgomery.

Working under a shared corporate philosophy of mutual respect and dedication to superior work, (left to right) Bobby Borden, Rory McKean, and David Payne survey the progress at the Alabama Baptist State Convention building site.

Combining more than 60 years of experience, the firm designs churches, schools, university buildings, and multifamily housing, including projects such as the Perimeter Church in Atlanta, Georgia, and Montgomery's own Job Corps Center, as illustrated above using the firm's in-house 3-D computer modeling.

THOMAS, MEANS & GILLIS, P.C.

The law firm of Thomas, Means & Gillis, P.C. is recognized throughout Alabama for its commitment to its clients and for its steadfast dedication to making the justice system work. The firm is proud of its role as a strong and successful client advocate. The proven and diverse legal experience of the firm's seven attorneys and a highly skilled support staff provide each client with a wealth of resources.

Founded in 1981, Thomas, Means & Gillis, P.C. is the successor firm and product of the merger of the practices of Massey, Means & Thomas, P.C. and H. Lewis Gillis. The three partners, Kenneth L. Thomas, Tyrone C. Means, and H. Lewis Gillis, have a combined 57 years of legal experience. Each partner is committed to the firm's founding mission to provide high-quality, uncompromising legal service in a professional environment that offers the finest resources available.

The firm's 25-member professional staff includes 7 attorneys, along with skilled paralegals, legal secretaries, administrators, and an investigator. "The employees of this firm all have one thing in common," said Means. "They are each committed to producing only first-quality products—for themselves, our clients, and this firm."

In all areas of representation Thomas, Means & Gillis, P.C. attributes its success to its willingness to dig deep and be thorough in its preparation. Photo by Fouts Commercial Photography.

Thomas, Means & Gillis, P.C. engages in the general civil and trial practice of law and has substantial experience in litigation for both plaintiffs and defendants in many different types of cases. Members of the firm have litigated personal injury, wrongful deaths, products liability, negligence, employment law, government law, fraud, and insurance cases within both the federal and state court systems and at the highest level of the appellate courts. The firm has also gained distinction for successfully trying a number of significant criminal cases. Gillis, a former Montgomery County chief deputy district attorney, has a stellar record as a criminal defense lawyer. He has also successfully represented a number of Alabama politicians and public officials in civil litigation, including a former Alabama governor, attorney general, and state representative.

The firm operates from a beautiful and spacious office on Zelda Court which was constructed specifically for the practice in 1990. The firm initially occupied only the bottom floor of the plush office space, but quickly grew to fill the two-story building. The office is equipped with the latest business technologies available, large comfortable conference rooms, a complete library, and kitchen facilities. Secured networked office computers allow each lawyer to share files and case information while maintaining confidentiality. The conference rooms are also used as client education rooms and are fully equipped for audio-visual presentations, which are used to inform clients about the legal process before them. These kinds of investments, and a commitment to on-going professional development, help ensure Thomas, Means & Gillis' clients receive the best resources and representation available.

In addition to its Montgomery office, the firm maintains an office in Birmingham to more conveniently serve clients. The firm's practice stretches throughout Alabama, and members are licensed to practice in a number of other states, including Kansas, Georgia, Texas, Pennsylvania, and the District of Columbia.

While Thomas, Means & Gillis, P.C. serves a broad client base, the firm has developed a specialized knowledge for representing public bodies and governmental agencies. Clients include such entities as the City of Montgomery, the City of Birmingham, and Alabama State University. Means has represented Montgomery County and the Montgomery County Sheriff since 1988 and was selected as county attorney in 1993. The firm also represents the Alabama Education Association and its members.

In all areas of representation the firm attributes its success to its willingness to dig deep and be thorough in its preparation. Members of the firm combine their substantial knowledge of the law with their skills as client advocates and their belief in the causes of their clients. "Many people unfortunately are lost in the justice system, and few have an understanding of what it takes to put a case together," said Gillis. "It is our job to guide them successfully through the process."

The lawyers of Thomas, Means & Gillis share an impressive array of credentials. Thomas was the first African-American lawyer to serve as a law clerk to a justice on the Supreme Court of

The three partners, (left to right) Kenneth L. Thomas, H. Lewis Gillis, and Tyrone C. Means have a combined 57 years of legal experience. Photo by Fouts Commercial Photography.

Alabama, while two other members of the firm, J. Mark Englehart and Anita L. Kelly, served as law clerks to federal judges. Means served as president of the Montgomery County Trial Lawyers Association and is currently on the executive committee for the state association. He is also general counsel to America's oldest black Greek-letter fraternity, Alpha Phi Alpha, of which he is a life member. Gillis has served as municipal court judge for the City of Montgomery since 1984, and Kelly, Cynthia W. Clinton, and Launice P. Sills are referees in the Family Court Division of the Circuit Court of Montgomery County. Each lawyer is an active member of the local, state, and national bar associations as well as other professional organizations

While the lawyers offer superior skill and expertise, they are quick to credit the tremendous support afforded by their well-prepared support staff. Recognizing that today's legal environment demands a full spectrum of expertise and a team approach to client needs, the lawyers meet with the staff bi-weekly to discuss case status and outline plans and strategies. In addition, the firm maintains committees to spearhead important projects, such as professional development, and even pays for employees to further their education. A framed print, placed strategically in the center of the work area, reads: "None of us is as strong as all of us"—a philosophy that runs true through both interoffice and client relationships.

As a result of this approach to service, Thomas, Means & Gillis, P.C. has been awarded the Martindale-Hubble Law Directory's highest accolade: an AV rating. This recognition, highly regarded in the legal profession, is both a professional and public confirmation of the firm's status as a respected and ethical legal services provider.

But respect for the members of the firm does not stop on the professional level. Thomas, Means & Gillis, P.C. and its individual members are committed to the betterment of the Montgomery area community, and each works diligently to support area youth and educational programs. Gillis, Means, and Englehart have been members of the prestigious Leadership Montgomery, which taps only the most upstanding citizens and professionals considered to possess extraordinary leadership potential.

Firm members are also active YMCA supporters, serving as board members and committee chairmen for a variety of programs. In fact, Gillis, Means, and Sills have been named Volunteer of the Year for the Cleveland Avenue YMCA. The firm generously supports education,

The firm's professional staff is committed to producing only first-quality products—for themselves, for clients, and for the firm. Photo by Fouts Commercial Photography.

contributing to the Tuskegee University Pre-Law Society and the Lowndes County Board of Education, among others. The firm also supports other local organizations, including the Montgomery Area United Way, the Junior League of Montgomery, Inc., the Lions Club, and Alabama Lawyers for Children. "All of us have families in this community, and it is important to us to be involved in community-based programs that have an impact on the welfare of area youth," said Thomas.

Over the years, Thomas, Means & Gillis, P.C. has remained true to its mission. In every aspect of its business, whether it be client relationships, professional skill, integrity, or community service, the firm consistently responds with the expected "first-quality product." *m*

The Alabama State Bar requires that we advise you that no representation is made that the quality of the legal services to be performed is greater than the quality of legal services performed by other lawyers.

COMMUNITY COMMUNICATIONS, INC.

There is a definite sparkle in the eyes of Ron Beers and Jim Turner when they talk about the stunning success of their young publishing company. And for good reason. It has only been a few short years since Beers first envisioned the possibility of building a company dedicated to helping communities promote themselves through a creative line of high quality publications. In short order, through a combination of Beers' dogged determination and enthusiasm for his product, and Turner's extraordinary creativity and resourceful management, the two have turned the vision into an exciting reality.

Established in 1989, Community Communications, Inc. is already well on its way to achieving its goal of becoming North America's leading publisher of quality books for commercial, civic, historical, and trade associations. In seven years, the company's annual revenues have increased ten-fold. Their publications have achieved national recognition and won prestigious printing and design awards.

"The fundamental key to our success has been an unwavering commitment to quality service to our sponsors, clients, advertisers, and readers," said Beers. "We try not to leave anything to chance when it comes to meeting our customers' expectations."

Formerly a long-time executive sales manager with another publisher, Beers tackled the challenge of starting his own enterprise with proven know-how, well-honed sales skills, a sound business plan, and unyielding determination. From a tiny, one-room office at the rear of a Montgomery area travel agency, Beers set the ball rolling. "You name it; I did it," Beers said. "From sales to production to delivery. I even drove a forklift to unload our first shipment of books."

Fully understanding exactly what it would take to succeed in the competitive world of publishing, Beers turned to LWT Communications President Jim Turner, a brilliant creative mind and one of Alabama's most respected advertising executives, for creative and management expertise. "Jim was willing to go out on a limb and be my production house on credit. Without his support, wisdom, and industry network, we would never have come this far," Beers said.

Today, Turner serves as chairman and chief executive officer of Community Communications, Inc. with responsibility for production and operations, while Beers serves as president with primary responsibility for sales and marketing. From a fully equipped office in Montgomery's Executive Park, which features state-of-the-art computer design technology, the two direct an energetic staff of nearly 50 skilled writers, editors, designers, and sales and marketing professionals.

To put it simply, Community Communications is in the business of promoting community image. Offering a broad line of products, ranging from elegant hardbound coffee-table books designed to last a lifetime to annually produced softcover membership directories and newcomer guides, Community Communications offers an innovative selection of products created to help its clients increase awareness and appreciation of their communities. Its flagship product line is the American Enterprise Series. "In nearly every community we work with, perception is the most important issue," Turner said. "Our American Enterprise book offers them an enriching opportunity to beautifully showcase their community and visually display its strongest attributes."

Community Communications creates its distinctive publications in close collaboration with a sponsoring agency, such as a Chamber of Commerce, Board of Trade, or ecomonic development agency. In exchange for the sponsor's active endorsement, Community Communications handles all aspects of advertising sales, production, and distribution. "It's a turnkey operation, and we accept all the risk," said Beers. "I believe we've created a win-win situation that effectively serves our sponsors, our advertisers, and our readers very well."

Recognizing the varying challenges facing

Jim Turner (left) serves as chairman and chief executive officer of Community Communications with responsibility for production and operations, while Ron Beers serves as president with primary responsibility for sales and marketing. Photo by Fouts Commercial Photography.

communities across the nation, each Community Communications publication is imaginatively conceived and designed to meet specific community needs and provide tangible benefits. Each product among the company's diverse selection of hardcover and softcover publications is thoughtfully created with a particular focus ranging from membership development and retention, to economic development, newcomer familiarization, corporate recruitment, and member and public relations. The creative minds at Community Communications combine interesting text, brilliant photography, and engaging design with quality materials and superior manufacturing to make its books editorially reliable and uncommonly beautiful.

At the outset, the company established a publishing goal of 12 hardcover books per year. With 15 major hardcover publications on the agenda for 1996, Beers and Turner have well exceeded their goals and are taking orders two years and more in advance. "The biggest challenge is helping our sponsors understand the logistics and production time needed to publish a hardcover book," Turner said. "The process is often long and complex, but we are committed to creating a superior product. We don't take shortcuts."

As a result, Community Communications enjoys an exceptional reputation with its clients and sponsors, as well as strong public demand for its books. Distributed via direct mail and conventional sales through bookstores, gift shops, and department stores, most of the company's American Enterprise Series books and American Heritage Series books have become regional bestsellers.

Community Communications has created a product with nationwide appeal. In its short history, the company has produced publications for communities across America from its Montgomery, Alabama, home to Naples, Florida; Buffalo, New York; Kansas City, Missouri; San Jose, California; Ft. Worth, Texas; Knoxville, Tennessee; Pittsburgh, Pennsylvania; Greensboro, North Carolina; and many more, including the book you are holding in your hands. In 1996 the company expanded into Canada, opening its first office in Toronto. Recognizing that its future is predicated on building long-term client relationships, Community Communications takes its place within each locale by becoming active in area Chambers of Commerce or Boards of Trade, working with local writers and photographers, and contributing softbound copies of the corporate profiles to area schools. "We've found the corporate profile sections of our enterprise books

The editorial staff at Community Communications works with sponsors and clients to produce a distinctive publication to showcase a community's strongest attributes. Pictured are (left to right) Lenita Gilreath, Mary Hughes, Linda Pegram, and Bonnie Harris. Not shown is Candy Strickland. Photo by Fouts Commercial Photography.

are valuable tools in teaching students about free enterprise and the business opportunities available right in their own communities," Beers said. And the company is equally committed in its own community, where it strongly supports the Montgomery Area Chamber of Commerce, the Business Council of Alabama, and a variety of educational, cultural, and charitable organizations.

On the strength of a distinguished reputation for excellence and integrity, the professionals at Community Communications are constantly at work dreaming, designing, and developing innovative new publications. "I truly believe no one else can generate the volume we do with the quality we ensure and the local commitment we provide," Beers said.

And while the company is soundly dedicated to the betterment of communities nationwide, it holds the greatest promise right here at home, where it is fast becoming one of Montgomery's most vibrant, vital, and growing business enterprises. **77**

MELTON, ESPY, WILLIAMS & HAYES, P.C.

With more than 85 years of experience, the law firm of Melton, Espy, Williams & Hayes, P.C., has built a solid reputation founded on long and distinguished service.

Oakley Melton Jr. founded the firm in 1964. After having established an excellent reputation with another Montgomery law firm, Melton set out to build his own firm with a passion for trial work. Today, in keeping with his original mission, the firm is primarily engaged in rendering litigation services for businesses, organizations, government agencies, and individuals.

disputes, civil rights, motor vehicle and personal injury accidents, employment discrimination, domestic relations, tax disputes, construction litigation, environmental cases, and business conflicts. The firm also practices administrative law, representing public agencies and local governments. Firm members practice before federal and state court systems and at the highest levels of the appellate courts of Alabama and the United States.

Because of its trial work expertise, the firm is often engaged by other lawyers to participate in their litigation cases. "We are often asked to associate with other firms on their cases. As a small firm, we benefit from their manpower and they benefit from our expertise," said Melton.

Members of the firm have played important roles in their professional and civic communities. Melton is a former president of the Alabama Bar Association and long-time chairman of the Alabama Supreme Court Advisory Committee on Civil Practice and Procedure. In addition, he and Williams have served as president of the Montgomery County Bar Association, and Williams has also served as a member of the State Board of Bar Commissioners since 1992. Espy and Hayes both served as president of the Young Lawyer Section of the Montgomery County Bar Association, and Hayes served as president of the Young Lawyers Section of the Alabama State Bar. Other professional affiliations of firm members include the American College of Trial Lawyers, International Society of Barristers, the Alabama Defense Lawyers Association, and the American Academy of Hospital Attorneys.

Melton, Espy, Williams & Hayes is a respected staple of the Montgomery legal community. Pictured are (seated left to right) Jim Williams, Joe Espy III, (standing) Les Hayes III, and Oakley Melton Jr.

With more than 85 years of experience, the law firm of Melton, Espy, Williams & Hayes, P.C., has built a solid reputation founded on long and distinguished service.

Melton, Espy, Williams & Hayes maintains an "AV" Martindale-Hubbell rating, the highest possible professional rating afforded law firms. In addition, Melton and Espy are included among *The Best Lawyers In America,* a prestigious directory published annually.

In 1973 Melton associated Joe Espy, a former Montgomery County district attorney and fellow graduate of the University of Alabama School of Law. In 1983 Jim Williams, a graduate of Cumberland School of Law at Samford University, joined the firm; and in 1984 Les Hayes, another University of Alabama Law School graduate, joined the firm.

The firm offers a wide range of legal services with a concentration in litigation. The firm has litigated diverse cases including products liability, health and hospital law, insurance coverage

The firm also takes on important civic responsibilities. Added to generous corporate charitable contributions, firm members have served on boards and committees of the Montgomery Area Chamber of Commerce, the Montgomery Area United Way, the American Heart Association, the YMCA of Montgomery, and their respective churches.

As the demand for legal services continues to grow, Melton, Espy, Williams & Hayes stands ready to meet the future by adapting to the changing needs of its clients. Already the firm has in-house automated research functions and participates in rigorous continuing education to stay abreast of a rapidly changing environment.

Melton, Espy, Williams & Hayes is a respected staple of the Montgomery legal community. Its heritage and past service in handling significant, and sometimes even landmark cases, is fundamental to its success. But without resting on its laurels, the firm keeps an eye to the future with Melton's original mission in mind—to provide the highest quality legal services to its clients. *m*

LWT COMMUNICATIONS, L.L.C.

*T*he team of professionals at LWT Communications believe their own success is best measured by the success of their clients.

This creative, highly energetic group takes a partnership approach to every client relationship it establishes, encouraging open communication and client participation at each stage of a creative project. The firm's goal is to combine intelligent fact-finding, creative know-how, and thorough results measurement to meet clients' marketing objectives and increase their profits.

LWT is particularly attuned to the need for accountability in today's increasingly competitive business world. The firm encourages and conducts evaluations of its work to determine effectiveness. "Our clients need to know if they are spending their marketing dollars effectively," said firm partner Jim Leonard. "We track results to determine what is working and adjust accordingly to make the total program as effective as possible."

Responsiveness and accountability have earned LWT an excellent track record for repeat business. In an industry were clients often come and go, many LWT clients have remained long-term marketing partners for over 20 years.

Founded in 1959, LWT Communications has the longest record of continuous service of any advertising agency in Montgomery. In more than 36 years of service, the agency has developed powerful marketing knowledge in such diverse fields as banking, politics, tourism and travel, hospitality, publishing, wholesale and retail grocery, real estate, automotive, chemical-agricultural, higher education, and package goods. The firm enjoys a well-established and growing client base made up of local, regional, and national accounts.

Central to the firm's client retention success is its uncompromising willingness to serve. LWT understands the demands of the marketing process. The need to stand apart in a cluttered world, looming deadlines, tight budgets, and understaffed departments plague marketers everywhere. LWT sees these situations as opportunities to provide a value-added service. "We have the resources, the energy, and the capability to offer our clients all the benefits of a fully-equipped, in-house marketing department," said partner David Allred. "We aim to be more efficient, effective, and every bit as responsive as an in-house staff."

Allred's assessment is confirmed by existing clients who willingly promote the firm and express gratitude for its priority attention to their accounts. "The size of a relationship is irrelevant," said Leonard. "Each client has top priority."

LWT has the technical capability to offer its customers a full line of communications options. The firm expertly provides services including counseling and planning, development of marketing strategies, creation and production of advertising for every medium from newspaper to CD ROM, art direction and print supervision, media research and placement, and more.

LWT uses these capabilities to create powerful advertising that sells. Creative minds review clients' businesses from every angle, carefully searching for the creative edge that will set it apart. The ultimate objective is powerful advertising created on time, on target, and on budget.

LWT Communications takes this same concerned and responsible approach into its community. The firm frequently donates creative services to promote local organizations and charity events. LWT Chairman of the Board Jim Turner, Allred, and Leonard are active community leaders, serving as directors on numerous civic, cultural, and educational boards.

While the firm frequently earns recognition for creative innovation in the form of awards presented by its peers, LWT is also commonly cited for advertising excellence by its clients' industries. LWT Communications' commitment to service, innovation, and quality product earned it the Montgomery Area Chamber of Commerce's Small Business of the Year Award in 1993.

LWT's success comes from a long-standing belief in hard-hitting, research-based marketing communications. The firm is equally committed to business integrity, quality service, and accountability. After more than three decades of success, LWT is positioned to lead the way in creative communications for decades to come. *m*

*T*he professionals at LWT Communications believe their own success is best measured by the success of their clients. Pictured (left to right) are David Allred, Jim Leonard, and Jim Turner.

HILL, HILL, CARTER, FRANCO, COLE & BLACK, P.C.

For more than 70 years, Hill, Hill, Carter, Franco, Cole & Black, P.C. has built a distinguished reputation founded upon a tradition of professional excellence and community service.

The law firm was founded by respected litigator and community leader Thomas B. Hill Jr. in 1924. He was joined by his brother, William Inge Hill, in 1931, and together they worked under the name "Thos. B. Hill, Jr. and Wm. Inge Hill." Over the years, the firm name developed as the partnership expanded. Other early members, such as James J. Carter, James T. Stovall and William Oldacre, also made notable contributions both to the firm's growth and to Alabama's legal community. Today, their heritage continues under the leadership of respected attorneys such as Ralph Franco, T. Bowen Hill III, Harry Cole, and Bobby Black.

The firm's principles are predicated on professional expertise, integrity, and client welfare. To ensure superior service, Hill, Hill, Carter integrates the talents of 21 attorneys and a skillful support staff to create an expert team targeted to meet each client's needs.

For years the firm operated from offices in the Hill Building at the corner of Washington Avenue and Perry Street. In 1992, it moved to newly renovated quarters up Perry Street, conveniently located near the Montgomery County Courthouse, the Alabama State Judicial Building, and the United States District Court. The complex features the finest automated communications and research technologies available to the legal profession.

Although Hill, Hill, Carter is a general civil practice law firm, various members have been recognized for their proficiency in specific practice areas, including litigation, real estate, estate planning and administration, and taxation. The firm is loosely divided into litigation and business sections, but lawyers from both sections interact regularly for the most thorough client representation.

Hill, Hill, Carter attorneys handle virtually every type of civil litigation at the trial and appellate levels in forums ranging from state and federal courts to regulatory boards and administrative agencies.

On the business side, the firm has established a strong reputation for representation of commercial real estate developers and financial institutions. It is also noted for work in residential real estate, business and commercial law, estate planning, mergers and acquisitions, taxation, and employee benefits.

As testament to the firm's emphasis on professional service, several members have served as presidents of the Montgomery County Bar Association and the Alabama State Bar Association. Others have served on the Alabama Board of Bar Examiners, taught at Alabama law schools, and published articles in professional journals. The firm is included in *Best's Directory of Recommended Insurance Attorneys,* five firm members are listed in the prominent national publication *Best Lawyers in America,* one is a Fellow of the American College of Trial Lawyers, another is a Fellow of the American College of Mortgage Attorneys, and still another is a Fellow of the American Law Foundation.

The firm and its members also support a broad range of civic and service organizations. Hill, Hill, Carter attorneys are visible community leaders who frequently serve state and local charitable, civic, cultural, educational, and religious organizations as volunteer board members and officers, through active participation with fund-raising campaigns and events, and in numerous other capacities, including coaching little league teams and tutoring under a local literacy program.

Hill, Hill, Carter, Franco, Cole & Black, P.C. enjoys a rich history, but the firm's commitment to the future is evidenced by its continued professional leadership, its commitment to superior client service, and its dedication to the welfare of its community. ■

The Alabama State Bar requires that we advise you that no representation is made that the quality of the legal services to be performed is greater than the quality of legal services performed by other lawyers.

Hill, Hill, Carter consists of 21 attorneys (most of whom are pictured above) who exemplify the firm's traditional principles of professional expertise, integrity, and client welfare.

A newly renovated facility at 425 South Perry Street houses the offices of Hill, Hill, Carter.

REID/O'DONAHUE & ASSOCIATES ADVERTISING, INC.

A sense of flair, evident from the moment one walks through the door, fills the air of Reid/O'Donahue & Associates' antebellum office in downtown Montgomery and confirms the quality of the work underway within.

Reid/O'Donahue is Montgomery's largest advertising and public relations firm. The nationally recognized full-service communications company provides a range of advertising, marketing, research, public relations, political media, and creative services to a nationwide clientele.

The professionals at Reid/O'Donahue live by the same philosophy they impress upon their clients: always expect more. As a result, the award-winning group has earned regional and national advertising accounts including Coca-Cola, KinderCare, Schlumberger, Rheem Water Heaters, Capitol Chevrolet, Blossman Gas, and Continental Eagle.

The firm was founded in 1980 by Chairman and Chief Executive Officer Bruce S. Reid, a Montgomery native recognized as a skilled media strategist and expert in creative broadcast production. Reid's name has appeared in *Advertising Age* as a national media specialist. Regionally acclaimed graphic designer Shannon O'Donahue joined Reid in 1982, taking on responsibility as president and creative director. O'Donahue has won numerous design awards. Tim Smith, vice president, joined the firm six years ago after being lured away from Jackson, Mississippi, where he worked for three outstanding agencies as owner, creative director, and broadcast producer. Claudia O'Donahue serves as vice president and production manager. She has a strong background in the printing industry and in print production.

Operating from the renovated 150-year-old Knox Mansion, the firm employs 30 professionals expert in management, creative copywriting, graphic design, marketing, and media buying. Together the group has established a reputation built on strong, results-oriented advertising. "We perform as partners with our clients," said Reid. "To be successful for them, we have to work as a team."

But the firm's success is not based solely on its creative achievements. The company employs state-of-the-art technologies to achieve maximum media-buying efficiency. Under the direction of vice president and media director Roberta Pinkston, who the Coca-Cola Company has repeatedly named one of America's most efficient media buyers, the firm uses the Media Management Plus/Smart Plus network computer system to analyze audience delivery research from Nielsen and ARBITRON, and transfer the data into useful tables, charts, and graphs for client review. The system allows station invoice audits, ensuring media deliver targeted audiences at promised costs.

Combining his firm's many strengths with his own interest in politics, Reid joined with high profile Republican strategists Rex Elsass and Brian Berry in 1994 to establish The Strategy Group for Republican Politics and Business, LLC. With offices in Austin, Texas, Columbus, Ohio, and Montgomery, Alabama, the three have served as media consultants for a number of political campaigns, while Elsass and Berry have held leadership positions within the Republican National Committee. Elsass was executive director for the Ohio Republican Party, and Berry worked for Bob Dole for three years before joining The Strategy Group.

In addition to its nationwide influence, Reid/O'Donahue has become an important contributor in its own community, providing pro bono creative services for the Montgomery Area Food Bank, Brantwood Children's Home, the Alabama Dance Theatre, the Montgomery Museum of Fine Arts, and others. "We decided the day we opened we would give back to the community whenever possible. It's our duty," Reid said.

At Reid/O'Donahue & Associates, impact is their job. From community theater to soft drinks and political candidates, Reid/O'Donahue delivers with a distinguished flair. *M*

The historic Knox House (circa 1850) is home to the creative talents of Reid/O'Donahue & Associates Advertising, Inc. Photo by Rus Baxley.

RUSHTON, STAKELY, JOHNSTON & GARRETT, P.A.

For more than a century, the law firm of Rushton, Stakely, Johnston & Garrett, P.A. has been a respected leader in Alabama's legal community. Founded in 1890, the Montgomery firm is composed of 35 attorneys, each skilled in major areas of the legal practice. The firm represents a broad spectrum of local, regional, national, and international businesses. It serves as an advocate for clients in all federal and state courts, before governmental agencies, and in corporate board rooms.

The firm's active and effective trial practice is conducted by attorneys experienced in virtually all areas of civil litigation. Several of the firm's attorneys have been selected as Fellows to the American College of Trial Lawyers. But the firm is equally recognized for its skill in other areas of legal expertise, including insurance, personal injury, professional liability, antitrust, business disputes, products liability, fraud, media litigation, health care, and environmental areas.

Rushton, Stakely, Johnston & Garrett's corporate, business, tax, and real estate attorneys have represented clients in business mergers and acquisitions, securities work of all kinds, including stock and bond issues, real estate and title work, tax matters, and estate planning. With an extensive client base, the firm represents parties in both the public and private sectors.

RSJ&G has also been recognized for its representation of clients in major antitrust litigations, including suits involving claims of price-fixing and market manipulation. Other common examples of the firm's business litigation experience includes cases involving allegations of securities fraud, litigation between owners, architects and contractors, and disputes that may arise out of the sale of businesses.

Rushton, Stakely, Johnston & Garrett also concentrates of product liability defense, warning design, and litigation supervision. The firm represents several international and domestic manufacturers and litigates major cases throughout Alabama and nationwide. Firm members have conducted seminars in Europe for corporations and businesses marketing their products in the United States.

The corporate and business practice of

Located downtown on Commerce Street, in the heart of Montgomery's business district, Rushton, Stakely, Johnston & Garrett is conveniently located to all local, state, and federal courts, where its lawyers and researchers work daily. Photo by Fouts Commercial Photography.

Rushton, Stakely, Johnston & Garrett is well known for its expertise in advising clients in starting, continuing, or acquiring businesses. The firm's corporate and business practice attorneys are a diverse group, with a breadth of experience that ranges from organizing a simple corporation or partnership to dealing with complex, multifaceted organizations.

Insurance defense is still another major component of the firm's practice. RSJ&G has represented virtually every major insurance company as well as many self-insurance programs in defense of personal injury suits, workers' compensation claims, and casualty claims of every description. Located downtown on Commerce Street, in the heart of Montgomery's business district, the firm is conveniently located to all local, state, and federal courts, where its lawyers and researchers work daily.

In addition to its law practice, the firm is involved in the activities of its surrounding community, contributing both time and resources to civic and charitable organizations. Firm members serve on the board of directors of the Montgomery Symphony, the Alabama Shakespeare Festival, and the Montgomery Area Boys' and Girls' Clubs. Recognizing the value of cultural arts to its community, RSJ&G contributed generously to the development of the Montgomery Museum of Fine Arts and is represented by a museum room that bears the firm name.

As a result of its professional strength, its respected leadership, and its community-mindedness, Rushton, Stakely, Johnston & Garrett, P.A. has earned a reputation both as a cornerstone of Alabama's legal profession and of the Montgomery area community. *n*

The Alabama State Bar requires that we advise you that no representation is made that the quality of the legal services to be performed is greater than the quality of legal services performed by other lawyers.

PETER A. LAND ASSOCIATES, INC.

As a teenager, Peter A. Land read management and leadership books while most of his friends were engrossed in mystery novels and comic books. The grandson of Charles A. Ashburner, the first city manager, Land was frequently stirred by written accounts of his grandfather's leadership, integrity, and accomplishments.

Peter Ashburner Land became fascinated with management. As a high school senior he was student body president of the sixth-largest high school in the South. He was recruited by The Citadel on a four-year leadership scholarship, and afterwards he entered the Air Force in 1958. He later earned an M.S. degree in systems management from the University of Southern California.

During his 24-year military career, Land held a variety of command and staff positions, retiring in 1982 as a colonel while serving as Vice Commandant of the Air War College at Maxwell Air Force Base. Land is credited with establishing the management consultation organization for the Air Force, a respected organization employing the latest in computer-based organizational development techniques and methodologies for Department of Defense clients worldwide.

It was those life experiences that led Land to establish his management consulting firm in 1983. The company serves clients throughout the United States, Europe, and Australia and is reeling with the success of Land's new book, *Managing To Get The Job Done.*

One of the most successful independent management consulting firms in the South, Peter A. Land Associates, Inc. provides management services in human resource and organizational development. In assisting its clients, the company reviews such organizational variables as interaction skills, leadership styles, goal clarity, communications, planning, accountability, and decision making.

He leads seminars and workshops on a wide variety of subjects with enthusiasm, clear direction, and purpose. There is a word for what Land does; it's called "edutainment." As he explains it, "The participants learn and practice critical management skills, but it's also a fun day." Land draws from personal experience and breathes life into concepts most managers understand but may not be able to apply effectively on the job.

The firm's client list reads like a virtual "Who's Who." Land works with Coca-Cola, Pennzoil, Yamaha, Atlanta Gas Light, Alabama Power Company, and the State of Alabama, just to name a few.

Land's new book has been endorsed by the coauthor of *The One Minute Manager,* Dr. Ken Blanchard. *Managing To Get The Job Done* is now in its third United States printing in paperback and was recently published in Russian. His book provokes calls and letters from throughout the world; a German translation is being considered.

Today's dynamic business environment, rife with re-engineering and the overhaul of long-held philosophical ideologies, has also helped propel the demand for Land's skills. In addition, our difficult legal environment is forcing other changes. "Nowadays, if we manage

Peter A. Land established his management consulting firm in 1983. His company serves clients throughout the United States, Europe, and Australia. Photo by Fouts Commerical Photography.

improperly, we are not only subject to lawsuits but to massive punitive damages as well. Companies are realizing that the consequences for having untrained managers is simply unacceptable."

Peter Land is doing exactly what he's known he would do all along . . . helping businesses become ever better. With effervescence, expertise, and energy, Land is bringing to light the resources that will help today's leaders manage to get the job done. 77

Land's new book, **Managing To Get The Job Done,** is now in its third United States printing in paperback and was recently published in Russian. Photo by Fouts Commerical Photography.

DEVEREAUX AND ASSOCIATES

Wanda Devereaux is known in legal circles as a strong-willed and meticulous litigator with a passionate commitment to her clients' welfare. Her firm, Devereaux and Associates, primarily concentrates on business law.

Representing a client base that ranges from large corporations to local small businesses, Devereaux and Associates handles business litigation, corporate law, administrative law, and estate planning and administration. The attorneys represent both plaintiffs and defendants in contract disputes, discrimination and employment cases, as well as litigating corporate shareholder disputes, corporate dissolutions, and collections.

In addition to their work before local, state, and federal courts, the attorneys represent clients before administrative agencies and regulatory bodies such as the Alabama Public Service Commission, the Alabama Department of Revenue, and a variety of state professional licensing agencies.

Devereaux devotes considerable time and resources to advising small businesses. "It's a personal commitment, that employs my business experience along with the legal expertise," said Devereaux.

The firm represents clients in divorce, child custody, and child support cases, and helps in the preparation of prenuptial agreements. They represent estates, prepare wills and trusts, and advise clients on estate planning, often working in cooperation with the clients' accountant or tax attorney.

James D. Hamlett, who had clerked for the firm, became an associate in 1995. His low key demeanor is the perfect foil for Devereaux's high energy. Both attorneys, graduates of the University of Alabama School of Law, evidence a strong love and respect for their profession.

In addition to her firm's reputation for providing intelligent, skilled legal representation, Devereaux has garnered praise for her contributions to Alabama's legal community. She has served as president of the Montgomery County Bar Association and as chairman of its ad hoc committee on capital murder defense. She is a trustee of the Alabama Bar Foundation; a member of the governing board of bar commissioners of the Alabama State Bar; and has served as a delegate to the 11th Circuit Judicial Conference.

Devereaux is a believer in "giving back" to the community through volunteer involvement. She has served on the board of the Downtown YMCA, the Montgomery Area United Way, Brantwood Children's Home, and SAYNO. She was an original member of the board of the child advocacy group Success by Six and takes an active role in several organizations dedicated to eliminating domestic violence. Devereaux was a member of the first class selected for Leadership Montgomery.

Ten years ago, Wanda Devereaux launched her private practice, a journey driven by professional challenge and the will to make a difference. Today, Devereaux and Associates is the culmination of that commitment, a respected and skillful advocate for its clients and the community. ▨

The Alabama State Bar requires that we advise you that no representation is made that the quality of the legal services to be performed is greater than the quality of legal services performed by other lawyers.

Devereaux and Associates is located in the historic Confederate Post Office building in downtown Montgomery. Photo by Fouts Commercial Photography.

Representing a client base that ranges from Fortune 500 corporations to local businesses, Devereaux and Associates handles business litigation, corporate law, administrative law, and estate planning and administration. Photo by Fouts Commercial Photography.

BROWN ASSOCIATES ARCHITECTS

For nearly 20 years, Brown Associates Architects has created lasting and progressive architectural projects found regionally and in the Montgomery area. The firm's work is diverse, from large scale planning to the final selection and coordination of furnishings and furniture. The firm's work covers a wide range of project types from office and commercial buildings to military construction, retail development, hotels, churches, and schools. It is recognized for its design work in the ever challenging health care industry. The firm has developed community based facilities to provide the constellation of services necessary for today's health care providers. One such project locally is Baptist Medical Park in Prattville.

The firm has played a role in preserving Montgomery's historic architecture. It was one of the first companies to restore a turn-of-the-century warehouse in the Lower Commerce Street Historic District, and it still occupies the beautifully restored brick building, one of several the firm has renovated, by the river.

At the other end of the spectrum, the firm helped create a vision for Montgomery's future—the Alabama TechnaCenter. This growing, high-tech, multiuse technology complex is located in east Montgomery, just off Interstate 85. The first building, The Institute for Advanced Information Systems, involved a partnership of state and local government, Auburn University, and private developers to develop the potential to nurture the growing software engineering community in Montgomery. Another facility in the park, the headquarters of the Alabama Rural Electric Association, has the state's largest water source ground loop heat pump system, and also demonstrates other design strategies for energy efficiency, a special interest of the firm.

Brown Associates Architects' projects for the military locally include several facilities and a Master Plan for the Air National Guard at Dannelly Field, the Security Police Building and Fire Station at Gunter, and restoration projects at Maxwell.

In every case, the process of developing a strategic plan with near-term objectives meeting a client's vision has resulted in a successful project. The result of this uncommon commitment to do things right and comprehensive approach to a client's needs has resulted in repeat business being the primary source of the firm's work.

The company has a strong commitment to community service. The firm's members have assisted Montgomery's Historic Development Commission, contributed design and construction guidance to Landmarks for the expansion and restoration of Old Alabama Town, and to Habitat for Humanity for projects in Montgomery. It also helped design and construct several historic markers and monuments in the area, provided support to Jubilee CityFest, and contributed to various activities of the Chamber of Commerce.

Brown Associates Architects has provided clients with cost-effective solutions through the employment of teams with specialized expertise, people who know what questions to ask and what answers will work. The firm's President, Don Brown, says: "Whatever type project we undertake, from medical centers to industrial development, we resolve the complicated strategic issues each of our clients face in today's dynamic business environment. We must produce work that meets near-term needs, provides for long-term flexibility, and always upholds the highest standards of quality desired by our client. Vision, determination, imagination, and professionalism are the core values shared by our firm with our clients." *m*

The Institute for Advanced Information Systems involved a partnership of state and local government, Auburn University, and private developers to develop the potential to nurture the growing software engineering community in Montgomery. Photo by Fouts Commercial Photography.

The process of developing a strategic plan with near-term objectives of meeting a client's vision has resulted in successful projects, such as the Parker Ryan building located on Carmichael Way in Montgomery. Photo by Gary Knight Photography.

The Alabama Rural Electric Association has the state's largest water source ground loop heat pump system, and also demonstrates other design strategies for energy efficiency, a special interest of the firm. Photo by Fouts Commercial Photography.

CAPELL, HOWARD, KNABE & COBBS, P.A.

Professional leadership, civic responsibility, and steady growth have characterized the Montgomery law firm of Capell, Howard, Knabe & Cobbs, P.A. since its founding. The firm, which began as the two-member partnership of Jack Capell and Fontaine Howard in 1947, is today a regional law firm of 31 lawyers—24 members and 7 associates.

Capell Howard is headquartered at 57 Adams Avenue, only a block from

Capell, Howard, Knabe & Cobbs offers a unique blend of tradition, professionalism, energy, individuality, and innovation.

both the Federal and County Courthouses. With an eye to the future and a commitment to the downtown area, the firm is expanding its firm-owned office complex to encompass a full quarter-block. The new facilities will feature modern conference rooms with sophisticated communications and computer technologies. The firm already employs computerized desktop databases that give lawyers instant worldwide information access.

Capell Howard is organized into three general departments—business law, real estate, and dispute resolution. Each department consists of a number of specialized practice groups. To achieve cost-effective and thorough client representation, lawyers in different departments or practice groups commonly work together on cases.

The firm's business practice covers the full range of planning, organizing, financing, and operating corporations, general and limited partnerships, joint ventures, limited liability companies, and other business enterprises. Its highly respected tax practice, its work as bond counsel, and its active securities practice are also integral to the business side.

Capell Howard's real estate lawyers provide counsel to numerous lenders and developers of commercial properties throughout the Southeast. The firm handles legal matters involving regional shopping centers and malls, industrial parks, office complexes, apartments, hotels, and condominium developments.

The dispute resolution department handles litigation at all levels of the state and federal judicial systems. The firm serves as trial and appellate counsel in a variety of complex lawsuits, with typical cases involving commercial, construction, surety, procurement, employment and labor, environmental, insurance, real estate, products liability, antitrust, unfair trade practices, workers' compensation, securities, financial transactions, or constitutional issues.

The firm also has a strong administrative law practice, representing clients before state and federal administrative and regulatory agencies such as the Equal Employment Opportunity Commission, the Environmental Protection Agency, the State Health Planning Agency, the Alabama Public Service Commission, and the Armed Services Board of Contract Appeals.

Recognizing the need for more cost-effective, less stressful alternatives to litigation, Capell Howard attorneys have taken a leading role in educating the bar, the judiciary, and the public about alternative methods of dispute resolution, such as arbitration and mediation. One firm member, a former federal judge, is a member of the national CPR Institute for Dispute Resolution. Another firm member chairs the Alabama State Bar Committee on Alternative Methods of Dispute Resolution and serves on the Alabama Supreme Court Commission on Dispute Resolution.

Honored by being selected the Alabama member of the prestigious State Capital Law Firm Group, the firm is uniquely able among Alabama law firms to offer its clients valuable access to legal information via a network of 50 of the foremost law firms in America.

The firm's tradition of professional leadership continues as eight firm members are named in the widely recognized directory *Best Lawyers in America,* three have served as president of the Montgomery County Bar Association, and several are active in Alabama State Bar committees and sections. Two firm members have held national leadership positions—one served as president of the American College of Mortgage Attorneys, and another formerly served as chairman of the board of the American Corporate Counsel Association. Members of the firm frequently speak and present papers at continuing legal education programs for other lawyers.

But Capell Howard contributions span beyond the professional realm. The firm and its individual members generously serve their community, giving of their time and financial resources. Firm members have served as president, chairmen, or in other leadership positions of numerous community organizations, including the Business Committee for the Arts, the Alabama Shakespeare Festival, the Montgomery Museum of Fine Arts, the Montgomery Civic Ballet, the Jasmine Hill Council, the Montgomery Area United Way, the Lighthouse, the Landmarks Foundation, and the Montgomery Area Food Bank. The firm is a significant supporter of the Montgomery Area Chamber of Commerce and is represented on the Chamber's Committee of 100.

Capell, Howard, Knabe & Cobbs, P.A. is proud of its heritage, but stays focused on the opportunities ahead. Offering a unique blend of tradition, professionalism, energy, individuality, and innovation, Capell Howard is well positioned to serve the Montgomery of tomorrow. 🄼

The Alabama State Bar requires that we advise you that no representation is made that the quality of the legal services to be performed is greater than the quality of legal services performed by other lawyers.

Jack L. Capell
Herman H. Hamilton Jr.
Rufus M. King
Robert S. Richard
Frank H. McFadden
John B. Scott Jr.
John F. Andrews
James M. Scott
Thomas S. Lawson Jr.
John L. Capell III
William D. Coleman
William K. Martin
Bruce J. Downey III
Henry C. Barnett Jr.
Palmer Smith Lehman
Neal H. Acker

Henry H. Hutchinson
Shapard D. Ashley
D. Kyle Johnson
J. Lister Hubbard
James N. Walter Jr.
James H. McLemore
W. Holt Speir III
Jim B. Grant Jr.
Christopher W. Weller
Chad S. Wachter
Ellen M. Hastings
Debra Deames Spain
C. Clay Torbert III
R. Eric Powers III
R. Brooke Lawson III

SIROTE & PERMUTT, P.C.

For a full half century, the highly regarded law firm of Sirote & Permutt, P.C. has been a leader in its field, offering its clients a full range of the highest quality legal services. The firm's reputation is founded upon prompt, thorough, and efficient service carried out by some of the finest attorneys in Alabama and the nation.

Founded by three prominent attorneys in Birmingham in 1946, the law firm has grown steadily to almost 100 attorneys and more than 300 support personnel. With offices in Montgomery, Birmingham, Tuscaloosa, Huntsville, and Mobile, the firm's influence and expertise stretch across Alabama.

Sirote & Permutt opened its Montgomery office in January 1991 under the direction of Fred Simpler, managing partner. Having served a number of Montgomery clients from its Birmingham office, the firm had established a solid client base in the Capital City. The new office, located in the prestigious Colonial Financial Center, would increase the firm's presence and offer immediate client access.

The full-service Montgomery office has since grown to include a staff of 6 attorneys and 14 support staff. The firm's diversified business practice extends to most aspects of litigation, real estate, labor, taxation, estate planning, health care, collections, banking, corporate and securities law, bankruptcy, probate, and tax-exempt and taxable bond financing, in addition to many other areas of practice.

The firm's broad practice is matched by the diversity of its clients. Sirote & Permutt established and expanded its practice by representing local, family-owned businesses. The firm remains committed to serving small and emerging businesses, but routinely represents some of America's largest publicly held corporations. In addition to businesses, the extensive Sirote & Permutt client list includes individuals, trusts and estates, and charitable and educational institutions.

With clients located not only throughout Alabama, but also in 42 other states, Europe, Asia, and Canada, Sirote & Permutt expertise reaches far and wide. Always determined to meet its clients' needs with efficiency and accuracy, the firm has been a leader in developing resources and technologies to enhance delivery of its services.

Sirote & Permutt pioneered the use of legal assistants in Alabama and has implemented state-of-the-art computer technology designed to bring clients responsive, cost-effective legal services. The firm's advanced telecommunications and information retrieval and management systems are networked statewide, giving each local office access to the firm's resources.

While Sirote & Permutt attorneys are noted for their broad spectrum of backgrounds, intelligence, and expertise, they are equally recognized for carrying on the firm's founding premise of philanthropy and community support.

Sirote & Permutt lawyers are visible throughout the community serving on boards of such worthwhile organizations as the Brantwood Children's Home and the Salvation Army. They are often seen on the sidelines coaching YMCA Little League teams, supporting the arts community through the Montgomery Museum of Fine Arts, and strengthening the business community through the Montgomery Area Chamber of Commerce.

In addition, Sirote & Permutt attorneys support and encourage professional development, frequently serving as faculty for Continuing Legal Education seminars and workshops. One attorney in the Montgomery office also serves as editor for the *Alabama Defense Lawyer's Journal*.

This well-balanced combination of legal skill, uncompromising service, and commitment to advancing technologies is certain to keep Sirote & Permutt, P.C. at the forefront of its profession well into the next century. *m*

The Alabama State Bar requires that we advise you that no representation is made that the quality of the legal services to be performed is greater than the quality of legal services performed by other lawyers.

Sirote & Permutt's Montgomery office is located in the prestigious Colonial Financial Center. Photo by Fouts Commericial Photography.

MCPHILLIPS, SHINBAUM, GILL & STONER, P.C.

One of the first things a visitor to the law firm of McPhillips, Shinbaum, Gill & Stoner, P.C. sees upon entering the foyer of the firm's historic Perry Street office is a framed picture of an American Indian with the following inscription: "To give dignity to a man is above all things."

Such is the mission upon which this law firm was established by attorney Julian McPhillips in 1978. Over the years, the firm has become recognized for its client advocacy work in cases involving personal injury, wrongful death, insurance fraud, product liability, employment discrimination, constitutional and civil rights, and criminal defense.

After graduating from Princeton in 1968 and the Columbia University School of Law in 1971, McPhillips worked in international law with a Wall Street law firm. He returned to his home state in 1975 and worked as an assistant attorney general in the Alabama Attorney General's office until 1977, when he resigned to conduct a strong, but unsuccessful, bid for the Attorney General's post.

McPhillips opened his own law office and practiced alone from a portion of the middle floor of the Perry High Building. His only assistant was a part-time secretary. Today the firm occupies the entire fully-renovated building, and McPhillips' one-time secretary, Regina Barron, is one of nine attorneys. The office environment is a hub of constant activity requiring the attention of more than 25 professional staffers.

The firm's partners, McPhillips, Kenneth Shinbaum, G. William Gill, and Allen Stoner are known for their aggressive and successful pursuit of client rights. "We are foremost committed to our role as client advocates," said McPhillips. "We will fight hard to win for our clients, but it is also our responsibility to make certain our clients understand the difficulties they may face throughout the process. To be successful, we must earn our clients' trust and work together."

After two decades of service, McPhillips and the firm have an impressive and diverse list of high-profile cases to their credit. Among others, McPhillips sued a former Alabama governor for using his office for personal gain—a controversial charge which ultimately led to the governor's resignation. The firm is well-known for its successful defense of cases involving the violation of First Amendment rights; and McPhillips has won acquittals in each of the four murder cases he has taken on, including two capital murder charges.

McPhillips is not an unlikely defender of the oppressed. A fierce competitor, he is the son of an Episcopal priest and a former football player and All-American wrestler at Princeton. He tried out for the Olympic wrestling team in 1968 and was a finalist in the 1972 Olympic tryouts. "We relish taking on tough cases; there is a certain satisfaction that comes with it," he said.

McPhillips, Shinbaum, Gill & Stoner encourages community involvement and support with equal enthusiasm. Firm attorneys and staff members are actively involved in civic, religious, educational, and charitable organizations. McPhillips personally spearheaded development of the F. Scott and Zelda Fitzgerald Museum, located in the beloved writer's Montgomery residence on historic Felder Avenue. He and his wife are also founding members of Christ the Redeemer Episcopal Church, which was organized in 1980.

Partner Stoner and associate Mary Goldthwaite were formerly deputy district attorneys of Montgomery County. Of counsel to the firm are Bill Honey, also a professor of law at Auburn University at Montgomery, and Gary Atchison, formerly general counsel to the Alabama Education Association.

While McPhillips, Shinbaum, Gill & Stoner is known for waging formidable battles, the lawyers emphasize that a challenging fight is only one part of the puzzle. The firm's ultimate mission remains as it has always been—solid, ethical client advocacy driven by justice. *n*

The Alabama State Bar requires that we advise you that no representation is made that the quality of the legal services to be performed is greater than the quality of legal services performed by other lawyers.

McPhillips, Shinbaum, Gill & Stoner's ultimate mission is to provide solid, ethical client advocacy driven by justice.

CHAPTER FIFTEEN

BUILDING GREATER MONTGOMERY

THE COLONIAL COMPANY

*I*n 1956 Ed Lowder founded The Colonial Company. After 40 years of growth, The Colonial Company operates across the Southeast through Lowder Construction Co., Inc., Coldwell Banker Lowder Realty, Colonial Insurance Agency, Inc., and Lowder New Homes, Inc.

The overall mission of The Colonial Company is to succeed through hard work, shared goals, and benevolent giving. Many of Montgomery's civic organizations (the United Way, the YMCA, the Red Cross, the Chamber of Commerce, and others) have benefited from the company's pursuit of this mission. As the company's business

Lowder New Homes has built over 5,000 new homes, from custom executive estates to garden homes, in communities like Wyndridge (shown here) and Halcyon Summit.

units have grown and prospered, Montgomery's economy has also benefited.

LOWDER CONSTRUCTION COMPANY

Involved in commercial office, shopping center, and multifamily construction throughout the Southeast, Lowder Construction is nationally recognized for its diverse construction capabilities.

Commercial office buildings in Montgomery include Interstate Park, Colonial Financial Center, the offices of Blue Cross Blue Shield, and historic renovations at 166 and 250 Commerce Street.

Montgomery shopping centers include McGehee Place Shopping Center, Montgomery Promenade, and Bellwood Shopping Village.

Lowder Construction is consistently ranked among the top 10 in apartment starts nationwide. Some multifamily communities in Montgomery include Vieux Carre Apartments, Willow Bend Apartments, McGehee Place

Apartments, and Vaughn Lakes Apartments.

LOWDER NEW HOMES, INC.

The largest home builder in Alabama, Lowder New Homes continues to maintain its position as one of the top 100 home builders nationally.

Lowder New Homes has built over 5,000 new homes, from custom executive estates to garden homes, in communities like Wyndridge, Young Farm, Bellwood West, Halcyon Summit, Highland Ridge in Prattville, and Deer Creek, a new 800-acre community.

COLDWELL BANKER LOWDER REALTY

Coldwell Banker Lowder Realty is consistently the area's leading residential real estate company. Whether in Montgomery, Prattville, Wetumpka, or Lake Martin, Coldwell Banker Lowder Realty provides unique and innovative real estate services. Its affiliation with the nation's leading real estate franchise gives clients access to unrivaled relocation services.

Wyndridge

COLONIAL INSURANCE AGENCY

Colonial Insurance Agency serves the Southeast as an independent agency. It focuses on the needs of the construction industry, property owners, financial institutions, wholesale, retail, manufacturer, and industrial clients, as well as meeting the personal insurance needs of individuals.

As complex as the operating environment is for each of The Colonial Company's business units, ultimately the reasons each succeeds are as simple as they are time-tested—hard work, shared goals, and giving back to our community a portion of the rewards. *77*

Halcyon Summit

COLONIAL PROPERTIES TRUST

*I*n an effort to enhance its ability to acquire and develop high-performing real estate, The Colonial Company established Colonial Properties Trust, a real estate investment trust. Originally founded in 1970 as Colonial Properties, Inc., Colonial Properties Trust completed its public offering in September 1993. Since the initial public offering, the company has quickly become one of the largest developers, owners, and managers of multifamily, retail, and office properties in the Southeast.

Colonial Properties Trust is a publicly held, fully integrated real estate company that owns a diversified portfolio of properties in Alabama, Florida, and Georgia, and is known for developing new properties, acquiring existing properties, managing, leasing, and selling commercial real estate.

Colonial Properties Trust is organized into three operating divisions—multifamily, retail, and office—each of which manages and leases its properties. In addition, with four decades of property management experience to its credit, the company has also established a large following in third-party management and leasing.

The office division provides outstanding developments in four major geographic areas in Alabama and Florida, managing and leasing in excess of 1.8 million square feet. Due to the outstanding quality of its properties, together with the professional expertise of its management personnel, the office division has maintained occupancy rates well above 90 percent throughout the last decade. Major office properties leased and managed within Montgomery include Interstate Park, located at I-85 and Perry Hill Road, and Colonial Financial Center, located in downtown Montgomery.

The retail division is a recognized expert in mall and shopping center leasing management. Retail management is responsible for over seven million square feet. Local retail properties include Montgomery Promenade, McGehee Place Shopping Center, Bellwood Shopping Center, and Olde Town Shopping Square.

The multifamily division is the largest division in the company, which owns and manages approximately 12,000 units throughout Alabama, Florida, and Georgia. Its Montgomery apartment properties include McGehee Place, Vieux Carre, and Willow Bend.

Colonial Properties' commercial sales division has been consistently recognized for its ability to perform in a highly professional and timely manner in meeting its clients' needs. Representing many individual investors and major corporations in accomplishing their real estate needs, the sales division of Colonial Properties is actively involved in all phases of commercial real estate in both the Montgomery and Prattville markets.

"Our objective is to continue on a path of consistent growth," said Senior Vice President John Stanley. "We must grow by investing in performing real estate if we are going to give our investors the kind of returns they expect." It would appear the mission is working. Since the company's initial public offering in 1993, its property holdings have increased by nearly 70 percent. The company is expected to reach $1 billion in total market capitalization in 1996.

True to their mission, "superior results through superior service with quality people," the people at Colonial Properties have never dreamed small. Through hard work, integrity, and professional skills, they have created a reality that has exceeded even their wildest dreams. *m*

*M*ontgomery Promenade

*M*cGehee Place Apartments (shown here), Montgomery Promenade, and Interstate Park Center were all developed by Colonial Properties Trust and built by Lowder Construction Co., Inc.

*I*nterstate Park Center

W. S. NEWELL, INC.

*I*n Alabama, the name W. S. Newell is practically synonymous with highway construction. If you have traveled almost anywhere in the Southeast, chances are you have crossed over massive stretches of Newell's highway handiwork.

But road construction is not all there is to the story behind this successful multimillion-dollar enterprise. W. S. Newell, Inc. is recognized throughout the Southeast for a variety of quality heavy construction work, including vast spans of highway, bridges, locks and dams, airport facilities, and more.

Company founder Billy Newell began his legendary construction career in 1953 on a shoestring budget with a borrowed Caterpillar bulldozer and a dream. His first job, a fish farm pond, earned him $300. A year later, Newell successfully completed his first job for the Alabama Highway Department, earning $100,000 as a project subcontractor. Not long thereafter, he successfully bid $750,000 for his first prime contract with the state highway department. The rest is history, as Newell proceeded to build a strong business and lasting relationships through responsive service and a "can-do" attitude.

By its 25th anniversary, W. S. Newell, Inc. had taken on and successfully completed more than $275 million in diverse heavy construction jobs, and Billy Newell had gained regional renown and respect.

Much of the company's success is directly attributable to Newell's personal drive, determination, and work ethic. But anyone close to the company is quick to note that Newell's wife, Sadie, has been essential to the company's astounding success and equally as committed to the business as her husband.

In the early days of fish ponds and borrowed equipment, Mrs. Newell ran the office and kept the books while her husband was on the job. For nearly 40 years, as the company grew and staff expanded, she remained central to its administration.

Although the Newells' sons, Sam and Keith, handle major management responsibilities as executive vice president and vice president, respectively, the senior Newell is still at the hub of daily operations, holding the title of president and chief executive officer. "This is his work; this is his hobby," said Newell's son, Keith. "It's all the time. If there's any spare time, he's out here at the office or riding on a job."

Road construction is at the core of the work that has sustained W. S. Newell, Inc. for more than four decades. The company built a major portion of Interstates 65 and 85 through Montgomery and much of Interstate 10 running through Mississippi and south Alabama. The company has for years competed with aggressive out-of-state road builders, but W. S. Newell has succeeded in earning more than 80 percent of its road construction business in Alabama, along with extensive work in Mississippi, Arkansas, North Carolina, Florida, and Georgia.

Although new business is taking on a variety of forms, highway construction remains at the center of W. S. Newell's future. The company recently won its second largest highway construction contract—a $27-million contract to build part of Interstate 78, which will ultimately connect Birmingham, Alabama, with Memphis, Tennessee.

According to Keith Newell, W. S. Newell, Inc. has the muscle to win prime projects because of its long-time commitment to quality work and superior service. "We pride ourselves on doing the best possible job in the most efficient manner. We are often recommended by former clients who attest to the fact that we do it right the first time."

A key example of the company's ability to handle complex, heavy construction work is its role in construction of the Tennessee-Tombigbee Waterway. This critical barge canal, which links the Tennessee River and the industrial Northeast to the Gulf of Mexico, is the largest civil construction project ever undertaken in the United States. Newell completed the excavation and related work on five of the waterway's many lock and dam systems. During the arduous process, the company excavated well more than 20 million cubic yards of earth.

W. S. Newell's waterway success is typical of its ability to take on challenging projects and meet client needs, even under the most difficult circumstances. In 1990 the United States Army let a contract in Fort Rucker called "Stage Field." In this contract Newell moved four million yards of dirt and constructed helicopter runways in just five months' time. The company took on the job and met the deadline. "We have a reputation for going the extra mile; that's why we get called

*N*ewell received its second largest highway construction contract—a $27-million contract to build part of Interstate 78, which will ultimately connect Birmingham, Alabama, with Memphis, Tennessee.

*R*ecognized throughout the Southeast for a variety of quality heavy construction work, W. S. Newell is responsible for work including vast spans of highway, such as the Corridor X project that connects Birmingham to Memphis.

Road construction is at the core of the work that has sustained W. S. Newell, Inc. for more than four decades. Shown here is construction of the U.S. Highway 82 Bypass located in Prattville, Alabama.

on so frequently for tough jobs," said Keith Newell.

A full-service operation, W. S. Newell is equipped to handle every phase of a construction project, from cost estimating to engineering and construction management. The company maintains a fully stocked equipment yard and a staff of experienced personnel second to none. At peak, the company employs up to 400 project personnel.

Employee loyalty and longevity are the rule, not the exception, at W. S. Newell. Some long-time employees have retired after a lifetime of service, and an extraordinary proportion of personnel have been with Newell for more than 25 years.

"Our reputation stems from the quality of our employees," said Keith Newell. "We have been blessed with loyal employees who have stayed with us and grown with us. W. S. Newell is as much a family as it is a business."

In addition to its heavy construction work, W. S. Newell is also noted for its site development work for large subdivisions such as Montgomery's prestigious Wynlakes Golf and Country Club community.

But the company is fast becoming one of the area's most prominent private developers in its own right. Towne Lakes, a luxurious subdivision in east Montgomery featuring 450 upscale homes, breathtaking landscaping, and welcoming rural surroundings, is a Newell development. In addition, W. S. Newell developed the Alabama TechnaCenter, an office park which houses some of Montgomery's most high-tech businesses, and the Montgomery Business Park on Congressman Dickinson Drive. The Montgomery community is eagerly awaiting the company's newest venture, the prestigious Deer Creek subdivision, which Newell will develop in association with Lowder and Aronov Realty companies.

As successful as the company has been, its low profile personality mirrors that of its founder. A native Montgomerian, graduate of Lanier High School, and World War II veteran, Billy Newell is a quiet contributor, loyal to his community in countless ways. He is actively involved in the Business Council of Alabama and a staunch supporter of the Montgomery Area Chamber of Commerce.

The dynamic growth in and around the Montgomery area and the Southeast are good signs for W. S. Newell, Inc. With decades of experience and a reputation for proven quality and dedicated service, the road ahead is paved for continued success. ***m***

In addition to its heavy construction work, W. S. Newell is also noted for its site development work for large subdivisions such as Deer Creek, an 800-acre development, located off Vaughn Road in Montgomery.

ARONOV REALTY

The diverse enterprises of Aronov Realty are intricately woven among the threads that have colored the tapestry of Montgomery living for nearly half a century.

Established in 1952 by Aaron Aronov, the company has become one of the South's largest diversified real estate development, management, and brokerage firms. Glittering examples of Aronov Realty's extraordinary contributions in office, retail, industrial, and residential real estate shine from one end of the Capital City to the other. But Aronov's influence spreads much farther.

In fact, the multifaceted real estate company owns or manages more than 150 properties in 15 states and is growing rapidly. The company's properties include more than 80 shopping centers and malls, thousands of apartment units, dozens of office buildings, resort developments, hotels, warehouses, and industrial buildings.

Having observed his father develop residential property as a sideline, Aaron Aronov embarked on his full-time career in real estate with both residential and commercial projects. In response to unprecedented demand for housing following World War II, he developed apartments and planned residential communities in Montgomery. Recognizing that suburban growth would necessitate convenient shopping and office facilities, he became a pioneer in shopping center development. In 1954 Aronov opened Normandale Shopping Center, then the second largest suburban shopping center in the Southeast.

Aronov has continued to introduce the latest concepts in retail to Montgomery and the Southeast. Examples in Montgomery include Eastdale Mall, Zelda Place, and Montgomery Towne Center.

Under the leadership of Jake and Owen Aronov, the company continues its legacy of residential and commercial property development. Aronov Realty is ranked among the top 25 retail real estate developers in the United States. The company's success is based on having served a variety of national and regional retailers well.

In addition to new development, Aronov manages numerous properties for individuals and financial institutions providing expert marketing, leasing, and management services. "We apply the same intensive management for others that we apply to our own properties," said Earl Martin, Aronov's senior vice president of asset management. As a result, the company is one of the

The five-story Carmichael Center opened in early 1995 and has become one of Montgomery's newest and most prestigious business addresses.

fastest growing managers of properties owned by others in America.

While its retail properties are spread across the country, Aronov may be known best locally for its residential and commercial property sales and for its prestigious office buildings and office parks.

The Aronov Building in the heart of Montgomery's downtown business district offers the distinction of an established downtown property and a location convenient to both the center of the city's government and business activity. The five-story Carmichael Center, which sits at the convenient intersection of Perry Hill and Carmichael Roads, opened in early 1995 and has become one of Montgomery's newest and most prestigious business addresses. And the distinctive Aronov Center, located in the company's Executive Park office park development, is home to Aronov's corporate headquarters and other leading central Alabama businesses.

Conveniently located just off the Eastern Boulevard in rapidly growing east Montgomery, Executive Park has become a highly regarded office location and is the home of prominent local businesses and such national concerns as IBM, Blue Cross Blue Shield, KinderCare, Inc., and Blount, Inc.

The company's mission includes creating quality living environments as well as outstanding places to work and shop. In expected fashion, Aronov took the lead in developing upscale multifamily residences in Montgomery with such

Aronov is known for introducing the latest concepts in retail to Montgomery and the Southeast, such as Eastdale Mall.

projects as the Hillwood and Vaughn Lakes luxury apartment complexes. Departing from the ordinary, the properties feature luxury amenities and at Vaughn Lakes beautiful lakeside balcony views. Aronov's Sea Chase Condominiums in Gulf Shores, Alabama, are yet another example of the company's ability to integrate luxury and affordability.

Aronov has developed high quality single-family residential neighborhoods in virtually every corner of Montgomery, including the prestigious Halcyon South on the growing east side, as well as such preferred subdivisions as Prattville East and Pecan Ridge in nearby Prattville.

Aronov has joined with another leading developer to create Montgomery's beautiful Deer Creek, one of the area's newest and most innovative neighborhoods. The Vaughn Road subdivision offers more than 800 acres of diverse residential options, accented by exquisitely landscaped recreational areas, lakes, and a neighborhood center.

Perhaps the most commonly visible indicators of Aronov's local presence are the bright red, white, and blue "Aronov Sold Another!" realty signs that pepper the landscapes of neighborhoods in Montgomery, Autauga, and Elmore Counties.

Backed by four decades of success, a corps of top-producing professional realtors, an advanced computer network that provides instant market data, and imaginative marketing and advertising programs, Aronov's residential real estate division has earned a 99-percent client satisfaction rating. Aronov sales professionals go the extra mile by taking time to explain the intricacies of home buying, and to understand their clients' lifestyles and special needs. A commitment to service is central to their ability to match the right home to the right homeowner.

In fact, it is this service-oriented approach to business that binds the enterprises of Aronov Realty. The company's 750 employees are service-minded individuals committed to producing consistent value for its clients.

Over the years, Aronov Realty has made extraordinary contributions to virtually every segment of its home community. The company is integral to the very fabric of quality living in Montgomery. And under the experienced leadership of a second generation, Aronov Realty is destined to continue its distinctive contributions to Montgomery and the Southeast. 𝍢

Aronov introduced the luxury apartment concept to Montgomery with its popular Vaughn Lakes apartment community.

Aronov is best known locally for its residential and commercial property sales.

RUSSELL CONSTRUCTION OF ALABAMA, INC.

Russell Construction of Alabama, Inc. has established a successful business by making quality the cornerstone of everything they do. Operating by the philosophy "Quality every day, not everyday quality," the 14-year-old company has grown to be a major player in Alabama's construction industry.

Now in its second decade, the company was founded by Steve Russell and Kay Russell, two former therapists who discovered their mutual enjoyment and appreciation of the building trade as they designed and built their personal residences. A native Montgomerian, Steve grew up with his father in the steel business and was familiar with the construction industry and the area's major players well before he decided to enter the business. Kay is a confident and capable woman who has, in her own words, "hammered and painted by the caboodles."

From the day they launched their business, the Russells made it a personal mandate to provide unsurpassed craftsmanship and customer service second to none. If they were to succeed in a highly competitive field, the Russells knew they would have to rise above the ordinary.

Today, that commitment is paying major dividends. Russell Construction and its staff of nearly 60 administrative and project employees have moved into a beautiful new building just off Interstate 85 in east Montgomery. The full-service company builds churches, health care facilities, light industrial buildings, office complexes, apartments, custom homes, and a variety of other projects. Recognized for solid workmanship and responsive service, Russell is called upon to handle some of the most demanding and unique projects in the area.

Because of a company-wide commitment to sound project management and efficiency, most of the company's business comes from repeat customers and referrals. Only about 10 percent of its work is derived from bidding—a tangible testimony to fine quality.

Although the company has grown dramatically, the Russells maintain active, hands-on management roles. Steve supervises production, sales, and estimating, while Kay oversees accounting, business management, and marketing activities. But to further ensure its mission for exceptional service and quality, Russell Construction hires experienced professionals who perform their crafts with the highest degree of pride and precision. The work of the company's carpenters, masons, and other specialists is widely respected.

Quality is evident throughout the company's portfolio of distinctive custom homes, restored churches, and beautifully renovated historical landmarks. Russell recently constructed an intriguing contemporary villa in one of Montgomery's most prestigious neighborhoods. Entrusted with the task of bringing the owner's vision of "a museum with living quarters" to life, Russell Construction produced a builder's masterpiece judged the most

Russell Construction, a full-service company, builds churches, health care facilities, light industrial buildings, office complexes, apartments, custom homes, and a variety of other projects.

masterfully built home in the nation by the Associated Builders and Contractors. Precision craftsmanship of limestone radius walls, barrel-vaulted ceilings, and a curved slate roof are among the complexities that earned Russell the group's National Excellence in Construction Award.

A hallmark of Russell Construction is its ability to handle highly unusual or otherwise complex projects. The company has proven itself superior in renovation work, construction of projects with unique design features, and the ability to work under difficult site, budget, and time conditions. Perhaps most notable is Russell's reputation for working efficiently in the midst of essential on-going operations at hospitals, nursing homes, industrial plants, and health clubs. For

Russell Construction has proven itself superior in renovation work and the ability to work under difficult site, budget, and time conditions. Photo by Fouts Commercial Photography.

more than four years, Russell crews have been on site at Montgomery Regional Medical Center building and renovating everything from doctors' suites to x-ray areas. To prepare for complex working environments, Russell conducts frequent in-house training sessions to enhance employee awareness and sensitivity to working in unusual circumstances. The company also goes the extra mile by carefully selecting the crew members for each job to ensure personalities and temperaments match work conditions.

While quality, professionalism, and flexibility are essential components of Russell's success, it is the full-service approach that attracts many clients. Russell professionals work with architects to bring their designs to life and to assist them with their knowledge of construction methods, materials, scheduling constraints, and costs. In addition, the company's start-to-finish capabilities include site location, zoning and building code compliance, financing, budgeting, and, of course, the construction itself. A recently added in-house design department completes the full-service menu.

"Whatever the project—a hospital, commercial office building, industrial facility, or home—we first and foremost want it to work for our client," said Kay Russell. To accomplish that, the company emphasizes preliminary scheduling, makes sure project staff are thoroughly knowledgeable about their respective projects, and lets the client's needs and desires prevail. "We work to help our clients get the absolute top dollar value in their project. Once we know their priorities and their desires, we do all we can to help them reach their goal," she said.

That approach has helped earn Russell an excellent reputation for effectively avoiding costly change orders, which is always a goal from the start. "We approach each project with the intention that the owner will be a close friend at completion. We are open and honest with the owners throughout the project."

Others would do well to learn from the Russell philosophy. After nearly 15 years in business, the firm has never faced a layoff due to lack of work, even during difficult economic times that affected others in the business. "If you do good work, there is always plenty to go around," Kay Russell said.

While the company is busily involved in a number of commercial office buildings, major apartment complexes throughout Alabama, and additional hospital and residential work, Russell employees found time to voluntarily construct a residence for Montgomery's Habitat for Humanity program. The Russells promote volunteerism and community involvement among their staff, encouraging and financing organizational memberships and other activities. Kay Russell serves on the Montgomery Area Chamber of Commerce CEO Roundtable and Education Task Force, on the board of directors for Habitat for Humanity, and as chairman of the Central Alabama Chapter of Associated Builders and Contractors.

In today's competitive business world, the term "quality" has almost become cliche'. It is often overused with little reverence for its meaning. But at Russell Construction of Alabama, quality has, in fact, become a way of life . . . a corporate mandate . . . the reason why the folks at Russell can take pride in knowing they provide quality every day, not everyday quality. *m*

*R*ussell Construction is busily involved in constructing a number of commercial office buildings and major apartment complexes throughout Alabama. Photo by Robert Fouts

*P*recision craftsmanship earned Russell the National Excellence in Construction Award. Photo by Fouts Commercial Photography.

JENKINS BRICK COMPANY, INC.

*I*n the 1880s John Michael Jenkins needed brick to build a factory for his beehive business. He couldn't afford the available brick, so he decided to make his own. Before he knew it, bricks had become more profitable than beehives, and a new enterprise was born. Today, more than a century later, his great-grandson, Mike Jenkins, is running that brick-making business—manufacturing an incredible 120 million bricks each year and distributing them throughout the eastern United States.

The company's first factory in Wetumpka still stands as Perkins Cotton Gin, and some of the original kilns from its second Montgomery plant can still be found on North Sixth Street. But Jenkins' bricks today are manufactured at a newer Montgomery plant and a Coosada plant, about 10 miles north of Montgomery. Huge clay pits, located about four miles from the plant site, supply more than 1,150,000 pounds of raw clay daily for processing.

With the exception of a brief hiatus, Jenkins Brick Company has consistently been a family-run enterprise. When John Michael Jenkins died in 1918, his son took over the operation until his own death in 1956. Mike Jenkins learned at the heels of his grandfather, and from an early age, aspired to carry on the tradition. After completing military service, working in the company's sales department, and earning a master's degree in ceramic engineering from Clemson University, the younger Jenkins took the helm at age 32.

Now in its second century of service, Jenkins Brick has crafted products that can be found in some of the most poignantly beautiful spots in America. Jenkins' bricks fill the sidewalks of Lafayette Square, across from the White House in Washington, D.C. They are found in Charles Square at Harvard University, in the Harbert Engineering Building at Auburn University, and on many other college campuses. The company gained nationwide recognition for its creative masonry at the renowned Alabama Shakespeare Festival Theatre in Montgomery.

While Montgomery and south Alabama are historically strong markets for Jenkins Brick, the company decided a decade ago to broaden its market base. Today about half of its brick takes to the rail market heading to Texas, Chicago, Cincinnati, New York, and Louisville, among other destinations.

In 1987 Jenkins split into two companies, Jenkins Brick Company for production, and Jenkins Brick and Materials Distribution for sales and distribution. One of the largest brick distribution companies in the nation, Jenkins Brick operates 15 distribution offices in Birmingham, Gadsden, Albertville, Albany, Panama City, Dothan, Opp, Sylvania, Mobile, Montgomery, Pensacola, Huntsville, and Tallahassee. In all, the two companies employ more than 300 associates.

As evidenced by these strategic moves, Jenkins Brick does not dwell on its time-tested past. Instead, management continually looks for new ways to build a stronger environment for productivity, healthy competition, and career security. "We are passionately pro-people," said Jenkins. "Our pay scales are competitive and our benefits are better than our competitors. From Huntsville to Tallahassee, our associates are absolutely the best people we can find."

A century of business success is cause for pride and reflection. Why the longevity? "The key is that those before us had it right. That doesn't mean we have it right, but we've had a strong foundation on which to build," said Jenkins—indeed, a foundation as solid as brick, based on rich historical perspective and visionary modern management. *n*

*J*enkins Brick Company manufactures a 120 million bricks each year and distributes them throughout the eastern United States.

WINTER COLEMAN REAL ESTATE

Many long-time Montgomerians remember a 1950s billboard that stood high above the bustling Court Square and displayed a picture of a young Irving Winter pointing and declaring, "I have a home for you!"

That billboard, patterned after a famous World War II "Uncle Sam Wants You!" poster, helped propel Winter's distinguished real estate career. His company, which celebrated its 40th anniversary in 1995, is one of the oldest and most recognized names in Montgomery real estate.

Winter opened an office on the second floor of an antebellum home at 17 Adams Avenue on November 1, 1955. He was the sales staff; his wife, Blanche, did everything else. Concentrating strictly on residential home sales, Winter grew his company quickly, and by 1961 he and a partner built a larger office at 444 South Perry Street.

Winter began his strategic move into commercial and investment properties in the mid 1960s when he joined with Realtor Frank Parquette to open Winter Parquette Realty. Growth and success prompted him to build a new company home in 1973. That building, at 300 South Hull Street near downtown, still houses Winter Coleman Real Estate.

The Winter real estate enterprise today is a second generation company specializing in commercial and investment real estate. The "Coleman" in Winter Coleman belongs to Irving Winter's son-in-law, Steve Coleman, company president, who joined the Winter Company in 1980. He is a Certified Property Manager® as designated by the Institute of Real Estate Management, an affiliate of the National Association of Realtors.

With a staff consisting of a property manager, on-site apartment managers, and a maintenance crew, Winter Coleman develops and manages a variety of commercial, multi-family and retail properties in Alabama. The company manages 7 Montgomery area apartment complexes, including the new $6-million, 136-unit McQueen Village apartment complex in Prattville. Winter Coleman's commercial properties include the Gunter Park Office Center, Carmichael Court Condominium Complex, 300 South Hull, and the Benkwith-Edwards Office Condominium Development.

While most of the company's properties are scattered throughout the Montgomery area, Winter Coleman still is involved in a number of national chain restaurant and retail properties in other southeastern states.

In addition to property management and development, Winter Coleman is one of Montgomery's foremost names in commercial and investment real estate sales and leasing.

Winter Coleman has made a conscious effort to stay small to ensure accessibility for its clients. "Our clients, whether property owners or tenants, can reach the chairman or the president with one telephone call. Each of our clients is a big cog in a small wheel."

As respected as they are professionally, both Winter and Coleman are also recognized community leaders. Winter has taken on leadership roles with the Cancer Society, Good Will Industries, Temple Beth Or, and others, while Coleman shares his time generously as a volunteer coach with the Montgomery YMCA, and as a board member for the Salvation Army, the Montgomery Jaycees, and the Standard Club.

For four decades, Winter Coleman has prospered under a business philosophy that calls for

*F*or four decades, Winter Coleman has prospered under a business philosophy that calls for industry knowledge and responsive client service. Photo by Fouts Commerical Photography.

industry knowledge, responsive client service, and professional and civic responsibility. As a second generation of management builds on that stable foundation, Winter Coleman Real Estate is positioned for many more decades of service to the Montgomery area. **𝓜**

*W*inter Coleman Real Estate is a second generation company specializing in commercial and investment real estate. Making up the leadership of the company is (left to right) Irving Winter, Steve Coleman, and Mae W. Coleman. Photo by Fouts Commercial Photography.

CASSELS REAL ESTATE

*I*t didn't seem particularly strange to Martha Cassels when one of her young real estate clients called her in a moment of crisis for help in finding an outdoor wedding location that would please his out-of-town bride to be. It seems Cassels is well-known for her willingness to go the extra mile for her customers. And, in the case of the newlyweds, Cassels escorted the groom all over town until they located just the right spot.

Martha Cassels, owner of Cassels Real Estate Company, has been in the realty business for more than 25 years. A former school teacher, she came to Montgomery from North Carolina in 1979. She opened her office at 623 South Perry Street in 1980 and has conducted business from that location ever since. With the help of two assistants, Cassels operates both a sales and a rental division, serving Montgomery, Elmore, and Autauga Counties.

"A realtor does not so much sell houses as she sells information. What people moving into a community need is a realtor who is intensely knowledgeable about this community and the opportunities that exist here," said Cassels.

As a result of her knowledge of the area and her industry expertise, Cassels is frequently the realtor of choice for businesses and industries bringing families to Montgomery. As a respected Certified Residential Specialist, she is also the choice of realtors from other locations who are sending valued clients to the Montgomery area.

Although Cassels exudes a colorful and vivacious personality that wins her clients over, she is quiet and subtle about her extraordinary

*W*elcoming new clients to their office with smiles and a genuine interest in their needs are (left to right) Danny Spears, rental division; Brenda Craig, sales associate; Martha Cassels, broker; Patti Stone, sales associate; and Cara Simonton, assistant to Martha Cassels.

professional accomplishments. She believes excellent service, honesty, and integrity speak for themselves. But the numbers speak, too. Cassels has achieved multimillion sales each of the past 15 years, and, on several occasions, she has posted the most home sales of any realtor in the Montgomery area.

Her success, she says, comes from hard work, intense market study, and sincere dedication to her customers. "The most important thing I do is listen. If I pay close attention to what my customers say, I will discover their individual needs and desires. Then I can go about the business of finding them the right home."

And Montgomery may be one of the best locations in the nation to place those homebuyers, Cassels says. Diverse terrains, a wide selection of residential neighborhoods, and varied price ranges offer tremendous choices for her customers. In addition, she says, a rock-solid economy means a consistently strong real estate market and peace of mind for home owners.

Cassels is an active member of the Montgomery Area Board of Realtors, the Multiple Listing Service, the Greater Montgomery Area Home Builders Association, and the Montgomery Area Chamber of Commerce. In conjunction with the Scott and Zelda Fitzgerald Museum Association, she and her husband, Samuel J. Cassels III, sponsor the annual Scott and Zelda Literary Contest for high school seniors and college students. "It's the teacher in me coming out," she says.

But the educator in Cassels actually comes out on a daily basis, and her customers are the beneficiaries. She is knowledgeable about financing options, area school districts, recreational activities, and employment opportunities. "It is my job to educate my customers so they can make an informed decision. There is nothing more rewarding than placing a family in a home that is right for them." *M*

*M*artha Cassels advises Barbara Winton during the planning process of the Winton's new home.

PH&J ARCHITECTS, INC.

*N*early 40 years of design excellence and an unyielding commitment to creating strong and timeless structures have made PH&J Architects, Inc. one of Alabama's foremost design firms.

Founded in 1957 as Pearson, Humphries & Jones Architects, the firm has grown in number and in stature because of its demand for design innovation, uncompromising client service, and the ability to handle widely diverse projects. The firm is a recognized specialist in institutional design work, including educational facilities, churches, hospitals, banks, and office buildings; but each PH&J structure is uniquely individual in design, reflecting careful attention to the owner's wants and needs.

PH&J designs of all kinds are found across Alabama, from a church in rural Pintlala, to university libraries in Auburn, in Tuscaloosa, and high-rise office buildings in downtown Montgomery.

While prominent, award-winning projects abound, perhaps the company's most notable current projects are four striking Montgomery office buildings designed as investment properties for the Retirement Systems of Alabama. The buildings, which house corporate and state offices, represent the heart of a downtown Montgomery renaissance.

The firm attributes its longevity and solid reputation to two primary characteristics, namely a sensitivity to client needs and senior partner involvement in each project. We are intent upon designing the quality into buildings that will stand the test of time. To succeed in the long term, we will invest the time and money up front.

PH&J invests in its community as well. The company has donated design services for renovating the historical headquarters building for the Montgomery Area United Way and for the facility assessment for the Montgomery Public Schools. PH&J employees are visible throughout the community, active in their churches and civic and professional organizations. The Alabama Council of Architects honored PH&J for its outstanding professional leadership by awarding the entire firm its President's Award, an honor normally bestowed on individual leaders.

Without question, PH&J designs have enhanced the quality of life in Alabama, and remains steadfastly committed to its home state—a decision that bodes well for Alabama landscapes and skylines for years to come. *m*

*F*or over 35 years, PH&J has specialized in designs for churches. The beauty and intimacy of this church sanctuary is an example of the sensitivity the firm has towards religious architecture.

*L*ocated in the garden district of Montgomery, Huntingdon College is an example of fine Gothic architecture. PH&J specified classical materials, such as brick and stone for the Sybil Smith Lebhertz Music Building located at the entrance to the campus.

*P*H&J served as lead architects for the revitalization of downtown Montgomery. A multi-building development owned and operated by the Retirement Systems of Alabama leases the new space as a portfolio investment of the fund. While office space is available to private businesses, more of the key state agencies, once scattered across the city, will have an opportunity to be efficiently located near the Capitol complex. Photos by Fouts Commercial Photography.

BALLARD COMPANIES, INC.

The Ballard Companies, Inc. have set a standard of excellence in the real estate industry. Since its founding as Ballard Realty in 1948, the company has played a leading role in commercial and residential real estate throughout the Southeast.

Ballard Realty was established by Eugene Ballard Jr., a businessman/attorney who saw opportunity in the housing demand and commercial real estate expansion that followed World War II. Today, under the leadership of his son Bowen Ballard, the company still predicates its growth on customer service and market demand.

Ballard Realty is a full-service real estate company offering expert property development, management, and brokerage services. The company's portfolio has grown to include properties in Alabama, Texas, Mississippi, Florida, Georgia, and South Carolina.

Sensitive to market need, Ballard developed Azalea Hill Apartment Suites and led the way in bringing luxury furnished corporate apartments to Montgomery. A new facility is currently under construction in Greenville, South Carolina. In the same spirit, Ballard responded to the growing need for quality elderly care facilities. Cedar Crest and South Haven Manor nursing homes, developed by Ballard, combine comfortable surroundings with specialized medical care to create uplifting living environments for Montgomery's elderly.

In the mid-1980s, Bowen Ballard conceived the idea of bringing a job-producing high-tech university-related Research Park to Montgomery. By 1993 he had joined forces with other community leaders to make the Alabama

Ballard developed Azalea Hill Apartment Suites and led the way in bringing luxury furnished corporate apartments to Montgomery.

TechnaCenter a reality. Ballard's 50,000-square-foot state-of-the-art TechnaCenter office building is leased to capacity, housing such high-tech enterprises as Computer Sciences Corporation and Palmer Wireless (Cellular One).

On the retail side, Ballard has developed a number of strategically located shopping centers, including Atlanta Crossing on the Atlanta Highway and Halcyon Village on Vaughn Road.

Ballard also developed some of Montgomery's finest residential subdivisions. The 320-acre Woodmere community was the city's first planned unit development featuring cluster housing, luxurious townhomes, and neighborhood parks.

The company's high-performing residential sales division is an independent entity owned and operated member of The Prudential Real Estate Affiliates, Inc. and specializes in new homes, corporate and military relocations, and residential resales. The Prudential Ballard Realty's service-minded realtors offer their clients the value-added benefits of the affiliation, including superior training, excellent home-buyer information tools, and a nationwide computer network for relocations and referrals.

At the Prudential Ballard Realty, quality sets the company apart from the competition. It can be seen in they way business is conducted, the quality of the properties for sale, and the caliber of agents that represent the company. Statistics from the Montgomery Area Association of Realtors

Multiple Listing Service reported that, when compared to other Montgomery offices, the Prudential Ballard Realty's Montgomery office was the number one company in closed volume for sales and listings for 1995.

Deeply committed to uncompromising professional service, Ballard is one of the few property management firms nationally to have earned the designation of Accredited Management Organization (AMO) through the Institute of Real Estate Management under the National Association of Realtors. The firm also includes three Certified Property Managers with more than 55 combined years experience and maintains state-of-the-art computer access to each of its management properties.

For years Ballard has been a driving force behind the economic development of Montgomery and surrounding areas. Bowen Ballard has served as past chairman and a member of the board of directors of the Montgomery Area Chamber of Commerce, past chairman of the Committee of 100, and as a member of the Auburn University at Montgomery board of advisors. He is currently chairman of Colonial Bank Central Region operations. As a general in the United States Air Force Reserve, his strong military involvement has been vital to the stability of Montgomery's important military community.

The professionals at Ballard have earned a reputation for unsurpassed industry knowledge, customer service, and professional dedication. As population shifts to the Sunbelt enhance regional real estate opportunities, Ballard is well positioned to grow with the expanding market. 𝄢

Montgomery Area Association of Realtors Multiple Listing Service statistics reported that the Prudential Ballard Realty was the number one company in listings and sales closed production for 1995.

ALTUS
92 FAVORITE!
STEAK·OUT

16

CHAPTER SIXTEEN

HEALTH CARE

Montgomery's extensive health care system provides the best in comprehensive care. Photo courtesy of Baptist Medical Center.

BAPTIST HEALTH SERVICES CORPORATION

The founding mission that drives Baptist Health Services Corporation calls for quality, compassionate service committed to enhancing the physical, emotional, and spiritual well-being of those it reaches. In the more than three decades since its establishment, Baptist has accomplished its mission through a far-reaching network of healthcare and wellness programs that have become vital to the well-being of vast numbers of Montgomerians.

Baptist Medical Center is Montgomery's largest healthcare facility and the hospital of choice for residents of Montgomery and surrounding areas. Photo by Rion C. Rizzo.

In 1954, Montgomery native and ordained Baptist minister Blount F. Davidson decided to pursue a dream that has grown to become one of the foremost healthcare organizations in Montgomery and the Southeast. The visionary Superintendent of Missions for the Montgomery Baptist Association, Davidson recognized a need for additional medical facilities in the Montgomery area and felt strongly that Montgomery Baptists should respond by embarking on a ministry for healing.

With aid from such civic-minded Montgomerians as J. B. Sylvest, Arthur Mead, N. J. Bell III, Sam Durden, and Frank Tripp, Davidson's dream became reality. After nine years of research, planning, and fund-raising, Montgomery Baptist Hospital opened its doors on July 29, 1963, with 131 doctors on staff and a 127-bed capacity.

From that moment forward, under the administration of W. Taylor Morrow, Baptist continued to add new services and facilities to answer the specific healthcare needs of the community.

A leader in progressive medicine since its founding, the hospital opened the first intensive care unit in central Alabama in the mid-1960s. Since then it has added five additional units, including the area's only Level III neonatal intensive care unit recognized by the state as a regional referral center.

As the hospital, whose name was changed to Baptist Medical Center in the 1970s, continued to make extraordinary "in-hospital" advances in technology during the next two decades, it became clear to administrators that the organization possessed the resources to meet the community's demand for important outside healthcare services.

To meet those demands, hospital officials created Baptist Health Services Corporation as the parent company of the hospital, allowing for the addition of valuable new programs. Baptist Health Services is comprised of four primary components: Baptist Medical Center, Baptist Health Care Foundation, Baptist Outreach Services Corporation, and Baptist Ventures, Inc. These individual entities combine to offer a network of healthcare services and programs designed to answer the diverse medical needs of the citizens of Montgomery and central Alabama.

In appreciation for its responsive service, the people of the Montgomery area have enthusiastically supported Baptist's continued growth and influence.

Today, under the direction of President and Chief Executive Officer Michael D. DeBoer, who rejoined the organization in 1994 after Morrow's retirement, Baptist Health Services Corporation continues to be Montgomery's largest healthcare provider and leading private employer with more than 1,550 full-time employees and an annual payroll of approximately $41.5 million.

The organization's growth is predicated upon what it calls "intelligent healthcare," or the vision to thoughtfully combine the finest in advanced, compassionate diagnostic and therapeutic care with a committed focus on wellness education and preventive care.

The licensed 454-bed Baptist Medical Center is a not-for-profit regional acute care referral center respected for its state-of-the-art facilities, compassionate approach to healthcare, and excellent staff. A leader in medical advancements, the hospital offers the area's only Sleep Disorder Center and the Baptist Center for Diabetes, the area's only program recognized by the American Diabetes Association for its educational programs and services.

In answer to identified community needs, the medical center also offers a Center for Advanced Surgery utilizing the latest laser and minimally invasive surgical technology; Meadhaven, the area's most established comprehensive addictive disease/emotional health treatment facility; and family centered maternity care that has made Baptist the most popular provider of childbirth services in the area.

In 1995 Baptist expanded its cardiac care services to include open-heart surgery. The hospital has implemented a comprehensive and progressive, multidisciplinary team approach to cardiac care which involves the collaboration of surgical staff, cardiovascular surgeons, cardiologists, the cardiac cath lab, the units that care for open-heart patients before and after surgery, and the cardiac rehabilitation department.

Located on the Baptist campus, the Parker Women's Pavilion is home to physician offices, the Breast Health Center, Women's Health Connection, Lactation Resource Center, and other services. Photo by Rion C. Rizzo.

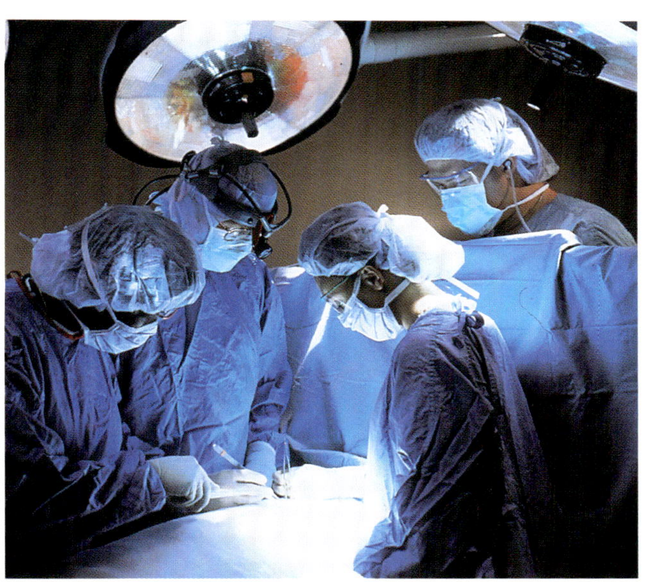

Baptist's open-heart surgery program includes open-heart surgery suites, a cardiac cath lab, a CVICU, and a cardiovascular step-down unit. Photo by Rion C. Rizzo.

To further enhance its cardiac care capabilities and in an effort to save lives, the hospital has established the Baptist Chest Pain Center for immediate reaction and care of those experiencing cardiac emergencies. In addition, Baptist built the Montgomery Cardiovascular Institute, located adjacent to the hospital.

To help prevent cardiac problems, Baptist offers the Healthy Heart Club, a free community outreach program which offers newsletters and programs on topics such as risk assessment, how the heart works, walking for the heart, how fat affects the heart, and other topics designed to teach people how to live "heart healthy" lives.

Baptist is also unsurpassed when it comes to emergency medical care, providing central Alabama with the newest, most advanced emergency department, staffed 24 hours a day, 365 days a year. While the medical professionals at Baptist Medical Center perform a staggering number of procedures each year, the staff remains committed to providing compassionate care in a concerned Christian environment. In an average year Baptist healthcare professionals will conduct more than 500,000 laboratory procedures, handle in excess of 32,000 emergency department cases, conduct 30,000 home health visits, handle more than 200,000 respiratory therapy procedures, perform at least 7,000 surgical operations, and deliver more than 2,400 babies.

The hospital's Morrow Medical Tower, which contains eight floors of physician office space, enhances physician efficiency and patient convenience. The building is connected to the medical center and to the Baptist Surgery Center, a same-day surgery outpatient unit. The surgery center includes eight operating rooms, a laser room for outpatient eye surgery, and houses the Montgomery Lions Eye Center.

Baptist's commitment to superior women's healthcare is evidenced by the Parker Women's Pavilion, which features offices for physicians specializing in women's health, child care for those visiting the center, the Breast Health Center, mammography services, a lactation resource center, a mastectomy and maternity clothing shop, and free valet parking.

The Parker Women's Pavilion is also home to Women's Health Connection, a valuable source of health information for women of all ages and sponsor of the popular Midlife Matters and Baptist Stork Club programs.

In addition to the offices located in the medical tower and Women's Pavilion, more than 100 physicians' offices surround the hospital's sprawling campus.

Perhaps as integral to Baptist's success as any of its programs and services is the hospital's commitment to technology. In addition to featuring the most advanced equipment available, from magnetic resonance imaging to safe, efficient unit dose dispensing systems for pharmaceuticals, Baptist became the first hospital in Montgomery to add a robotic assistant for minimally invasive surgery. "AESOP" is the first and only robotic medical device to receive FDA clearance, and Baptist is one of the first hospitals in the country to begin using it. "Baptist is committed to providing the community with the latest in medical technology while keeping costs under control," said DeBoer. "This technology allows us to utilize hospital staff in the most effective manner, shorten operating time, and better serve the patient."

Further testimony to its dedication to progress is Baptist's role in the advancement of healthcare education. The hospital sponsors hands-on learning opportunities, including a medical residency program and medical clerkship in internal medicine conducted jointly with the University of Alabama School of Medicine, a 12-month School of Medical Technology approved by the Committee on Allied Health Education and Accreditation of the American Medical Association, and registered nurse clinical training provided for Auburn University, Auburn University at Montgomery, and Troy State University nursing students.

At Baptist, students learn and patients benefit at the hands of one of the region's most respected medical staffs, which includes 325 healthcare professionals. These highly skilled physicians and specialists are some of the nation's leading experts in clinical specialties ranging from allergy to urology.

Proud of its association with a respected and highly credentialed group of physicians, nurses,

Family centered maternity care includes 10 LDR suites, traditional labor and delivery rooms, a surgical suite, and the Neonatal Intensive Care Unit—recognized by the state as the area's primary Level III neonatal intensive care referral center. Photo by Rion C. Rizzo.

technicians, and medical staff, the hospital offers professional educational programs conducted by nationally and internationally recognized faculty, provides unparalleled clinical and technical support, ensures the highest standards of safety, and provides an aggressive marketing program to promote the hospital's services and programs.

In addition to its role as a modern medical complex featuring superior staff and technology, Baptist serves the community with a range of wellness programs and services designed to help people live healthier lives.

"As we look ahead, all signs point to a renewed emphasis on helping people to reduce their risks of illness and disease while teaching them to live healthier lives," said DeBoer. "We're

Baptist's Emergency Department and Chest Pain Center, the area's newest, most advanced facilities, are open 24 hours a day, seven days a week.

positioned for the task because we have been focused on preventive care for many years."

As a result of that focus, Baptist has established an array of outreach services. Among others, the programs include the Physician Finder program which helps those new to the community or in need of a specialist locate a doctor, and the Senior Advantage membership program designed to meet the needs and address the concerns of people 55 and older.

The popular Baptist Wellness Connection disseminates information focusing on preventive measures and conducts special lunchtime seminars designed to help families attain and maintain a healthy lifestyle.

Concerned for the emotional impacts associated with the trauma of disease, serious illness, and death, the hospital also provides numerous support groups, including the Alzheimer's disease family support group, caregivers' support group, mother-to-mother discussion group, bereavement support group, and more.

In addition to its diverse "in-hospital" programs, Baptist Health Services operates facilities such as PriMed, an immediate care, minor emergency medical facility with convenient locations in Montgomery, and SportsFirst Health and Racquet, Montgomery's most complete family health and fitness center.

In recognition of the trend in healthcare calling for home-centered care, Baptist also provides Baptist Home Services, which offers three unique home-oriented alternatives to hospitalization—Baptist Hospice, Baptist Home Health, and Private Duty Nursing. The organization has also established Bell Oaks, a retirement community designed to offer affordable, comfortable living for active senior adults.

In answer to still another community need, Baptist recently turned its attention to nearby Prattville, Alabama, beginning development of the 50-acre Baptist Medical Park located at the corner of U.S. Highway 14 and McQueen-Smith Road. The project's first phase features a three-story, 50,000-square-foot medical office building able to accommodate approximately 25 physicians. An adjacent 25,000-square-foot ambulatory services facility will include diagnostic testing and imaging, outpatient rehabilitation, and other ambulatory services. Plans for future development include an acute care hospital, recovery care center, nursing home, and birthing center.

Recognizing that the cost of medical care can exceed the scope of available financial resources, Baptist established the Baptist Health Care Foundation in 1972 to raise and administer charitable contributions in support of Baptist Health Services Corporation and its efforts to provide for the healthcare needs of the community.

Over the years, the work of the Foundation board of directors and staff has led to new levels of accomplishment. With the concerned support of community donors, the Foundation has provided funding for needed programs and services. As technology advances and the cost of new medical technology rises, the Foundation plays an integral role in confirming Baptist's continued healthcare leadership.

The work of the Foundation and its donors have provided for such technologies as magnetic resonance imaging, surgical lasers, neonatal unit equipment, the Lifeline Emergency Response System, Montgomery Lions Eye Center, and the Bell Oaks Retirement Community. In 1995 the Foundation sponsored its first annual "Birdies for Babies" golf classic and raised more than $40,000 for the hospital's neonatal intensive care unit.

Vital outreach organizations such as Baptist Hospice receive annual support from community contributions. In addition, the Foundation Scholars Program recognizes meritorious students

SportsFirst Health and Racquet, a family-oriented club, has aerobic classes, Cybex machines and free weights, a cardiovascular fitness center, swimming pools, tennis and racquetball courts, children's programs, and much more for the family.

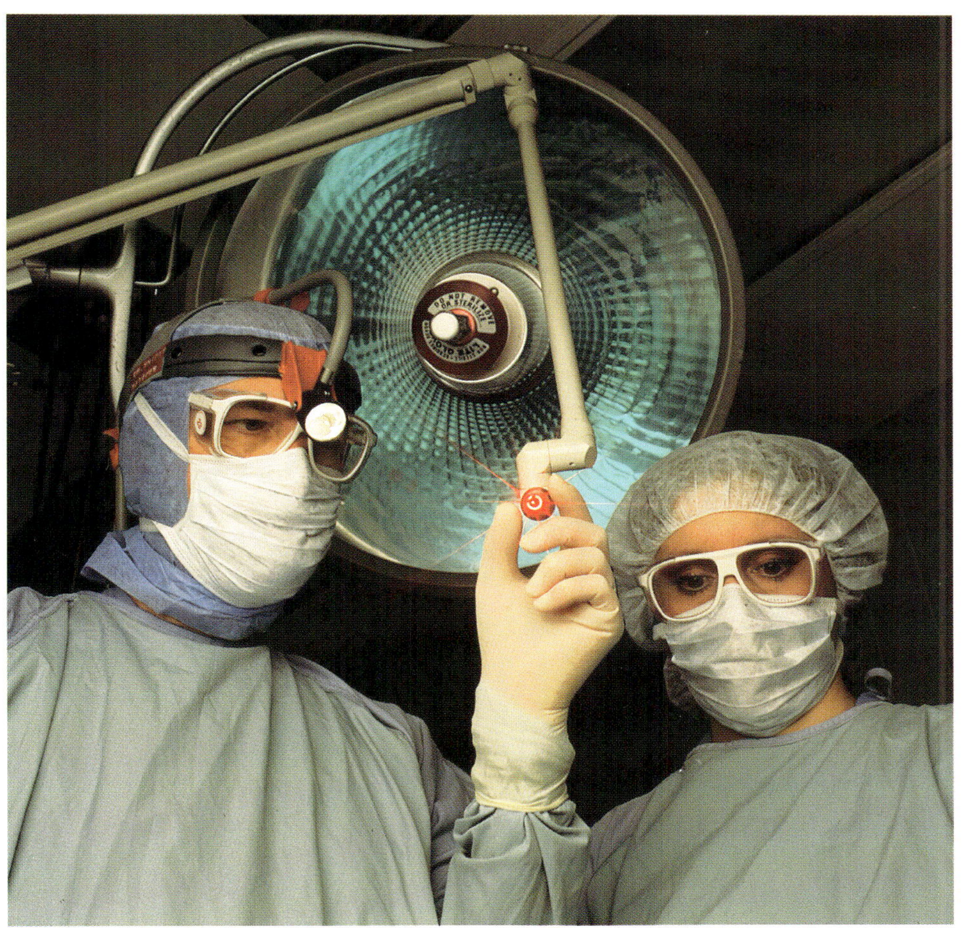

The area's most advanced surgerical program, the Baptist Center for Advanced Surgery, uses the latest technology, such as lasers, which often results in faster healing and a shorter hospital stay.

Baptist's sense of community commitment does not stop with the Foundation. Baptist employees clearly live by the same sense of compassion that runs throughout the organization. In addition to generously staffing seminars, health screenings, and wellness events, Baptist employees are major contributors to the Montgomery Area United Way, give generously of their time and resources to their Partners In Education schools, conduct blood drives, and have given nearly 100,000 pounds of food to Montgomery Baptist Association Food Distribution Centers.

Baptist Health Services Corporation is a shining star on the healthcare horizon whose points extend into every segment of its community. From open-heart surgery to rehabilitative services, from community outreach to compassionate support groups, Baptist remains committed to serving all the healthcare needs of Montgomery and the surrounding communities.

Successfully balancing a combination of compassion, knowledge, skill, and vision, Baptist has found the formula for intelligent healthcare. *m*

in the medical and nursing curriculum with six annual scholarships.

When it comes to serving the people of its own community, there is little doubt Baptist Health Services Corporation is one of the most dedicated philanthropic organizations in Alabama.

During the past five years, the organization has donated more than $1.5 million in used office furniture and computer equipment to area schools. In 1995 Baptist launched an assistance program to help meet the medical supply needs of Montgomery County's 54 public schools and joined with the American Heart Association of Montgomery to conduct a "Schoolsite" program designed to educate area school children in grades kindergarten through 12 about healthy lifestyles.

In addition, each year Baptist Medical Center and the Baptist Health Care Foundation join with the Montgomery Council of the Telephone Pioneers of America to sponsor Camp Bluebird, an uplifting three-day retreat for adult cancer patients on the beautiful waters of Lake Jordan.

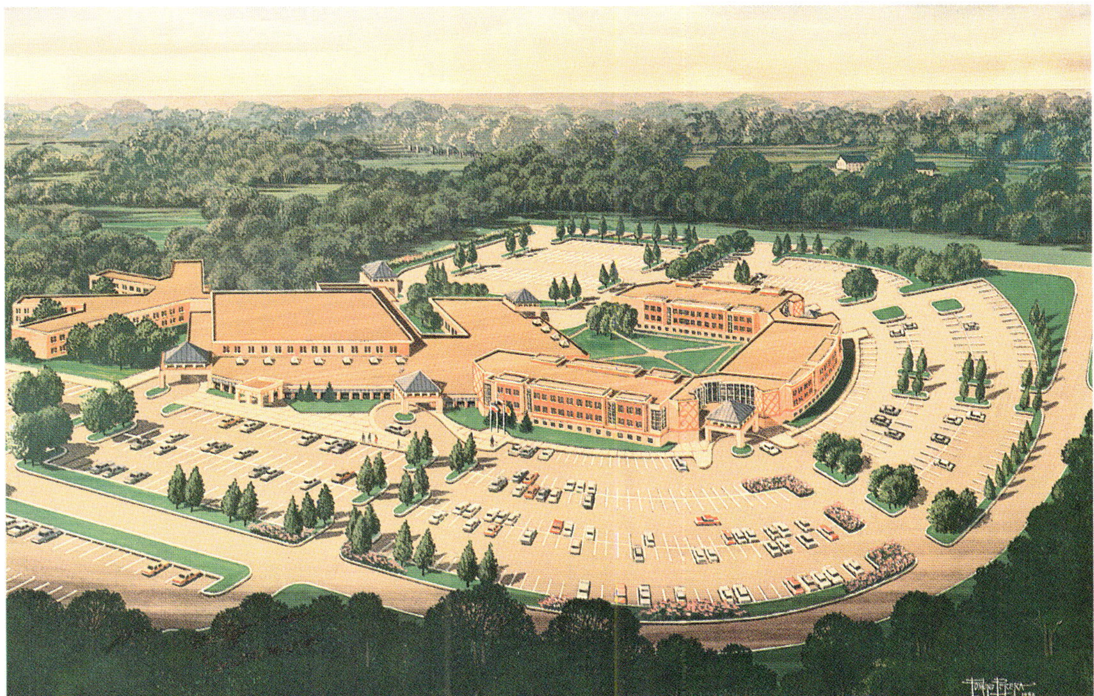

The Baptist Medical Park, located in Prattville, will house a three-story physician office building and an outpatient facility, including diagnostic lab and x-ray services, physical therapy, and an after-hours clinic. Photo by Fouts Commercial Photography.

JACKSON HOSPITAL & CLINIC, INC.

FIFTY YEARS OF DISTINGUISHED SERVICE

Since its humble beginning 50 years ago, Jackson Hospital & Clinic has been a dependable, dedicated provider of superior health care for the citizens of central Alabama. Celebrating its golden anniversary in 1996, Jackson Hospital is proudly commemorating a distinguished past and looking forward to a promising future as one of the region's premiere health care organizations.

In 1946 when the hospital was established by Dr. Franklin Jackson, the 36-bed facility was composed of three small frame houses connected by wooden archways. Located on the south half of Montgomery's centrally located Forest Avenue, the hospital included one large operating room and another small suite for emergencies and minor surgical procedures. It was common for medical staff to place large blocks of ice in front of window fans to cool the unair-conditioned facility—the available technology of the times.

Finding his hospital in increasing demand, Dr. Jackson, in association with four other founding physicians, soon recognized the vital need in central Alabama for a true community hospital. The doctors believed to grow successfully, the organization should be void of private gain. Indicative of that commitment, the doctors joined with seven other physicians in 1949 to create Jackson Hospital & Clinic, Inc., a not-for-profit organization.

The institution's founders also developed an open staff membership for physicians, limited only by their qualifications and good character. Exemplifying extraordinary commitment and vision, these 12 leaders charted a strong course for quality care, a tradition which Jackson Hospital maintains today.

"This institution was a gift to the community when the original investors made it a not-for-profit organization," said Jackson's Chief Executive Officer Donald M. Ball. "From day one this hospital has been community-oriented. Its roots are grounded in this community. As a result, everything we do is in response to the needs of central Alabama."

The next 25 years marked a notable increase in the number of highly qualified specialists representing various fields who joined the hospital's medical staff and brought about the need for expanded physical facilities. The hospital's early development featured a variety of medical innovations, including the advent of an obstetrical unit, a medical records library with credentialed personnel, carpeting in patient rooms, attractive homelike furnishings, and a lessening of the dreary hospital image.

In 1972 Jackson Hospital received national recognition as the only hospital at the time to receive its accreditation with a perfect rating from the Joint Commission on Hospital Accreditation. Recognition of its superior service continues today as Jackson consistently receives its accreditation on time, along with compliments on the maintenance of quality medical care delivery.

Still situated on its original location, Jackson has become an impressive health care facility encompassing an 11-city block area. One of Montgomery's leading employers, the hospital employs some 1,300 professionals and is licensed for 409 beds, ranking it among the largest health care institutions in Alabama.

Long one of the finest facilities in central Alabama, Jackson has initiated construction plans for an exciting new replacement hospital which will begin construction in 1996. "It seems appropriate, upon our 50th anniversary, to celebrate the future in this way," said Ball. The striking,

Long one of the finest facilities in central Alabama, Jackson has initiated construction plans for an exciting new replacement hospital which will begin construction in 1996.

In 1946 when Jackson was established, the 36-bed facility was located on the south half of Montgomery's centrally located Forest Avenue.

Jackson Hospital's hallmark is personal attention and quality care. Photo by Robert Fouts.

state-of-the-art facility will feature a glass-enclosed two-story lobby, a grand staircase, patient tower, and optimal emergency room facilities. Located adjacent to the existing hospital, the facility will replace the original east and west wings. With construction handled in phases to avoid patient inconvenience, the facility is scheduled for completion in 1998.

Interestingly, in 1995 Dr. Thomas Stroud Jackson of Clio, Alabama, nephew of the hospital's founder, generously contributed $250,000 toward the hospital's new emergency unit in honor of his uncle's "inspiration and encouragement."

"With all of its amenities, this new facility puts Jackson in a strong position to rapidly adapt to Montgomery's medical needs. It is designed with a vision for the future and a flexibility that will allow us to effectively adapt as health care needs change," said Ball.

SUPERIOR SERVICE AT EVERY TURN

The professionals at Jackson Hospital take great pride in their reputation for providing personal, compassionate medical care enhanced by the latest technological advances available to the health care industry. The hospital's full complement of medical staff represents a wide range of specialties, and many of its more than 300 physicians are respected leaders in their fields. Jackson is particularly noted regionally for its outstanding neurological, orthopedic, and pain management specialties.

Supplementing the compassionate care of fine

physicians and a nursing staff considered among the community's most competent and dedicated, is a Patient Representative Program which provides warm, personal interaction with individuals trained to address questions or concerns during hospitalization. Congenial American Red Cross volunteers are a familiar staple, unselfishly delivering smiles, compassion, and information to patients and their families.

While the human element is integral to Jackson's mission, the hospital has long led the way in recognizing community need and responding with the finest in equipment and facilities. Jackson Hospital is the only health care institution in a 12-county area offering a dedicated inpatient oncology unit. The Frank McGough Oncology Unit is the focal point for a specialized care program designed solely for the care of cancer patients. A highly skilled multidisciplinary medical team, each member with a focused commitment to the compassionate care of cancer patients and their families, provides the area's finest in oncology treatment.

In the same spirit of family-centered care, Jackson Hospital has created an extraordinary obstetrics unit designed to turn each birthing experience into a pleasant memory. Expectant mothers are afforded the advantage of the LDRP birthing concept which brings labor, delivery, recovery, and postpartum into one area. A state-of-the-art central monitoring system enables physicians to trace the progress of each patient from monitors strategically placed throughout the unit.

Located on the fourth floor of the hospital's

north wing, the unit contains eight comfortably furnished suites, a large nursery, and gives new mothers the opportunity to include family members of their choice throughout the birthing process.

In addition to other specialized units, including advanced coronary care and surgical intensive care units designed for critically ill patients needing constant observation and treatment, a colorful and comforting pediatrics unit, a fully equipped physical therapy department, an inpatient psychiatric services department designed to provide therapeutic, short-term care for adult patients, and a radiology department equipped with the most advanced diagnostic tools available, Jackson has established a comprehensive outpatient services department to serve patients requiring certain types of surgery, diagnostic testing, and treatments that can be performed without an overnight stay.

In 1987 Jackson reached beyond the confines of the hospital and purchased land conveniently located just off Interstate 85 near Carmichael and Perry Hill Roads where the Institute for Total Eye Care is housed. The state-of-the-art facility provides comprehensive ophthalmic care, including a widely recognized program for the recently developed radial keratotomy surgery to correct near-sightedness.

In the spirit of family-centered care, Jackson Hospital has created an extraordinary obstetrics unit designed to turn each birthing experience into a pleasant memory. Photo by Robert Fouts.

While Jackson Hospital's hallmark is personal attention and quality care, it is also committed to bringing the latest technologies to the community. In keeping with its mission to provide cost-effective health care, the hospital has begun implementation of an advanced computerized patient information system which not only allows communication within the hospital but also across an entire network of physicians' offices, laboratories, insurance carriers, and other health care providers. "The staff in one department can view a patient's entire clinical pathway instantly," said Ball. "Plus, it gives us a huge database which collects and trends information that will help us respond more quickly to local patient care needs. It will be an incredible advantage for our patients and our physicians."

Although Jackson Hospital has invested in cutting-edge technology, skilled staff, and excellent facilities to maintain its industry leadership position for five decades, the hospital does not rest on its laurels. Administrators and staff at every level are engaged in a multiphase continued quality improvement program to effectively identify their customers' desires and build responsive work systems to ensure they are met. "Health care is a rapidly changing industry," said Ball. "To stay ahead, we have to be willing to go the extra mile to ensure our services are everything they should be."

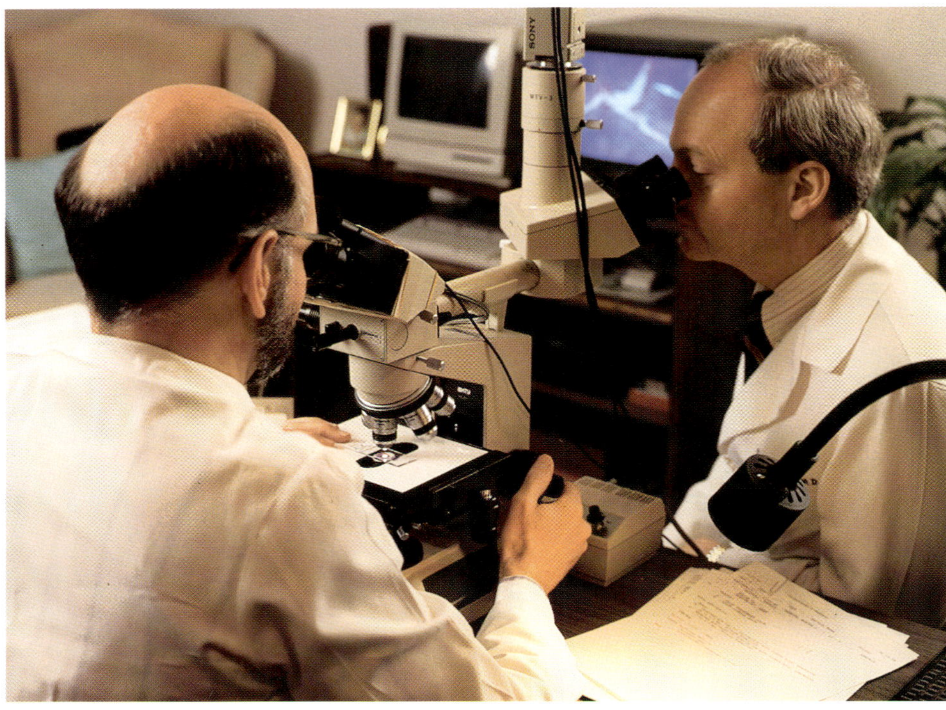

Jackson Hospital has invested in cutting-edge technology, skilled staff, and excellent facilities to maintain its industry leadership position. Photo by Robert Fouts.

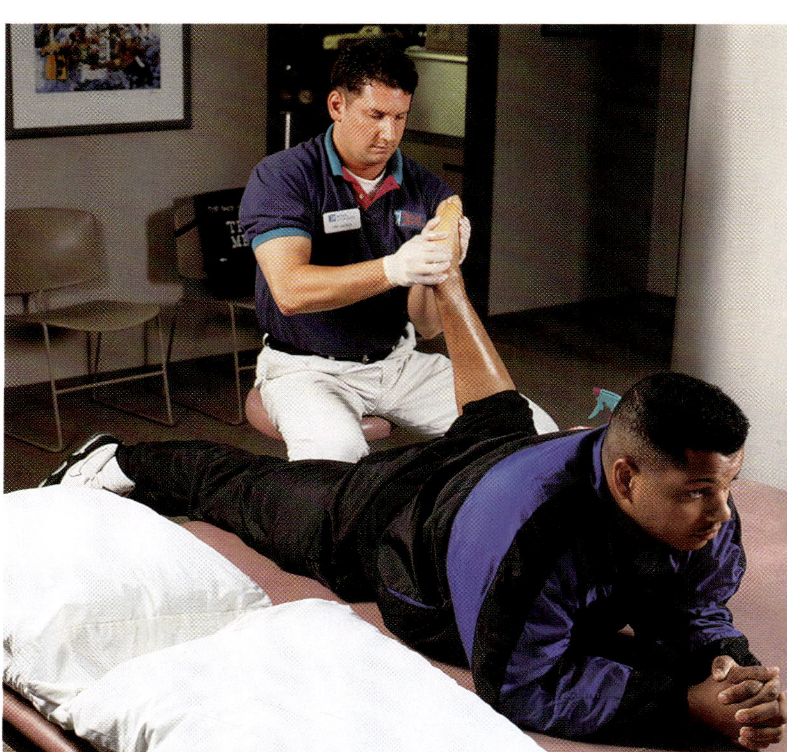

In addition to other specialized units, Jackson provides a fully equipped physical therapy department. Photo by Robert Fouts, courtesy of Rehab Associates.

Recognizing that opportunities for excellence will always be greater than available resources, the Jackson Hospital Foundation was established in 1976 to assist, advance, and strengthen the hospital in its ministry of health.

The foundation accomplishes its objective by identifying, encouraging, and securing the philanthropic support that enables Jackson to maintain its high standards of excellence. Tax-deductible contributions are used to purchase sophisticated equipment which otherwise might not be available in the area, as well as to fund special projects, such as the hospital's intensive care waiting room and the Frank McGough Oncology Unit.

SPECIAL PROGRAMS

The professionals at Jackson Hospital are concerned not only for the medical welfare of their patients, but also for the medical well-being of their community as a whole. "It is this hospital's responsibility to take preventive medicine and wellness to the people of this community, as opposed to waiting for them to come to us," said Ball.

Evidence of that commitment, Jackson Hospital sponsors a diverse variety of outreach programs designed to educate and promote wellness. Drawing from the resources of a highly skilled medical staff, the hospital frequently offers community health fairs and provides free health screening and information programs.

One of Jackson's most eagerly anticipated outreach programs is the annual Community Challenge, a highly effective wellness and community relations program sponsored each year by the Jackson Hospital Foundation. Endorsed by the Governor's Commission on Physical Fitness, Community Challenge is a citywide, day-long sporting event that promotes health awareness and physical fitness among area employers. While funds raised go to the hospital's foundation, the program promotes goodwill and sportsmanship throughout the community.

Jackson's popular speaker's bureau is a free public service that brings into the community knowledgeable speakers expert on a broad range of topics, including patient rights and confidentiality, neurology, communicating effectively, cardiovascular care, and many more.

Jackson's innovative Parent Path program is designed to help inform couples planning to start a family about the many life changes that may be

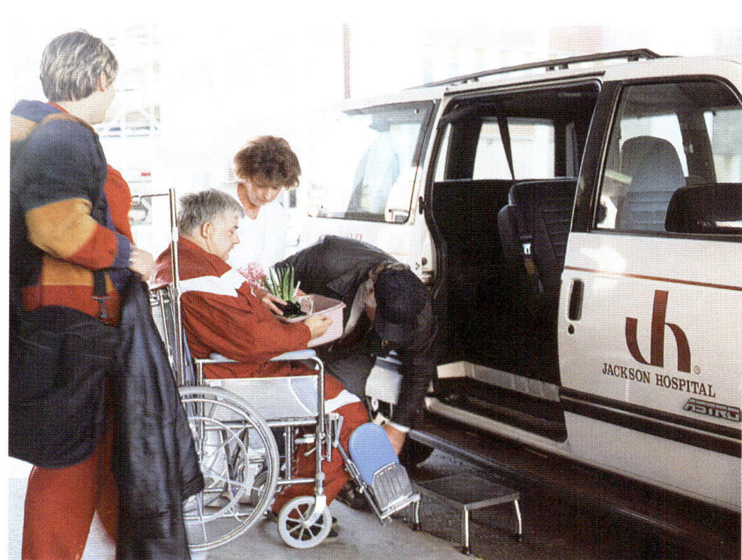

Through its caring spirit, vision for excellence, and unparalleled professionalism, Jackson Hospital & Clinic, Inc. has provided the citizens of Montgomery and surrounding areas with special health care for generations. Photo by Robert Fouts.

ahead. The educational program includes quarterly newsletters with useful information on parenting and planning, health assessments prior to pregnancy, and a wide range of seminars from experts in child care, health, and wellness. The hospital also covers all the bases when it comes to educating expectant families, offering a variety of childbirth preparation classes, including Prenatal Orientation, which welcomes expectant parents to the hospital's beautiful obstetrics unit; a grandparents class, which presents new concepts in childcare; a sibling class, to familiarize older children with the obstetrics area; a C-Birth class, designed for couples who will experience the birthing process by Cesarean section; a Lamaze class, to prepare both partners for labor and delivery; and a breast feeding class to prepare the expectant mother for breast feeding her newborn.

When it comes to top-of-the-mind awareness, there are few advertising slogans more familiar to Montgomerians than "Need a Doctor? Call our Nurse." Jackson's convenient physician referral program puts skilled registered nurses within easy reach by telephone to help patients find the right physician for their needs. Simply by telephoning the service, patients will not only receive a knowledgeable referral but also assistance in making a first appointment, a reminder of appointment date and time, and a post-visit evaluation to determine the patient's satisfaction.

The hospital has also introduced a well-received nutrition program called It's the Right Way—The Healthy Weigh. This medically sound, eight-session weight management class includes nutrition counseling with a registered dietician, a complete nutrition and fitness manual, and fun and interesting cooking demonstrations.

Also as part of the hospital's role in promoting wellness community-wide, Jackson produces and distributes a quarterly health care magazine, *Partners*, which provides easy-to-read, informative articles on an array of health care topics from weight training for beginners to glaucoma.

Seniors throughout the community enjoy Jackson's Senior Citizen Services which provide valuable savings on a variety of items from meals in the hospital cafeteria to items in the pharmacy, and travel, special attractions, and movie discounts.

Through its caring spirit, vision for excellence, and unparalleled professionalism, Jackson Hospital & Clinic, Inc. has provided the citizens of Montgomery and surrounding areas with special health care for generations. And for the generations to come, Jackson is well positioned with the technology, skill, and focus needed to continue its health care leadership into the new millennium. That's why, for total health care, so many central Alabamians *Consider Jackson First*. 𝍖

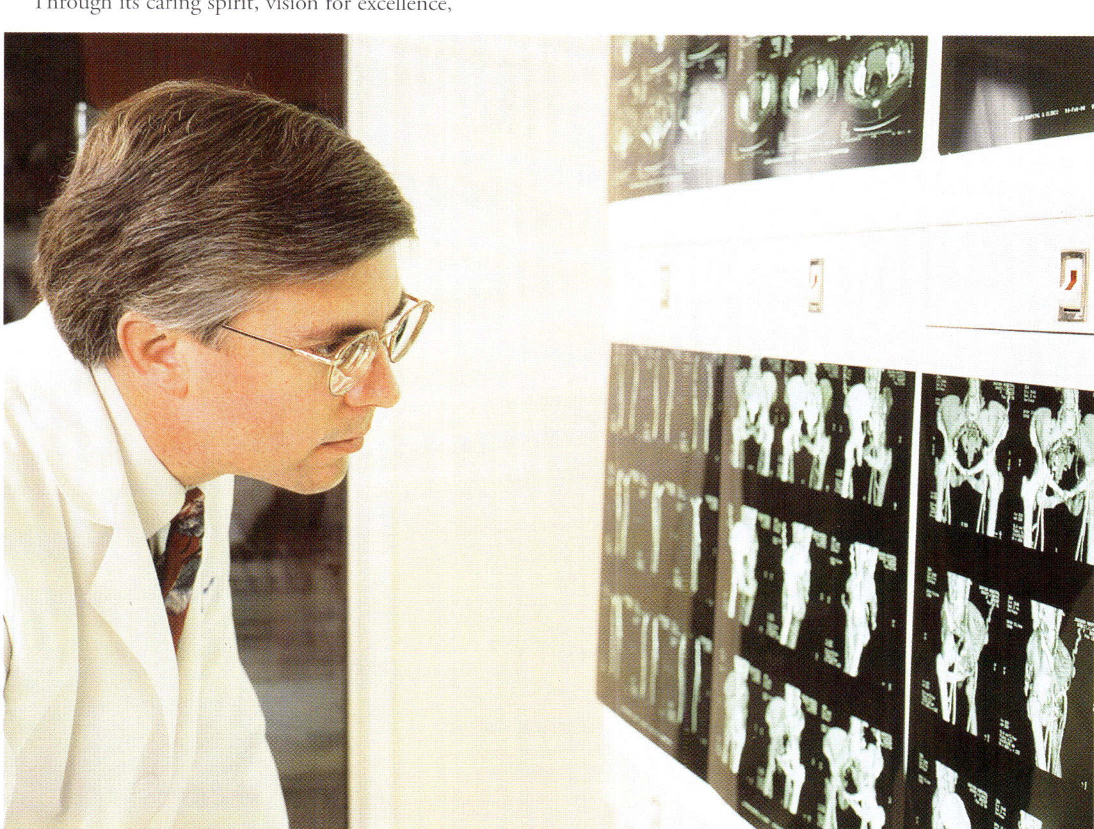

One of Montgomery's leading employers, the hospital employs some 1,300 professionals, ranking it among the largest health care institutions in Alabama. Photo by Robert Fouts.

ADVANCED ORTHOPEDIC
SURGICAL SPECIALISTS, P.C.

Born into a family of educators from Danville, Virginia, Dr. Pinchback was the first in his family to pursue medical training. He completed his undergraduate education at Johnson C. Smith University in Charlotte, North Carolina. Graduating in 1971 with a Bachelor of Science degree in biology, Dr. Pinchback earned his M.D. degree in 1975 from Meharry Medical College in Nashville, Tennessee, and served his internship at Providence Hospital in Southfield, Michigan, from 1975 until 1979. Between 1965 and 1969, Dr. Pinchback performed his orthopedics residency in a rotation through the four hospitals of the Northwest Detroit Affiliated Hospitals, Inc. He worked in hand surgery at Harper Hospital in Detroit and also performed pediatric orthopedics at T. C. Thomas Children's Hospital in Chattanooga, Tennessee, and Scottish Rites Hospital in Atlanta, Georgia.

It was during Dr. Pinchback's second year in medical school, as he assisted an orthopedic surgeon in a South Boston, Virginia, hospital, that he discovered his interest in orthopedics. "I found orthopedics intriguing for a number of reasons," said Dr. Pinchback. "In this field we have an opportunity to work with patients of all ages, most of whom are relatively healthy with the exception of their bones or joints. It is rewarding to be able to bring them back to full health. In addition, it is a challenging field, offering more surgical procedures than any other specialty."

After being aggressively recruited by a Montgomery-area hospital management firm, Dr. Pinchback moved to the Capital City in 1979 and opened an office at 25 Washington Avenue. A fact-finding trip to the Montgomery area prior to his move was only the doctor's second trip to Alabama, the first having been as a Johnson C. Smith University band member playing at nearby Tuskegee Institute. The temperate weather, coupled with a warm reception, a progressive medical environment, and the discovery that several medical school classmates were practicing in the area,

Dr. Pinchback moved to the Capital City in 1979 and opened Advanced Orthopedic Surgical Specialists, P.C. Photo by Paul Robertson.

prompted Dr. Pinchback and his family to make the move.

After nearly eight years in Montgomery, Dr. Pinchback moved his practice to its present location at 1329 Mulberry Street, near the Jackson Hospital complex.

A fellow of the American Academy of Orthopedic Surgeons and certified by the American Board of Orthopedic Surgeons, Dr. Pinchback has earned regional recognition in his field of medicine. He provides considerable service to Montgomery Regional Medical Center, where he serves as chief of the medical staff, and he is also on staff at every other hospital in the Montgomery area, including Baptist Medical Center, Jackson Hospital, East Montgomery Medical Center, and the Veterans Affairs Hospital in Tuskegee, Alabama. Dr. Pinchback's sterling professional credentials include membership in the American Academy of Orthopedic Surgeons, North American Medical Association, Montgomery County Medical Society, and Alabama State Medical Association. A noted speaker and community leader, Dr. Pinchback is equally active in the Montgomery area community, taking on leadership roles in a variety of church, educational, and civic groups.

During more than 20 years in orthopedics, Dr. Pinchback has earned a respected reputation among his peers and patients as a dedicated and knowledgeable physician. But he shares those sentiments for his colleagues, expressing pride in the quality of medical care available in the

The health care professionals at Advanced Orthopedic Surgical Specialists, P.C. are focused on the goal of providing the finest, most complete orthopedic health care in the state of Alabama. Photo by Fouts Commercial Photography.

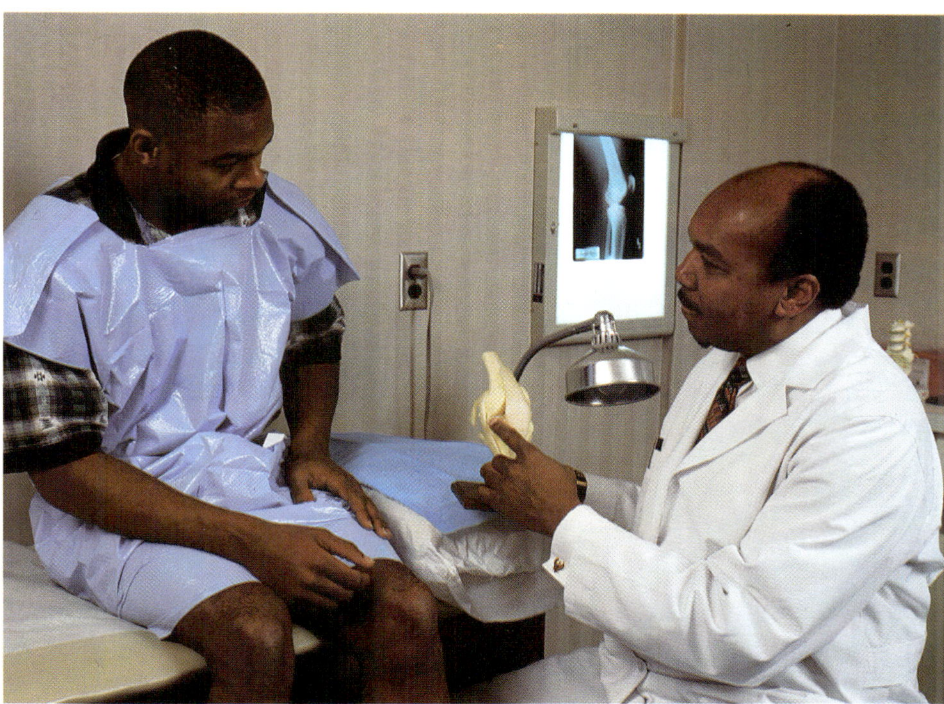

Dr. Pinchback and his staff encourage open communication between patients, physicians, nurses, and any other health care professionals involved in the patient's care. Photo by Fouts Commercial Photography.

Montgomery area. "I am proud to be part of the Montgomery medical community because our physicians provide consistently high quality care, operate established practices, and practice responsibly."

THE STAFF

The health care professionals at Advanced Orthopedic Surgical Specialists, P.C. are focused on the goal of providing the finest, most complete orthopedic health care in the state of Alabama. Under the direction of founder and medical director Dr. Warner Louis Pinchback, the respected practice is achieving its goal by combining attentive, thorough, and personal care with the finest technologies available in the practice of orthopedics.

A professional staff of ten, including one registered nurse, exercise physiologist, a patient care coordinator, an orthopedic technician, and administrative personnel, assist patients in the spacious, two-level complex.

Working in one of the most dynamic and progressive fields of medicine, Dr. Pinchback and his staff rigorously follow changes and developments in orthopedic technologies. Their work in arthroscopic and joint replacement spine surgeries requires extensive knowledge and skill in the use of rapidly developing techniques and materials. The practice of "orthopedics has more surgical procedures than any other medical specialty,"

said Dr. Pinchback. "That fact, combined with the technological dynamics of the field, challenges us to stay on the cutting edge."

ARTHROSCOPIC SURGERY

Advanced arthroscopic joint surgery has dramatically changed the way physicians like Dr. Pinchback manage knee, ankle, shoulder, wrist, and elbow injuries and conditions. What once required large, painful surgical incisions is now accomplished through tiny punctures using special noninvasive techniques. The result, according to Dr. Pinchback, is less pain and faster recovery.

SPINE AND BONE

Advanced Orthopedic Surgical Specialists' primary concentration is in the treatment and study of bones, joints, muscles, and certain nerve ailments, but Dr. Pinchback also has a strong interest and extensive experience in treatment of the spine and lower back problems. The professionals at Advanced Orthopedic Surgical Specialists provide comprehensive management of back problems, including lower disk ailments, problems of instability, and disorders requiring complex spinal surgery. Dr. Pinchback offers individual evaluation, diagnosis, and treatment of all spinal disorders, including back problems relating to injuries from work-related sources.

PHYSICAL THERAPY

Because of a commitment to total patient care, Advanced Orthopedic Surgical Specialists maintains one of the finest physical therapy facilities available in the Montgomery area. Located on the second floor of Dr. Pinchback's fully-equipped Mulberry Street office, the elevator-accessible department offers the latest technology innovations in equipment and therapeutic technique. "It is important to us to provide advanced physical therapy right here in our office, not only for the patient's convenience, but also for thorough treatment," said Dr. Pinchback. "If our patients have questions regarding therapy or the healing process, I am right here, and I know exactly what kind of therapy they are receiving."

The state-of-the-art physical therapy facility includes separate areas for active and passive therapeutic exercise. Among the amenities are raised exercise mats for easier access, ultrasound and electrical stimulation equipment, Med-X equipment, and the only piece of therapeutic equipment proven to specifically isolate an exercise for lumbar spine muscles. Recognizing the demands on his patients' time, Dr. Pinchback and his skilled clinicians work with each patient to develop a complete treatment plan that meets individual needs, schedules, and lifestyles.

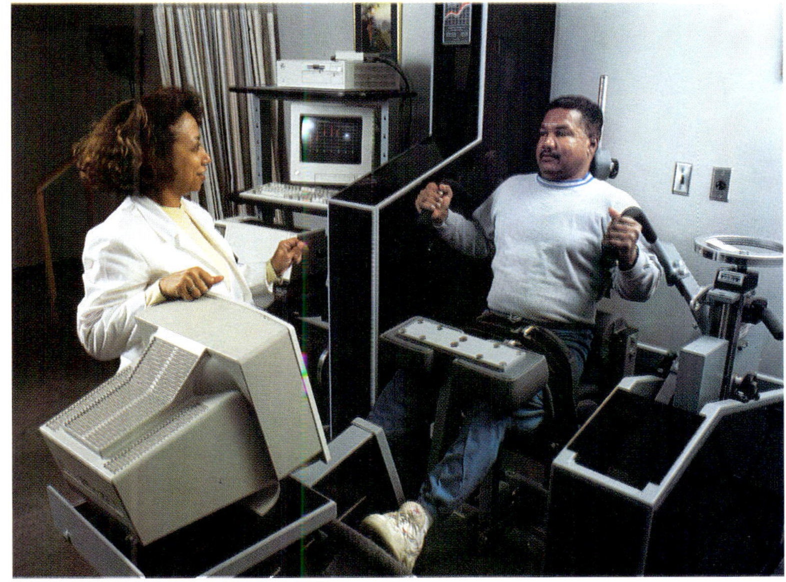

Working in one of the most dynamic and progressive fields of medicine, Dr. Pinchback and his staff rigorously follow changes and developments in orthopedic technologies. Photo by Fouts Commercial Photography.

FRACTURES AND SPRAINS

In addition to its specialized treatment of spinal problems and its extensive physical therapy program, Advanced Orthopedic Surgical Specialists also provides comprehensive treatment for broken bones and related sprains, including casting or surgery when needed. An in-house x-ray facility is yet another convenient amenity of the full-service orthopedic practice.

JOINT IMPLANTS

Joint implant technology is another of the most rapidly changing orthopedic procedures. The procedure has improved dramatically since the first artificial joints were implanted, and Dr. Pinchback is an expert in the most advanced joint implant techniques, including cementless implants. "Today's replacements are made of strong, light-weight metal alloys and plastics. They can restore full use of a joint with an improved range of motion and elimination of pain and deformity," said Dr. Pinchback.

ARTHRITIS

In addition to these specialty areas, Advanced Orthopedic Surgical Specialists treats patients suffering from varying types of arthritis, America's number one crippler, and sports-related injuries affecting weekend warriors, amateur athletes, and professional competitors. "The goal with any treatment we undertake is to return our patients to quality lifestyles as quickly as possible," said Dr. Pinchback. "To suffer from a joint or bone ailment, when you feel fine otherwise, is a frustrating experience. We recognize the dilemma our patients face, and we realize the strain is both physical and emotional."

OTHER SERVICES

In an effort to treat the whole patient as efficiently as possible, Dr. Pinchback and his staff encourage open communication between patients, physicians, nurses, and any other health care professionals involved in the patient's care. "We want our patients to take an active role in their own care and treatment. We value their input and their involvement because we believe it helps speed the healing process."

To facilitate that kind of communication, Advanced Orthopedic Specialists coordinates a number of special programs, including a support group which meets periodically to offer information and emotional support to patients and their immediate family members. The practice also publishes a quarterly patients newsletter, *Bone Talk* to keep patients up-to-date on the constantly changing field of orthopedics and upcoming special events or programs that may be useful to their treatment, therapy, or injury prevention. In service to Montgomery and surrounding communities, Advanced Orthopedic Surgical Specialists also provide speakers for community

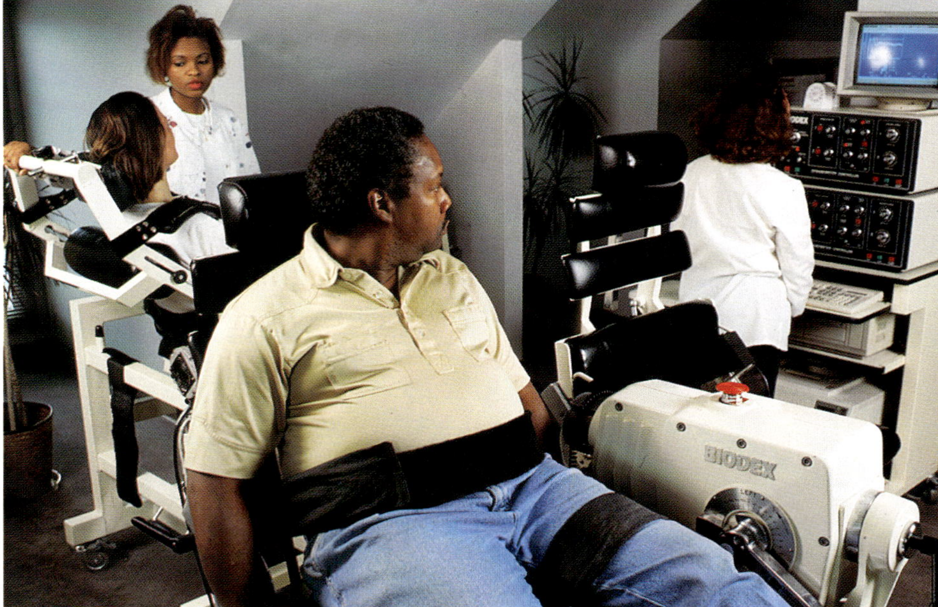

Because of a commitment to total patient care, Advanced Orthopedic Surgical Specialists maintains one of the finest physical therapy facilities available in the Montgomery area. Photo by Fouts Commercial Photography.

A concern for patients and a sincere interest in finding the most productive path to wellness, set Advanced Orthopedic Surgical Specialists apart as one of the finest orthopedic health care providers in Alabama. Photo by Fouts Commercial Photography.

Advanced Orthopedic Surgical Specialists, P.C. is located at 1329 Mulberry Street, near the Jackson Hospital complex.

and civic organizations to present information on a variety of orthopedic-related topics.

These kinds of value-added services, combined with concern for patients and a sincere interest in finding the most productive path to wellness, set Advanced Orthopedic Surgical Specialists apart as one of the finest orthopedic health care providers in Alabama. The large practice continues to grow, with the vast majority of new patients turning to Dr. Pinchback and his staff on the basis of referrals from other satisfied patients. "We think of ourselves as highly service oriented, and we believe our patients feel the same way. They are often quick to recommend us to others," said Dr. Pinchback.

The professionals at Advanced Orthopedic Surgical Specialists are committed to maintaining and expanding their fine reputation by doggedly pursuing their founding mission. Said Dr. Pinchback, "We will continue to provide the finest comprehensive orthopedic care in Alabama by doing it right the first time, every time." **𝍎**

COLUMBIA REGIONAL MEDICAL CENTER

There is little doubt the Catholic nuns who founded Montgomery's first hospital nearly a century ago would be astounded and gratified by what has become of their contribution.

The gleaming five-story Columbia Regional Medical Center that covers 13 acres at the bustling downtown corner of Ripley Street and Adams Avenue is far different from the Daughters of Charity's Saint Margaret's Hospital that opened in the historic Watts Mansion on the same spot in 1903.

As would be expected after nearly 100 years of service, the hospital has grown and changed at every level. Its facilities, technologies, and services are on the leading edge of health care in Alabama. But progress aside, each change has been driven by the nuns' founding mission—a mission that has never wavered: To meet patient needs with quality, cost-effective, and compassionate health care.

For Saint Margaret's Hospital, the early decades were characterized by rapid structural change necessitated by astounding growth. Within the first decade after its founding, the hospital constructed a two-story addition, connected by bridge to the main facility. Soon after, a second wing was added; and in 1940, Saint Margaret's responded to community need by building Mariel Hall, home to the hospital's new School of Nursing.

In the years that followed, Saint Margaret's Hospital established a respected reputation for compassionate health care and broad vision of its role in the community. Located in the heart of downtown Montgomery, the hospital served all patients in need and frequently cared for state politicians and business leaders who worked within walking distance of the facility.

In 1989, as dramatic change began to impact the health care industry, Humana, Inc. purchased Montgomery's oldest hospital, and the facility was renamed Humana Hospital-Montgomery. Four years later, Humana hospitals nationwide were organized under a new hospital company, Galen Health Care, Inc., and the Montgomery hospital was renamed Montgomery Regional Medical Center. Several months later Galen Health Care, Inc. merged with Columbia Healthcare, Inc., and in February 1994, a union between Columbia Healthcare, Inc. and Hospital Corporation of America established the largest hospital chain in the world.

As a result of those changes, the hospital became known as Columbia Regional Medical Center in mid-1996 and is one of three Columbia health care facilities in Montgomery. Recognized nationally for superior management

Columbia Regional Medical Center's facilities, technologies, and services are on the leading edge of health care in Alabama.

and a progressive approach to health care, Columbia also owns Columbia East Montgomery Medical Center, the Montgomery Surgical Center, and hospitals in nearby Prattville, Selma, and Andalusia. In addition to its acute care and ambulatory facilities, Columbia also owns Montgomery's Columbia HomeCare for patients needing medical care at home following hospitalization.

"Columbia brings great strength to this hospital in the form of tremendous resources, innovative management, buying power, and much more," said Columbia Regional Medical Center Chief Operating Officer Ron O'Neal. "Continued investment in this hospital not only serves our patients, but the community as well by enhancing the value of Montgomery's downtown area and allowing us to provide premiere health care service."

According to O'Neal, the 700 medical, administrative, and support professionals who serve Columbia Regional Medical Center understand their mission is more than meeting medical needs as they arise. "We must keep pace with the latest developments in medical science; we must

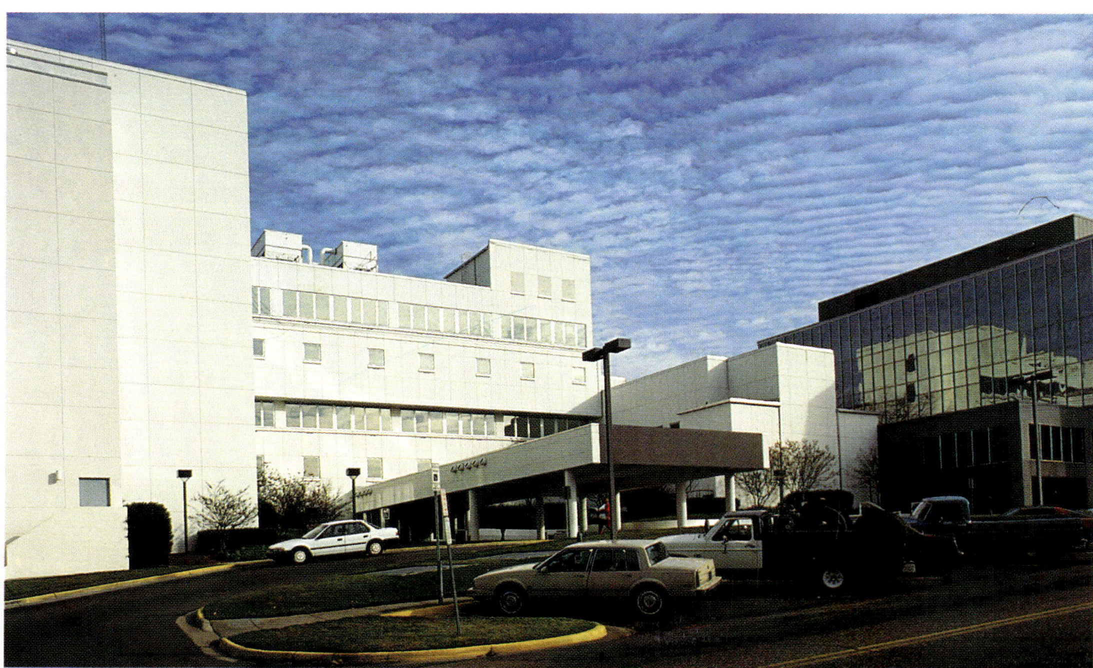

The gleaming five-story Columbia Regional Medical Center covers 13 acres at the bustling downtown corner of Ripley Street and Adams Avenue.

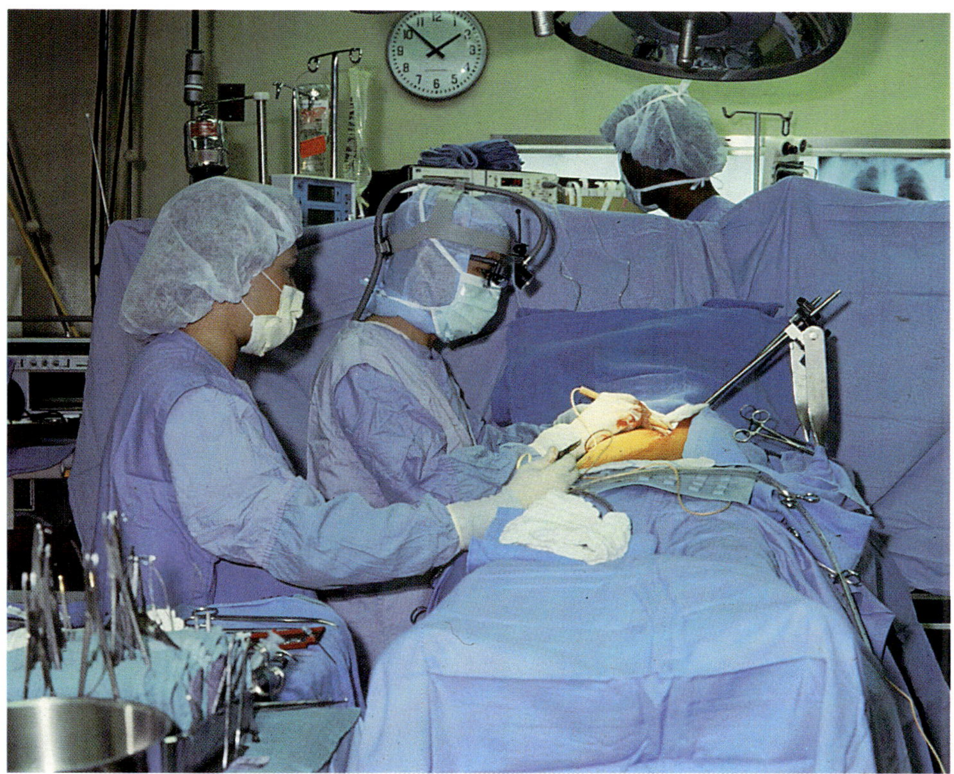

The hospital's fully equipped surgical department is equipped with general and cardiac suites as well as a urology suite. The surgery area also includes a seven-bed intensive care unit, a 10-bed cardiovascular surgery unit, and two cardiac catheterization labs.

recognize health care needs unique to this community and respond proactively to meet those needs; and we must provide educational programs to help prevent disease," he said.

At Columbia Regional Medical Center those "musts" have become reality in the form of superior facilities, cutting-edge technology, a highly respected medical staff, and extraordinary medical specialty care programming.

PREPARING FOR THE TWENTY-FIRST CENTURY

Columbia Regional Medical Center is a 250-bed acute care medical/surgical hospital located on a sprawling downtown campus which includes the hospital, a six-story professional office building, the Troy State University School of Nursing building, and other adjacent buildings leased to health care concerns such as the American Heart Association. An adjacent multi-level parking garage and free valet parking provide a welcome convenience for visitors to the bustling downtown area.

The main hospital building has five floors, along with a basement laboratory which includes the outpatient receiving area, histology, microbiology, chemistry, and hematology departments and a blood bank. A welcoming corridor and glass-enclosed entrance on Ripley Street provide

access to the main lobby, a beautifully decorated and comfortable area in close proximity to the admitting office, gift shop, and information desk. The first floor also includes respiratory care, radiology, and physical therapy departments, an endoscopy suite, outpatient department, and the emergency department.

The hospital's fully equipped surgical department is located on the second floor with general and cardiac suites as well as a urology suite for cystoscopies, and a recovery suite with six open bays and one closed bay. The surgery area also includes a seven-bed intensive care unit, a 10-bed cardiovascular surgery unit, and two cardiac catheterization labs. In addition, the second floor is home to the EP lab, Echo department, EKG department, hospital pharmacy, cafeteria, medical staff library, doctors' dining

room, environmental services department, and other administrative areas.

The third floor includes a 12-bed specialized cardiac care unit, a 25-bed cardiac care step down medical unit, a 25-bed cardiovascular stepdown unit, and a telemetry monitoring room. An additional 25-bed stepdown cardiac unit is also located on the third floor for post-cardiac catheterization recovery.

The fourth level is home to the hospital's recently expanded and comfortably renovated Womens' and Childrens' Center, which services Montgomery's successful Gift of Life program for indigent families. The obstetrical wing includes four private labor and delivery rooms, one semi-private LDR, a cesarean section room, a delivery room, and a two-bay recovery area. A 16-bed Level 1 nursery and an 8-bed Level 2 nursery are conveniently located adjacent to a 16-bed postpartum area. Testimony to its commitment to community need, the hospital has joined with the BellSouth Telephone Pioneers to build lasting relationships with Gift of Life families through such enriching programs as "Teach This Child to Read." Completing the services on the fourth floor is a 14-bed pediatric unit.

The hospital's fifth floor includes a 32-bed surgical unit, a 14-bed renal metabolic unit, an acute renal dialysis unit with five open bays and a 14-bed neuro/med surgical step down unit.

With patient concern at the forefront of its business philosophy, Columbia Regional Medical Center has completely renovated the interior of

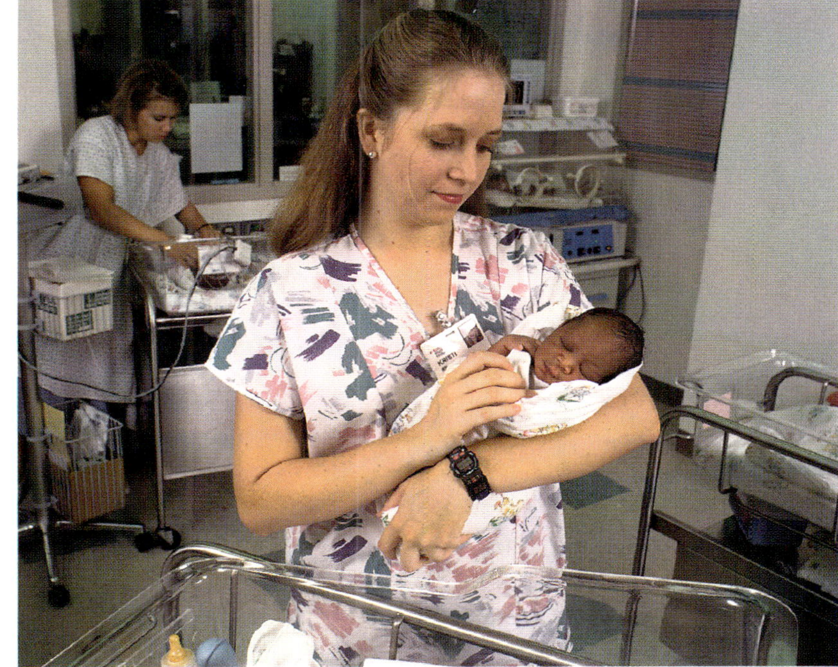

The hospital's obstetrical wing includes a 16-bed Level 1 nursery and an 8-bed Level 2 nursery, conveniently located adjacent to a 16-bed postpartum area.

each floor to exude a soothing warmth and comfort essential to a healing environment. Also, for comfort and convenience, the hospital provides overnight accommodations in its tower rooms for out-of-town family or visitors.

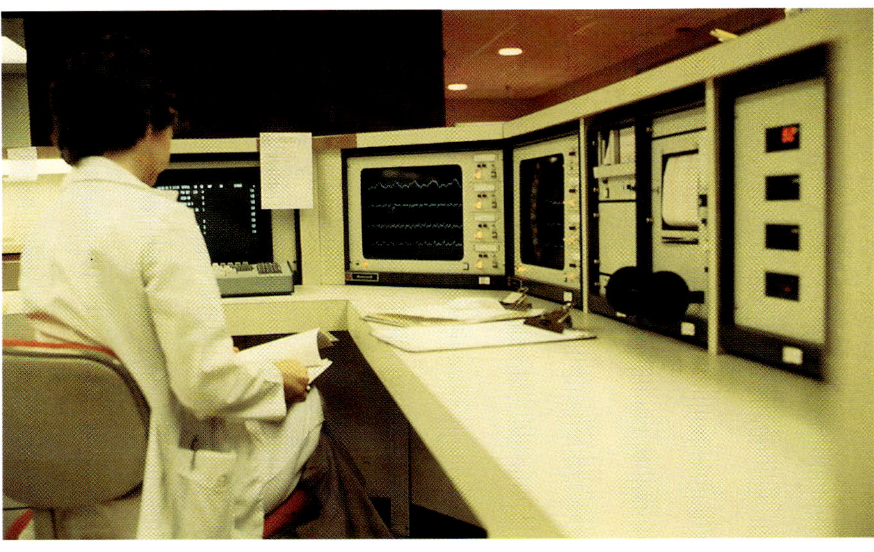

The hospital's renowned Heart Institute has combined the most up-to-date technological procedures with skillful, compassionate professionals to lead the way in the cardiac field throughout central Alabama.

But to supplement its full-service facilities and to enhance its value both to its patients and to its medical professionals, Columbia Regional Medical Center has implemented some of the world's finest health care administration technologies.

The hospital was first in Montgomery to install the "Meditrol" system, a new computerized medication distribution, which accurately places each patient's medications and supplies at the nurse's fingertips, ensures proper dosage levels, and enhances hospital security and safety. "The value with this system is three-fold," said O'Neal. "It improves efficiency, serves our patients more responsively, and saves money through enhanced safety and security."

Columbia Regional is part of the advanced "Meditech" system, a state-of-the-art, fully integrated patient information system. Meditech integrates all hospital data for a complete single-source patient management file. "Columbia will have Meditech in each of its hospitals," said O'Neal. "If one of our patients goes into a Columbia hospital in another state, we can easily exchange patient records." With Meditech, doctors' offices are tied to the hospital via a personal computer, providing direct on-line access to patient reports. In addition, the hospital will have a full range of documented patient information to help administrators analyze the hospital's

resource allocation. "We have studied every nook and cranny of this hospital for efficiency, and we are doing everything we can to ensure we are performing at peak potential," said O'Neal.

RESPONDING TO NEED

Over the years, Columbia Regional Medical Center has recognized weaknesses in local health care offerings and has moved quickly and competently to fill the gaps.

For nearly two decades, Montgomery's first hospital has been first in cardiac health care. Since the 1970s, cardiac catheterizations and open-heart surgery have been performed at Columbia Regional Medical Center. The hospital's renowned Heart Institute has combined the most up-to-date technological procedures with skillful, compassionate professionals to lead the way in the cardiac field throughout central Alabama. Operating two cardiac catheterization/angioplasty labs, three open-heart surgical suites, a dedicated open-heart intensive care unit, a dedicated cardiac intensive care unit, and phase I, II, and III cardiac rehabilitation programs, the institute offers the area's most complete array of cardiac diagnosis, treatment, and rehabilitation procedures.

Among the procedures routinely performed at the Heart Institute are bypass graphs, stent therapy, laser angioplasties, automatic implantable cardioverter defibrillators, radiofrequency ablation, and electrophysiology studies. Each year, the institute performs more than

1,500 cardiac catheterizations. For patients recovering from cardiac care, the hospital sponsors the popular Heart of Montgomery Club, which offers cardiac patients and their families educational seminars, cooking and exercise demonstrations, social events, and more.

In much the same progressive spirit, Columbia Regional Medical Center was also first in Montgomery to develop a diabetes treatment center. Located on the fifth floor of the hospital, the center treats patients both on an in- and out-patient basis, with an emphasis on education and helping patients learn to live with diabetes. "The community needed a program of this type, and we stepped out," said Margaret Mehearg, director of public affairs. "Doctors can arrange diabetic consultations for their patients, and the center often provides open classes for the public." The hospital's Central Alabama Wound Care Center®, located across the street from the main facility, is yet another innovative health care service, specializing in the aggressive treatment of chronic wounds that will not heal under ordinary care. Only the second clinic of its kind in Alabama, the center is staffed by Columbia Regional Medical Center physicians expert in a variety of medical specialties from podiatry to plastic surgery and endocrinology. "The Wound Care Center has a tremendous success rate," said Mehearg. "Many patients who had previously accepted the pain and inconvenience of long-term wounds have found help through the center's concentrated effort."

Responding to the growing need for quality

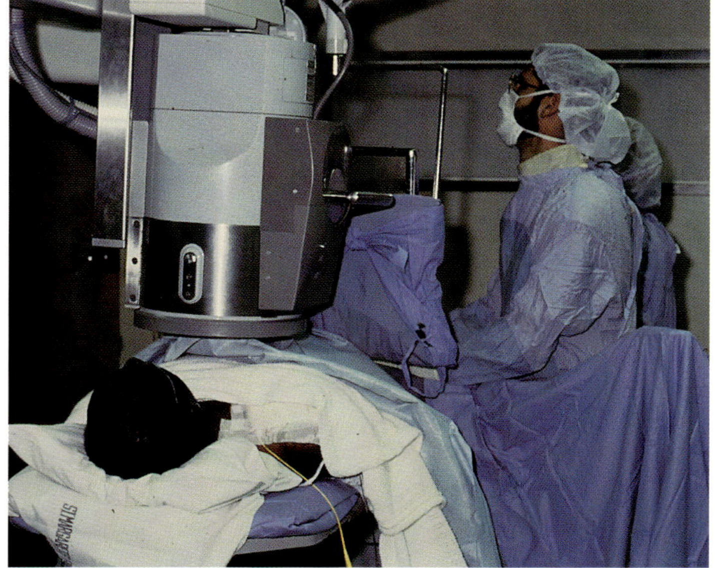

Columbia Regional is part of the advanced "Meditech" system, a state-of-the-art, fully integrated patient information system. Meditech integrates all hospital data for a complete single-source patient management file, ensuring the finest patient care.

health care for the elderly, the hospital has established the Senior Healthcare Center to serve senior patients over the age of 65. In association with the physicians of Mulberry Medical Associates on Mulberry Street, Columbia Regional has opened the center with the goal of enhancing the quality of life for seniors and finding ways to keep them active and independent for as long as possible. "As health care providers, it is up to us to recognize and respond to the social care needs of our community," said O'Neal.

TAKING A BROADER VIEW

Since its unassuming founding nearly 10 decades ago, Columbia Regional Medical Center has been as strongly committed to the welfare of its community as it has been to the welfare of its patients. One of Montgomery's most proactive forces in disease prevention, the hospital conducts an aggressive and far-reaching array of field education programs promoting topics of interest from baby safety classes to nutrition and heart health issues. Other outreach services include a strong speaker's bureau, which features many of the hospital's most respected physicians and other health care professionals, and an informative quarterly magazine, *Columbia OneSource: Montgomery's Guide to Healthy Living,* which is distributed throughout central Alabama.

Committed to enhancing the quality of life in its community beyond the realm of health care, Columbia Regional Medical Center is an active Partner in Education, supports the Montgomery Area Chamber of Commerce, and has taken a leading role in Montgomery's beautification of the downtown area.

Still upholding a commitment to its century-old founding mission, the professionals at Columbia Regional have created a progressive health care institution dedicated to medical excellence and compassionate service. Columbia Regional Medical Center has successfully combined tradition with technology to establish itself at the forefront of contemporary health care in Alabama. *m*

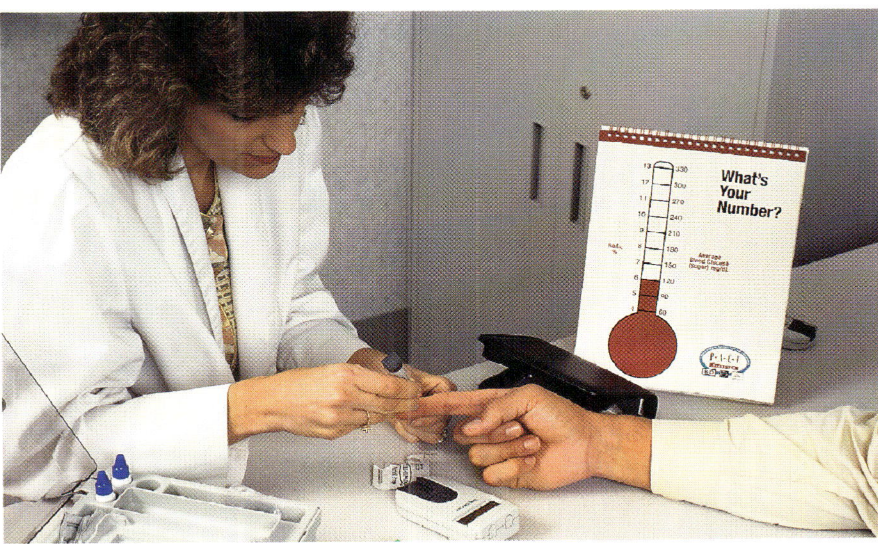

C*olumbia Regional Medical Center is committed to enhancing the quality of life in its community.*

A *welcoming corridor and glass-enclosed entrance on Ripley Street provide access to the main lobby, a beautifully decorated and comfortable area in close proximity to the admitting office, gift shop, and information desk.*

SOUTHEASTERN CARDIOLOGY CONSULTANTS, P.C.

Southeastern Cardiology Consultants, P.C. is recognized throughout central Alabama for offering a uniquely comprehensive range of cardiac medical services, from initial diagnosis to treatment and follow-up. Operating with the finest facilities, equipment, and resources available, the skilled physicians and clinical staff attract patients from as far south as Andalusia, Alabama, and as far north as Birmingham, Alabama.

The practice was founded in 1981 by Montgomery native Thomas J. Wool, M.D. shortly after he completed a fellowship in cardiology at the University of Alabama in Birmingham. Since its establishment, the practice has grown dramatically to include seven of the most highly respected clinical cardiologists in Alabama.

The other physicians in the practice are Kenneth J. Wool, M.D.; Kevin L. Sublett, M.D.; Beverly A. Stoudemire, M.D.; Karl J. Crossen, M.D.; Mark J. Hsu, M.D.; and J. Lee Grigsby, M.D. Doctors Thomas Wool, Kenneth Wool, Kevin Sublett, Karl Crossen, Beverly Stoudemire, and Mark Hsu are Fellows of the American College of Cardiology, and each of the seven doctors is board certified in one or more specialties, including cardiology, internal medicine, or electrophysiology. The physicians have achieved the highest level of training available and have been recognized by other cardiologists across the nation for their accomplishments.

The physicians of Southeastern Cardiology Consultants perform invasive cardiology procedures including cardiac catheterization, percutaneous transluminal coronary angioplasty, directional coronary artherectomy, laser angioplasty, and intracoronary stent placement. Noninvasive services include a complete range of diagnostic testing from nuclear cardiology studies to pacemaker management and transtelephonic monitoring. The physicians, cardiac trained nurses, and skilled clinical staff also provide patient consultation, cardiac rehabilitation programs, preventive and educational programs, and nutritional counseling.

In addition to its main office on Forest Avenue, off Interstate 85 and near Jackson Hospital, the group maintains seven satellite offices, including offices at Montgomery's Baptist Medical Center and East Montgomery Medical

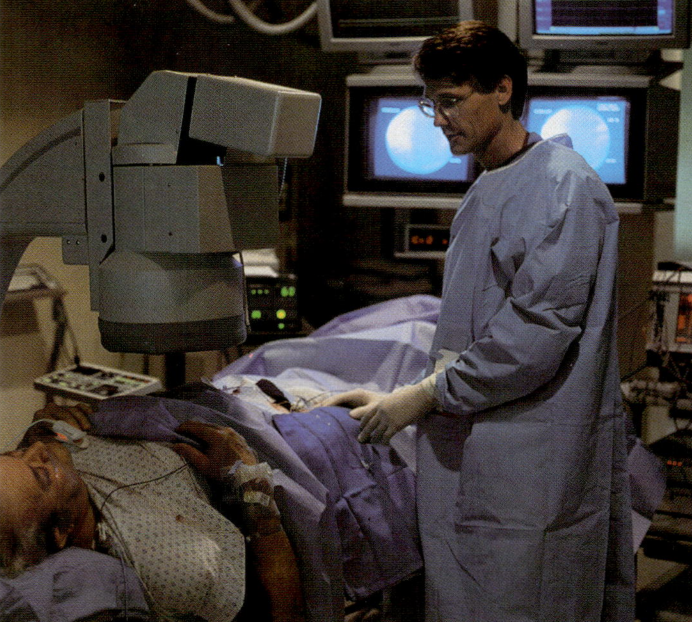

Dr. Karl Crossen completes an electrophysiology study. This procedure is performed to determine the cause of irregular heart beats or rhythms.

Center. The physicians also maintain an office in Selma and outreach clinics in Union Springs, Troy, Greenville, and Evergreen.

Recognizing a need for cardiac care services in smaller Alabama towns and rural areas, the physicians work hard to service primary care physicians in outlying areas and make their expertise available whenever requested.

A number of the physicians of Southeastern Cardiology Consultants are respected as experts in specialized areas of cardiology. Dr. Crossen, a board certified electrophysiologist, is known for his work in radio frequency ablation. Four of the doctors are interventionalists and recognized experts in such invasive therapeutic treatments as balloon angioplasty and transcatheter therapy. Dr. Hsu, also an electrophysiologist, is noted for his work in noninvasive diagnostics such as transesophogeal echocardiology. The group's nuclear imaging capability and staff expertise is noted statewide.

Since its founding, Southeastern Cardiology Consultants has been dedicated to building a practice second to none in terms of skill and resources. The physicians confront the technological dynamics of their ever-changing specialty by staying at the forefront in education and preparedness. In addition to maintaining their own rigorous continuing medical education programs, the physicians of Southeastern Cardiology Consultants are often called upon to present public awareness programs and address professional seminars.

Patient education is vital to the treatment of a patient newly diagnosed with a heart disorder.

These recognized specialists are able to sustain the demands of their fast-paced practice with the support of a highly skilled 50-person support staff. The staff includes registered nurses, a full-time research coordinator, certified medical assistants, certified nuclear technologist, certified

Perhaps the most exciting sign of the group's commitment to its future in Montgomery is its planned One Heart Center. This progressive state-of-the-art facility will be one of Montgomery's premiere facilities for complete cardiology service that will carry the cardiac

cardiac patients, allowing the physicians and staff to concentrate their training and expertise to achieve the highest quality cardiac care.

Backed by a technically sound clinical staff and some of the most advanced medical equipment and facilities available, Southeastern Cardiac Diagnostics provides a full range of testing services, including electrocardiogram, nuclear cardiac imaging, arrhythmia monitoring, echocardiography, duplex carotid imaging, arterial and venous doppler analysis, and a pacemaker clinic.

The center's nuclear cardiac testing expertise and capabilities are widely recognized. Each member of the nuclear staff has been extensively trained and works under the direct supervision of a certified nuclear technologist and a nuclear trained cardiologist. The physicians use advanced Single Photon Emission Computerized Tomography to provide a complete range of nuclear cardiac imaging, including thallium stress testing and MUGA scans. The ability to perform dypyridamole thallium stress testing on those patients who are not candidates for a treadmill test allows the physicians to gain valuable information only recently available through advancing technologies.

Southeastern Cardiac Diagnostics also provides a variety of arrhythmia monitoring services, including event monitoring, which helps screen patients with episodic symptoms such as palpitations and syncope.

The center's echocardiographic imaging tests are conducted under the supervision of a registered diagnostic cardiac sonographer. Its wide variety of echocardiographic testing includes the

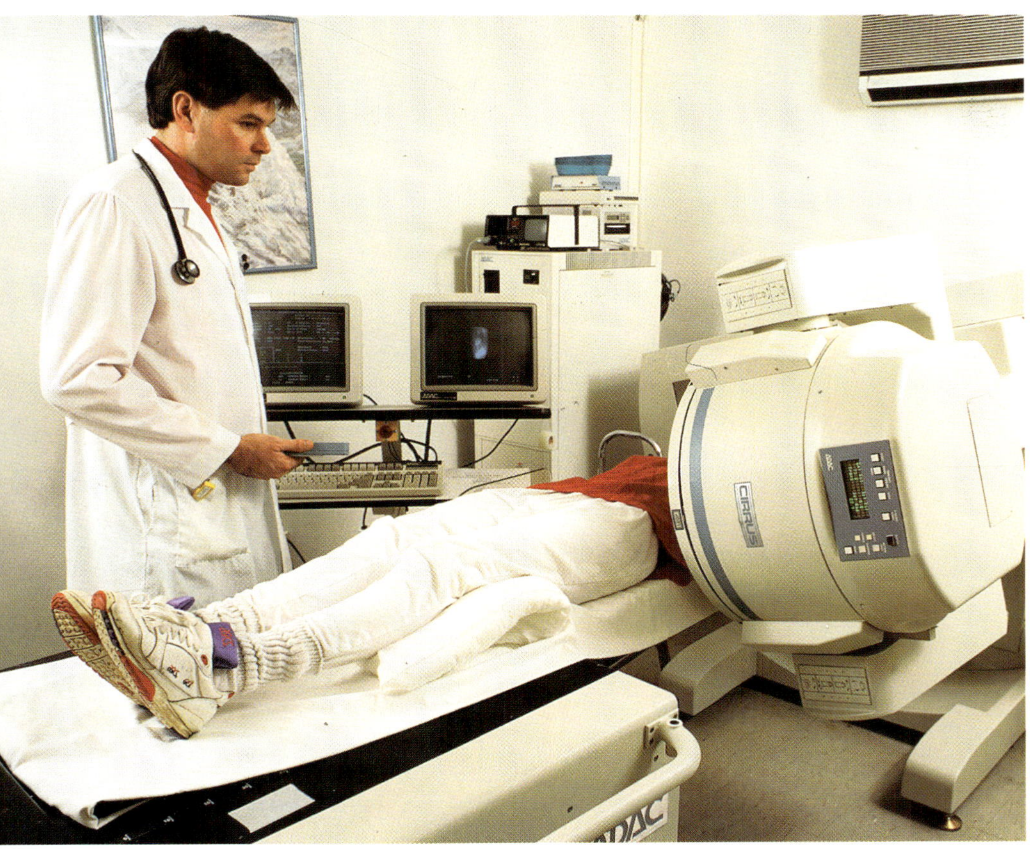

Combining state-of-the-art technology and a highly trained clinical staff enables Southeastern Cardiac Diagnostics to provide the highest quality noninvasive cardiac imaging.

EKG technologist, certified echostenographers, technicians, and administrative support staff. The specially trained physicians, nurses, and clinical staff have built a supportive team environment to provide responsive, compassionate, and thorough patient care.

As health care reform approaches and managed care options take shape on the medical horizon, it is clear the number of medical specialties will decline. But the expertise, skill, and competency required for quality heart care means an excellent future for the kind of superior cardiac services provided by Southeastern Cardiology Consultants.

As baby boomers age and prevention and treatment technologies improve, the field of cardiac care will continue to expand. The physicians and staff at Southeastern Cardiology are addressing the future by continuing to develop their expertise and looking to add soon more quality physicians.

patient through every phase of care from diagnosis to treatment and on to rehabilitation.

SOUTHEASTERN CARDIAC DIAGNOSTICS

A division of Southeastern Cardiology Consultants, P.C., this diagnostic arm of the practice provides cardiac testing services to more than 100 physicians in Montgomery and the surrounding area.

Founded in 1987 by the physicians of Southeastern Cardiology Consultants, South-eastern Cardiac Diagnostics limits its services to the special needs of

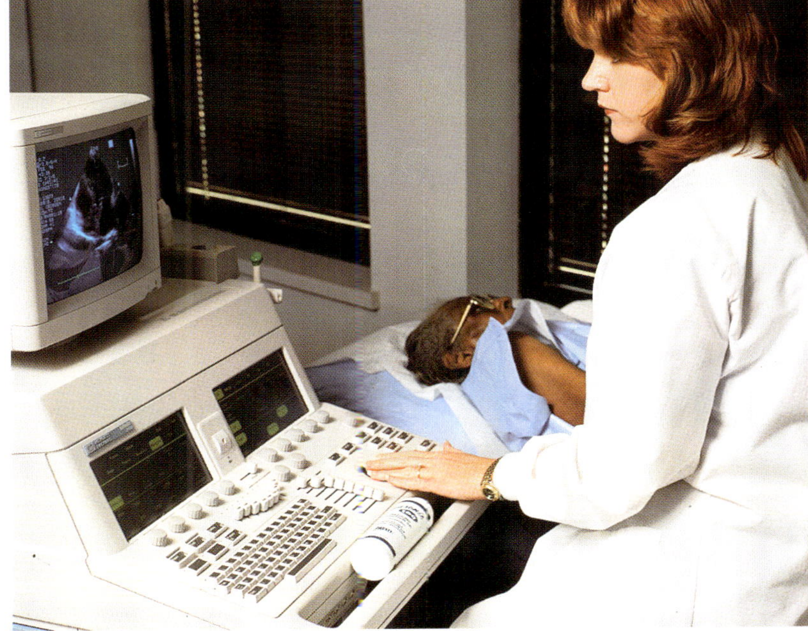

noninvasive Two-Dimensional M-Mode for evaluating the heart, the Two-Dimensional M-Mode with Color Flow Doppler for a useful analysis of blood flow through the heart, and

Dr. Ken Wool, along with the other physicians in the practice are Fellows of the American College of Cardiology and have achieved the highest level of training available.

Transeophageal Echocardiography for patients who are not candidates for transthoracic echocardiography.

High quality duplex carotid imaging allows physicians to visualize plaque or clots within the carotid artery, and arterial and venous doppler analysis indicates various blood flow abnormalities, such a clots in the upper and lower extremities.

Southeastern Cardiac Diagnostics services not only other cardiac care physicians but also physicians of other specialties who turn to the doctors and staff for their specialized expertise. At the completion of testing, the diagnostic center provides other physicians with thorough documentation, reporting, and interpretation of the test results.

Although Southeastern Cardiac Diagnostics uses the area's finest equipment and technologies and offers the superior clinical skills of a highly trained staff, each doctor believes that personal concern and trusting relationships go a long way in enhancing a patient's experiences and building a road to better health. The physicians of Southeastern Cardiology Consultants and Southeastern Diagnostics commonly work 12- to 16-hour days with an emphasis on spending the time necessary to understand and address each patient's individual needs.

ONE HEART CENTER

Evidence of Southeastern Cardiology's commitment to providing its patients the finest in cardiac diagnosis and testing is its new One Heart Center to be located conveniently at the junction of Interstate 85 and Forest Avenue. This fully integrated state-of-the-art health care facility, scheduled to open in the summer of 1997, will include every amenity for single-source cardiac diagnosis and testing. It will serve Southeastern Cardiology patients as well as patients referred from other area physicians.

The beautiful, ultramodern building will include four floors efficiently designed to house facilities for diagnostics, examination, out-patient treatments, and administrative offices. "Our vision is to build a full-service cardiac care facility that will offer our patients comfort, peace of mind, and the finest resources," said Allen Goree, director of administration. "At the same time, our doctors will be able to work more efficiently out of a single facility and will be able to spend more time working directly with their patients."

Along with concern for efficiency and flexibility, One Heart Center has been designed with sensitivity for the human element. Because cardiac patients are often facing difficult and traumatic life experiences, Southeastern Cardiology has been careful to design a warm, comfortable facility which, when combined with compassionate care and sensitivity, can enhance the healing process.

The building's glass-enclosed center lobby area will be accented with cherry paneling, granite, and stone to create a sense of warmth and openness. The inviting interiors are designed to make it easy for patients to find their way throughout the facility.

The ground floor of One Heart Center will

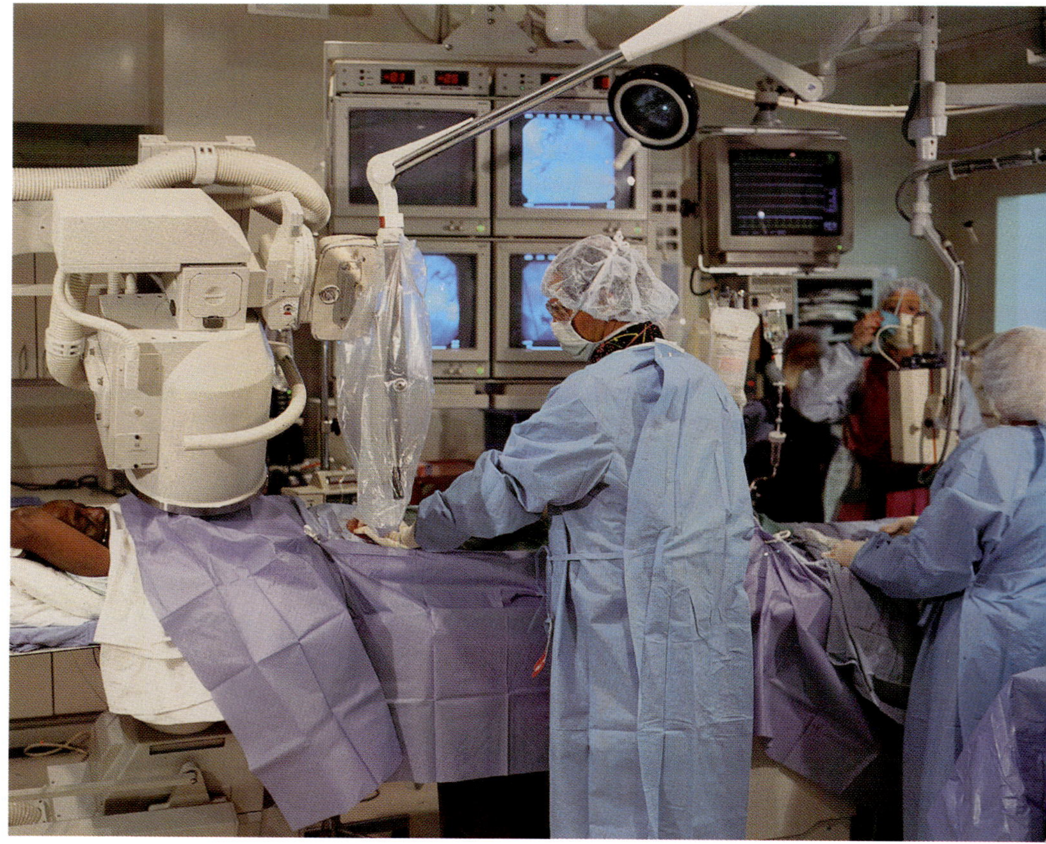

Dr. Tom Wool performs a diagnostic heart catherization. This procedure is routinely performed to visualize the patients' arteries supplying blood to the heart. Once strictly an inpatient procedure, it can now be performed on an outpatient basis.

house Southeastern Cardiac Diagnostics, with separate areas for invasive and noninvasive diagnostic testing, while the second floor includes examination rooms and a fully equipped cardiac rehabilitation facility. "Our doctors will be able to examine a patient upstairs, take a few steps downstairs to monitor a test, and return to patient exams in short order," Goree said. "The whole idea is to provide better service for our patients."

The third and fourth floors will include administrative offices and facilities for specialists, such as dieticians and psychologists, who play significant roles in the healing and rehabilitation of cardiac patients.

One Heart Center designers also included a state-of-the-art audiovisual room where patients will have access to the latest information regarding their diagnosis and available treatments. A large screen television will visually display cardiac treatments as cardiac care nurses offer patients insight into their conditions. "Education and information are essential to the patient care process," said Goree. "We want our patients to understand how to live with heart disease or how to avoid getting it. Our goal is to enhance their lives and the quality of their lives."

In all, the patient-centered facility will cover some 90,000 square feet, including an underground parking garage and a delicatessen. Centrally located and easily accessible to all Montgomery hospitals, One Heart Center will offer the citizens of central Alabama the ultimate in cardiac care.

The physicians and staff at Southeastern Cardiology Consultants, P.C. recognize that sophisticated technology and clinical skills are not enough. They take a personal interest in their patients and are concerned for their well-being. Testimony to their commitment is evidenced through their offering of the finest in clinical care, equipment, and facilities.

As Goree points out, "There is no reason for a patient to look beyond Montgomery for superior cardiac care. The dedication, the quality, and the know-how are right here." *m*

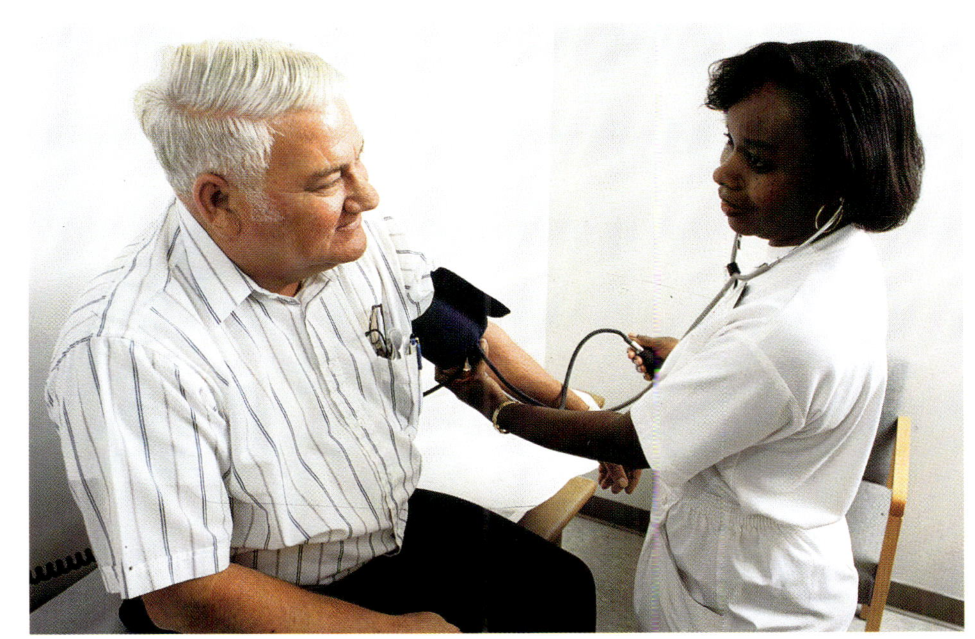

The highly trained support staff of Southeastern Cardiology provides personal, individualized attention, which they consider to be the heart of health care.

E*vidence of Southeastern Cardiology's commitment to providing its patients the finest in cardiac diagnosis and testing is its new One Heart Center to be located conveniently at the junction of Interstate 85 and Forest Avenue.*

ADVANCED MEDICAL IMAGING CENTER

dvanced Medical Imaging Center, located at the corner of Lawrence and High Streets near downtown Montgomery, is dedicated to providing high quality, state-of-the-art diagnostic imaging services in a personable, caring manner, while focusing on both patient and physician needs.

More than 300 physicians throughout Alabama refer patients to the center, which offers a variety of diagnostic services including magnetic resonance imaging (MRI), CT scans, ultrasound, nuclear medicine, mammography, routine radiography, and fluoroscopy. Three radiologists, certified by the board of the American College of Radiologists, are on hand full-time to provide experienced patient treatment and care.

The center is affiliated with U.S. Diagnostic Labs of West Palm Beach, Florida, the leader in outpatient diagnostics. This relationship ensures the ever-growing Advanced Medical Imaging Center state-of-the-art technology and professional support. Although the facility is only a few years old and its resources remain on the cutting edge of medical technology, advances and changes aimed at serving physicians and patients with greater responsiveness and accuracy are always on the drawing board. Immediate

additions include new ultrasound equipment and an upgraded CT scanner.

The center opened in 1991 with three technologists, two support staff, and an administrator. It has quickly grown to 18 full-time employees and performs more than 16,000 exams each year. Lisa Noyes, director of marketing, attributes much of the center's success to its hand-picked staff of experienced technologists and radiologists, as well as to its ability to provide the finest in equipment and diagnostic resources.

The 10,000-square-foot building, specially designed by its eight founding physicians for efficiency and performance, offers separate areas for each patient service and an individual work station for each technologist. As evidence of its progressive approach to patient care, the center was the first imaging center in the United States to feature an open MRI scanner (no tunnel), making MRI exams easier and more comfortable for all patients including the claustrophobic and large patient. MRIs are instrumental in establishing the status of orthopedic injuries to areas such as the back or knees, thus eliminating the need for exploratory surgery. The new, innovative scanner at Advanced Medical Imaging has attracted the attention of physicians from across the state who send their patients to Montgomery for MRI evaluation.

"It was a market that had not been addressed in this area," said Noyes. "In some cases, if the patient was claustrophobic, he or she had to be put sleep or heavily sedated to have the exam, but that is no longer a problem with the open scanner."

Advanced Medical Imaging prides itself on providing the highest quality film and laser images, as well as prompt and convenient service, two criteria that are important to physicians and patients alike. For the referring physician, the center guarantees the finest in professionalism at every stage of the patient's imaging process, which begins with prompt, convenient test scheduling and continues with personalized attention from highly trained staff and state-of-the-art imaging capabilities. The center has an esteemed reputation for careful, accurate interpretation of examination results, and for maintaining an open line of communication between its physician clients and its physician/technical staff.

For added convenience, the center automatically faxes the diagnostic report to the referring physician immediately after it is typed, usually within two hours of the procedure's completion. The center also hand-delivers the original report and films, if requested, in less than 24 hours.

At the Advanced Medical Imaging Center,

Advanced Medical Imaging Center, located at the corner of Lawrence and High Streets near downtown Montgomery, is dedicated to providing high quality, state-of-the-art diagnostic imaging services. Photo by Paul Robertson Photography.

patients enjoy an atmosphere of interest and courtesy in a modern, pleasant setting. They are treated cordially, as welcome guests, as well as individuals who deserve the utmost in respect and dignity during their treatment. Examples of the center's careful attention to patient concern are the individual dressing rooms and waiting rooms, designed to provide complete privacy for each patient and visitor.

The employees of Advanced Medical Imaging are concerned with providing prompt attention to the patient. In addition, the staff strives to expedite insurance billing by filing insurance forms for the patients and works closely with all insurance companies to achieve the most responsive service.

In light of the dynamics of the health care industry, especially in regard to rapidly changing technologies, Advanced Medical Imaging has made it a primary goal to stay on the leading edge of technologies and to continually work to provide patients with the finest equipment available and the utmost in support and services.

The multimodality center provides separate specialty areas for each of its fields of treatment. The center's computed tomography scanning procedures include a variety of applications ranging from revealing the normal anatomy of the brain, abdomen, or pelvis, to distinguishing tumors and abscesses and evaluating their trauma to the body.

Nuclear medicine technologists implement radioactive tracers to detect specific forms of disease and injury. Working in tandem with a high-tech computer, the ultrasound sonographic technique can be used to evaluate pregnancies, diagnose gall bladder, vascular, and other diseases. The center's laser camera makes images sharper, so they can be evaluated in closer detail.

Advanced Medical Imaging Center is also an ACR-FDA accredited mammography facility with four registered mammography technologists on duty. A radiologist is available to monitor patient studies and for consultation regarding test results and specific imaging recommendations. In an effort to be further responsive to patient needs, the center offers flexible operating hours and emergency services.

Recognized for its concern for the health of area citizens and community welfare, the center received a grant from the Montgomery City Council to provide mammograms free of charge for women without insurance. An additional grant from the Occupational Industry Center

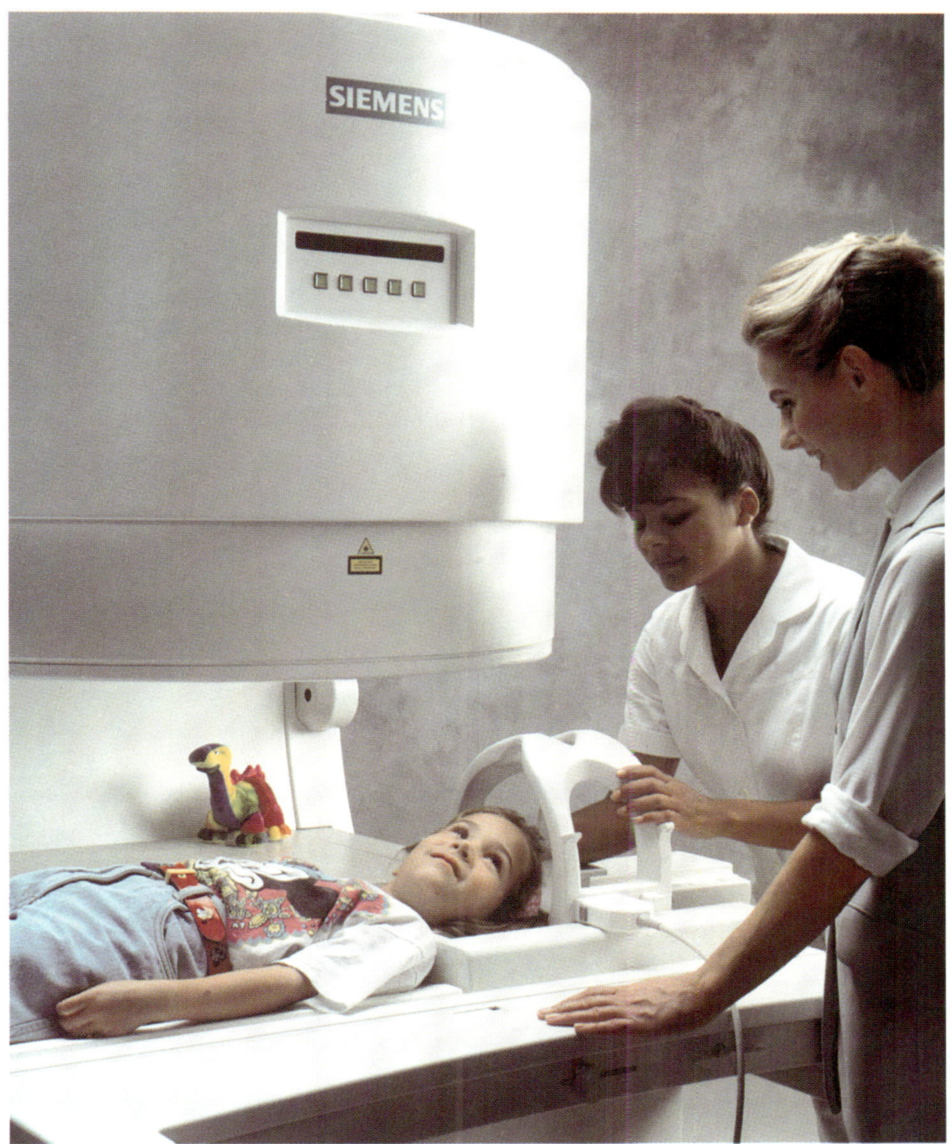

As evidence of its progressive approach to patient care, the Advanced Medical Imaging Center was the first imaging center in the United States to feature an open MRI scanner (no tunnel), making MRI exams easier and more comfortable for all patients.

enables Advanced Medical Imaging to provide the same service for women outside the Montgomery city limits.

In addition to technical resources, the center makes staff time and expertise available for community support programs. Advanced Medical Imaging is an active member of the Montgomery Area Chamber of Commerce and supports the Capital City Kiwanis Club.

With a wealth of resources and a reputation for service quality to match, Advanced Medical Imaging is able to attract some of the finest, most qualified medical personnel in the area. "Montgomery is a wonderful place to work in the medical field because the people here sincerely care for others," said Noyes. "The working atmosphere is positive and upbeat; it's a sophisticated city with a small town aura, where everyone cares and makes every effort to work together."

Working together is at the very core of the success Advanced Medical Imaging has experienced during the past half-decade. Cooperatively bringing together the valuable skills of physicians, medical staff, and experienced administrators, Montgomery's Advanced Medical Imaging Center provides the finest in diagnostic services and patient support in central Alabama.

BLUE CROSS AND BLUE SHIELD OF ALABAMA

Blue Cross and Blue Shield of Alabama's Montgomery Sales and Service Center is the central Alabama base for one of the state's leading corporations. The Montgomery Blue Cross office has been serving 21 counties across south central Alabama for more than 40 years. The local staff of over 41 includes marketing, sales, and customer service representatives, administrative personnel, and registered nurses.

An independent member of the national Blue Cross and Blue Shield Association; Blue Cross and Blue Shield of Alabama operates four district sales and service offices and nine satellite offices throughout the state.

The company provides health, prescription drug, and dental coverage to more than 2.1 million Alabamians, through group health and dental benefit plans offered to companies ranging in size from huge corporations to businesses as small as three employees. They also offer coverage to individuals and provide supplemental coverage for Medicare participants through the C Plus plan.

Blue Cross is Alabama's leader in managed care with specialized programs designed to control rising health care costs. The Preferred Care program controls costs through contracts with hospitals, physicians, pharmacies, and other health care providers. Blue Cross and Blue Shield was Alabama's first company to put together a statewide network of physicians. Today this network of Preferred Medical Doctors (PMD) is the largest network in the state and one of the largest in the nation.

Blue Cross also contracts with pharmacies through the Participating Prescription Drug Program. More than 97 percent of the state's pharmacies participate in this program.

The company's Managed Care Programs use Blue Cross registered nurses working with the doctor, patient, and family in making the best decisions for the subscriber.

The company's specially developed ACE software, an acronym for Analyze, Compare, and Explore, offers more ways to manage health care costs and services. The innovative software tracks health-related information according to factors such as demographics and geography and helps Blue Cross to pinpoint and research unusually high costs or problem areas.

Blue Cross has also put advanced computer technology to work with its new InfoSolutions, a medical information network. InfoSolutions is a database and electronic access network that allows Blue Cross, physicians, pharmacies, diagnostic facilities, labs, and other health care providers to communicate and share medical information with one another. Blue Cross is committed to improving communications among the medical community to enhance medical care and reduce unnecessary duplicate tests.

Blue Cross and Blue Shield also cares about the communities in which it works and is particularly active in the United Way and many health-related charities. The company's major commitment has been the establishment and support of the Alabama Child Caring Foundation. The Foundation provides health coverage to thousands of Alabama's children. It meets the needs of children whose parents are not eligible for Medicaid, yet do not earn enough to buy insurance. Blue Cross matches dollar-for-dollar all contributions, in addition to covering all administrative costs.

Blue Cross and Blue Shield of Alabama, and its Montgomery office, are working hard to further strengthen their reputation as "The Caring Company." The Montgomery staff, like all Blue Cross employees, are committed to responding to the needs of every customer with a sense of urgency and compassion and to doing all they can to make the capital city a quality place to live. **𝓃**

Blue Cross and Blue Shield of Alabama, and its Montgomery office, are working hard to further strengthen their reputation as "The Caring Company."

ALABAMA PROSTHETICS
& ORTHOTICS

Concerned, compassionate, and knowledgeable are the three words that best describe the people and the service at Alabama Prosthetics & Orthotics.

An innovative and progressive practice located in a modern, fully-equipped facility at the corner of Narrow Lane Road and Narrow Lane Parkway, Alabama Prosthetics & Orthotics is Montgomery's newest provider of artificial limbs and orthopedic braces, opening their doors in 1988.

The professionals at Alabama Prosthetics & Orthotics recognize the importance of the role they play in enhancing the quality of life for their patients who are in need of artificial limbs or orthopedic bracing. "We approach each patient and each situation with great care because every one of our patients is a human being with a specific lifestyle and very specific needs," said company cofounder Teri Powers-Watts. "It is our job to provide them with the finest devices available that will afford them the greatest potential for a full life."

A family-owned business established in 1988 by Teri and her husband, Preston Watts, Alabama Prosthetics & Orthotics is committed to technical quality and personal concern.

The company ensures that each custom-made product is meticulously designed for optimum comfort and support with the most advanced materials on the market. A combination of high-tech carbon and epoxy laminate creates artificial legs that may weigh as little as two pounds.

"There are many types and combinations of limbs," said Teri. "Our primary concern is to design a brace or a limb to match a patient's physical needs and lifestyle needs."

Alabama Prosthetics & Orthotics ensures technical quality by providing a combination of highly skilled service providers with the finest equipment available in the industry. Teri holds a degree in engineering mechanics and bioengineering from the University of Illinois. She and her husband have a combined 30 years' experience in the field, and both are certified prosthetists and orthotists. Their associate, Gordon Bosker, holds a degree in rehabilitation engineering and has more than 15 years of practical experience.

The offices feature a complete inventory of high-tech manufacturing equipment ranging from sewing and metal working rooms to a state-of-the-art cast-reading computer system that digitizes cast measurements, sends them to a cast-carving machine, and creates precision-measured cast designs. The only one of its kind in the area, the computer-driven machine helps ensure comfort, fit, and stress-free durability.

Because of its commitment to technological progress, Alabama Prosthetics & Orthotics is widely recognized for knowledgeable, innovative service. The company encourages professional development for each staff member and maintains a continuous research and development program to explore new possibilities in a dynamic industry.

Alabama Prosthetics & Orthotics shares information quarterly with more than 600 physicians in central Alabama through a quarterly newsletter which is designed to put the latest information in prosthetics and orthotics at their fingertips.

At Alabama Prosthetics & Orthotics, this technical skill is combined with personal concern in a supportive, family-oriented treatment environment. Said Bosker, "Every one of our patients is dealing with a difficult life circumstance. We may have the ability to help them

through it and, in many cases, to work with them for the rest of their lives. Our patients deserve the best we can give in knowledgeable, respectful, and considerate service." 🎵

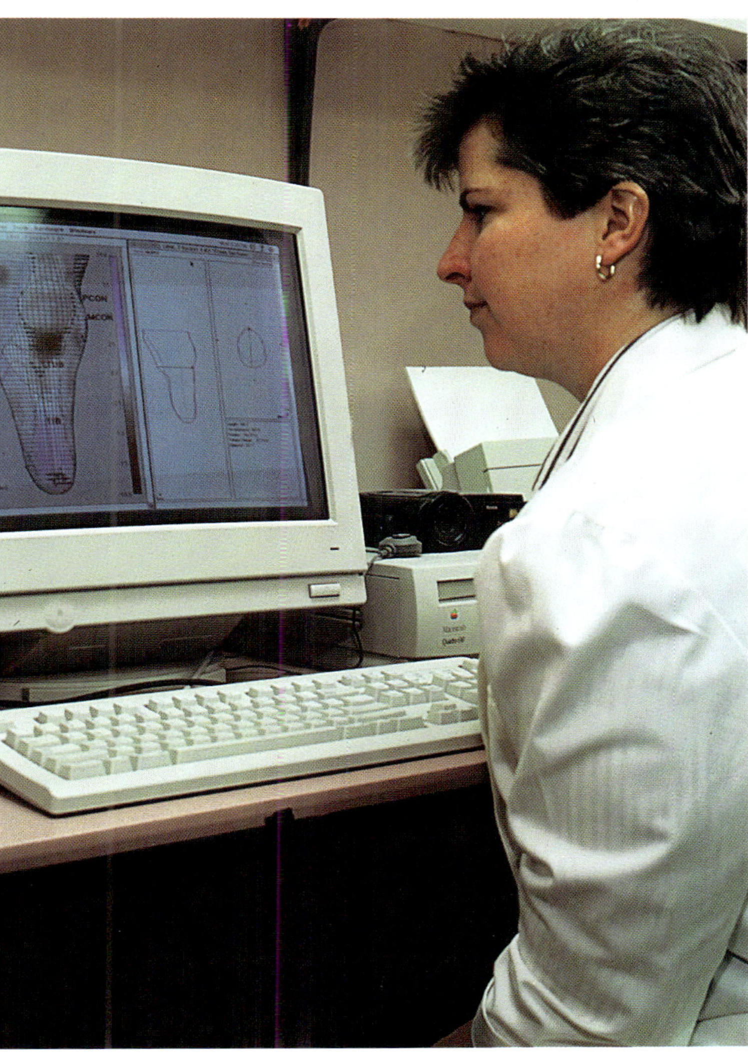

Alabama Prosthetics & Orthotics, Inc. provides the cutting edge in modern technology such as computer aided designs in prosthetics.

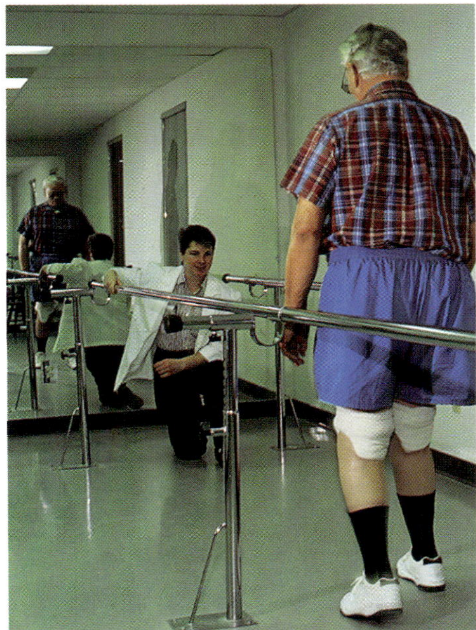

Alabama Prosthetics & Orthotics, Inc. custom-designed gait analysis lab has 20 foot parallel bars and mirrors for the most natural gait that can be achieved by the amputee.

MONTGOMERY FAMILY MEDICINE, P.C.

The doctors and staff of Montgomery Family Medicine, P.C. have made it their business to provide the finest in cutting-edge family health care while maintaining a comfortable, client-centered practice where their patients feel welcome.

Since Dr. Brian Elrod started in practice in 1990, the patient base has grown rapidly and now offers the skilled services of two additional physicians, Dr. Rick Graves and Dr. Jeff Mathis. Each is a certified diplomate of the American Board of Family Practice. Serving their patients from spacious offices conveniently located near major medical centers, the doctors, all native Montgomerians, are committed to bringing their hometown the best family medical care possible.

Fundamental to the practice, however, is the fact that their commitment to quality health care does not stop with technical precision. Their commitment goes even deeper, as they and their compassionate professional support staff make it a point to give patients a kind of personal-touch service that is difficult to find in today's medical environment.

each new patient receives a sit-down, face-to-face introduction to the practice, its services, and its policies. Courteous staff members call in advance to confirm an appointment date. Little things, like birthday cards signed personally by the doctors, set this practice apart and make it clear patient care is the top priority.

One of the largest family medicine practices in the area, Montgomery Family Medicine is trained to serve all ages and to handle more than 90 percent of all potential medical problems.

In addition to its reputation as one of Montgomery's finest family providers, the practice has built a strong corporate client base by providing pre-employment physicals, screenings, and workers' compensation examinations. The doctors stay up to date and on the progressive edge of their work by taking part in professional development programs including seminars, conferences, and journal reviews.

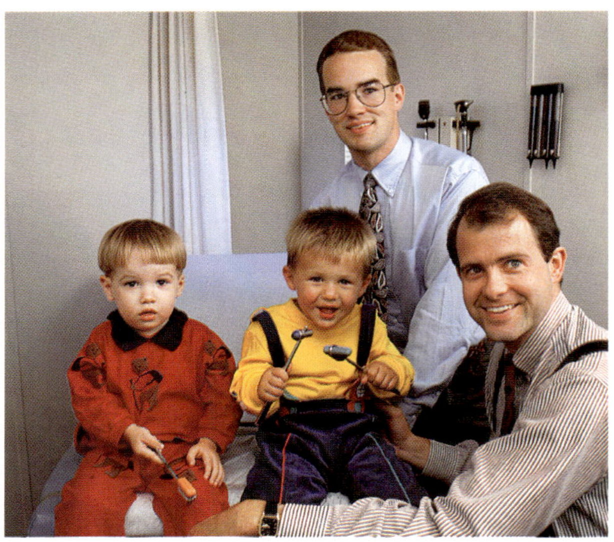

One of the largest family medicine practices in the area, Montgomery Family Medicine is trained to service all ages and to handle more than 90 percent of all potential medical problems. Pictured are (sitting) Dr. Brian Elrod and (standing) Dr. Jeff Mathis.

According to Dr. Graves, the dramatic changes on the horizon for the health care industry will contribute to the growth of family practice. "As hospital stays shorten and health care moves more toward home care, each family will need a doctor to provide that line between the hospital and the home . . . to mobilize the necessary services. As family doctors with varied skills, knowledge, and expertise, we are ready to be there for our patients."

The doctors of Montgomery Family Medicine are committed not just to their patients, but also to the community they call home.

Founded by (left to right) Dr. Brian Elrod, Montgomery Family Medicine, P.C. has grown rapidly and now offers the skilled services of two additional physicians, Dr. Rick Graves and Dr. Jeff Mathis.

"We chose family practice because we think the family is important," said Dr. Elrod. "It is a personal, community-based type of medical service that allows a doctor to care for the members of a family and follow them through their lives."

The state-of-the-art medical equipment and facilities at Montgomery Family Medicine are complemented by good, old-fashioned service. The trained staff takes time with each patient to listen and build relationships. Prior to a first visit,

"Strong and healthy family units are the foundation of stronger communities," said Dr. Mathis.

Doctors Elrod, Graves, and Mathis offer the families of Montgomery proven medical skill, a respected and established practice, and extraordinary patient sensitivity. For each of the doctors and staff at Montgomery Family Medicine, quality medical care is a personal commitment. *m*

OB/GYN ASSOCIATES
OF MONTGOMERY, P.C.

Bound by a passion for their work and a sincere desire to build lasting patient relationships, the physicians of Ob/Gyn Associates have built one of Montgomery's finest medical practices dedicated to women's health care.

The practice was established in 1991 when Greg Waller, M.D., a Huntingdon College graduate, returned to Montgomery after completing his residency training at the University of Mississippi. Although he was afforded other opportunities, including a Mayo Clinic Fellowship, Dr. Waller saw greater long-term potential in building a practice in the Capital City.

Dr. Waller opened an office in the Medical Office Building adjacent to East Montgomery Medical Center on Taylor Road just as the hospital completed a beautiful renovation and expansion of its obstetrical unit. In five short years the practice has enjoyed exponential growth, and Waller has been joined by University of Mississippi colleagues Allen Dupre, M.D., James R. Dockery Jr., M.D., and Keith Martin, M.D.

"It was important for us to establish a group that shares the same philosophy of patient care," said Waller. "With a four-doctor group, we can ensure our patients have the benefit of a sharp, rested physician at all times. When I can't be with a patient, I can be sure she is receiving the best of care. And the same holds true for each of us."

As testimony to the group's patient-first philosophy, the physicians treat patients at three local hospitals, and maintain two Montgomery offices along with a satellite office in nearby Prattville. "The first priority is patient preference and convenience. This group has the flexibility to be where the patients need us," said Dupre.

Committed to establishing patient relationships based on sensitivity and respect, the doctors are quick to acknowledge the value of their professional staff. "We have brought in staff who parallel our philosophy of treating our patients as we would our own families," said Waller.

Ob/Gyn Associates also employs the finest technologies available. The office includes state-of-the-art ultrasonographic equipment, in-house laboratory facilities, and is fully equipped for minor surgical procedures. The doctors have access to central monitoring equipment at each hospital in which they practice. The centrally located monitors allow them to closely trace the progress of each unborn baby simultaneously.

In addition to obstetrics, the physicians perform a full range of gynecological surgical procedures (including laparoscopy and laser surgery. They also have a keen interest in infertility and a strong patient following in fertility assistance.

While obstetrics and gynecology are among the most demanding specialties in medicine, the physicians discount the long hours in lieu of the associated rewards. "It's easy for me to wake up in the middle of the night and attend a delivery," said Dr. Dupre. "It's uplifting and rewarding."

Sensitive to both the physical and emotional needs of their patients, each physician exudes a relaxed, compassionate approach to his work. "We make it a point to spend time with each patient and involve them in the decision-making process," Waller said.

The professionals at Ob/Gyn Associates approach each day with an unwavering commitment to quality health care. Their efforts have been well rewarded. "While we have been successful in our practice, we have also been enriched by the people of Montgomery and their overwhelming acceptance," Dr. Waller said. "In appreciation, we intend to be here for a long time, providing the finest in women's health care."

The physicians of Ob/Gyn Associates have built one of Montgomery's finest medical practices dedicated to women's health care. Pictured are (left to right) Allen R. Dupre, M.D.; Gregory A. Waller, M.D.; and James R. Dockery Jr., M.D. Not pictured is Keith Martin, M.D.

Attention
Please DO NOT
remove anything
from the card
catalogue. What's
in there is suppos-
to be there, no
matter what it looks
like. Scrap paper
is at circulation
desk, or on top of
card catalogue.
Thank you!

EDUCATION & QUALITY OF LIFE

Montgomery has made a commitment to education and quality of life. The area's educational institutions challenge scholars and those seeking to enhance practical skills. Photo courtesy of Huntingdon College.

AUBURN UNIVERSITY AT MONTGOMERY

*I*n the three decades since its founding in 1967, Auburn University at Montgomery has established a respected reputation for educational excellence and community service. As the urban campus of a century-old land grant institution, AUM blends the traditional view of the university as a community of scholars with the contemporary view of the university as an integral part of its surrounding community.

Following the institution's mission to foster and exemplify excellence in teaching and learning through the avenues of instruction, research, and service, the university's forward-thinking faculty and staff have created an educational environment that encourages open inquiry and communication. AUM is dedicated to providing its students with an education that will be of enduring value.

Under the leadership of Chancellor Roy H. Saigo, Auburn University at Montgomery not only presents the finest traditions of the liberal arts, business, the sciences, nursing, and education, but also provides support for the functions of government, regional economic growth, and cultural enrichment through the arts.

AUM's easily accessible 500-acre campus is located approximately seven miles east of downtown Montgomery between Interstate 85 and Highway 80. The contemporary campus features five classroom buildings, a ten-story library tower, a student center, a physical education teaching complex, two student housing areas, and various support facilities.

With a distinctively diverse student body that represents six of the world's seven continents, AUM's enrollment consistently stays around 6,000. Minority students comprise approximately 29 percent of the student population. The university's role as a vital provider of adult education is evidenced by the fact that 85 percent of its students work full- or part-time, and 42 percent are over the age of 25.

AUM is committed to meeting the needs of a rapidly changing world by continually focusing on the quality of its instruction and research, as well as by expanding its outreach services to a growing surrounding community.

Dedicated efforts focused on staying abreast of academic and technological advances, and incorporating new technologies into university operations and instructional programs are central to the university's maintenance of excellence in education. With increasingly sophisticated uses of technology in the classroom and each academic major requiring a computer component, AUM students graduate prepared to compete in today's high-tech, global marketplace.

In addition, AUM provides its students with the experience needed to develop job skills required in the professional world. Academic internships, ranging from writing and editing to assisting senior administrators in state government, give students the practical on-the-job experience they will need upon entering the workforce.

The university has also become a significant contributor of useful research data addressing societal, economic, and environmental concerns locally and regionally. Students benefit from opportunities to conduct research as well as to present papers at professional meetings and to publish their research findings.

A *UM's Library Tower houses the library as well as several administrative offices and centers.*

ACADEMICS

Fully accredited by the Southern Association of Colleges and Schools, Auburn University at Montgomery offers a strong academic program that has earned a solid reputation for its attention to meeting student needs, maintaining small class environments, engaging distinguished instructors, and providing a well-rounded educational experience.

Seventy-five percent of AUM's full-time faculty hold the doctorate or terminal degree in their fields of expertise. And the university is distinctive in that nearly 70 percent of the courses are taught by full-time professors.

Flexible class schedules in more than 90 areas

A *nursing class meets outdoors with Moore Hall and the Library Tower as a backdrop.*

State-of-the-art technology benefits AUM's graphic design students.

of study make AUM an attractive choice for students who are working toward their chosen career goals. Whether they need daytime or evening classes or even weekend college, AUM has the right schedule for the working or non-working student. Considerate scheduling, combined with reasonable tuition rates, scholarships, and financial aid programs, makes a quality education affordable and possible.

AUM's School of Business ranks among the top 20 percent of business schools in the nation, with both its undergraduate and graduate programs accredited by the American Assembly of Collegiate Schools of Business. AUM is one of only five universities in Alabama to hold such a distinction.

The School of Education's nationally accredited programs prepare students for careers in teaching, counseling, and administration. A teacher-in-residence program, in-depth field experiences, and partnerships with local schools give students a broader perspective and the benefit of practical knowledge.

The School of Liberal Arts offers seven undergraduate degrees and an interdisciplinary Master of Liberal Arts degree, the only one of its kind in Alabama. The popular and critically acclaimed Theatre AUM stages five major productions each year and offers students experience in all aspects of theater.

AUM's nationally and state accredited nursing program provides comprehensive education in the techniques, theories, and management of nursing. Since February 1989, more than 85 percent of all AUM nursing graduates have passed the national nursing licensure examination.

Ten degree programs are available within the School of Sciences. The university's medical technology program is one of only three university-based programs in the state with accreditation from the American Medical Association. The legal assistant program is the only American Bar Association accredited program offered by a public university in Alabama. And the university's public administration program is one of only three in the state accredited by the National Association of Schools of Public Affairs and Administration. AUM also offers strong pre-professional programs and enjoys a high acceptance rate for its applicants looking to continue their educations in professional schools.

THE CENTER FOR GOVERNMENT AND PUBLIC AFFAIRS

AUM's Center for Government and Public Affairs contracts for consulting services and training designed for governmental employees involved in public management, governmental accounting, and information systems. Under the direction of Dr. Keivan Deravi, the center trains thousands of government workers each year and serves as a bridge between the university and federal, state, and local governmental agencies. The center is committed to using its considerable resources to enhance the quality of life in communities throughout Alabama and beyond.

Having gained national acclaim for the development of an innovative econometric model used in economic analysis and forecasting, the center has become a popular choice for economic insight at the state and regional levels.

The center's Alabama Certified Public Manager program provides a systematic approach to developing and training managers in state and local government. The program operates under the guidance of the State Advisory Board to the Alabama Certified Public Manager Program, as well as in accordance with the standards set forth by the National Consortium of Certified Public Managers.

The Governmental Accountant and Auditor Training Program is designed to provide continuing professional education for individuals responsible for maintaining the integrity of accounting, auditing, and finance functions in state and local government. The program also provides continuing professional development for governmental officials, agency directors, and

The university boasts an average pass rate of above 98 percent on the medical technology licensing examination. In February 1995, the pass rate was 100 percent.

department heads responsible for making financial decisions.

All Alabama state employees have access to Computer Competency Training designed to help users develop the skills necessary to effectively use, administer, and manage the newest information systems technology.

In addition to training courses and programming, the center is also committed to using its services to improve the economic quality of life for surrounding counties in need of economic development assistance.

CONTINUING EDUCATION

With educational and creative programs designed for personal and professional development, youths and senior citizens, AUM's Division of Continuing Education is yet another way the university impacts surrounding communities. The division's commitment to lifelong learning can be seen in its wide variety of programs ranging from youth camps to high technology training.

Programs take the form of noncredit courses, seminars, teleconferences, certificate programs, business contracts, conferences, and special functions. Courses and programs often reflect contemporary thought and development, both personal and professional.

The AUM School of Business is the home of Southern Business & Economic Journal, *now in its 18th year of publication. The school also provides polling and marketing research to firms throughout the United States.*

AUM provides computer training and state-of-the-art software to help professionals prepare for a future in cyberspace.

"We see ourselves as the hub of the wheel whose spokes reach out to all parts of the university and the community," said Dr. Alan Hackel, dean of continuing education.

The division sponsors a variety of innovative programs, and partners quarterly with the Montgomery Area Chamber of Commerce to present the Business Breakfast, a well-attended event which features speakers of national and international note able to address topics of interest to business, civic, and academic leaders.

The Division of Continuing Education assisted nearly 300 companies with their training needs in 1994 alone, and the university's Camp AUM received the 1994 Program of Excellence Award from the National University Continuing Education Association, Region III.

The award-winning camp program offers four weeks of creative summer camp activities for children ages 8 to 12. In addition, AUM's Youth College brings more than 100 educational and recreational programs to children and teenagers.

The need for lifelong learning is more apparent now than ever before, and AUM lies at the cutting edge of it all, ready to provide a full array of training services to help area residents, businesses, and organizations meet their personal and professional goals.

THE CENTER FOR BUSINESS AND ECONOMIC DEVELOPMENT

AUM's Center for Business and Economic Development has gained the respect of business leaders statewide for its resourceful ability to project its knowledge base into real world issues facing Alabama businesses, industries, and government. Under the direction of Dr. John Veres, the center works with university faculty to provide research expertise and consulting services in accounting, information systems, economics and econometrics, marketing, management and business administration, public administration, statistics, and quantitative methods.

At any given time, the center will be responsible for widely diverse projects, from reviewing employment procedures for local law enforcement agencies to helping a corporate giant such as the Boeing Company select competent supervisors.

The center has earned a reputation as an important Capital City resource, and many Alabama state government agencies frequently turn to Dr. Veres' operation for management and administrative support.

The center commonly joins with AUM's Center for Government and Public Affairs to foster support for surrounding communities by helping them find and obtain economic development funding sources. The two entities recently presented the well-received Economic Development Initiative Conference, where county representatives learned how to ferret out grant opportunities and write strong grant applications. The two units also collaborate on the Alabama Consumer Confidence Index, a useful economic tool which gauges consumer sentiment statewide.

Relationships developed through the Center

for Business and Economic Development are beneficial both to the communities served and to the university, providing businesses with resources for greater efficiency and educators with an ongoing study of changing community needs.

COMMUNITY INVOLVEMENT

AUM is the eighth largest employer in the Montgomery area. With more than 1,200 employees, the university's total economic impact on the city was nearly $78 million in 1993. In academic year 1994-1995, the university drew 42 percent of its students from outside Montgomery County, resulting in an economic impact of almost $15.5 million.

In addition to the value of its direct economic impact, the university plays a vital role in spawning advanced technological development essential to Montgomery's future.

Joining with the Montgomery Area Chamber of Commerce, land owners, investment bankers, and others to bring a high-tech research park to the Capital City, AUM was a leading proponent behind the development of the Alabama TechnaCenter, which opened its gates in 1991. The first facility to be built in the 200-acre park, the Institute for Advanced Information Systems, serves as a teaching site for many of AUM's open enrollment and contractual computer courses.

Also housed in the Institute is the university's Advanced Technology Group, which brings together the expertise of the Center for Business and Economic Development, the Division of Continuing Education, and the Center for Government and Public Affairs. ATG offers computer training, consulting, design, and support services geared to public and private sector technology needs.

In a spirit of educational cooperation and service, AUM participates in cross-enrollment agreements with other area institutions, including Alabama State University, Huntingdon College, and Faulkner University, and is exploring other cooperative efforts to expand educational offerings and reduce duplication of programs.

Recognizing the significance of Montgomery's military community, the university has maintained a long-standing program of graduate study in political science and public administration with Air University on Maxwell Air Force Base, and is continually looking for ways to expand its educational services to Air Force personnel and their families.

On the strength of its steadfast commitment to educational excellence and community service, Auburn University at Montgomery has become a more vital force in achievement, constantly propelling its students and its community forward to the realization of their greatest potential. ∎

A*UM offers Montgomery area children and teens more than 100 educational and recreational programs.*

A *commencement processional crosses the campus of AUM, which is accredited by the Commission on Colleges of the Southern Association of Colleges and Schools to award the bachelor's, master's, specialist, and doctoral degrees.*

ALABAMA STATE UNIVERSITY

ounded in Marion, Alabama, in 1867, Alabama State University was America's first state-supported academic institution founded for the education of blacks. After nearly 130 years of glorious history, the university today serves a diverse student population by embracing the best of the past and pursuing a progressive, visionary future.

At his inauguration on April 28, 1995, Dr. William Hamilton Harris, an author, a Fulbright Scholar, and the university's 10th president, lauded the school's historic significance and looked with vigor upon the work yet to be accomplished. "Those of us who have responsibility for the present and future development of Alabama State University must, and rightly do, recognize and appreciate the institution's past and those who labored to keep it alive. Their work reminds us of how successive generations build upon the efforts of their predecessors and of how interdependent we are."

Today, Alabama State University serves about 5,500 students from 39 states and 21 foreign countries. While the university's past is rich with

ASU provides exceptional academic programs ranging from biomedical research to theater, and from music media technology to accounting.

valiant struggle and overwhelming accomplishment, Dr. Harris sees its greatest opportunity in its future. "The transformed ASU will serve Alabama, especially greater Montgomery, as a comprehensive regional university of impeccable quality that is a model for others to follow as the nation meets its needs for educational excellence and cultural diversity."

A full-time faculty of nearly 250, more than half of whom possess doctorate degrees, prepares students in 40 programs of study leading to the associate's, master's, and education specialist's degrees. Plans are under way to offer doctoral programs in the near future. ASU boasts approximately one faculty member to every 20 students, creating a personal environment where teachers share their concern and extra time on an individual basis.

Alabama State University offers seven academic units, including the colleges of arts and sciences, business administration, and education, along with the division of aerospace studies, school of music, university college, and school of graduate studies. With all areas accredited by the Southern Association of Colleges and Schools and the Alabama Department of Education, ASU provides exceptional academic programs ranging from biomedical research to theater, and from music media technology to accounting.

During the past 10 years, ASU's biomedical research department has received $13 million in federal research grants, offering talented students far-reaching opportunity and an extra edge in gaining graduate-school admission.

Numerous academic programs are administered by instructors of national renown, including Dr. Tommie Stewart, director of the Theater Arts Program. Dr. Stewart, known to many by her stage name, Tonea Stewart, is a star of film and television and a recent inductee into the Black College Alumni Hall of Fame.

While quality academics is the highest priority, ASU ensures its students receive a well-rounded education in an environment that fosters academic, social, physical, and emotional development. More than 70 different organizations, including professional clubs, athletic teams, sororities, and fraternities, are available for the choosing.

Intercollegiate athletic programs include men's football and baseball, women's volleyball, and men's and women's basketball, tennis, and track and field. The university's commitment to athletic and academic development is evidenced in the construction of the $20-million Joe L. Reed Acadome, a state-of-the-art basketball arena with 7,400 seats and superb facilities for everything from classes to commencements, and concerts to athletic competitions. The beautiful new Olean Black Underwood Tennis Center, a lighted complex of 12 tennis courts, offers home-court advantage for ASU's women's and men's tennis teams, who took first and second place respectively in the 1995 Southwestern Athletic Conference championships.

All of this bustling activity takes place on a sprawling 105-acre landscaped campus featuring a welcoming combination of historic, traditional, and contemporary buildings. A tree-filled and

While quality academics is the highest priority, ASU ensures its students receive a well-rounded education in an environment that fosters academic, social, physical, and emotional development.

flowering urban campus, ASU is just a short walk from Alabama's Capitol and government complex. It conveniently adjoins Interstate 85 and is only about two miles from the interchange of Interstates 85 and 65.

Historic landmarks, such as the Bell Memorial, which was transferred from the school's original Marion location and is sounded on special occasions, and the stately Bibb Graves Tower, an inspiring and prominent structure completed in 1928 and incorporated into the university's logo, adorn the campus with charm and character. Modern structures, including the 11-story C. Johnson Dunn Tower, which houses 1,800 students, and the Levi Watkins Learning Center, filled with more than 200,000 volumes, periodicals, microfilm, and audiovisuals, represent the university's commitment to the students of tomorrow.

Alabama State University is determined to make these fine educational provisions and more available to all who desire them. Most ASU students, who competitively demonstrate financial need and academic merit, receive financial assistance in the form of loans, scholarships, grants, and part-time university employment. But in addition to the students on campus, ASU seeks to serve the community outside its gates. A recently revitalized Continuing Education Department is intended to serve community needs and, in Dr. Harris's words, to help build a "new relationship in which the fortunes of Montgomery—and indeed those of our state—

The Levi Watkins Learning Center is filled with more than 200,000 volumes, periodicals, microfilm, and audiovisuals, representing the university's commitment to the students of tomorrow.

and the fortunes of Alabama State University are intricately and inextricably intertwined."

At Alabama State University, a profound heritage is the constant reminder of what can be accomplished in education. With that as its foundation, ASU is positioned to face the challenges of today and tomorrow. For its part as an impetus to a better Alabama, Alabama State University has set its sights on increasing cultural diversity, preparing its students in international understanding for global competition, boarding the information superhighway, and pursuing all

possible venues for information sharing and transfer, embracing all opportunities for technological development, and reaffirming its commitment to making education available to all who seek it. 🔲

Alabama State University serves a diverse student population by embracing the best of the past and pursuing a progressive, visionary future.

THE MONTGOMERY ACADEMY

The Montgomery Academy is dedicated to uncompromising academic excellence. For more than 35 years, The Academy has operated like a well-oiled machine, its component parts working in precision synchronization to train young minds.

The Montgomery Academy's mission is "to provide a challenging academic atmosphere in a unique environment where each person's contributions are recognized and respected." Photo by Lyn Bonham.

Motivated students, dedicated instructors, a challenging college preparatory curriculum, innovative teaching techniques, involved parents, first-class facilities, successful athletic programs, and fine arts offerings have driven an academic machine that produces well-rounded young men and women prepared to succeed in the world.

Headmaster A. Emerson Johnson III joined The Academy in 1991. He oversees the activities of two campuses, 860 students, and a professional staff of 85, of whom 62 percent hold graduate degrees.

Founded by a group of local business and civic leaders, The Academy opened its doors to 108 students in 1959. The school's original mission— "to provide a challenging academic atmosphere in a unique environment where each person's contributions are recognized and respected"— remains its driving philosophy.

Since its first graduating class in 1963, the school has sent forth more than 1,000 students, many of whom have sent their children to The Academy and support the school generously with their time and money.

From 1962 until 1988, The Academy accommodated all grades from its Vaughn Road campus. But expansive growth and a desire to provide an unparalleled learning environment led The Academy to construct the $3.1-million Lower School Campus on Perry Hill Road.

The new facility opened in 1988 and serves grades kindergarten through four. An expansive, recessed library is at the center of the structure, emphasizing the school's commitment to academic exploration. Color-coded doors and hallways direct children to their classrooms, which are purposely separated from the specialty classroom wing where science, computer and language labs, and art and music rooms are located.

Prior to the 1995-1996 school year, The Academy expanded and renovated its Middle School, which serves the fifth through eighth grades, and completed the phenomenal $1.3-million Garzon Library, serving both the Middle and Upper Schools.

In addition to general classrooms, the Upper School includes two large computer laboratories, a state-of-the-art language laboratory, a stately music room, private music lesson classrooms, and two courtyards.

"We have worked hard to create an environment where our students will want to learn," said Lynn Beshear, Director of Admissions. "These facilities come to us solely through the generosity of our donors. No tuition money ever goes to bricks and mortar. There is too much other work to be done with those funds."

This excellent learning environment, combined with a 12-to-1 student/teacher ratio, has produced 151 National Merit Semifinalists and Finalists, and 78 National Merit Commended Students since 1962. Each year, 100 percent of the graduating seniors enroll in college. But students aren't the only ones who excel. Two Academy teachers are Fulbright Scholars, two are Klingenstein Scholars, and another is an IDEA Fellow.

In addition to its challenging academic programs, The Academy fields 23 men's and women's athletic teams for students in grades 7 through 12. New tennis courts and a new gymnasium will further enhance the thriving athletic program.

According to Jeff Boggan, Director of Development, "What our students accomplish prior to graduation is truly exceptional. We are graduating young adults who are prepared to excel in the world before them." *M*

The phenomenal $1.3-million Garzon Library, serves both Middle and Upper School students. Photo by Lyn Bonham.

TROY STATE
UNIVERSITY MONTGOMERY

*I*n a word, TSUM spells "opportunity." Troy State University Montgomery is Alabama's only comprehensive university dedicated to meeting the special needs of adult working students. TSUM serves more than 3,400 students by offering associate, undergraduate, and graduate degrees.

A member of the Troy State University System, TSUM traces its origin to Troy State University in Troy, Alabama. Beginning as a resident center at Maxwell Air Force Base in 1965 and designated a branch campus of TSU in 1966, the university earned accreditation by the Southern Association of Colleges and Schools in 1983.

Under the direction of President Glenda McGaha-Curry, the university has gained national attention as a model for developing the metropolitan community university of the twenty-first century. Innovative programs including flexible class scheduling and expert instructional service to area businesses are only a sampling of the programs that set TSUM apart.

Approximately 80 percent of all TSUM students are employed at more than 900 businesses in the Montgomery area. "Consider the impact of working students who can take what they've learned at night and put it to work on the job the next day," said Dr. Cam Martindale, vice president for institutional advancement. "It's good for the student, and it's good for the business."

Because the typical TSUM student is employed, has a family, and is in school to prepare for career advancement, the university schedules classes at night, on weekends, and through progressive distance learning programs.

The only institution in Montgomery to offer credit courses by television, TSUM has a nationally respected television curriculum. TSUM also offers more than 65 college level contract courses that allow for home study at an individual pace.

TSUM extends its resources beyond typical academic degree programs to meet the educational requirements of area business and industry. The university shares its faculty expertise and provides on-site training in areas ranging from computer information services to human resources management.

Troy State University Montgomery recognizes the military's importance to its community by offering classes at Maxwell and Gunter Air Force

TSUM has over 3,400 students in over 900 different businesses and places of employment. Dr. Martindale (standing) reports that what the students learn at TSUM, they take to work with them.

Bases. As testimony to the university's responsive service to this vital population, 15 percent of all Air Force generals are graduates of the Troy State system, and of those, 60 percent obtained their degrees from TSUM.

Although flexibility and educational opportunity are at the forefront, TSUM's primary commitment is to excellence in teaching. The university employs highly qualified faculty who combine their educational and professional experience to help students integrate theoretical concepts and practical applications.

Central to the university's mission is its role as a contributor to economic development in the area. For nearly 20 years, TSUM has been integral to the revitalization of downtown Montgomery. Campus renovations, including upgrades at historic Whitley Hall and the Davis Theatre for the Performing Arts add beauty and stature to the area.

This kind of growth, coupled with TSUM's economic impact of nearly $24 million annually, validates the university's position as one of the most vital entities in Montgomery.

Since 1985, TSUM student enrollment has risen by nearly 75 percent, and the university is poised for even greater accomplishments to come. Dr. McGaha-Curry said, "This university will continue to reach out and build new alliances of business, government, and educational agencies who share our vision and our desire to elevate Montgomery to a new level of prominence." TSUM is the Evening University of Montgomery. *77*

New students often comment on how they are treated with respect and consideration as working adults through the admissions and registration process and in the classroom.

TRINITY PRESBYTERIAN SCHOOL

quarter of a century ago, a group of community leaders and concerned parents came together with a vision to build a school that would bind academic excellence with a Christian perspective. They dreamed of creating an academic environment that would equip young people to reach their God-given potential mentally, physically, and spiritually, realizing this is a cooperative effort with support from both home and church.

That dream has become reality in Trinity Presbyterian School. Today one of Montgomery's foremost educational institutions, Trinity is recognized for demanding academics, superior educators, outstanding athletics, and a nurturing, family environment.

Headmaster Brian Willett, who joined Trinity in 1976, took on the challenge of building a young and growing school because he saw "an opportunity to be part of an educational program that espoused sincere concern for every student, both personally and educationally."

Trinity School opened in a local church in 1970 with 200 students and 15 instructors. Today the multimillion-dollar campus services 965 students, covers 32 acres, and includes 140,000 square feet under one roof. A recent $3.5-million expansion added a state-of-the-art kindergarten complex, a breathtaking elementary science laboratory, 22 new classrooms, lower school administrative offices, a 700-seat gymnasium, six-court tennis complex, and baseball, softball and soccer fields. Those amenities were added to existing facilities that included two libraries with extensive computer capabilities, a second gymnasium, four fully-equipped science labs, band and choral facilities, a multipurpose assembly room, and football stadium.

Because of its family-centered focus, Trinity has grown on a single site to keep siblings, family, friends, and faculty in close proximity to one another. The result is a rare esprit de corps that runs throughout the Trinity family.

Extraordinary parental involvement is evident in the family-like atmosphere. From banquet coordinators to band boosters, generous Trinity parents help keep the engines humming. Involved parents also help Trinity students respond to the school's challenging academic program. Students graduate with a minimum of a college prep diploma, but 10 advanced placement courses enhance the curriculum. Trinity has graduated 25 National Merit finalists and semifinalists. Thirty eight percent of Trinity graduates in the past five years have earned college scholarships based on merit. These successes are accomplished at the hands of a skilled staff of 80 dedicated

Trinity's award-winning science program involves kindergarten through twelfth graders in the scientific process by using the latest emerging technologies to prepare them for future leadership roles.

instructors, 65 percent of whom have master's degrees or higher.

Elementary administrator Dr. Darlene Mullen suggests preparation for such performance begins early for Trinity children. "We offer students an accelerated academic program, which, when coupled with our enrichment activities, gives them an opportunity to discover their diverse gifts and to develop those gifts in an environment designed to nurture the total child."

The school also encourages athletic participation as an opportunity to build self-esteem, healthy bodies, and appreciation for teamwork. Trinity fields 18 boys' and girls' teams that work out, practice, and play on some of the area's finest fields and indoor facilities. The Trinity coaches promote a strong work ethic which results in frequent Division 2-A championship appearances.

Academic and athletic programs are supplemented with Christian studies. "We endeavor to create an environment in which young people can discover that one's faith and perspective influence how one ultimately chooses a life direction," said Willett.

This balanced approach fulfills the dream of those who founded Trinity Presbyterian School. **Ⅲ**

The music and drama departments of Trinity Presbyterian School continue to provide creative musical and dramatic productions for the community's enjoyment.

THE MONTGOMERY YMCA

*E*xtraordinary community support for the Montgomery YMCA is the single best testament to its tremendous strength, influence, and impact.

For 128 years, the YMCA has been a stable influence on the lives of Montgomery's youth. Many of today's community leaders were part of the YMCA family as children, and, in appreciation, still steadfastly support the institution with donations of their time and resources.

Founded in 1868, the organization's growth has come at the hands of long-time staff and dedicated lay leaders committed to its purposes. The YMCA's historic timeline is replete with contributors, supporters, and milestones far too many to name. But clearly, one of the most significant events in the YMCA's history was the hiring of William C. Chandler in 1948, still at the helm today. Under his direction, the organization has grown to a membership of more than 40,000 and annual individual participation of more than 70,000.

With a budget of nearly $9 million, the Montgomery Y is a member of the YMCA's Metro 25, the largest 25 YMCAs in the Southeast by budget. These funds come from contributions, fees, grants, and membership dues. Scholarships are an integral part of the YMCA's commitment to ensuring opportunities for all who wish to participate.

The Montgomery YMCA is fortunate to have strong financial support. But it is impossible to put a price tag on what it buys. The Y operates seven full-service branches located in every corner of the city, along with four branches in Wetumpka, Tuskegee, Greenville, and Pike County. The YMCA also operates special branches at Camp Chandler and Camp Grandview, along with branches dedicated to swimming, soccer, teen leadership programs, and "Good Times," before-and-after-school child care.

The YMCA sports program includes a vast array of activities, including football, cheerleading, soccer, miniscoccer, karate, tennis, swimming, basketball, wrestling, T-ball, track and field, gymnastics, and volleyball. In addition, the Montgomery YMCA was the first in the state to construct an indoor soccer arena for this exciting new sport.

But the Montgomery YMCA's most far-reaching recognition comes in response to its innovative youth leadership programs, including Youth In Government, the International Youth Camp, and direction of national conferences on Christian values and national affairs. The Montgomery YMCA has provided the leadership for the Alabama Youth Legislature and the Alabama Youth Judicial Programs for nearly 50 years and has contracted with the Montgomery Lion's Club to run its international youth camp.

The Y accomplishes these programs with the help of a dedicated and energetic staff. Composed of more than 500 employees, approximately 100 of whom serve full time, the YMCA staff is made up of committed individuals. More than 500 individuals voluntarily serve on YMCA boards and committees, and still more willingly give of their time to coach, tutor, and mentor at-risk youth.

"There is an extra sense of community behind this organization," said Dale Osterman, executive director of the Y's downtown branch. "The continuity of the leadership here, along with the Y's established place in this community, has strengthened its effect."

The Montgomery YMCA is a microcosm of its community. Its reach stretches through every neighborhood and across every walk of life. Each YMCA program is dedicated to building character. To validate its success, one need look no farther than YMCA's own committee meetings and sidelines. *⚏*

*E*ach YMCA program is dedicated to building the character of area youth.

*T*he YMCA is composed of more than 500 employees and more than 500 committed volunteers who willingly give of their time to coach, tutor, and mentor the children of the Montgomery area. Photo by Paul Robertson.

GREEN GATE SCHOOL

Twenty years ago, as a college student and part-time teacher's aide, Yvonna Richardson knew her life would somehow always include Green Gate School. Today she and her husband own Green Gate Schools of Alabama and operate its two Montgomery campuses. A skillful educator and manager, Mrs. Richardson administers daily operations, while her husband, retired Air Force Colonel Kenneth Richardson, plays a dual role as Headmaster and sixth grade instructor.

For Mrs. Richardson, Green Gate School is truly an affair of the heart. Not only has she watched the operation grow and prosper, but she has also cultivated a nurturing environment that has an identity all its own. Small classes, close-knit relationships among teachers, students, and parents, and genuine concern are the cornerstone of Green Gate's success.

Green Gate's original campus was built on McGehee Road in 1971 and served children in prekindergarten through third grade until 1994, when it expanded to offer classes through the sixth grade. Brilliant colors, classroom computers, and stimulating artwork fill the schoolhouse, offering signs of energy and creativity.

In 1995 Green Gate School was awarded a contract to operate the state-of-the-art Helen Hunt Early Learning Center owned and developed by the Retirement Systems of Alabama. Located in downtown Montgomery, the center combines a convenient location with the finest facilities available. Designed for children at every turn, the progressive building offers countless amenities, including two indoor playgrounds with soft, spongy floors, a HVAC unit that purifies the air to hold down illnesses, and even alluring little bathrooms located inside make-believe castles.

Between its two campuses, Green Gate School serves approximately 300 children. Green Gate purposefully maintains small classes to ensure one-on-one attention. Experienced, caring, and skillful teachers implement innovative instruction techniques, including cross-teaching, which allows high achievers to move ahead as appropriate. "We are small enough to meet each child's individual needs, whether challenging them to move ahead or slowing down to be certain they fully understand," said Richardson.

And, while academic excellence is Green Gate's top priority, the school sponsors on-campus after-school activities including a Cub Scout pack, a Girl Scout troop, dance, music, gymnastics, art, and manners lessons. "Our parents can go off to work without worrying that their child is missing those important extra opportunities," said Richardson.

Recognizing the challenges working parents faced in finding secure and stimulating child care, Green Gate was the first private school in Montgomery to offer extended-day child care and after-school pick-up. Green Gate's Summer Fun program serves working parents as well, offering their children full-time summer fun in a joyful and academically enriching atmosphere.

Green Gate's success can be measured by the number of children who, after leaving the school, place easily into other fine private and public schools in the Montgomery area. Green Gate's reputation for academic excellence has also made it the choice of many military and international families stationed in the Montgomery area.

For Richardson, lifelong friendships and a sense of accomplishment are her greatest rewards. "After 20 years, I have parents come in who were actually students of mine . . . now they're bringing their own children to us."

For Green Gate School, there could be no greater compliment than a parent's trust, for it is testimony to a job well done and to the school's continuing tradition of excellence.

Green Gate School has cultivated a nurturing environment designed to meet the needs of each individual child.

Small classes, close-knit relationships among teachers, students, and parents, and genuine concern are the cornerstone of Green Gate's success.

JOHN M. PATTERSON STATE TECHNICAL COLLEGE

For more than 30 years, John M. Patterson State Technical College has been a valued educational resource and a significant contributor to the economic development of central Alabama.

The institution was founded to provide quality educational opportunities and services responsive to individual, business, and community needs. This commitment to its three-pronged purpose has resulted in a strong curriculum, superior instructors, and quality, flexible programming.

The school was established in 1961 and constructed on a 46-acre parcel of donated land at the junction of Montgomery's Southern Bypass and Highway 231. The $1-million facility opened its doors to 162 students.

In 1974 the State Board of Education named John Patterson a technical college and authorized the school's associate degree in applied technology, setting the stage for what has become one of Alabama's premiere occupational institutions.

Today J. P. Tech serves more than 1,000 students per quarter, offering a diverse curriculum ranging from industrial maintenance to cosmetology. The college has 21 departments offering over 25 program areas, all accredited by the Alabama State Board of Education and the Council on Occupational Education.

Because more than two-thirds of its students work full- or part-time, J. P. Tech accommodates the demands of their strenuous schedules by offering classes at all hours of the day, evenings, and weekends.

businesses. We are driven by their needs," said Industrial Coordinator Jack Edwards.

J. P. Tech's ability to service its customers is further enhanced by skilled instructors, each one a respected professional skilled in his or her area of instruction. Their hands-on experience enlivens the teaching process and brings to bear practical, on-the-job insight. The college strategically supplements its staff expertise with Occupational Advisory Committees which evaluate training programs and bring insight into industry trends and technological advances.

When new industry moves into the area, instructors work on site, receiving intensive hands-on experience they share with students. "It's a win-win situation," said Edwards. "The industry wins because they get skilled workers; we win because we gain valuable knowledge we are able to impart to our students; and the community wins because our people are more employable."

In that same spirit of partnership, J. P. Tech supports the work of the Alabama Industrial Development and Training program. While AIDT provides upfront training and development, J. P. Tech maintains the necessary on-going operational training to make sure a strong workforce is consistently available.

But J. P. Tech is not concerned only with meeting today's occupational needs. The college's innovative Tech Prep program brings occupational training to high schools to make an early impact on the students who will not attend a traditional college. "We identify these students, introduce them to the opportunities these programs offer, and help them plan so they can get a head start on their careers," said Edwards.

It is through programs like these, and a willingness to go the extra mile for education, that John M. Patterson State Technical College is bringing to central Alabama the training resources its people need to succeed in a dynamic and growing economy. **m**

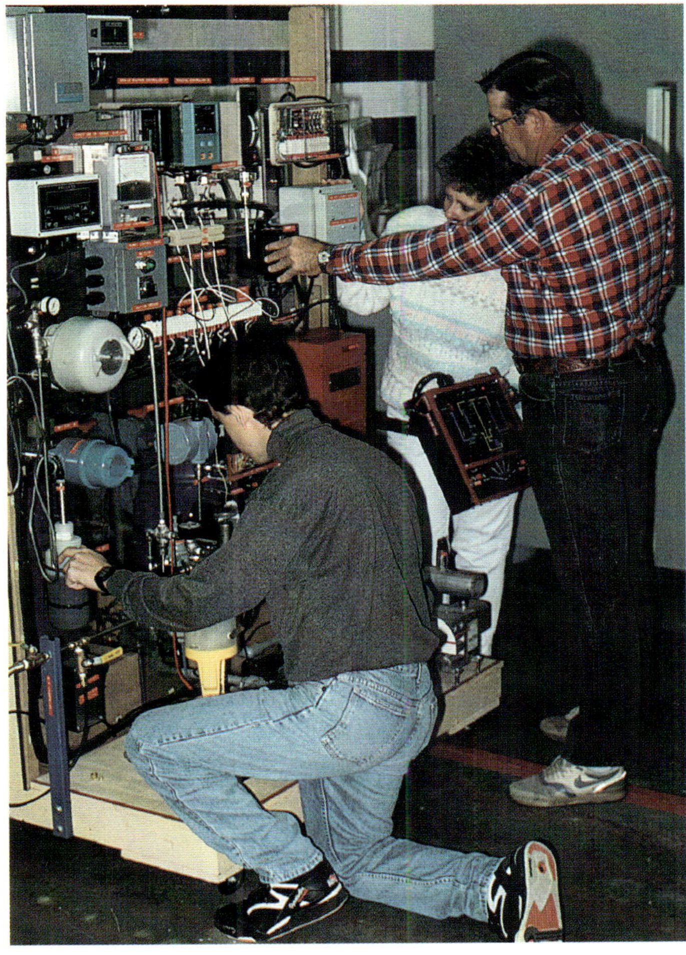

A *willingness to go the extra mile for education is what John M. Patterson State Technical College brings to central Alabama.*

J*ohn M. Patterson State Technical College is a valued educational resource and a significant contributor to the economic development of central Alabama.*

The professional staff at John Patterson frequently develop industry-specific curriculum, tailored for the special training needs of local industry, and offer on-site instruction. "Our first priority is to work as a partner with area

MARKETPLACE

The area's retail establishments, service industries, and automobile dealers vitalize the economic life of the Montgomery area. Photo by Robert Fouts.

CAPITOL CHEVROLET, INC.

Capitol Chevrolet, Inc. is not only one of Montgomery's top automobile dealers, but also the number one Chevrolet dealer in Alabama and a mainstay in Montgomery's automobile industry. The company recently celebrated its 77th anniversary, a significant milestone for any company, but especially so for one that has been family owned and operated since it was founded by Thomas D. McGough Jr. in 1919.

*F*rank E. McGough Jr. now serves as president and owner of Capitol Chevrolet.

In 1922 the organization formerly known as McGough Motor Truck Company became McGough Motor Co., and the company moved from its location on Moulton Street to Dexter Avenue in downtown Montgomery to sell Hudson and Essex cars. In 1928 the company again moved to a new building at 243 Catoma Street.

In 1931 McGough Motor Co. won the Chevrolet franchise and began a new era in Montgomery's automobile industry. The company quickly grew and soon sold Oldsmobiles, as well. In 1948 General Motors required its franchises to sell only Chevrolets, so the Oldsmobile dealership became Capitol Motor Co.

McGough's two sons, Frank and Tom McGough III, grew up schooled in the automobile industry and trained at an early age to take over the reins of their father's enterprises. The new dealership offered the perfect opportunity for Tom McGough to test his skills. His brother, Frank, took over McGough Chevrolet, now named Capitol Chevrolet, Inc.

Since those early days, Capitol Chevrolet has continued to be a leader in the automobile industry. It has grown and prospered, becoming today one of the leading Chevrolet dealerships in the United States under the leadership of Frank McGough Jr., who took over after his father's death in 1982.

Like his father, Frank Jr. learned the business from the bottom up, first as a boy washing cars on the lot, and then years later as service manager, used and new car sales manager, and leasing manager.

The Capitol Chevrolet umbrella encompasses Capitol Imports, added in 1988, the Geo franchise, a GM-Toyota joint venture compact, and Capitol Smart Cars Sales and Rentals.

Automobiles cover 14 acres at the Capitol Chevrolet headquarters on the Eastern Bypass, and it takes more than 200 employees to run the massive enterprise.

The company's move from downtown to the Eastern Bypass in 1970 proved to be a profitable one for Capitol Chevrolet and an example of visionary leadership. Despite advice to the contrary, McGough elected to move the company, which turned out to be such a boon to car sales that other dealerships soon followed in his footsteps, quickly turning the Eastern Bypass into an automobile dealers' mecca.

The company specializes in the sale of both new and used cars and trucks, but it also takes pride in a well-stocked parts department, an excellent body shop, and a service department manned by well-trained technicians schooled in the GM tradition, tested for their expertise and certified to practice their craft.

The service department, directed by Manager John Rogers, has 53 employees and is equipped with 52 bays featuring state-of-the-art diagnostic equipment designed to service computerized automobile components.

Under the direction of Manager Mike Warren, the paint and body shop handles approximately 50 cars each week from 32 bays equipped with advanced equipment including frame-alignment and front-alignment machines. It is the only shop in the city with three down draft paint booths. The paint shop also mixes its own paint to assure the highest quality color matches on customer cars. The DuPont paint used carries a four-year warranty.

Edwin Moates, manager of the parts department, stresses that the success of his department is largely due to high quality GM parts, as well as a knowledgeable, experienced staff. Those qualities, along with competitive pricing, makes Capitol Chevrolet's parts department one of the finest in Alabama.

But it is the sales department that makes any dealership a player in the marketplace, and Capitol Chevrolet's is a powerhouse. The company reached $110 million plus in sales in 1995, and its record continues to grow. McGough

*T*he company takes pride in its service department, which is manned by well-trained technicians schooled in the GM tradition and tested for their expertise and certified to practice their craft.

*I*n 1988 Capitol Chevrolet added Capitol Imports to its line of fine cars.

attributes the success of the company's sales record to a dedicated and caring sales staff that is motivated to do whatever is necessary to satisfy each customer.

The company motivates its sales staff to strive for excellence by awarding each month's top sales professional with its "Sales Professional of the Month Award." Special recognition goes annually to the company's top producer. Evidence the incentive programs have their own rewards is the company's selection as WAKA-TV's Best of Montgomery for three years in a row.

The Capitol Chevrolet leasing department, under the direction of Manager Don Mims, has experienced resounding success since it was first established in 1978. The company leases vehicles to individuals and business accounts, and offers leasing on new or used vehicles on their lot or any other lot, including other brands, makes, and models—yet another example of Capitol Chevrolet's dedication to customer service. Among the company's long list of satisfied clients are the Alabama Education Association, Jackson Hospital, Montgomery Beverage Co., and more.

Despite its extraordinary success, Capitol Chevrolet has managed amazingly well to maintain its family-like atmosphere with a close-knit group of employees who are concerned about their customers and each other.

That concern carries over visibly into the community as well. In 1995 Capitol achieved 100 percent participation in the Montgomery Area United Way campaign. The company's corporate citizenship is driven directly by McGough's own example. Committed to the welfare of his community, McGough is a former United Way

chairman, president of the Jackson Hospital Foundation, a board member of the Montgomery Chamber of Commerce and the YMCA, and a member of the Rotary and Lions Clubs. He also serves as president of the Super Savings Chevy Dealers Association.

A dedicated sales staff, excellent leadership, and concerned employees all dedicated to serving customers with the utmost care in sales and service ensures Capitol Chevrolet will be celebrating anniversary milestones in Montgomery for years to come. ▨

*T*he Capitol Chevrolet umbrella also encompasses Capitol Kia and Smart Cars Sales and Rentals.

GAYFERS

A simple enterprise that started as Pollak's Dollar Store in the center of bustling Montgomery in 1868 is today part of a 17-store regional division of one of America's largest retailers.

The Civil War had ended only a few years earlier when the little kerosene-lighted store opened on Montgomery's Court Square. The city was rebuilding and expanding, and Pollak's was destined to grow up with it. Indeed, more than a century-and-a-quarter later, Montgomery has become an economic and cultural leader in the South, and that humble little store has become the tradition we know as Gayfers.

The journey has been a long and prosperous one. Names and ownerships have changed along the way, as testimony to the store's growth. But its role as a community leader, in business, fashion, and service, has remained steadfastly consistent.

During the Gay Nineties, Montgomery was the place work-weary farmers could stop and relax after selling their wagon loads of cotton. They went to Pollak's for the fancy corkscrew suits, cutaways, and other fashions of the times.

In the early 1900s the H. B. Claflin Company purchased the store and changed its name to Montgomery Fair. In 1914 Montgomery Fair became part of Mercantile Stores Company, Inc.,

Gayfers aggressively offers exceptional service, selection, fair pricing, and flexibility—a combination that builds customer relationships and keeps them coming back.

an association that remains in place today. For the next three decades, the Court Square department store built its reputation for quality goods and superior customer service. With new merchandise lines and expanding departments, Montgomery Fair became one of the leading department stores south of Birmingham.

Shortly after World War II, the store opened its first full branch about 60 miles to the northeast in Opelika. The exciting new store would serve all of east Alabama. And in 1957 Montgomery Fair continued its mission to "grow with the city" by opening an ultramodern facility in Montgomery's Eastbrook Shopping Center.

In 1965 the store was again on the cutting edge in Alabama's retail industry, serving as a glittering multimillion-dollar anchor store in the trendy new $10-million Montgomery Mall. The gala opening extravaganza for the 171,360-square-foot department store attracted dignitaries from across the state, including former Governor George C. Wallace, who did the ribbon-cutting honors.

The store's rich history continued with the addition of new branches and relocations in response to demographic changes, but in 1971, the well-known Gayfers name was added to that of Montgomery Fair, linking two illustrious Southern retailing names and extending their spheres of influence. During the '70s, Gayfers reached into neighboring Georgia and responded to Montgomery's eastward growth by opening a full-line store in the elaborate Eastdale Mall.

In 1992 and 1995, respectively, Mercantile merged its Augusta, Georgia-based J. B. White group and four Gayfers/Maison Blanche stores into the Montgomery-based Gayfers group. The mergers added 11 stores located in South

Gayfer's Montgomery-based division operates more than three million square feet of retail space and three distribution centers. It is the fastest growing group in Mercantile stores.

Carolina, Georgia, Mississippi, and south Alabama.

Today, the 17-store regional group, under the direction of President Robin E. Sanderford, is headquartered in spacious new offices located adjacent to the Eastdale Mall Gayfers store. The Montgomery-based division, which is the fastest growing group in Mercantile stores, operates more than three million square feet of retail space and three distribution centers. Expansion plans for eight new stores are on the books for 1997 and 1998. In Montgomery alone, between its two department stores, the Gayfers Home Store, and a distribution center, the company employs nearly 1,000 people.

This kind of success is no accident, for since its founding, Gayfers has aggressively offered exceptional service, selection, fair pricing, and flexibility—a combination that builds customer relationships and keeps them coming back.

With its highest priority being customer service, Gayfers carefully selects and trains its sales associates, emphasizing product knowledge and professionalism at every turn. The company provides intensive training before an associate ever greets a customer and continues on-going customer service education throughout each associate's career. "We have many associates who are on a first name basis with some of their customers and fully understand their fashion preferences," said Group Fashion/Promotion Director Rhea Kirk. "We work hard to build those relationships and offer a little something extra that makes their shopping more pleasurable."

In the retail business, friendliness goes a long way, but knowledge is every bit as important. In its tradition of excellent service, Gayfers offers an array of some 25 convenient customer services and programs, ranging from free gift wrapping to the free services of a personal shopper, and a 60-day interest free Quick Credit Account. It is the sales associates and customer service representatives on the front line who must understand, promote, and provide these diverse services.

When it comes to selection, Gayfers is second to none. Recognizing the store's popularity among a widely diverse clientele, Gayfers buyers scour the market for high quality, competitively priced clothing, shoes, accessories, and cosmetics for men, women, and children. In response to its customers' demands, Gayfers offers a full range of choices from private boutique and designer fashions to value sportswear. "I believe we have been truly unique in our ability to satisfy a very mixed customer base," said Kirk. Other unique offerings include the Gayfers' Kids' Club and Grandparents' Club, two more ways the store builds loyalty with special savings programs.

Over the years, Gayfers has also been in the forefront with flexibility and a desire to "give the customers what they want." The store stays keenly aware of trends in fashion design and housewares and responds quickly with products in demand. The beautiful Gayfers Home Store, located adjacent to the Eastdale Mall store, offers everything for the home from bath mats to bone china, and is just one example of Gayfers' willing flexibility. "As we anticipated, the '90s is the decade for coming back to the home," said Kirk. "Our departments grow as customer need grows."

But Gayfers does more than just attend to customer needs. The company has a long history of meeting community needs and encourages all managers and associates to be involved in their communities as well as their jobs.

Each summer Montgomerians look forward to the Gayfers Charity Sale event which raises funds

The beautiful Gayfers Home Store, located adjacent to the Eastdale Mall store, offers everything for the home.

for local charitable organizations. In return for a ticket purchase (which goes to the charity), contributors are able to take advantage of bargains. Then, in the fall, Gayfers sponsors the "Glitter, Glamour, and Glitz" gala fashion show to raise funds for endeavors of local charitable organizations. "We have an obligation to give back to our community, and we give as we can, not expecting anything in return," said Kirk.

The humble country store is a thing of the past, but its mission of leadership and service lives on. Perhaps that is why Gayfers has become a Montgomery tradition—a rich tradition of shopping excellence. ⬛

With its highest priority being customer service, Gayfers carefully selects and trains its sales associates, emphasizing product knowledge and professionalism at every turn.

THE KYSER COMPANY

When the Kyser Furniture Leasing Company was established in the late 1960s, it was designed to meet a market need for high- quality temporary home and office furnishing needs. Today, the five furniture businesses that make up The Kyser Company fill virtually every furniture need imaginable.

With the establishment of Kyser Furniture Leasing, Kyser Fine Furnishings, My Room, Kyser OfficeWorks, and Manufacturers Bedding Outlet, the Kyser Company has made it easy and affordable to find furniture and accessories for every need, from temporary office or apartment furniture to top-of-the-line home furnishings and specialty children's furniture.

Kyser Fine Furnishings offers one of the largest selections of top quality, name brand furniture in the Southeast.

"Over the years we saw voids in the market," said company founder Kyle Kyser. "Montgomerians had to go to Atlanta or Birmingham for quality home and office furniture. We're proud of this community, and we wanted Montgomery to have just as much to offer. Now, customers from Birmingham and Atlanta are coming here."

The Kyser furniture leasing business sprang up in response to the construction of garden apartment complexes that called for furniture a step above the standard rental property fare. As customers began to purchase items from the rental warehouse, it became clear to Kyle Kyser and his brother Jerry, who helped establish the company, that Montgomery needed a store that could offer competitively priced, upper-end furniture. The

response to Kyser Fine Furnishings was tremendous—so much so that the company has expanded its beautiful 40,000-square-foot showroom and warehouse on the Wetumpka Highway four times.

For more than 25 years, Kyser Company furniture enterprises have grown, carefully and consistently, with market demand. Why such success? Because the company has recognized customer desires and answered them, stocked only the finest furnishings, created aggressive pricing programs, and hired experienced, thoroughly trained sales and service associates. Each Kyser Company business is founded on those principles. To that end, Mr. Kyser said, "We have made it our mission to provide fine furniture that is aggressively priced without asking our customers to give up anything in the way of quality or service."

KYSER FINE FURNISHINGS

Kyser Fine Furnishings offers one of the largest selections of top quality, name brand furniture in the Southeast. That selection, coupled with one of the most experienced sales staffs in Alabama, has contributed to a local reputation second to none.

The store carries furniture recognized around the world for quality. In 1981 Kyser opened a Century Showplace Gallery, followed by a Drexel Heritage Gallery in 1985, and a Henredon Gallery in 1989. Each gallery features 6,000 to 8,000 square feet of furniture groupings dedicated to each renowned manufacturer. Kyser is one of the largest Century dealers in the Southeast and one of the largest Drexel Heritage dealer in Alabama. Its commitment to these quality manufacturers allows Kyser to sell aggressively and maintain consistently competitive prices.

The Kyser sales and service staff works to make the buying experience an enjoyable one. Each sales associate is knowledgeable and experienced; decorators offer innovative and cost-saving ideas from furniture arrangement to fabric selection, and delivery personnel service to customers quickly with care and precision. When furniture is delivered, the Kyser staff intalls it, arranges it, and polishes it for immediate enjoyment.

My Room is Montgomery's only furniture store dedicated solely to top quality furniture for children's and guests' bedrooms, specializing in space-saving modular furniture that can be expanded as children grow and their needs change.

MY ROOM

My Room is Montgomery's only furniture store dedicated solely to top quality furniture for children's and guests' bedrooms. Established in 1993, My Room carries a wide selection of children's furniture and accessories, including bunk beds, futons, daybeds, desks, computer desks, chairs, and tables. The store specializes in space-saving modular furniture that can be purchased in segments and expanded as children grow and their needs change. But the store is also full of traditional, country French, and contemporary bedroom furnishings. My Room opened in response to what Kyser saw as an increasing need for youth- specific furniture. From its location on Burbank Drive behind Eastdale Mall, My Room has become a popular shopping place for parents, grandparents, and children of all ages.

In addition to low prices on new and used office furniture, Kyser OfficeWorks offers computer-aided design and drafting capabilities, furniture specification and procurement, inventory and move management services, and interior design.

KYSER OFFICEWORKS

Kyser entered the office furniture business in the mid-1970s, so "new and growing Montgomery businesses would be able to do their office furnishing business in Montgomery," said Mr. Kyser. After operating from a portion of its main showroom, Kyser opened its OfficeWorks store in 1992 in a 30,000-square-foot remodeled showroom on Spruce Street. An authorized Steelcase dealer and member of the Office Furniture USA franchise, OfficeWorks represents more than 100 quality top manufacturers. Its franchise network provides the benefit of high volume buying and offers customers name brand office furniture and accessories at 50 percent off manufacturer's retail prices every day.

But in addition to low prices on new and used office furniture, the OfficeWorks professionals offer computer-aided design and drafting capabilities, furniture specification and procurement, inventory and move management services, and interior design by ASID interior designers. OfficeWorks customers include banks, law firms, hospitals, state agencies, architects, and engineers. Responding to market trends, the company is moving rapidly into the home office arena.

Kyser Furniture Leasing is central Alabama's oldest and largest furniture leasing store, offering a wide selection of furniture, accessories, entertainment systems, and appliances.

KYSER FURNITURE LEASING

Kyser Furniture Leasing is central Alabama's oldest and largest furniture leasing store. Established in 1968, the business offers lease, lease/purchase, and sales arrangements. With a wide selection of furniture, accessories, entertainment systems, and appliances, the East South Boulevard store offers solutions for temporary apartment, home, or office living arrangements.

"We frequently work with businesses and corporations that are moving to Montgomery. We create temporary office and living arrangements for their staff while they are exploring and developing permanent arrangements," said Kyser Chief Financial Officer Jack Parrish. "When they are ready to make their permanent moves, Kyser Fine Furnishings and OfficeWorks have what they need for the long-term."

MANUFACTURERS BEDDING OUTLET

Kyser entered the bedding business in 1988 and now runs nine stores in Montgomery, Birmingham, and Huntsville, with more on the drawing board. Manufacturers Bedding Outlet is the largest independent dealer of Serta bedding in Alabama and one of the largest Sealy and Simmons dealers in the state.

Each store showcases more than 50 bedding sets from which to choose, and unlike other dealers, Manufacturers Bedding Outlet offers same-day delivery of sets purchased before 2 P.M. Recognized for its commitment to lowest price and largest selection, MBO goes even a step further for customer satisfaction by providing a 30-night in-home sleep warranty and free disposal of old bedding.

With all of these offerings, one might wonder what's left for Kyser to accomplish. But according to both Mr. Kyser and Mr.

Parrish, expansion is definitely part of the company's future. As in its successful past, however, growth will happen only in response to real market need. That will ensure Kyser's continued ability to provide its value-added touch—the distinctive quality, service, and pricing for which the company has come to be known. **⁊⁊**

Each Manufacturers Bedding Outlet store showcases more than 50 bedding sets from which to choose, and unlike other dealers, offers same-day delivery of sets purchased before 2 P.M.

Bibliography

Bruccoli, Matthew J., Scottie Fitzgerald Smith and Joan P. Kerr, Eds. *The Romantic Egoists: A Pictorial Autobiography from the Scrapbooks and Albums of Scott and Zelda Fitzgerald.* New York: Charles Scribner's Sons, 1974.

Dees, Morris S., Jr. *Current Biography.* 56.1 (January 1995): 6-10.

Greenhaw, Wayne. *Montgomery: The Biography of a City.* Montgomery, Alabama: The Advertiser Company, 1993.

Zinsser, William. "I Realized Tears Were Becoming Part of the Memorial." *Smithsonian*, September 1991: 32-43.

Enterprises Index

Index

n

This book was set in Adobe Garamond Book and Italic, Futura Extra Bold, and Stuyvesant at
Community Communications, Montgomery, Alabama, and printed on 80 lb. Warren Flo Text.

m